STUDIES ON GOTTLOB FREGE AND
TRADITIONAL PHILOSOPHY

IGNACIO ANGELELLI
University of Texas

STUDIES ON GOTTLOB FREGE AND TRADITIONAL PHILOSOPHY

D. REIDEL PUBLISHING COMPANY / DORDRECHT-HOLLAND

Printed in The Netherlands

PARENTIBUS UXORIQUE DEDICATUM

PREFACE

I wish to express, first of all, my profound gratitude to Professor J. M. Bocheński, without whose assistance the present work would have not been possible. To be concise, I would like to state that his contribution to this book may be viewed at three levels: (1) that of the general *spirit*, (2) that of the specific ideas, theses or approaches which are expressed in its pages, (3) that of this work *qua* doctoral dissertation. The general spirit which has guided my research coincides with that underlying Professor Bocheński's own works, in particular his *Formale Logik* (München 1956). Moreover, the particular occasion which suggested my investigation was a statement included in that book according to which the literature in the field still lacked a detailed work on Frege (p. 317).

I wish, likewise, to express my gratitude to other professors of the University of Fribourg for their generous help. I mention especially Professors P. Wyser, M. D. Philippe, N. Luyten, and V. Kuiper.

I have also benefited from Professor E. Specker's lectures at the Eidgenössische Technische Hochschule (Zürich) and from Professor Olof Gigon's lectures at the University of Bern.

From an earlier period I wish to express my gratitude to the professors of the philosophy department of the Universidad Nacional de Buenos Aires, especially the late Professor Francisco Romero.

The Swiss National Library (Bern) has greatly facilitated access to bibliographical sources, and the library of the University of Münster (Westphalien) has kindly provided microfilms of Frege's *Nachlaß*.

Last but not least, my sincere gratitude is also addressed to the Universidad de Buenos Aires and to the Swiss Confederation for their generous long-term financial assistance.

Fribourg, Switzerland IGNACIO ANGELELLI
May 1965

CONTENTS

0. INTRODUCTION

0.1 The aim, the method and the structure of the present work

The question motivating the present work is: *what is really the significance of Frege with respect to the philosophical tradition*? Of course this question may also be viewed as a particular case of the more general one: what is the significance of modern "Grundlagenforschung" or modern logic with respect to the philosophical tradition? The problem is of the type *quid sit* rather than of the type *an sit*, the latter enjoying nowadays an unanimously affirmative answer. Our aim is therefore to provide more precise answers to the question regarding the *nature* of Frege's relations with the philosophical tradition. Such relations may be considered under different aspects. In one of these aspects Frege's significance with respect to the philosophical past has already been largely dealt with; this is his purely formal logical creation. And perhaps the above mentioned unanimity is mostly restricted to Frege *qua* logician.

Nevertheless, Frege's formal logic – Frege's *Begriffsschrift* – was within Frege's thought a mere *adminiculum* or *organon* (to use ancient terminology), serving only the purpose of providing a control of the derivation of arithmetic from logic.

Logicism and philosophy of *number* are the central aspects of Frege's system, from which all the rest – not only his logic – has to be understood.

Even semantics is related to number within his philosophy, because the much stressed Fregean distinction between signs and designata (which is obviously a condition *sine qua non* for any semantics) was largely motivated by Frege's antiformalist conception of number (= numbers are not signs). As to the relation to number of the other aspects of his thought, it is easy to observe how close it is. *Class* is Frege's way of dealing with numbers; predication theory, existence, the distinction

"Merkmal–Eigenschaft", properties of properties, the sharp distinction of individuals and concepts, all this happens to be different in Frege from traditional formulations and doctrines, for from the outset Frege viewed *number* as an entity concerning concepts and not the individuals falling under those concepts.

Now, although much has been written in recent years on aspects of Frege other than formal logic proper, there is not yet a full evaluation of the significance of these aspects with respect to the philosophical past, in particular the great Aristotelian tradition. The aim of the present work is to contribute to such an evaluation.

Almost ten years ago Frege's bibliography was set forth in I. M. Bocheński's *Formale Logik* (1956), but a book on Frege was still counted among the desiderata of logical literature.[1] Since then many pages have been written on Frege: articles, academic reports, dissertations, chapters of books, and books. In this vast amount of Fregean bibliography some interesting possibilities concerning the insertion of Frege – of Frege *der deutsche Mathematiker*[2] – in the philosophical tradition have not yet been considered, and some critical points of Frege's own doctrines have not been discussed.

The present work is not intended to be a presentation of or an introduction to Frege's doctrines (though it may be so in some respects). It presupposes a general knowledge of Frege's main doctrines and terminology, as well as of the main recent discussions on Frege.

Fregean terminology or doctrines are explained only so far as is necessary for each single discussion. (For instance, from an explanatory point of view, Frege's ideas on number should have been presented at the beginning, and not in the last chapter.)

As has been said, Frege's different aspects are distributed according to a hierarchy, in which his insight into *number* has the central place.

Nevertheless, in looking for an answer to our primary question, the *method* used has been analytical rather than synthetical; thereby, of course, the deep unity of Frege's thought has continually been taken into account.

Some of the philosophically relevant aspects of Frege's philosophy have been, so to speak, isolated, and the general question of his significance in the context of the philosophical tradition has been reiterated in reference to each single aspect. Thus the general question has split into a set of particular investigations, which is reflected in the title of the present work.

Incidentally, it should be observed that the question of Frege's relations with the philosophical tradition does not involve the opposition "Frege versus the philosophical tradition". The opposition suggested by the title of the present work is merely a methodological one, having perhaps some remote *fundamentum in re* in that Frege was not a *professor* of philosophy.

The main particular investigations making up the present research are *ten* in number, each of them forming a special *chapter*. In some cases the investigation of an aspect has been sub-divided into other partial studies.

Given any feature of Frege's thought (say his theory of "Stufen" or his complaint that traditional logic did not distinguish class-membership and class-inclusion), the possibility of establishing connections between it and the philosophical past presupposes, of course, a thorough critical discussion of that aspect in Frege himself. Once this is done, one may ask what is Frege's contribution to philosophy (in that respect), or inversely, what the philosophical tradition may contribute (in that respect) to Frege. A particular point of Frege's system may *clarify*, *challenge* or help to understand in some other way a certain fragment of the philosophical tradition; in such a case we would generally speak of *applications* of Fregean doctrines to the philosophical tradition. On the other hand, some feature of the philosophical tradition may likewise clarify, challenge or simply provide a sort of *illustrious background* to a Fregean doctrine.

Each one of these 'Studies on G. Frege and Traditional Philosophy' is intented to satisfy simultaneously, at least in some degree, the following three conditions:

(1) that they be a critical discussion of some fragment of Frege's thought;

(2) that they be an application of Fregean doctrines to the philosophical past;

(3) that they be a study of some feature of the philosophical tradition which seems *necessary* for a better understanding of Frege's doctrines, and this in two ways: (a) intrinsically (i.e., a Fregean doctrine is confusing or not easily intelligible unless it is situated in the whole context of Western philosophy), (b) extrinsically (i.e., a Fregean doctrine, clear

enough in itself, may be better appreciated in its full significance by comparing it with some similar doctrine of the philosophical tradition).

Certainly it is not possible to fulfill equally all these conditions for each single aspect of Frege. This is only a methodological "ideal" which governed the present research.

In some cases (for instance, Chapter 5, "Merkmal-Eigenschaft"), point (2) could be adequately carried out; in other cases (for instance, Chapter 2, "Semantics", or Chapter 6, "Function"), point (1) is elaborated much more than points (2) or (3); on the other hand, there are instances of almost exclusive treatment of point (3a) (Chapter 1, "Ontology"), or point (3b) (Chapter 7, "Levels . . ."). This unavoidable disproportion in some of the particular studies of the present work should not conceal their real significance; even in the case of Chapters 1, 4, or 7 the Fregean context is essential.

Some relations between Frege and contemporary philosophy have also been considered. Although this was not the main intention, it was necessary, in some cases, to discuss other interpretations of Frege or to mention possible applications of Fregean themes to post-Fregean philosophy.

The multiplicity and variety of the many studies gathered in the present work is an effect of the author's seeking as many applications and connections between Frege and Western philosophy as possible, and also of his wish to provide those references (in traditional philosophy) which are necessary for a better understanding of Frege.

0.2 Frege's scientific program and philosophy

An adequate evaluation of Frege requires first of all a consideration of his scientific program. This program is clearly stated in the very early pages of the Fregean *corpus*, i.e., in the *Vorwort* to the *Begriffsschrift* of 1879.

Do arithmetical propositions belong to the class of propositions which may be proved in a purely logical way (*rein logisch*), or to the class of truths which must be established by recourse to empirical facts? Frege's philosophical logicism consists simply in being a priori persuaded that the first alternative must be the case, for, as Leibniz said, number is a sort of transcendental[3] and the science of number must be very akin to ontology or metaphysics. This central argument of philosophical logicism does not appear in the *Begriffsschrift* of 1879 but is clearly stated five years later.[4] In his *Begriffsschrift* of 1879 Frege affirms that in order to decide whether arithmetical theses are "*verités de raison*" it is necessary to have a rigorous deductive apparatus, such that any intuitive (empirical and *even a priori intuitive*[5]) element may be detected. This is why Frege does logic, and this is why he does symbolic logic.[6]

The formal machinery which Frege constructs for that purpose is called "Formelsprache des reinen Denkens", because by utilizing it one can rigorously decide how far pure reason alone (not even with the help of *reine Anschauung*[7]) can go and is called "*Begriffsschrift*" because *Begriff* and not *Anschauung* is Frege's concern; had Frege been Kantian, he would have written an *Anschauungsschrift*.[8]

Frege's scientific program is conceived in dialogue with Kant and Leibniz; thus it naturally becomes part of the philosophical tradition.[9] This suggests that to consider Frege outside this historical connection is to risk missing something valuable in him. There is an important case where the potential risk could become an actual impossibility of *seeing* the significance of Frege's doctrine: logicism.[10]

It should be stressed that Frege kept a prudent silence in regard to the impact of his work on the development of philosophy.[11] To official philosophers of his time Frege was *ein deutscher Mathematiker*[12] and for the German mathematicians he was an author of curious byproducts.[13]

In fact, Frege's way was as different from that of his "professional" colleagues – professors of mathematics – as the way from Thebes to Athens is different from the way from Athens to Thebes. Frege was doing foundational research.[14]

To this extent he naturally belonged to the family of philosophers. In fact, he was easily recognized by all true philosophers; by those who dealt with the same problems (Russell), by those who dealt with related problems (Husserl[15]) and even by those who started developing quite different questions (Heidegger[16]).

0.3 The bibliography

As concerns Frege's writings, one should distinguish between *published* and *unpublished* works. A complete list of the former is to be found elsewhere.[17] All the items belonging to that list have been considered here, although only some of them have been quoted. On the other hand, the *inedita* have been for the most part taken into account; for reasons beyond the author's control, however, texts from the *Nachlaß* cannot be quoted here.[18] Such quotations would have, at most, entailed a simplification of our arguments. The *Nachlaß* does not essentially enrich the content of Frege's published works, apart from showing how this content was applied to new situations (for instance Russell's paradox or Hilbert's doctrines), or how it was formulated in a more perspicuous way (for instance, "subject-predicate", "Sinn-Bedeutung" for predicate-terms, etc.).

With regard to philosophers other than Frege, my particular approach is mentioned in the next section.

0.4 History of philosophy re-examined

The choice of authors making up the bibliography of the present research has been influenced by a criterion which requires some comments.

Attention has been paid to authors who are not easily classifiable in the up-to-now standard divisions of the history of philosophy. These authors fall within the period of modern philosophy (*Neuzeit*), but the content of their works is rather mediaeval or classic. Without entering into difficult characterizations it is possible to give a sort of "ostensive" definition of these authors by referring to the about 600 names recorded in Rabus [1], from the Reformation to Kant.

These authors have been disregarded by the leading philosophical or logical historiography. As to the former see, for instance, *Überweg*. As to the second, it may be observed that Prantl was unable to complete his *Geschichte* beyond the 15th century, and Bocheński [1] and Kneale [1] for their part have negatively judged the period subsequent to the Middle Ages.[19]

Apart from Rabus and perhaps other older expositions of the history of philosophy, research on these authors has up to now been only a minor concern in philosophical historiography.[20] Nevertheless, this situation has begun to change; the forthcoming edition of *Überweg* will pay special attention to these authors[21], and in general an advanced systematic research is being done.[22]

Indeed, a great deal of the extensive material recorded by Rabus [1] is far from being formal logic proper (a fact which supports Bocheński's and Kneale's judgment), and its interest is more from the point of view of general philosophical studies such as philosophy of logic, methodology, ontology, semantics, etc. But these are precisely the studies whose revival characterizes our contemporary philosophy.

0.5 Abbreviations. Terminology

The following abbreviations will be employed:

UF = das Fallen eines Einzelnen unter einen Begriff
UO = the relation of subordination between two concepts
IF = UF between two concepts.

An individual proper *falls under* (UF) a concept; a concept *falls within* (IF) another concept (cf. 3.2).

KU = *καθ' ὑποκειμένου κατηγορεῖσθαι* (de subjecto dici)
EU = *ἐν ὑποκειμένῳ εἶναι* (inesse)
K = *κατηγορεῖσθαι*

For these terms, cf. Sections 1.2, 4.2.

Further, the current logical symbolism is used. The titles of Frege's works have been abbreviated according to a convention explained in the bibliography.

Fregean terminology is used without necessarily being explained and without necessarily referring the reader to some other chapter where that terminology may be explained. The English renderings chosen for Fregean terms are familiar to students of Frege.

Where there is no danger of confusion with *accidents* which are *predicated* of *substances* (accidental predication), *the term "predicate"* (*"predication"*) *as short for "universal"* (*"singularity–universality"*) is sometimes used. This is in accord with both the intention of *Categoriae* (KU) and the terminology prevailing today.

The term "unsaturatedness" is employed according to three senses: (1) unsaturatedness of names, (2) unsaturatedness of entities, (3) unsaturatedness as the peculiar Fregean combination of both (1) and (2).

REFERENCES

1. Bocheński [1], p. 317.
2. Cf. note 12.
3. Cf. Section 10.6.
4. UFT (1885) contains a particularly clear and concise formulation of logicism, but GRL (1884) already includes the same ideas.

5. For the pure intuition cf. BG, § 23 ("...selbst durch eine Anschauung a priori...)." Also GRL, §§ 90, 91.
6. BG, *Vorwort*, p. IV ("... Damit sich hierbei nicht unbemerkt etwas Anschauliches eindrängen könnte ..."). But see the more impressive statement in GRL, § 91: "Um diese Übelstände zu vermindern [i.e., to detect non-logical factors in demonstration], habe ich meine Begriffsschrift erdacht."
7. I expand in this way Frege's statement in BG, p. IV below. Cf. note 5 here.
8. This is of course a free interpretation of the word "*Begriffsschrift*", but I think it is adequate to Frege's insights.
9. "... wir gelangten zu einer Verbesserung der Ansicht Kants" (GRL, § 109). This is the result (1884) of the program sketched in 1879 (BG, *Vorwort*). Frege thinks that "außer von Kant noch wenig in dieser Richtung geleistet worden ist" (COH, p. 324). For Leibniz cf. BG, Vorwort.
10. Cf. Section 10.6.
11. Of course Frege was not supposed to know history of philosophy.
12. Marty [1], p. 56. Mortan [1] contains (*Anhang*) the best biographical references on Frege, including a publication of the *Gutachten* of Frege's academic life.
13. Cf. BG (reprint Olms), *Vorbemerkung*. Frege's lack of success among mathematicians is notorious, cf., for instance, GRG, I, p. XI, note; also Linke [1].
14. Cf. Chapter 1, note 5.
15. Husserl's *Philosophie der Arithmetik* was written in close relation to Frege's GRL, as Frege's *Nachlaß*, particularly, shows. There were misunderstandings between both thinkers, of course. See for instance Section 3.6, and even deeper differences may be indicated; cf. Section 2.26.
16. Heidegger [4]: "G. Freges logisch-mathematische Forschungen sind meines Erachtens in ihrer wahren Bedeutung noch nicht gewürdigt, geschweige dann ausgeschöpft." This was written in 1912. Heidegger rightly points out the significance of Frege's notion of *Begriff*. (Reference provided by A. Battro.)
17. Frege, *Kleine Schriften* (cf. bibliography).
18. As far as I know, only Bartlett [1] and Sluga [1] provide extensive quotations from the *Nachlaß*; also Bocheński [1], 39.01.
19. Kneale [1], p. 298; Bocheński [1], p. 297.
20. For instance Wundt [1].
21. Cf. Wilpert [1], p. 89.
22. Above all Risse [1]. Examples of active research in the field are also: Schüling [1], Greniewski [1] (for Poland), Pereira Gomez [1] (for Portugal), Muñoz Delgado [1] (for Spain), etc.

1. ONTOLOGY

Summary and general remarks. Taking for granted that much of the content of Frege's works is ontology (1.1), our problem is not whether or not in Frege there *is* ontology, but rather to pursue further the analysis of those aspects of Frege's thought which call for a comparison with traditional ontology.

One such aspect is the relation of *predication* or, in other words, the relation between an object and a property. Modern logic and modern *Grundlagenforschung* (and Frege in particular) in systematically dealing with such a relation have been doing something quite familiar to philosophers since Plato. In this respect, *Logik*, *Metaphysik* and *Grammatik* (to use H. Scholz's terms) fully coincide.

The demand for a deeper analysis of such a well-established coincidence necessitates emphasizing a fact whose significance seems to have been ignored. Traditional ontology has two dimensions (to use an algebraic metaphor): (1) substance–accident, (2) singular–universal. This is briefly described as the *ontological square* (1.2).

An important consequence of the existence of these two dimensions is that the term "property" becomes ambiguous, as does the expression "relation between individual and property". A property of a thing may be an accident; then the property is not at all a universal but an individual. On the other hand, a property of a thing may be a universal ("property" in the sense usual today). The same applies to other terms like "attribute", "predicate", etc.

As a result, the initial enthusiastic association *à la* Scholz of ontology and modern foundational research must be re-examined.

In the present work a first step towards this re-examination is accomplished. This consists in a general presentation of the ontological square and its history (1.2–1.4.6).

Unfortunately this history seems to be one of ambiguities rather than of clear doctrines. Aristotle appears to be responsible for the ontological square (1.2), as well as for having introduced ambiguities, with regard to it (1.3). The philosophical tradition, in its turn, seems to have inherited both the Aristotelian distinction as well as the Aristotelian ambiguity (1.4). Although as centuries went on the ambiguity seems to have imposed itself upon the distinction (in such a way that the ontological square is actually deformed, 1.44), there are exceptions, and the misunderstanding of Russell-Leibniz (1.43) is a striking example of this, not to mention some curious irregularities in Frege's technical terminology or in that of other contemporary authors (1.45 and 1.46). In a final section (1.46), some applications of the ontological square in the present work are mentioned.

From such a first critical approach a general conclusion can already be drawn, which is actually the main conclusion of the present chapter on ontology. It may be summarized in the following way.

It is true to say that classical ontology has explicitly considered two dimensions whereas this distinction is not "officially" introduced in contemporary philosophy. But it is equally true to affirm that the distinction of the two dimensions is far from having been well preserved in the past, whereas it is still discernable (though not acknowledged) in Frege and other recent authors (belonging, in particular, to foundational philosophy).

The reasons for considering this point at length are the following: (1) the necessity mentioned above of qualifying hasty identifications between Fregean and classical ontology, (2) the fact that the knowledge of the distinction between the two ontological dimensions in classical ontology is a necessary prerequisite for any successful understanding of the connections between Frege (or Fregean philosophy) and the philosophical past in matters of ontology, (3) the fact that throughout the present work the ontological square is referred to, (4) last but not least, the circumstance that, independently of its applications, the ontological square is in itself a remarkable *lieu de rencontre* of old metaphysics and new logic, which has been rather neglected by students of old metaphysics and to which new logic makes one sensitive.

1.1 Contemporary logic and ontology

Without engaging in the old dispute about the two senses of "metaphysics"[1] one may at least assume that "first philosophy" contains, as a significant part, the program of a science investigating entities in general.[2] It is *this aspect* of the Aristotelian doctrine which (a) in modern philosophy received the name "ontology"[3], (b) in contemporary philosophy has been again adopted[4], and (c) more recently has suggested comparisons with the new philosophical movements originating in foundational research.[5]

Comparisons of the ontology of modern philosophy with Frege's work (or in general with philosophy arising from foundational research) are only natural. Individuals, properties, membership-relation[6], identity, etc., are a common subject-matter[7]; even semantics is included in the ontological program of modern philosophy.[8]

The same applies to a comparison of Frege's work with ontology in contemporary philosophy. The significance of Pichler [1] has already been pointed out for the development of "new ontology"[9], and we need only to compare Frege's conception of functions as concerning *Gegenstände überhaupt*[10] with the title of the first chapter of Pichler [1]: 'Die Ontologie als Wissenschaft von den Gegenständen überhaupt'.

The impression that there exists a wonderful harmony (even in spite of mutual misunderstandings) may be confirmed by comparing statements of such authors as H. Scholz and M. Heidegger: if on the one hand Heidegger says that however we look at it the structure of things is a *subject-property* structure[11], on the other hand Scholz affirms that logical laws (predicate calculus) concern nothing else than subjects and properties.[12]

It is a conclusion of the present work that Frege's new approach to predication theory enables one to see why in the philosophical tradition logic and ontology have been so drastically separated one from the other.[13] Such a Fregean contribution is of course a new fact confirming even more the close relationship between modern logic and old ontology. The rest of the present chapter is devoted to qualifying that relationship in the particular respect of the two dimensions of ancient ontology.

1.2 The ontological square ('Categoriae', 1a, 20–1b, 10)

I shall first quote the text to be analysed in the present section:

> *Τῶν ὄντων τὰ μὲν καθ' ὑποκειμένου τινὸς λέγεται, ἐν ὑποκειμένῳ δὲ οὐδενί ἐστιν, οἷον ἄνθρωπος καθ' ὑποκειμένου μὲν λέγεται*

τοῦ τινὸς ἀνθρώπου, ἐν ὑποκειμένῳ δὲ οὐδενί ἐστιν· τὰ δὲ ἐν ὑποκειμένῳ μὲν ἐστι, καθ᾽ὑποκειμένου δὲ οὐδενὸς λέγεται, – ἐν ὑποκειμένῳ δὲ λέγω ὅ ἔν τινι μὴ ὡς μέρος ὑπάρχον ἀδύνατον χωρὶς εἶναι τοῦ ἐν ᾧ ἐστίν, – οἷον ἡ τὶς γραμματικὴ ἐν ὑποκειμένῳ μὲν ἐστι τῷ σώματι, – ἅπαν γὰρ χρῶμα ἐν σώματι, – καθ᾽ ὑποκειμένου δὲ οὐδενὸς λέγεται· τὰ δὲ καθ᾽ ὑποκειμένου τε λέγεται καὶ ἐν ὑποκειμένῳ ἐστιν, οἷον, ἡ ἐπιστήμη ἐν ὑποκειμένῳ μὲν ἐστι τῇ ψυχῇ, καθ᾽ ὑποκειμένου δὲ λέγεται τῆς γραμματικῆς· τὰ δὲ οὔτε ἐν ὑποκειμένῳ ἐστὶν οὔτε καθ᾽ ὑποκειμένου λέγεται, οἷον ὁ τὶς ἄνθρωπος ἢ ὁ τὶς ἵππος, – οὐδὲν γὰρ τῶν τοιούτων οὔτε ἐν ὑποκειμένῳ ἐστὶν οὔτε καθ᾽ ὑποκειμένου λέγεται. – ἁπλῶς δὲ τὰ ἄτομα καὶ ἕν ἀριθμῷ κατ᾽ οὐδενὸς ὑποκειμένου λέγεται, ἐν ὑποκειμένῳ δὲ ἔνια οὐδὲν κωλύει εἶναι· ἡ γὰρ τὶς γραμματικὴ τῶν ἐν ὑποκειμένῳ ἐστίν.

The following scheme is intended to reproduce the content of the quoted text: *Categoriae*[14] la, 20–1b, 10. (Elements taken from other passages are either supplemented with quotation-references in the figure itself or are justified in the course of the present section.)

THE ONTOLOGICAL SQUARE

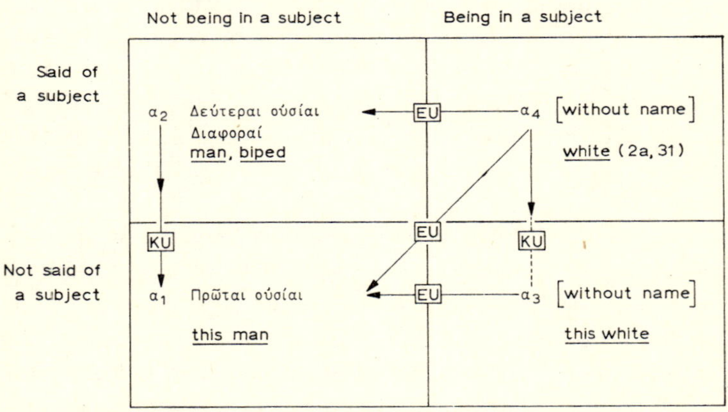

This passage of *Categoriae* is traditionally understood as making a distinction between universal substances, particular substances, universal accidents and particular accidents. The history of commentaries on the *Organon* provides an extensive number of paraphrases and presentations of this text.[15] Boethius' text and other ancient commentators[16] illustrate our quoted passage by means of a diagram similar to ours above: a square in each of whose vertices one of the four classes of entities is located. The Aristotelian text explicitly states that this is a classification of *entities*, but it is of course contrary to traditional Aristotelianism to call universals entities *simpliciter*. In fact, Ioannes a Sancto Thoma elegantly modifies the formulation.[17] Still, universals do enjoy an objective being, and *ens rationis* falls under *ens communissime sumptum*.[18]

The classification of entities into four classes is achieved by means of two relations: *to be in a subject*[19] and *to be said of a subject*.[20] Let us abbreviate their names by $\mathrm{EU}(x, y)$ and $\mathrm{KU}(x, y)$ respectively.

D1 $\mathrm{KU}(x, y) =_{\mathrm{df}}$ (the name of x is said of y) and (the *logos* of x is said of y).[21]

Remarks. The *logos* of x is said of y for we say that y is x (but the sense of the latter "is" is not further explained; cf. also 3a, 28). That the name of x is said of y means simply that y is called x (cf. 2a, 32). The text does not provide any rule which would enable us to decide to what extent the name of x may be modified in its function of being applied to y (I mean grammatical changes of number, gender, etc.). Another designation for KU (although appearing in a context where only substances are meant) is perhaps "συνωνύμως λέγεσθαι".[22]

D2 $\mathrm{EU}(x, y) =_{\mathrm{df}}$ (x ὑπάρχει τῷ[23] y) and (x is not a part of y) and (it is impossible for x to be χωρὶς[24] of y) and (the name of x is sometimes[25] said of y) and (the *logos* of x is never said of y).[26]

By means of these two relations, the four classes of entities are described in the following way:

D3 $\alpha_1 =_{\mathrm{df}} \hat{x}\,(x \sim \varepsilon\, D'\mathrm{KU})\ \&\ (x\, \varepsilon\, \text{Ɑ}'\mathrm{KU})\ \&\ (x \sim \varepsilon\, D'\mathrm{EU})\ \&\ (x\, \varepsilon\, \text{Ɑ}'\mathrm{EU}).$

D4 $\alpha_2 =_{\mathrm{df}} \hat{x}\,(x\ \ \varepsilon\, D'\mathrm{KU})\ \&\ (x\, \varepsilon\, \text{Ɑ}'\mathrm{KU})\ \&\ (x \sim \varepsilon\, D'\mathrm{EU})\ \&\ (x\, \varepsilon\, \text{Ɑ}'\mathrm{EU}).$

D5 $\alpha_3 =_{\mathrm{df}} \hat{x}\,(x \sim \varepsilon\, D'\mathrm{KU})\ \&\ (x\ ?\ \text{Ɑ}'\mathrm{KU})\ \&\ (x\ \ \varepsilon\, D'\mathrm{EU})\ \&\ (x\ ?\ \text{Ɑ}'\mathrm{EU}).$

D6 $\alpha_4 =_{\mathrm{df}} \hat{x}\,(x\ \ \varepsilon\, D'\mathrm{KU})\ \&\ (x\, \varepsilon\, \text{Ɑ}'\mathrm{KU})\ \&\ (x\ \ \varepsilon\, D'\mathrm{EU})\ \&\ (x\ ?\ \text{Ɑ}'\mathrm{EU}).$

(The symbolism employed here is that of *Principia Mathematica* or that current in modern logic.)

The following fact should be considered, implied by D1 and D2:

$$(x, y).\ \mathrm{EU}(x, y) \supset \sim \mathrm{KU}(x, y),$$

i.e., if something inheres (EU) in something else, then it will not be said (KU) of the latter. It is clear that the term "subject" is ambiguous[27]: to be a relatum in KU is not equivalent to being a relatum in EU. Members of α_4 are said *de subiecto* (with respect to accidents) but are *in subiecto* (with respect to substances).

Class α_1 includes all *substantiae primae* and only these. (This is often stated in Chapter 5 of *Categoriae*.[28]) *This man* and *this horse* are the examples Aristotle prefers (cf. our diagram). It should be noted that no element of α_1 is a referent in any of the two relations.

For class α_2 the text gives the designations of *substantiae secundae* and *differentiae*.[29] It seems that traditional paraphrases do not make clear enough that class α_2 is *not* composed of entities which are only referents in KU.[30] The distinction α_1–α_2 does *not* correspond to the distinction *D*'KU–*Ɑ*'KU.[31] This is related to the fact that in traditional logic *animal* is predicated not only of the subject *Socrates* but also of the subject *man*. In my diagram I have expressed this fact by a special KU-arrow *within* the fragment α_2 of the ontological square.

In classes α_3 and α_4 the relation of inherence (EU) appears. Referents in such a relation are traditionally called *accidents*[32] (α_3 = singular, α_4 = universal accidents). The relation of inherence may originate in α_3 as well as in α_4. This is clear in the basic text itself. It should be stressed that subjects of inherence are not only members of α_1, i.e., individuals "proper" as one would think today, but also members of α_2.[33] This is a most important fact, which has a parallel in predication theory.

In classes α_3 and α_4 some difficulties appear. In the definitions above three question marks have been inserted where the situation is doubtful. The first one, in D5, is due to the fact that we do not know whether a particular accident (class α_3) is supposed to belong to the converse domain of KU. This doubt is justified, for simple reasons of symmetry would require particular accidents as relata of KU as well. If a member of α_4 – say the universal accident *grammar* – is said to be a relatum (in KU) of another universal accident – say *science* – it would be most natural to have *grammar* being said (KU) of *this grammar*, as *man* is said of *this man*. But this is already to touch a critical point in Aristotelian and Western ontology. To indicate this fact a dotted line has been inserted in the diagram (instead of an arrow).

The two other question marks (in D5 and D6) are due rather to our requirements of symmetry, but still they are meaningful questions within the system of *Categoriae*. I do not know whether there are answers in the Aristotelian *corpus*.

Again, traditional accounts do not seem adequate in that they do not make clear that KU is a relation which may apply *between members* of α_4, i.e., *between universals*: universals are subjects of predication. (In fact, it should be noted that KU is exemplified by Aristotle only for such cases.)

Members of α_2 and α_4 may be called *universals*, although this term is not used by the author of *Categoriae*. Not only the whole tradition, but the text itself allows us to use that term for members of α_2.[34] It seems correct to extend the term to members of α_4, and speak along with tradition of *universal accidents*; but this is again the critical point: the distinction singularity-universality in the accidental realm is not respected by the very author who introduced it.

Members of α_1 and α_3 are explicitly called *individuals* in the text itself.[35]

The text analysed in the present section seems to be an exception in the Aristotelian corpus. In the next section we shall observe that a relatively clear treatment of the two ontological relations (KU and EU), such as *Categoriae* offer, is lacking in the main works of Aristotle.

1.3 Universal–singular, substance–accident[36] in other works of Aristotle

It seems that the following two points characterize the situation of Aristotle's main works (apart from *Categoriae*) in what concerns the present question.

(1) When the distinction singular-universal is stressed, this is done for the realm of substantial entities, not for accidents.[37]

(2) When the distinction substance-accident is stressed, the distinction singular-universal is rather disregarded.[38]

We may speak of an Aristotelian ambiguity in the special sense that a required distinction of universality-singularity *within accidents* is not respected. The distinction is required by the system, but the author of the system proceeds as if it could be dispensed with. There is a text where the question of the One and the Many in categories apart from substance is mentioned, but this seems a rare exception.[39] Thus "accident" becomes an ambiguous term, on the one hand close to "universal" ("attribute", "predicate") in so far as it is *said of* substances, on the other hand close to "individual", in so far as it is always thought of as a real entity.[40]

Distinguished contemporary Aristotelian scholars (Ross, Tricot, De Rijk, Owens) do not help the reader on this point. They easily assume that accidents are universals, or they vaguely allude to "degrees" of universality in the accidental categories.[41] Perhaps this is natural in so far as one investigates Aristotle *ex Aristotele ipso* or from traditional standards. The contrary applies if one has in mind the Fregean question: "Eigenname oder Begriffswort?"[42], i.e., if one demands a sharp distinction of individuals and concepts[43], which in a sense was not possible traditionally because of the idea of essence.

1.4 Universal–singular, substance–accident in the philosophical tradition

General remarks. The fourfold division of entities – or of *entia* and *intentiones,* to adopt the weakened terminology of Ioannes a Sancto Thoma[44] – belongs to philosophy up to the present day.[45] The two dimensions of the ontological square *are there* even among thinkers who would perhaps not accept the Aristotelian doctrine of categories (whose essence is the distinction substance–accident and not, of course, the "ten" categories). Philosophers seem to be classifiable into those who are consistent and explicitly acknowledge the two dimensions, and those who prefer ambiguity.

In so far as in the present section we aim at pointing out the presence of the two ontological dimensions in Western philosophy, there may result a false image of the philosophical past, as if both dimensions had been more clearly distinguished than what they actually were. Indeed, for the tradition in general I think that the ambiguity prevails over the distinction in this question. But here I wish to stress that the distinction *has* also been made.

1.41 *Middle Ages and Renaissance*[46]

A few examples indicating the Mediaeval and Renaissance vicissitudes of the ontological square will be given here.

Let us begin with Porphyry (*qua* significant for the Middle Ages). Porphyry simply *eludes* the question of the individuality of accidents. This is obvious because he describes the "columns" of categories and he even says that *in each* category there are *species infimae*, but when it is time to know where the accidental *species infimae* are supposed to be attached, the author of the *Isagoge* suddenly decides to consider only substances.[47]

Algazel's *Metaphysics* introduces as *prima divisio entis* the couple substance–accident; and as *secunda divisio* the couple universal–particular.[48]

Kaufmann, D. [1] – a critical history of the theory of divine attributes in Jewish philosophy of the Middle Ages – centers on the basic concepts of *substance*, *accident* and . . . *predicate*. These many pages are not understandable without a careful distinction of the two ontological dimensions. Actually this distinction is *not* made by the author, but how else could one duly appreciate some of his crucial statements?[49]

John of Salisbury [1] contains a clear restatement of the doctrine of *Categoriae*.[50] It could be observed that this is not surprising since this author is simply commenting on the Categories, and it would be easy to accumulate evidence for the survival of the ontological square from such commentaries. Nevertheless, John of Salisbury's text is not merely a résumé; he consciously takes *Categoriae* as clearly explaining "what things are universal, and what ones singular, what ones substances and what ones accidents".[51]

In Aquinas' vocabulary "accidens" and "praedicatum" seem to partially overlap.[52] Duns Scotus offers a strong restatement of the ontological square.[53] Ockham uses "accidens" in two senses; the key term for one of them is "inhaerentia", for the other "praedicatio".[54] The same double meaning is again recognizable in "accidentale" and "accidere".[55] In the latter we are provided an example where the term "accidere" is supposed to mean the same as "praedicari". In the article "inesse" we find again a combination of both perspectives.[56]

Paulus Venetus – in contrast to Porphyry – frankly speaks of individuals within accidental categories.[57] For the relation *aequale* there is an individual: *hoc aequale*; for *binarius* (= two) the individual *hic binarius*; for *triangulus* the individual *hic triangulus*.[58]

There is a well known distinction in traditional philosophy, which clearly reflects the two senses (universal and singular) of "accident".

This is the opposition *accidens praedicabile* and *accidens praedicamentale*, also called logical and ontological accident, respectively. In the 16th century an Aristotelian scholar will correctly ask, after his exposition of Porphyry's *Isagoge*, whether such an entity as *haec albedo* is to be called an accident.[59] The answer is that it is an accident in the sense in which accident is opposed to substance, but not in the sense in which accident is opposed to the other four predicables. In the latter, accident is opposed to essence.

Suarez asks – once more – why there is not a distinction of primary and secondary accidents, corresponding to the same distinction in substances. Suarez's explanation contains the interesting point that that is only a terminological failure: philosophical vocabulary is *de facto* such that individual accidents are not called primary accidents with respect to their universal predicates.[60]

Pacius teaches that everything is either substance or accident, and, again, either universal or particular.[61] In Keckermann we find some interesting ontological theses about individual accidents; individual accidents do not "migrate" from one subject to another, one individual accident – *as any other individual* – cannot be (inhere) in more than one subject.[62] Keckermann also gives a curious example of individual accident: logic qua inhering in the mind of Aristotle.[63]

1.42 *Descartes, Port-Royal, Locke, Reid*

A few examples concerning the history of the ontological square in modern philosophy will be given here.

In Descartes reality is divided first into substances and attributes (*façons*, modes, qualities) and afterwards attributes are divided into those existing in the things themselves and those existing only in our minds, a particular case of the latter being universals.[64] Thus "attribute" becomes a highly equivocal term, with a meaning ranging from singulars to universals. Thus, too, some theses[65] given by Descartes about attributes cannot be immediately translated into the "predicate-theoretical"[66] language of contemporary logic.

Port-Royal in one sense invites one to compare substance-mode with Frege's individual-concept (because the "unsaturatedness" of modes is very much stressed [67]) but on the other hand *L'Art de Penser* also introduces the (supposedly different) dimension of singularity–universality[68] and this may as well (or better) be a candidate for comparisons with Frege's *Gegenstand* and *Begriff*.

Locke's achievement in this context may be described as an effort to deprive universal substances (essences) of their "substantive" function (at least, of course, with respect to *our* knowledge of essences). In terms of the ontological square this means that EU (inherence) no longer has any relata among universal substances. The only sense of "substance" is *being under*, *supporting*[69], which Locke is obliged to maintain for otherwise one would not be able to conceive how simple ideas (qualities) "should subsist alone nor one in another".[70] In Locke the idea of individual accidents is still alive[71] and it is Locke who gives the most suggestive explanation of why our vocabulary lacks proper names for individual accidents.[72]

Reid sees an "objection to generalizing" in that even if by abstraction we may consider the attributes of a subject separately from the subject, this will not make them capable of being also attributes of another subject; the weight of one guinea cannot become the weight of another guinea. Reid's solution consists in restating the doctrine of *Categoriae*.[73] Thus "attribute" means an individual (accident) as well as a universal.

1.43 *Leibniz–Russell*

It is easy to appreciate how the idea of individual accidents is preserved in Leibniz's thought if one considers what Russell calls a text of "capital importance for the comprehension of Leibniz's philosophy".[74]

Leibniz has an ontological axiom according to which accidents – more precisely: individual accidents – cannot inhere in more than one subject.[75] This is not new, but I want to stress that Leibniz does have such an axiom. Individual accidents, say *this white*, are individuals, just as well spatio-temporally located as any other (but inhering, not self-subsisting). While it does not seem absurd to think of a particular white as inhering in this particular piece of paper, in the case of relations one would be led to the disagreeable result of making of every couple of entities related by some relation R a sort of *Siamese twins*, "joined by cartilaginous band from the one's right to the other's left side".[76] On the one hand, there would be the universal relation R, on the other hand its individual instances transforming any couple of related terms into

Siamese twins. *This* is the "awkward discovery" made by Leibniz, not the mere fact of having found that there are relations.[77]

To approach the problem in another way, it should be observed that relations were most familiar in traditional philosophy[78]; the problem began when the *individuals* of universal two-place predicates were looked for *in rerum natura*.[79] If "*aRb*", "*cRd*" are true sentences (*a*, *b*, *c*, *d*, being four distinct objects) then there is no trouble as long as one leaves "*R*" designating a vaguely floating universal entity, the same for both sentences. But this is Russell's approach to relations, not Leibniz's. Leibniz requires that the *R* relating *a* and *b* be *not* the *R* relating *c* and *d*, as Socrates is not Plato although both are specifically the same.[80] Actually one should write $R_{a,b}$ to designate that individual instance of *R* applying between *a* and *b*. The awkwardness of this is due to the fact that $R_{a,b}$ cannot be thought of except as a concrete and physical individual . . . as a sort of cartilaginous band between *a* and *b*. This leads Leibniz to split $R_{a,b}$ into two "monadic" accidents, inhering in the referent and relatum respectively.[81] He prefers to give up thinking of $R_{a,b}$; he adopts the easy way out of putting $R_{a,b}$ "in the mind".[82] The relation does not become a subjective entity because of being "in the mind" – much less an accident inhering in the mind (as Russell suggests[83]). It enjoys a pure objectivity and in this shadowy realm of *entia rationis* $R_{a,b}$ and $R_{c,d}$ smoothly become the universal *R*, which is no longer awkward. *Principia Mathematica*'s "*R*", "*S*" and other symbols for relations designate entities belonging to that shadowy realm.

An achievement of symbolic logic has been to provide an adequate symbolism for universal relations enjoying objectivity in the mind, but not for individual relations in the sense of Leibniz's (classic) ontology. It is wrong to oppose such an achievement to a so-called Leibnizian "reductionism"[84] of relational propositions to subject-predicate ones. Leibniz did not primarily "reduce" propositions or sentences but awkward cartilaginous bands.

When Russell approaches Leibniz he seems to assume what in the next section we shall consider a degenerate ontological square.[85] A characteristic of the latter is that the two dimensions of *Categoriae* collapse into one, which may be indifferently called "attribution", "inherence", "predication", etc. The terms of this relation are called "subjects", "substances", "substrata" on the one hand, and "predicates", "attributes", "accidents", "affections", on the other. The latter are assumed to be universals, the former individuals.[86]

An approach like Russell's is harmless when applied to those chapters of Aristotelianism where the two relations of the ontological square are not clearly distinguished, but this approach fails in such cases as Russell's criticism of Leibniz's philosophy of relations. It is up to further research to see whether other aspects of Russell's criticism (for example, that concerning the identity of indiscernibles[87]) also fall under the same objections.

1.44 *'Parallelism' of singular–universal, substance–accident*

The two original dimensions have undergone a transformation which may be described in the following way:

(1) Substance–accident is assigned to the world of "real things", i.e., to metaphysics or ontology.

(2) Singularity–universality is assigned to the world of "concepts" or "words", i.e., to logic and grammar.

(3) There is a parallelism – a sort of isomorphism – between the world of logic and grammar and the world of things.

We may represent this situation by the following schema:

Real things (metaphysics, ontology):	substance–accident
	↕ ↕
Concepts, words (logic, grammar):	subject–predicate

Certainly the ambiguities of the Aristotelian *corpus* lie at the origin of such a deformation of the ontological square. In fact, Trendelenburg, a representative of the above version of the ontological square, finds support in the Aristotelian texts themselves.[88] "Authentical judgments" are for Trendelenburg an "image" of how things are in reality.[89] "Judgments" are made up of subject and predicate. But what are subject and predicate? Are they names?

They are names, but they are also concepts.[90] Thanks to the fact that predicates are *also* concepts, Trendelenburg can speak of universality–singularity without committing himself to nominalism.[91] But it should be clear that this is a clandestine way of preserving the dimension of universality, because "officially" Trendelenburg seems to have understood "predicate" in a purely linguistic sense; this is precisely the point of his thesis about the "grammatical" origin of the Aristotelian categories.[92] Under "subject–predicate" or "judgment", Trendelenburg mixes grammar and logic, concepts and words, and all this is called "formal" as far as it is opposed to the "real"[93] world of substances and accidents.[94]

A typical traditional procedure consists in *saying* that universality–singularity is just something "irrelevant", but *making* at the same time *much use* of that distinction. *Intellectus facit universalitatem*[95]; in this sense universality is something incidental, something just "happening" to a thing[96], and one may dispense with analysing it. On such an assumption it may be banished from the *Transzendentalphilosophie* and thrust into "general logic".[97] In the frame of transcendental idealism there are "substances" and "accidents", both being always "real".[98] This is made to correspond with categorical judgments whose structure is subject–predicate. And here, under "predicate" (or "concept") universality takes refuge[99]; it continues to be an essential thread throughout the *Critique of Pure Reason*, where, so to speak, it is used but not mentioned.[100]

1.45 *Husserl. Pseudo-properties of properties: Carnap, Ingarden, F. Kaufmann*

In the Husserlian notion of "moments" of a thing we find an impressive analogon of individual accidents. Each piece of red paper has its *individuelle Röte*, which is an *Einzelfall* of the *Spezies Röte*; the individual rednesses (*Rotmomente*) are only equal (*gleich*) among themselves.[101]

In an early text[102] Husserl comes across a sort of vestige of the ontological square. J. Bergmann[103] had introduced a classification of "ideas" by means of two criteria: singular–universal, concrete–abstract. Husserl's criticism of this appearance of the ontological square is interesting because he says that such a classification does not allow for giving a place (*placieren*) to some special kinds of entities. I understand that Husserl means that in Bergmann's classification there is no room for "higher predicates" or ideal entities (species, etc.). If my interpretation is correct, Husserl's criticism would be particularly interesting for, in fact, those are the things which cannot be immediately annexed to the ontological square (because of the peculiarities of the Aristotelian predication theory[104]).

A curious way of observing how the two ontological dimensions are intimately related in different periods of the history of philosophy is to consider a sophism whose "secret" lies in passing from one of these dimensions to the other. The Greek commentators Simplicius and Elias comment on this sophism precisely within their analysis of *Categoriae*.[105] A version of the sophism is, for example: man is white, white is a colour, man is a colour. Husserl considers this sophism (in another variant) as an illegitimate application of the principle *nota notae est nota rei*.[106] In Husserl's language this sophism consists in passing from a thing to one of its "moments" and from this to a universal entity (universal with respect to the "moment", not to the thing).

Carnap's solution of the sophism would be different. He views *colour* as a property of properties, for instance as a property of the property *white*; therefore, in the Fregean or modern logic's theory of predication, *colour* will not "descend" to the individual. Nevertheless, such a solution of the sophism depends itself on a grave ambiguity. In fact, when Carnap[107] gives the example "the word 'colour' designates a property of properties", we must assume a change in the meaning of "property", because otherwise an *abstract* object (as a property is supposed to be) would be a colour, i.e., a visible entity. Obviously *colour* is not a property of properties, if "property" is to preserve its usual meaning.[108] From the point of view of classical ontology (or Husserl's theory of *moments*) colour is a property of an accident (moment).

In Husserl's school there has also been an ambiguous use of "property", similar to Carnap's. Ingarden [1] formulates a paradox concerning *properties of properties*[109]; he says that on the one hand a property of a property of an object is not a property of the object, but on the other hand he points out that a property of a property of an object should still be thought of as "belonging" to the object.

This paradox disappears as soon as one observes that Ingarden [1] works with *two* senses of "property"; that a property of properties should "belong" to the individual is plausible on the assumption that properties are Husserlian *moments* (as Ingarden says) or that "accidens non excedit subiectum suum"[110] (to use a classical formula).

Having observed such an ambiguity in Carnap's and Ingarden's use of "property", it would not seem unlikely to find something similar in the works of F. Kaufmann, an author depending both on Husserl and on the Vienna circle, and who rejects the idea of properties of properties.[111] (This rejection is one of his basic insights, from which he tries to make meaningless the higher-order predicate calculus.) In fact the main examples of properties of properties discussed by F. Kaufmann (*Farbe*, *Helligkeit*) suggest that he had in mind Husserlian "moments", which makes his argument suspicious. There is even a more definite objection to F. Kaufmann's theories, namely, that his properties of properties seem to be visualized rather as class-inclusion (Frege's UO). As a result, F. Kaufmann's discussion would be vitiated by *two* kinds of pseudo-properties of properties: the first, where properties of properties are mixed up with accidents (or moments), the second, where properties of properties are just concepts of a wider extension.[112]

It would not be difficult to accumulate further examples of modern philosophers of logic who are still entangled in the ancient difficulties of the ontological square.[113]

1.46 *Frege*

A comparison of Frege's *Ungesättigtheit* with the first chapter of Book Z of Aristotle's *Metaphysics* may suggest an immediate identification. Aristotle opposes substances to other things which have the peculiarity that they involve an essential reference to the former. And from Aristotle to Kant passing through Port-Royal there are "quasi-things" whose characteristic is to be *ens entis* rather than *ens* proper.

If one stays in the line of Scholz, in the sense of comparing classical ontology with contemporary "predicate-theoretical" logic[114], the above mentioned identification would impose itself as obvious.

But a closer inspection shows that the first chapter of Book Z of *Metaphysics* conceals a grave ambiguity with respect to the two ontological dimensions. Therefore, a comparison of Frege's "Ungesättigtheit" with traditional philosophy is not possible unless one previously answers the question whether "traditional" unsaturatedness applies to one or both of the two ontological dimensions (assuming that it is already established that one or both of these dimensions is to be found in Frege's system, say, that *predication* is *falling under a concept*).

A term which frequently recurs in Frege's texts is: "(un)selbständig". This word appears first, perhaps, in BG[115] in an important context. We may say that to understand the term "selbständig" in GRL is equivalent to having some insight into Frege's philosophy of numbers.[116] In a late paper, published in 1918[117], Frege uses "(un)selbständig" in another significant context.

Therefore it is appropriate to analyse more deeply Frege's conception of *selbständig*. In so doing one is brought to consider the two ontological dimensions. First, because Frege himself uses "selbständig" with connotations which strongly recall some traditional ontological theses[118]; secondly, if one looks for the possible sources of Frege's term or for the philosophical history of the term itself it seems that the most accurate accounts one may obtain are formulated by means of the two ontological dimensions.[119]

If one is puzzled by some irregular uses of the important term "Eigenschaft" in Frege's books, it seems necessary to take into account the two ontological dimensions. Frege in fact uses in some cases "Eigenschaft" in the sense of individual accident.[120] This happens, for instance, in the context of his philosophy of number in GRL.[121]

Frege's rejection of predicates of predicates in the explicit sense appears as a most suggestive fact in the history of philosophy. But shall we compare it with Aristotle's "there is no accident of accident"?[122]

In Frege's *Sinn* there is perhaps some need for taking into account a distinction between *aspects* of a thing and *concepts* under which the thing falls.

At the same time (at least in natural languages) there are senses lacking a reference. Now, while this may be easily formulated by saying that there are empty-concepts, it would be a *tour de force* to say that there are empty-aspects.[123] If "the Morning Star" has a sense but lacks a reference, it is natural to think of that sense as an empty concept, but it is unnatural to think of it as an "empty aspect of Venus". This is due to the fact that aspects are meant to be concrete properties, rather similar to individual accidents. Individual accidents which do not inhere were already a difficult question for classical ontologists and theologians.

Two other applications of the ontological square in the present work are the following: (1) The semantics of so-called "general" or "common" names may have been influenced by the relation of *inherence*. The name of an accident (universal accident) includes a reference to the substance, in the sense that (individual) accidents must inhere in substances. The metaphysical stress on the dependence of accidents upon substances increases the importance of the "denotation" (as opposed to the "connotation") of names of concepts belonging to the "accidental" sphere. *White things* (to take Mill's example of denotation) are not only important as containing the instances of a universal, but also as subjects "in which" such instances can exist.[124] (2) The standard form of the Aristotelian predication theory can be explained only in terms of the two ontological dimensions.[125]

REFERENCES

1. A rich critical history of the problem of the two metaphysics is to be found in Owens [1], Part 1, Chapter 1. The author records the different views since the Greek commentators until our times.
2. Aristotle [2], Γ, 3, 1005a, 22: *ἅπασι γὰρ ὑπάρχει τοῖς οὖσιν ἀλλ'οὐ γενει τινὶ . . .* is the reason given for counting the "axioms" as part of the *philosophia prima.*
3. For the appearance of this name, cf. Ferrater Mora [1], where the use of "ontology" before Wolff is studied.
4. Pichler [1].
5. Scholz-Hasenjaeger [1], p. 13 below, and note. For Leśniewski, cf. Luschei [1], p. 28. By "foundational research" I simply refer to the following text of Frege: "Wenn ich die Arithmetik mit einem Baume vergleiche, der sich oben in eine Mannigfaltigkeit von Methoden und Lehrsätzen entfaltet, während die Wurzel in die Tiefe strebt, so scheint mir der Wurzeltrieb, in Deutschland wenigstens, schwach zu sein. Selbst in einem Werke, das man dieser Richtung zuzählen möchte, der *Algebra der Logik* des Herrn E. Schröder, gewinnt doch bald der Wipfeltrieb wieder die Oberhand, bevor noch eine größere Tiefe erreicht ist . . ." (GRG I, p. XIII).
6. Signo ε es litera initiale de vocabulo graeco *ἐστι* (Peano [1], I, § 1).
7. The subject-matter of logic is for Frege *die Gesetze des Wahrseins* which are the logical laws, only secondarily the *Schlußregeln* (cf. Bartlett [1], p. 3). "Logic" is said also to contain such subjects as *Verneinung* (negation), *Subsumption, Unterordnung* (subordination), *Identität* . . . (UGG_2 (III), p. 428). If Frege speaks here of "logical" relations he is merely the victim of a situation he himself helped to destroy (cf. Chapters 5 and 7).
   For "ontology" in modern philosophy, let us consider the following text of Baumgarten: "Ontologia [= die Grundwissenschaft, says the author in a footnote] (ontosophia, metaphysica, metaphysica universalis, architectonica, philosophia prima) est scientia praedicatorum entis generaliorum" (Baumgarten [1], § 4). Or the well known definition of Wolff: "Quoniam Ontologia de ente in genere agit, ea demonstrare debet, quae onmibus entibus sive absolute sive sub data quadam conditione conveniunt" (Wolff [1], § 8).
8. Baumgarten [1], *sectio* VIII of "praedicata relativa entis" is devoted to "signum et signatum".
9. Jacoby [1] and [2].
10. For example, FUB, p. 17, GRG I, p. 7.
11. Heidegger [1]: "Was ist demnach ein Ding? Ein Kern, um den viele wechselnde Eigenschaften herumliegen, oder ein Träger, dem diese Eigenschaften aufliegen, etwas, was anderes besitzt, an sich hat. Wie wir es auch drehen und wenden, der Bau der Dinge zeigt sich so . . ." (p. 25).

"Was ist also ein Ding? Antwort: Ein Ding ist der vorhandene Träger vieler an ihm vorhandener und dabei wechselnder Eigenschaften . . .
Die überlieferte Wesensbestimmung der Dingheit des Dinges können wir in den bekannten und geläufigen Titeln festhalten:

1. Unterlage – was immer schon dabei steht, sich auch mit eingestellt hat.
2. Substantia – accidens.
3. Träger – Eigenschaften.
(4. Subjekt – Prädikat)" (p. 26).

The last couple, subject-predicate, belongs to the structure (*Bau*) of the sentence, and corresponds (*genau angemessen*) to a similar structure of the thing (substratum–property, p. 28). Heidegger [3], § 33 should be also considered here.

12. "... diese Sätze [logical laws] sprechen von nichts anderem als von Individuen und Eigenschaften" (Scholz-Hasenjaeger [1], p. 13). The same is implied by Hilbert–Ackermann [1], p. 50; Lorenzen [1], § 1, etc., etc.
13. The absolute separation of "logic" and "reality" is expressed with particular force by Clauberg, who acknowledges (in agreement with tradition) that both disciplines (logic and metaphysics) are equally universal, but "inter Metaphysicae ac Logicae subiectum infinita est distantia, quatenus nullum esse reale commune habent" (quoted in Ferrater Mora [1], p. 39–40).
14. On the authenticity of *Categoriae* see De Rijk [2].
15. Let us consider Jungius' paraphrase of the Aristotelian text:
"Secunda Divisio. Entium, sive eorum, quae sunt, quaedam de Subjecto dicuntur, in Subjecto vero nullo sunt, ut Substantiae Universales, sive Genera vel Species Substantiae, ut *homo*, *animal*, *corpus*.
Quaedam in Subjecto sunt, de Subjecto vero nullo dicuntur, ut Accidentia praedicamentalia singularia, ut *haec superficies*, *hic color*, *haec Virtus*.
Quaedam et de Subjecto dicuntur, et in Subjecto sunt, ut accidentia universalia, sive Genera et Species Accidentium praedicamentalium ut *Superficies*, *color nigrities*, *sapor*, *dulcedo*.
Quaedam neque de Subjecto dicuntur, neque in Subjecto sunt, ut Substantiae singulares sive individuae, ut *Socrates*, *Cicero*, *Bucephalus*" (Jungius [1], p. 16).
Boethius calls the division of entities into ten categories the *divisio maxima*, the present classification into four classes of entities the *divisio parvissima*. But unfortunately Boethius does not provide further explanations as to how both divisions and how the two fundamental relations (singular–universal, substance–accident) should be combined (Boethius [1]).
16. Cf. Prantl [1], Vol. I, p. 685. Also Boethius [1]. We find the square in such important editions as Averroes [1] and Pacius [3].
17. Ioannes a Sto. Thoma [1], p. 476:
"Atque ita in hoc tertio antepraedicamento distinguit Aristoteles duplex genus entium, scilicet substantiam et accidens, et duplex genus intentionum, scilicet universalitatis et singularitatis."
18. Fernandez–Garcia [1]: *distinctio ens–res*. It is interesting to consider also the following earlier text:
"Thus the word 'thing' may admit of a wider extension, whereby it may apply to universals, even though Aristotle says that the latter are to be understood as abstracted from particular things in such a way that they would have no existence in the absence of the aforesaid" (John of Salisbury [1], p. 140 = Book II, Ch. 20).

19. ἐν ὑποκειμένῳ εἶναι.
20. καθ' ὑποκειμένου λέγεσθαι.
21. Aristotle [1], 2a, 19–27.
22. "to be predicated univocally", Aristotle [1], 3a, 33; 3b, 9; cf. Simplicius [1], p. 52.
23. "Belongs to" (approximately).
24. "Separately" (approximately).
25. The possibility of *sometimes* predicating the name will actually develop into a wider theory of predication (cf. Section 4.2).
26. Aristotle [1], 2a, 27–34.
27. "Subiectum in praesentia non sumitur eodem modo; cum enim asseritur aliquid dici de subiecto, accipitur subiectum pro subiecto praedicationis; at cum dicitur, aliquid esse in subiecto, usurpatur pro subiecto inhaesionis" (Gasconius [1], II, 67a). Cf. Simplicius [1], p. 53, 25.
28. For example, 3a, 7–15.
29. Aristotle [1], Chapter 5, in particular 3a, 7–32.
30. Cf. Jungius' paraphrase (quoted above) and especially Boethius [1].
31. This is clear in Aristotle [1], 1b, 13; 1b, 20–24; 2b, 19 and especially the passage 3a, 33–3b, 10.
32. The term συμβεβηκός does not appear in *Categoriae* but we follow tradition, for example, Boethius [1]. Cf. also Van Auben [1], 399–400.
33. This is not clear in the basic text (1a, 20–1b, 10) but it is obvious in 2b, 1–3. "Tam primae quam secundae substantiae subiiciuntur accidentibus", says Pacius [2], *cap.* 3, n. 3. This is a fundamental point in traditional *ontology* whose effects on traditional *logic* may be easily foreseen. If properties (accidents) inhere in *man* as well as in *this man*, one may presume that they will also be said of *man* as well as of *this man*.
    Do individual accidents inhere also in universal substances? The basic text (1a, 20–1b, 10) does perhaps allow this (taking for example "ψυχή" in 1a, 26 as a universal). But thereby we would be forcing the text in a question which is precisely the weak point of Aristotelian ontology: singularity-universality in accidents.
34. Aristotle [1], 3b, 17.
35. τὸ καθ' ἕκαστον (2a, 35–2b, 3); ἄτομα καὶ ἓν ἀριθμῷ (1b, 6); ἄτομα (3a, 35). The individuality of members of α_3 is explicitly assigned by 1b, 6 and 4a, 14–17. 11a, 20–36 cannot be used for this because there τὰ κάθ' ἕκαστα seems rather to designate subordinate concepts.
36. For the meaning of these terms cf. Bonitz [1], articles καθόλου and οὐσία. *Universal* is described not only by means of "being predicable of" but also by the Greek term ὑπάρχειν; this is the origin of the traditional double characterization of universals as being said *de multis* and being *in multis*, "universale in praedicando" and "universale in essendo". The definition of EU in *Categoriae* (cf. Section 1.2) still serves to characterize the opposition substance–accident in the main Aristotelian works, except that now accidents may *always*, not only *sometimes*, be said of their substances. (This corresponds to a predication theory different from that of *Categoriae*, cf. Section 4.2.)
37. Aristotle [1], *Perihermeneias*, 7, 17a, 38–40, boldly divides *ta pragmata* into universals and singulars, but the only examples given are *man* and *Callias*. In Aristotle [4], B, 3, 195b, 13–15, we may be momentarily attracted by the fact

that such terms as "genus", "individual", "accident" appear together, but this is useless for the purposes of the present research because there the term "accident" means rather *what is incidental*. Aristotle [2], B, 6, 1003a, 7ff. illustrates the distinction universal–singular by means of *Socrates, animal, man*. Aristotle [2], Δ, 6, 1015b, 16–34, actually refers to both dimensions but the distinction universal–singular is considered only for substances.

38. Perhaps the most significant passage exemplifying this is Aristotle [2], Z, 1: the main opposition there is between substance and non-substance; if some hint at universality–singularity is to be found, this concerns only substances. Aristotle [2], Γ, 2, contains also an important formulation of the metaphysical program. The dominant opposition is again *ousia* vs. *non-ousia*, but it is impossible to find an explicit or adequate reference to the other dimension.
39. Aristotle [2], N, 2, 1089b, 20–28. We quote Ross' paraphrase:
"In the categories other than substance there is another problem as to how things are many; no doubt, since they do not exist apart, they are many through the substratum taking on many qualities, &c.; but there must be a matter for each category, only it cannot be one existing apart from substance" (Vol. II, p. 469). Cf. also:
"The special difficulty attaching to the minor categories is that of assigning to each a matter which shall render plurality possible without being separable from substance . . ." (*Ibid.*, p. 477).
40. It may be inferred from such passages as Aristotle [2], *Λ*, 5, 1071a, 20 (until the end) that accidents are individuals because (a) universals do not exist (1071a, 19) and (b) if substances would disappear, all other things would likewise disappear, which means that accidents do exist (when substances exist). The same could be inferred from the first lines of *Λ* plus Pseudo-Alexander's commentary (in Aristotle [2.1], Vol. II, p. 643, note 1). But this tends simply to confuse the reader. Sometimes accidents are individual, real entities; sometimes they are predicated of substances, i.e., they are universals. (Of course, examples of accidents being predicated of substances are to be found everywhere in the main Aristotelian works, apart from *Categoriae's* peculiar first pages; that is in fact the standard, in opposition to *Categoriae*, Aristotelian predication theory; cf. Section 4.2.)
41. Tricot (in Aristotle [2.1], Vol. 1, p. 289, note 1) depending on Alexander and Bonitz; Ross (in Aristotle [2], Vol. 1, p. 323) also depending on Alexander. For the second point, Ross in Aristotle [2], Vol. 1, p. LXXXVII; also Ross' commentary on *Metaphysics* I, 1054, b, 35, where an expression equivalent to "Porphyrian tree" appears, but where, as in Porphyry, complete obscurity reigns as to which are the bases of the *accidental* Porphyrian trees.
De Rijk [1], p. 70–71, deals with the present question, and he affirms that the reason is to be found in the peculiarities of "the" Aristotelian theory of predication. But "the" Aristotelian theory which he means is that of *Analytica Posteriora*, and moreover a theory which Aristotle seems to propose only incidentally ("if we are to legislate"). Therefore, the predication theory meant by De Rijk does not seem to explain – as he suggests – why Aristotle is silent about singular–universal in accidents.
Owens [1] does not appear to consider at all the problem of singularity–universality in accidents. This is all the more significant as this study is especially concerned with universal–singular relations (but apparently only in the substantial domain).

A particular case is Scholz, who approached classical texts on ontology from a perspective of modern predicate-calculus. May "huparchein" always be translated into contemporary predicate-theoretical standards? (cf. Scholz–Hasenjaeger [1], p. 13, note). One may conjecture that Scholz, according to such an approach, would have translated the famous "non est accidens accidenti" (*Metaphysics*, Γ, 4) with "there are no predicates of predicates". But this, especially from the point of view of the whole tradition, would be a most questionable version. Also, in Scholz [2] it is said (p. 140) that to define the existence of classes as their non-emptiness is to be Aristotelian rather than Platonist; this may be correct in itself, but Scholz supports his statement by evoking such Aristotelian theses as "*ta pathe* do not exist apart from substances". Now, does "pathe" designate individual or universal accidents? Scholz's well-known comparison of old ontology with modern logic should perhaps be re-examined; in doing so the *two* ontological dimensions should be taken into account.

Owen [1] is a recent discussion related to the ontological square. The author stresses that the Aristotelian texts do not sufficiently support the thesis that individual accidents cannot be found in more than one subject. This thesis is viewed by the author as "a dogma" originating with Aristotle's interpreters. The author also stresses that such a dogma entails many difficulties. But the absence of the dogma in Aristotle raises in fact even more difficulties, which are not accounted for by Owen [1].

42. GRG II, § 151 (in the analysis of contents).
43. Cf. Sections 2.61 and 6.4.
44. Cf. Section 1.2, note 17.
45. Cf. Sections 1.45 and 1.46.
46. In the Renaissance I include the second scholastics. (For this term "second scholastics", cf. Giacon [1]. For the usual "restricted" conception of "Medieval philosophy", cf. De Wulf [1], n. 15 and 449.)
47. Porphyry [1], *Isagoge*, 2a, 5–13. Aaron [1], Section 2, finds it strange that Porphyry poses the problem (of universals) in terms of thing-universals only (thing-universals as opposed to qualities or relations). Actually within the framework of a strict Aristotelianism it would be strange to find somebody paying attention to the problem of universals within the accidental domain. *It is* indeed strange to find so many authors (especially in the Middle Ages) stressing the singular–universal question in the case of accidents. Incidentally, Aaron [1] makes extensive use of the opposition thing–universal and qualities or relations (pp. 3ff, 26, 33, 36, 40, 104, 176, 191, 217–8, 234, 237), but the connection of this modern-philosophy terminology to its source – the ontological square – is not clear. (The author gives one reference to *Categoriae*'s individuality of accidents on p. 10.)
48. Algazel [1], *Tract. primus, div. prima, div. secunda.* The second section of the *divisio secunda* is entitled: "Universale non potest habere plura singularia nisi unumquodque discernatur ab alio." This involves something akin to the principle of indiscernibles, but with an awareness of the two dimensions of classical ontology.
49. For example: "Ich will einen allgemeinen Satz vorausschicken: alle Substanzen oder Accidenzen oder auch Attribute von Substanzen und Accidenzen mit denen man in dieser Hinsicht auf ihn [God] hinweist, sind weder in großem noch in kleinem Umfange auf den Schöpfer anwendbar" (Kaufmann [1], p. 54).

50. "In like manner, and with due proportion, those quantities and qualities which are individually present in primary substances may also be called "primary", while those quantities which are abstracted from particular things by an analogous process [quadam ratione similitudinis] may be termed "secondary". The same holds with the other predicaments" (John of Salisbury [1], p. 161 = Chapter 3, Book 3).
51. *Ibid.*, p. 156.
52. Schütz [1], article "accidens", b), third line.
53. "Ubi notandum est quod natura non se habet ad suppositum sicut universale ad singulare, quia in accidentibus etiam invenitur singularitas sine ratione suppositi et in substantia nostra natura assumpta est a Verbo, secundum Damascenum, non tamen suppositum nostrae naturae" (Duns Scotus [1], p. 558). Also: "Quia ita impossibile videtur unum accidens esse in duobus subiectis, sicut unam formam substantialem esse in duobus materiis" (quoted by Fernandez Garcia [1], p. 745, *effata*: "Accidentis unius unum est subiectum"; referring to *Op. Oxon.* III dist. I, q. 2, n. 4).
54. Baudry [1].
55. *Ibid.*
56. "Uno modo idem est [Ockham is explaining the meanings of "inesse"] quod inhaerere realiter sicut accidens inest subiecto et forma materiae. Alio modo idem est quod praedicari."
The term "inesse" will be enthusiastically adopted by Leibniz (Couturat [1], p. 10).
57. Paulus Venetus [1], *tract.* 1, *cap.* XVI, *de praedicamentis.*
58. This is an interesting background, which may be taken into account in regard to the famous Berkeley discussion of the idea of *triangle.*
59. Gasconius [1], II, 55b. Cf. *De Natura Accidentis* in Aquinas [2].
60. Suarez [1], 39, 1, 1 and 16; cf. the text quoted above in note 50.
61. Pacius [2], *cap.* 2, n. 16 and 20.
62. Keckermann [1], *Index*: "Accidens . . . numero unum de subiecto non migrat in subiectum . . . numero unum in subiectis numero diversis esse nequit . . ."
63. *Ibid.*, *Liber I*, *cap.* 5 (p. 72): "Sic Logica quae fuit in Aristotele, non fuit idea vel species, sed Logica individua et singularis." Keckermann adds: "Scholasticorum Canon huic pertinet: Accidentia numerantur ad numerum subiectorum."
64. Descartes [1], §§ 51, 57. Gilson [3], p. 46, gives a list of passages where Descartes refers to "choses particulières et universelles".
65. For example, Descartes [1], § 52 *in fine*, asserts that when we come across a property we may conclude that *there is* a substance having that property. This is not the ontological argument . . . but probably an obvious argument about properties understood as individual accidents. *Ibid.* n. 61, Descartes examines the *distinction modale*; he considers four cases of distinction: (i) between a mode and a substance, (ii) between two modes of the same substance, (iii) between a mode of a substance and another substance, (iv) between a mode of a substance and a mode of another substance. Obviously, this is conceived in terms of properties-of-a-given-individual.
66. Contrary to Scholz's program, cf. Scholz [7], for example, p. 414.
67. Port-Royal [1], *Première partie, Chapitre* 2: "On ne sçauroit nier ce rapport du mode, qu'on ne detruise l'idée qu'on en avoit."
68. *Ibid.*, *Chapitre* 6.
69. Accidents "stick on" substances; substances are "under-propping" (Locke [1], II, 13, § 20).

70. Locke [1], II, 23, § 4.
71. "In the notice that our senses take of the constant vicissitude of things, we cannot but observe that several *particulars*, both *qualities* and substances, begin to exist" (Locke [1], II, 26, § 1, italics ours).
72. "This is further to be observed concerning substances, that they alone of all our several sorts of ideas have particular or proper names, whereby one only particular thing is signified. Because in simple ideas, modes, and relations, it seldom happens that men have occasion to mention often this or that particular when it is observed" (Locke [1], III, 6, § 42).
73. "On this account, if one should say, that the whiteness of this sheet is the whiteness of another sheet, every man perceives this to be absurd" (Reid [1], p. 327, *Essay* V, Ch. 3).
"To this I answer, that the whiteness of this sheet is one thing, whiteness is another; the conceptions signified by these two forms of speech are as different as the expressions; the first signifies an individual quality really existing and is not a general conception, though it be an abstract one; the second signifies a general conception, which implies no existence, but may be predicated of every thing that is white, and in the same sense" (*ibid.*).
74. In such terms Russell [1], § 10, describes a passage of Leibniz's polemics with Clarke (in Leibniz [1], vol. VII, p. 400–401).
75. "Car deux sujets differens, comme A et B, ne sauroient avoir precisement la même affection individuelle, un même accident individuel ne se pouvant point trouver en deux sujets, ny passer de sujet en sujet" (Leibniz [1], *loc. cit.*).
76. *The Concise Oxford Dictionary of Current English* (1949), article "Siamese".
77. Russell [1], § 10: "After he has seemed for a moment to realize that *relation* is something distinct from, and independent of, subject and accident, he thrusts aside the awkward discovery." If Russell means *universal* relation (that R which applies between a and b as well as between c and d), then (1), it is not true to say that Leibniz rejects them, for he still assigns to them an objective ontological status in the mind (cf. note 83); (2), moreover, Russell's statement would not fit with the Leibnizian text where *individual* relations are meant (cf. note 79). If Russell means *individual* relation (that $R_{a,b}$ which is an individual instance of R applying between a and b), then the Leibnizian discovery is indeed so awkward that one wonders how Leibniz could do otherwise than to thrust it aside. But the second alternative seems improbable.
78. "Itaque plena omnia relationum in mundo, nec res ulla nascitur, quin infinitae propemodum cum ea nascantur relationes" (Keckermann [1], Lib. I, cap. XII = p. 115).
79. The fragment quoted by Russell [1], § 10, does not mention individual accidents but only accidents. It is obvious, however, from the immediately preceding context that Leibniz is simply abbreviating "accident" for "individual accident". The fragment quoted by Russell is intended by Leibniz as an *example* of his previously formulated thesis about individual accidents (cf. our note 75).
80. Leibniz would say: $R_{a,b}$ and $R_{c,d}$ *conviennent seulement* (*loc. cit.*, p. 401 above). For a modern approach to these "concrete" properties cf. Küng [1] and [2].
81. Cf. following note.
82. Leibniz says, in the English translation quoted by Russell: "You will not, I believe, admit an accident which is in two subjects at once. Thus, I hold, as regards relations, that paternity in David is one thing, and filiation in Solomon

is another, but the relation common to both is a merely mental thing, of which the modifications of singulars are the foundation" (in Russell [1], Appendix, *ad* § 10).

83. Russell [1], § 10. The critical phrase "being in the mind" has primarily an objective sense in traditional philosophy. Leibniz himself would say, for example, that necessary truths are *dans l'entendement* (Leibniz [1], Vol. V, p. 76).
84. Dependent on Russell's interpretation are Maritain [1] (n. 40, b), Scholz–Hasenjaeger [1], § 84. Bergmann [1] is perhaps the only adequate approach to Leibniz in the present questions; but still it would seem that even Prof. Bergmann does not point to the ultimate source of Leibniz's difficulty with relations, i.e., the awkwardness of individual instances of relations. Leibniz's difficulty was to find a model – a sound model – for *hoc aequale*, not for *aequale* (to take Paulus Venetus' example of a relation and its individual instance, cf. note 57).
85. In particular Russell [1], § 4.
86. In such a context it is meaningless to speak of properties "migrating" from one subject to another (cf. note 75) and in fact Russell does *not* consider *this* aspect of Leibniz's ontology (for example, Russell [1], § 67, where the text quoted in our note 75 is paraphrased but the phrase on migration of properties is *curiously dropped*).
87. Russell [1], § 23.
88. For instance Trendelenburg [1], pp. 14–15.
89. "Wo ein Urteil im eigentlichen Sinne vorliegt, so daß es die Sache aussagt, wie sie wird, ist das Subject die erzeugende Substanz (*οὐσία*). Die ausgesagten Begriffe (*κατηγορούμενα* im eigentlichen Sinne) setzen das Subject voraus, und, inwiefern sie nicht Substanzen sind, sind sie, real gefaßt, in der Substanz *συμβεβηκότα*" (Trendelenburg [1], p. 210).
The "authenticity" of a "judgment" is determined by Aristotle's ruling on correct predication (*Analytica Posteriora* I, 22; cf. Trendelenburg's text referred to in the preceding note).
90. The clandestine introduction of concepts under the heading of "predicate" is clear, for example, in the following text: "Hiernach erscheinen die Kategorien als die allgemeinen Begriffe, unter welche die Prädikate des einfachen Satzes fallen . . . Die Kategorien sind die allgemeinsten Prädikaten" (Trendelenburg [1], p. 20).
One may compare this use of "Fallen unter" with Frege's. This is an occasion to appreciate the importance of Frege's stressing the necessity of distinguishing names and designata.
In the text quoted in note 89 we had already seen the expression "ausgesagten Begriffe"; the same phrase occurs in p. 19 of Trendelenburg [1]. The "judgment" is analysed into subject–predicate, but "predicate" ambiguously covers linguistic as well as non-linguistic entities (i.e. universals, concepts).
91. Cf. for instance the description of categories as *die allgemeinen Begriffe* in the text quoted in the preceding note.
92. Therefore, in the polemic between Trendelenburg and Bonitz about the significance of the categories, it appears how ambiguous the very formulation of the problem is.
93. For the opposition "formal" and "real", cf. Trendelenburg [1], p. 18, below.
94. How *essential* predication is to be understood, remains obscure in the "parallelism" version of the ontological square. Trendelenburg [1], p. 16, mentions

this kind of predication without, however, saying whether or how it fits with the correspondence between substance–accident and subject–predicate. In the text quoted in note 89, there is only a negative reference.

95. This is an old and fundamental approach to universals.
96. A typical Aristotelian scholar of the 16th century would teach that the division of entities into singulars and universals is a "divisio subiecti in accidentia, nam cuilibet rei sive enti accidit ratio universalis et singularis; ut enim superius diximus, res ipsa neque per se universalis est, neque singularis, sed potius illud ei convenit per abstractionem intellectus, hoc vero per condiciones particulares" (Gasconius [1], II, 67a, below).
Kant teaches that in concepts there is a *Materie* and a *Form*. The former is the *Gegenstand* (here, obviously, as in Gasconius: *Gegenstand* = *res*, indifferent or neutral with respect to universality and singularity; not *Gegenstand* = existing individual given, for instance, in the *Anschauung*); the latter is the *Allgemeinheit*. Now, universality is always made by us, *jederzeit gemacht* (Kant [2], §§ 2, 4, 5).
97. As Kant puts it: "er [i.e., the distinction singular–universal] keinen Unterschied in der Beschaffenheit der Dinge, sondern nur des Gebrauchs der Begriffe, ob sie im allgemeinen oder aufs einzelne angewandt werden, anzeigt" (Kant [4], Erst. Abschn., C, fourth note).
98. Eisler [1], "Akzidenzen".
99. Cf. text quoted in note 96.
100. Heidegger also seems to support the "parallelism" version described in the present section (cf. Heidegger [1], p. 28). A recent version is the following: "Aristotle's position in logic, that every proposition is reducible to subject–predicate form, is paralleled by his metaphysical doctrine that the world consists of substances with attributes" (Körner [1], p. 21).
101. Husserl [1], 1, §§ 31, 34, 39. As for the other dimension cf. Husserl [1], *I. Untersuchung*, § 15, where universality is described in the following terms: "Fähigkeit, auf eine Vielheit von Gegenständen prädikativ bezogen zu werden".
102. Husserl [2], *Erster Artikel.*
103. Bergmann, J. [1], § 5, 2 and 3.
104. Cf. Section 5.32.
105. Elias [1], p. 153; Simplicius [1], p. 54, lines 15–20.
106. Husserl [1], I, 41.
107. Carnap [1], p. 216 (or Linsky [1], p. 222). Cf. Carnap [7], p. 20, and also Simpson [1], pp. 272, 277, 291, 295–6.
108. Reichenbach [1], p. 53 and [2], pp. 27–28 suggests that "property" has to be understood in two senses. One of them involves the so-called "specific properties" of an entity; a specific property of x is for instance the individual motion of x and it is only of this specific property that we may predicate the (higher property?) of *being slow*. Unfortunately, Reichenbach does not develop this question systematically. Let us only observe that "specific properties" are, in classical terms, individual accidents.
109. Ingarden [1] p. 73: "Indessen führt bekanntlich anderseits gerade die Annahme von Eigenschaften der Eigenschaften zu einer Antinomie. Zugleich müßte man zugeben daß es in dem Seinsbereiche eines Gegenstandes etwas gibt (nämlich die Eigenschaften der Eigenschaften), das zugleich außerhalb dieses Bereiches liegt. Denn indem die Eigenschaft das dem Gegenstande in einer Hinsicht Zukommende ist, kommt sie ihm mit allem und jedem, was in ihr selbst "ent-

halten" ist, zu. Somit muß sie mit allem und jedem in ihr Unterscheidbaren in den Seinsbereich des betreffenden Gegenstandes fallen. Wenn dagegen das der Eigenschaft Zukommende dem entsprechenden Gegenstande nicht zukommt, so liegen, wie es scheint, mindestens die vermeintlichen Eigenschaften der Eigenschaft außerhalb des Seinsbereiches des betreffenden Gegenstandes."

110. Schütz [1] article "accidens". This impressive thesis of classical ontology underlies the paradox discussed by Ingarden [1].

111. F. Kaufmann [1] (pp. 18–19) and [2].

112. F. Kaufmann [1] *ibid.*: "Wie steht es aber demgegenüber mit der Behauptung, daß eine bestimmte Eigenschaft E_1 (z.B., eine bestimmte Farbe) eine bestimmte "Eigenschaft" E_2 (z.B. eine bestimmte Helligkeit) habe? Da zeigt es sich, das eine Eigenschaft (Farbe) E_1 als bestimmt überhaupt nur dann gelten kann, wenn feststeht, ob sie die "Eigenschaft" E_2 (bestimmte Helligkeit) besitzt oder nicht." The situation described by this text may be expressed by the following schema:

Farbe

↓

bestimmte Helligkeit → *bestimmte Farbe.*

Now this is (in my view) quite similar to the familiar schema

animal

↓

rationalis → *homo.*

In fact, F. Kaufmann seems to have in mind that *rationalis* is not a property of a determined *animal* (*homo*) for it is only due to *rationalis* that one may speak at all of a "determined" *animal.* Thereby F. Kaufmann apparently assumes that to speak of a property of an object *a* implies that *a* is "already" a sufficiently determined entity, regardless of its having or not having the property in question (*ibid.*). Actually his rejection of properties of properties seems also to involve the pointing out of an ambiguity in "property" rather than to reject as absolutely meaningless the locution "properties of property" (*ibid.*).

F. Kaufmann denounces the meaninglessness of this phrase in the famous (Fregean) example of existence as property of properties (*ibid.*). He says, that it is *unsinnig* to assign a spatio-temporal property (i.e., "to have three individuals in such a place and such a time") to a property which is not a spatio-temporal entity.

It is curious that F. Kaufmann has not discussed examples of a more properly mathematical nature (for instance, *to be local* as a property of properties of functions).

In any case, it should be observed that F. Kaufmann's pretended "Ausschaltung" of the infinite from mathematics (cf. the title of F. Kaufmann [1]) largely depends on these ontological subtleties; for instance, he partially eliminates the possibility of speaking of sets of sets by referring to his doctrine on properties of properties (cf. F. Kaufmann [1], p. 98–99).

113. Bolzano [1] (§ 178) discusses sentences of the form "*A*, als ein *C*, ist *B*", i.e., the so-called "reduplicative" sentences. For instance, "Cajus, als Musiker, ist unübertrefflich" is interpreted by Bolzano as meaning that "die Beschaffenheit *C* des *A* hat die Beschaffenheit *B*". But this would not be readily admitted by Frege as an example of properties of properties; for the same reasons Frege would be suspicious of the examples of "types" and "orders" given by Crahay [1], p. 48.

114. Cf. for example Scholz [7]: "... über der eigenschaftstheoretischen Ontologie des Aristoteles eine unanfechtbare eigenschaftstheoretische Logik zu konstruieren ..." (p. 414).
115. BG., p. 17.
116. Cf. Chapter 10.
117. GED.
118. GED., pp. 67–68: *Vorstellungen* are not *selbständig*; they require a subject, a *Träger*; moreover, "Jede Vorstellung hat nur einen Träger", which corresponds to the Leibnizian (traditional) axiom that an accident cannot inhere in more than one subject.
119. Trendelenburg [1], which is a possible philosophical source of Frege (cf. BG, *Vorwort*). The *Selbständigkeit* of individual substances is determined in a *double* way: negatively or logically as that which is not a predicate, and "really" (*real*) as that which is not in (does not inhere in) another entity (p. 21, note 2; also pp. 53–54).
120. GRL, §§ 21–25, cf. Section 10.11; GRG II, p. 125; GED p. 61, cf. Chapter 2, note 82. It is not clear to me whether in this late text Frege perhaps is aware of the equivocal use of "Eigenschaft". Grossmann [1], IV, does not seem to consider the possibility of an "ambiguity" in the term "Eigenschaft". Cf. also Chapter 2, note 65.
121. Cf. 10.11.
122. Cf. note 41.
123. Cf. Chapter 2, in particular Section 2.24.
124. Cf. Section 2.62.
125. Cf. Section 4.2.

2. SEMANTICS

Summary and general remarks. Before his paper 'Sinn und Bedeutung', Frege had described his own semantics as if it were dyadic (names-content, meaning), but he actually viewed names as having a double semantical dimension (2.1).

That double semantical dimension will later on be called *Sinn–Bedeutung* by Frege, a distinction which here is examined first for "proper" proper names (excluding sentences, in spite of the fact that they are, for Frege, proper names too) (2.2).

After a general presentation (2.21), some historical comparisons are made (2.22). Next, the question of the equality of senses is discussed (2.23).

A special section is devoted to the examination of the possible identification of senses and concepts (2.24).

A conflict of different trends is to be observed in Frege's semantics (2.25). The idea of the ontological analysis of an entity into its various ways of being given, and the idea of the (supposedly) plausible interchangeability of the equi-referential names are two opposite motivations coexisting in Frege's semantics since the *Begriffsschrift* (§ 8) of 1879. The second of these motivations was combined with a pragmatic tendency in Frege to "identify" entities serving equally some assigned purpose, and the result is in my view a grave ambiguity in the term "Bedeutung" (and "Sinn") (2.26) – *Bedeutung* not as reference, but as *importance*.

The suggested ambiguity of "Bedeutung" is perhaps the best way to make sense of Frege's odd doctrine of sentences as proper names of the truth-values (2.3).

Some aspects of Frege's analysis of subordinate sentences are considered next (2.4). Frege's aim in this analysis is to show that where sentences cannot be interchanged *salva veritate*, it is because such sentences do not denote a truth-value. From Frege's discussion of subordinate sentences we consider: (1) his exclusion of some pseudo-subordinate sentences which seem to be names of concepts (this touches the question sense-concept) (2.41), (2) his incidental remarks about the necessity of ensuring reference to well-formed expressions (2.42), (3) his distinction of indirect and customary sense or reference (2.43).

Afterwards, Frege's notion of *Vorstellung* and his conception of objectivity are examined, which is necessary in order to evaluate his Platonism (2.5).

Next, his semantics of predicate-terms will be examined. Here, again, the ambiguity of "Bedeutung" may be a valuable help in our interpretation of Frege (2.6).

An attempt is made to show that there is a curious misunderstanding about a so-called semantical principle of *Grundlagen der Arithmetik* (2.7).

The chapter concludes with a brief exposition of Frege's idea of analyticity, a priori, and definitions (2.8, 2.9).

2.1 Sense and reference before 'Sinn und Bedeutung'

> If not the philosopher, who else would consider such questions as: Is Socrates the same as Socrates sitting?
> (Aristotle, *Metaphysics*, 1004b).

2.11 *Begriffsschrift* (§ 8)

In BG Frege speaks many times about signs, and he assumes a dyadic semantics according to which a sign has or designates a content (*Inhalt*).[1] Identity is approached as a relation between signs; namely a relation stating that two names have the same content: *Inhaltsgleichheit*.[2] But if names are *voces significativae ad placitum*[3] it would seem that statements of identity are irrelevant to content, as much as it is arbitrary to designate a thing by means of one or another name. This is a fortiori valid for the scientific language called *Begriffsschrift*, which is supposed to reflect only "conceptual" content, i.e., that "which counts for deduction".[4] Frege in fact considers such an objection against the incorporation of a special sign for identity into the *Begriffsschrift*. His reply consists in pointing out, (1) that in some cases it is practically convenient to introduce a shorter designation for the same thing (= definitions by abbreviation) and, (2) that it is *not always* true that the various names of one thing are just a multiplication of *ad placitum* designations; different names make a difference.

Frege illustrates the second point by the following example. Let us imagine a circle in which there is a fixed point *A*. Let us consider the following property *B*: *to be an intersection of the circle and a straight line rotating around A*. The point *A* – until now determined only by direct intuition: "the point *A*" – may be also determined as "the *B* which corresponds to that position of the rotating straight line in which it becomes perpendicular to the diameter starting from *A*".

In this presentation of Frege's example I have stressed the fact that *B* is a property or concept. Frege does not. On the contrary, he seems to take "*B*" as a name which is successively applied to different entities (points), as if "man" were a name of Peter when applied to Peter.[5] This is in sharp contrast with later doctrines of Frege.[6] Nevertheless, it seems clear that he has in mind what he would later call a property, because the name "*B*" is said to have an undetermined meaning (*Unbestimmtes*) as long as a concrete position of the rotating straight line is not assigned.

By his example Frege shows that the same entity may be determined in more than one way. This fact is the reason for having more than one name for the same entity without merely accumulating *ad placitum* designations. Each name, then, reflects the various ways of determining the entity in question. If there is not an underlying variety of *Bestimmungsweisen* in the thing, the variety of names remains purely arbitrary, irrelevant to content, and then only practical reasons for having shorter expressions (definition by abbreviation) may be considered.

The new sign "≡" is defined as stating the identity of the content of the two names it relates.[7]

It is surprising to suddenly find – together with the definition of the new sign – the rule that names related by that sign may be interchanged in any context. This is obviously inconsistent with respect to the view that different names of a thing express different aspects of the thing.

But my central criticism of Frege's discussion is that the "official" formulations of his semantics ("names have one content": *dyadic* semantics) are not adequately reproducing the core of his own argument, namely, that (in some cases) different names not only designate the same thing but also each of them expresses a particular aspect.[8] This is already sense and reference: only the famous terminology "*Sinn*" and "*Bedeutung*" is lacking here.[9] The point is not trivial, since Frege himself in this respect has done injustice to his own text of 1879.[10]

In these "preliminaries" of sense and reference it is also important to observe the close association of *concept* and *sense*: the point *A* may be determined not only by direct intuition, but also by "describing" it as falling under the concept *B*.

2.12 *Grundlagen der Arithmetik* (§ 67)

In the discussion leading to the famous definition of number, Frege examines several examples of definitions by abstraction, one of which is the passage from parallelism to identity of direction: "the straight line *a* is parallel to the straight line *b*" should mean the same as "the direction of the straight line *a* is the same as the direction of the straight line *b*".[11] But for Frege such a definition is still insufficient because it does not provide a criterion for dealing with objects which (being or not being in themselves directions) are not *given as* directions of some line. England is an example of such an object, and if we know that England is not the direction of some line, this is not precisely due to our definition. Before identifying two directions – *given as* directions – it is necessary to be able to say, about any object at all – *not* necessarily given as a direction – whether or not it is a direction. Frege next considers the possibility of defining in the following way: "*q* is a direction if there is a straight line *b* of which *q* is a direction".[12] But obviously this still presupposes a criterion for deciding what is a direction. Frege also rejects an alternative interpretation of such a definition, according to which one would say: "an object is a direction if it is introduced by means of that definition". The formulation and the rejection of this interpretation make up the content of the § 67 of GRL, a semantically interesting text. This text is not clear in all its details, but we shall nevertheless quote it in full and try to analyse it.

> Wenn man sagen wollte: *q* ist eine Richtung, wenn es durch die oben ausgesprochene Definition eingeführt ist, so würde man die Weise, wie der Gegenstand *q* eingeführt ist, als dessen Eigenschaft behandeln, was sie nicht ist. Die Definition eines Gegenstandes sagt als solche eigentlich nichts von ihm aus, sondern setzt die Bedeutung eines Zeichens fest. Nachdem das geschehen ist, verwandelt sie sich in

ein Urteil, das von dem Gegenstande handelt, aber führt ihn nun auch nicht mehr ein und steht mit andern Aussagen von ihm in gleicher Linie. Man würde, wenn man diesen Ausweg wählte, voraussetzen, daß ein Gegenstand nur auf eine einzige Weise gegeben werden könnte; denn sonst würde daraus, dass *q* nicht durch unsere Definition eingeführt ist, nicht folgen, daß es nicht so eingeführt werden könnte. Alle Gleichungen würden darauf hinauskommen, daß das als dasselbe anerkannt würde, was uns auf dieselbe Weise gegeben ist. Aber dies ist so selbstverständlich, und so unfruchtbar, daß es nicht verlohnte, es auszusprechen. Man könnte in der Tat keinen Schluß daraus ziehen, der von jeder der Voraussetzungen verschieden wäre. Die vielseitige und bedeutsameVerwendbarkeit der Gleichungen beruht vielmehr darauf, daß man etwas wiedererkennen kann obwohl es auf verschiedene Weise gegeben ist. (GRL § 67)

Let us abbreviate by "*A*" the interpretation of the previously given definition which Frege discusses in this text. It will not be examined *how A* is an interpretation of the definition but only Frege's criticism of *A*.

"To introduce an object" is used by Frege here to mean the same as "to introduce a new name (by definition)".[13] In definitions – as Frege says since BG – one does not have a sentence about objects but a rule about signs.

The formulation of *A* mixes different levels of language: on the one hand the object *q* (a direction) and on the other hand a discourse about names (say "*q*"). This confusion of languages is Frege's *first criticism* of *A*. The result of such a confusion is that the way in which an object is introduced would be regarded as a property of the object, which it is not as soon as we substitute "introduction of an object" by "assignment of a meaning to a new name". One could reply that, (1) Frege himself allows for transforming the initial metalinguistic definition into a sentence of the object language[14], (2) *to be called by a name* is actually a property of the object.[15] But Frege does not mean this; he means – I think – that one cannot make of a name of a thing (or of a way of this thing's being given) the *only* name of that thing (or the *only* way of that thing's being given). Neither the title of § 67 in the analysis of contents (of GRL) nor the text itself are clear in this respect, even if Frege's words are literally read, for the way in which an object is designated (the way in which an object is given) *is* a property of the object, and *is* a mark of some concept under which the object falls. That Frege has in mind something different is suggested by a later parallel text:

> ... weil die Weise wie ein Gegenstand gegeben ist, nicht als dessen unveränderliche Eigenschaft angesehen werden darf, sintemal derselbe Gegenstand in verschiedenen Weisen gegeben werden kann. (GRG I, p. 18 note)

Here Frege adds the adjective "unveränderlich"; and the compound expression "unchangeable property" is indeed a rare jewel in his vocabulary. Still, the new qualification is insufficient. The reader naturally understands the new expression as meaning *inseparable accidents* (*propria*) but this, again, is not what Frege means, for the fact that something is an inseparable accident does not entail that one is obliged to view the substance (having that accident) *only* as having that property ("corvus est niger" but one may also say "corvus" and simply consider this animal *qua corvus*, not *qua* black[16]). "Unchangeable property" in my view has to be interpreted in the following manner: a way in which a thing is being given is not its unchangeable property because the thing may be given also under other aspects and hence may be called by other names.

According to this interpretation of Frege's first criticism of *A* we may easily understand his *second criticism*. If one accepts *A*, one is compelled to assume that an object *can* be given in only one way. *A* implies that the object *cannot* be found "under" or "behind" any other designation (or way of being given) than the one fixed by the definition. This argument is reiterated in the above quoted text of GRG I.

Frege himself thinks that objects can be given under different guises, that therefore they may be called (without accumulating *ad placitum* names) by different designations, that one recognizes the object under its different presentations, and that the cognitive value of identity statements is precisely grounded on the basic ontological fact of a *morceau de cire*'s sameness.

GRL § 67 thus contains everything for sense and reference except the famous terms "*Sinn*" and "*Bedeutung*". Curiously, Frege keeps giving "official" formulations of his semantics which do not duly reflect his actual analysis. For example, in a paper published one year after GRL, Frege still defines identity statements as those in which it is said that two signs have the same *content*[17]; it will take some years to split this *dyadic* semantics into a tryadic one of *sense* and *reference*.[18]

2.2 'Sinn' and 'Bedeutung' (proper names)

2.21 *Presentation*

Sinn und Bedeutung[19] begins by formulating the following dilemma concerning the nature of identity: Is identity a relation between objects or is it a relation between names? Frege proceeds as if the "official" formulations only of his previous semantics should be taken into account, and he says that in BG he had assumed the second possibility. The reason supporting the view ascribed to BG is the necessity of preserving the cognitive value of identity statements, preventing them from collapsing into triviality; since if identity were a relation between things, every object would be identical to itself and no object would be identical to any other. Frege's lack of interest for such "trivial" properties was already obvious in GRL as concerns "one" and "existent".[20] Now the fact is that identity statements are *not* always trivial; often sentences of the form $a = b$ (not: $a = a$) contain a significant increase in knowledge. Therefore it remains that identity has to be a relation between names. But this is itself another objectionable solution: if names are "voces significativae ad placitum", a relation between names is also as arbitrary and irrelevant to content as the fact that an entity is being called in this rather than in that way. We have tried to escape triviality but now we are thrown into arbitrariness, which is again disproved by the fact that some sentences of the form $a = b$ have a cognitive value.

This perplexing situation is overcome by introducing some distinctions. A sign may be considered either *as a sign* or *as a figure*[21] (*Figur*). If the relation of designation, which holds between a name "*a*" and an object, is *the same* as that which holds between another name "*b*" of that object and the object, i.e., if one has to write *Designation* ("*a*", object) and *Designation* ("b", object) without further qualifications, then "*a*" and "*b*" in "$a = b$" are different only as figures; as signs they are the same. Now the fact that two figures "*a*" and "*b*" are applied to some object is *ad placitum*, and identity statements lose any cognitive value. But the relations of designation between "*a*" or "*b*" and the object are *not* the same (of course, except when "$a = b$" is a mere abbreviation); "*a*" presents the object under a particular aspect, different from that of "*b*". Thus we see that the semantic situation has to be expressed by a tryadic relation: *Designation* ("*a*", aspect_a, object). Frege holds that "*a*" does not designate the object in the same way as "*b*" does, and that "*a*" and "*b*" are different not only as figures but also *as signs*.

We see now that the initial dilemma of SUB (Is identity a relation between names or between signs?) has to be reworded in a more precise fashion: Is identity a relation between names *qua figures* or between things?

One may thus criticise for two reasons Frege's assertion that in BG the first possibility had been chosen. Frege is not only forgetting the "informal" analysis of BG § 8; he is even projecting a later distinction (signs *qua* signs, signs *qua* figures) on the "official" formulations of that early work.

"The Morning Star" and "the Evening Star" are not only different as figures, they are also different as signs: they give the object (Venus) in different ways. These different ways are not "divorced from the object and wedded to the word"[22]; they are primarily different ways of the object's being given, and if one speaks of different ways of designation, it is simply because each way of designation *answers* to a way of being given. The very half page, where "*Sinn*" and "*Bedeutung*" are first mentioned in the Fregean corpus, contains *three* explicit references to the effect that the famous distinction is primarily an *ontological* one, quite trivial indeed.[23] And it is not necessary to recall BG § 8 and GRL § 67.

Designation ("*a*", aspect$_a$, object) is afterwards transformed into two partial statements: "*a*" expresses (*ausdrücken*) a sense (*Sinn*), and refers to or denotes (*bedeuten, bezeichnen*) a reference (*Bedeutung*).[24]

2.22 *Some historical comparisons*: *Aristotle*, *Brentano*

The idea that an entity is given in many ways or under many aspects is indeed fundamental; it is universally accepted in Western philosophy and needs no illustration. Let us consider only some remarkable cases. Aristotle mentions in the *Physics* (and of course in the corresponding series of commentaries one may find the same idea) that a subject may be "one numerically" though "two in form"[25]; he applies this idea in the analysis of movement. Frege would say that one has to recognize there the same entity under different aspects.

In more recent times, Brentano distinguishes three dimensions in the semantics of names: (1) a name *announces*[26] that someone is using it, (2) a name *means*[27] something, (3) a name refers to an object, *designates* or names an object.[28] "Founder of logic" or "teacher of Alexander the Great" name Aristotle *through* two different meanings. Aristotle may be called by many names because meanings are incomplete and each of them gives only a certain side or aspect of the thing.[29]

In Frege one does not have the pragmatic dimension (point 1) and "Bedeutung" is used precisely in an opposite sense; what Brentano calls "bedeuten" in point (2) would be Frege's "expressing a sense".

The above division is given by Brentano only for what he calls *selbstbedeutende Namen*, i.e., names of real entities or individuals, not names of fictitious universals or concepts. Thus one should not worry about the lack of the definite article before "founder of logic" and "teacher of Alexander the Great": Brentano means in both cases Aristotle, not concepts under which Aristotle falls.

Frege probably would have considered the pragmatic dimension of signs as psychologism; nevertheless, that dimension is essentially involved in indirect speech, which Frege was forced to deal with.

2.23 *Equality of senses*

In "perfect" or "scientific" languages, a sign has only one sense, and it is certain that *there is* a reference.[30] In natural languages, and especially in the case of simple proper names ("Aristotle"), there is ambiguity as to which is *the* sense.[31] Furthermore, natural languages have the defect of not excluding fictitious proper names, expressions which are grammatically correct and have perhaps a sense, but which lack a reference.[32]

While the direction going from names to references is univocal, the inverse direction, starting from the *Bedeutung* and going to the names, is not univocal.[33] By definition, more than one sense is associated with the same reference. Now, the further fact that even for perfect languages more than one name is associated with a sense[34] immediately introduces the question of equality of senses: given two non-equiform signs having the same reference, it may be asked whether they express the same sense.

Frege did not start from a general thesis that every name has a sense and a reference, but from the fact that in some cases (= non trivial identity statements) a certain distinction (two senses vs. one reference) is to be introduced, and this not primarily in the name (semantics) but in the things (ontology). Now, Frege generalizes and states that names (supposedly without restrictions) have a sense and a reference.[35]

This may be accepted, but one should not forget that his *generalization* is not accompanied by further indications as to the identity of sense. All we know may be summed up in the following two points: whether two names have the same sense is decidable, (1) when one of them is intended to be only an abbreviation of the other, or (2) when "one agrees" that one of them involves a cognitive increment (with respect to the thing) in comparison to the other.

It is thus difficult to treat equality of senses with Fregean instruments alone.

The primary *ontological* significance of "*Sinn*" and "*Bedeutung*" should comfort us in the sense that the question of equality of senses[36] is no more "mysterious" than such old problems as to whether *Socrates* is the same as *Socrates sitting*. To be at a loss to discover the identity of the senses of two names without realizing this, is to be involved in a pseudo-problem. To scrutinize the form of a name in order to detect its sense, or to let the equality of senses depend on mechanical changes in the group of signs making up a name[37] is to engage in a method which is neither Frege's original approach nor has been adequately clarified by him.

There is an interesting example of how the disregard of the ontological significance of *Sinn–Bedeutung* may foster pseudo-problems. R. M. Martin [1] is a recent attack on the theory of sense and reference, understood according to Church's version rather than according to Frege's original texts. The author assumes that senses may be construed (playing with the meager conditions laid down for them) as quite arbitrary entities, i.e., as entities which obviously depart from those which a semanticist might expect from a "sense of a name"; to illustrate this by means of a striking example, the author affirms that senses may be construed as guardian angels of words. Thereby the author stresses that the guardian angels are, "of course", of the expression, not of the thing named. But precisely the contrary is the case; the guardian angels are not of the expression but of the thing.[38] Now, guardian angels of the things is a possibility admitted even by R.M. Martin [1].[39] And they are a commonplace in classical ontology – where Frege's *Sinn* and *Bedeutung* was born; guardian angels used to be called accidents, properties, *rationes* or aspects under which a thing is considered, and there was a linguistic device for concentrating all the light upon them: *reduplicatio*.

As to the identity of the senses of sentences, it will be of course interesting to look for criteria fixing it (cf. Bartlett [1]), although it can hardly be called a question of identity of *sense* if by "sense" one means *Art des Gegebenseins* or aspect.

2.24 *Sense and concept*

As has been emphasized in the preceding sections, senses of names are aspects of things (just as references of names are the things themselves). Entities in Frege as well as in traditional ontology are supposed to be exhaustively classified into singulars and universals. One of Frege's contributions to philosophy is precisely the fact of having stressed very much such a distinction, which was partially blurred because of the idea of essence and because of there being *another* powerful distinction, namely, substance–accident. Given any entity, traditional philosophers would first of all ask: Is it a substance or an accident? Frege, on the contrary, would ask: Is it a singular or a universal?

Thus the question arises whether senses of names (aspects of things) are for Frege singulars or universals. From the point of view of classical ontology they would be conceived rather as singulars, in the sense of individual accidents, Husserlian "moments", etc.

Now, Frege does not speak of singulars and universals but of *objects* and *concepts*. Fregean concepts are universals, but Fregean objects include not only traditional particulars but also any entity which happens to be the designatum of a saturated expression, for instance and paradoxically the designatum of the expression "the universal concept *man*".

Consequently, one has to determine first of all whether the Fregean texts view senses as concepts or as objects. If senses are Fregean concepts they certainly are traditional universals as well; but if senses are objects in Fregean terminology, then there will be no other alternative than to patiently accept a new consequence of unsaturatedness.

There are at least three reasons suggesting that senses are concepts.

(1) There is a sort of "duality" between concepts and senses, according to which senses would be concepts *qua* concepts of some object. Stressing the idea that senses are aspects of a thing, Frege says that each name of a thing (apart from referring to the thing) illuminates the thing only under a particular aspect or side (*nur einseitig beleuchtet*) and that an exhaustive knowledge of an entity according to all its aspects is unattainable.[40] This

exhaustive knowledge is characterized by the following condition: one should be able to decide, for any given sense, whether or not it belongs to the object in question. This is curiously similar to the *scharfe Begrenzung* of concepts required by Frege: one should be able to decide, for every object, whether or not it falls under the concept in question.

In BG the discussion on *Inhaltsgleichheit* leads to the consideration of the fact that many names are placed in correspondence with one thing; the apparent superfluousness of this is rejected because each name involves a particular *Bestimmungsweise* of the thing. In UWB[41] Frege considers the situation in which the same name or sign is applied to several similar things ("man" to Peter and John) and he escapes the apparent equivocation of this by saying that such a name is not a designation of the individual things but of the concept common to them.

This curious situation may be described in the following way: when viewing *many things* (correlated to one name), Frege speaks of the concept (common to them), when viewing *one thing* (correlated to many names), he speaks of the sense (of each name).

This would suggest that senses are concepts taken as concepts or properties of a given object. In the famous presentation of "ramified" types, the first edition of *Principia* also views concepts as "concepts of an object *a*", and thereby the authors of *Principia* do not seem to imply any change in the meaning of the term "concept".

(2) To fix a sense seems to be the same as to choose a concept. Frege in SUB distinguishes simple and compound proper names: "Aristotle" and "the disciple of Plato", etc.[42] In BG the distinction is between the geometrical point *A* as given directly to intuition ("the point *A*") or as given by a description ("the *B* such that . . ."). Intuition-description is a disguised way of saying intuition-concept (a fundamental philosophical distinction inherited by Frege), and we have already stressed the fact that "B" in the geometrical example of BG is the name of a concept.[43] It should be observed that disagreements or fluctuations in determining the sense of proper names seem to be reduced to *simple* names; "Aristotle"'s sense will be for one person *Aristotle's being disciple of Plato and Master of Alexander the Great*, for another *Aristotle's being born in Stagira and Master of Alexander the Great.*[44] A scientific language should avoid such fluctuations of sense, but one may ask *how* the fluctuation of sense is to be avoided or *how* a sense is to be fixed for "Ari-

stotle". Frege does not answer this question, but obviously the only possible way is to choose a *concept* (under which the object, here Aristotle, falls) and to build a description.

(3) There are "empty senses" (the expression is not Frege's). Frege stresses that it is possible to have names expressing a sense but lacking a reference; the task of a perfect language will be to ensure reference for all well-formed expressions.[45] The examples in SUB[46] of reference-less expressions which have a sense should be compared with the examples of pseudo-definite descriptions in GRL, where the non-fulfillment of the two conditions of existence and uniqueness deprives those descriptions of *content*[47], but where one can still "grasp" another *Inhalt*. Now this *Inhalt* is in GRL a concept.

If one wishes to identify senses with concepts in SUB this also may be supported by Frege's identification of *Bedeutung* of proper names with *Gegenstand*.[48]

Against the identification of senses with concepts there is, independently of Frege, an important objection, namely, that aspects of things (senses of names) are thought of as "concrete" entities, "accompanying" the thing, while concepts, on the contrary, are conceived as abstract universals common to many things. Now, although Frege was a victim of the ambiguities of the term "*Eigenschaft*"[49] (concrete and abstract) and although he systematically applied the traditional notion of individual accidents in the case of *Vorstellungen*[50], he was not aware of (or at least did not explicitly consider) that distinction. Had he become aware of it, he would have seen that between aspects of things (senses) and concepts there is the *nuance*, if not the abyss, which separates the concrete and the abstract.

But we should look rather for *actual Fregean* references to the possible identity of senses and concepts. After having considered some hints in favor of this identification, let us concentrate on an opposing argument.

Insofar as *sense* is a semantic notion, it is necessary to consider how senses may be named.

In direct speech, i.e., where signs designate (denote, etc.) their reference (*Bedeutung*) and only "obliquely" point at their sense (cf. 2.43), there is of course no way of designating *in recto* a sense apart from using the phrase, "the sense of the name so and so". Frege in fact indicates that he approves of such a device.[51] (Incidentally, it should be observed that we have been deliberately incorrect in giving some examples of senses for the word "Aristotle"; Frege does not give "Aristotle's being disciple of Plato ..." etc., but "*the* disciple of Plato ..." etc.; italics ours.) This is a name (or description) of Aristotle, i.e., of the *Bedeutung* of "Aristotle" and not of the *Sinn* of "Aristotle". Here we have a curious mistake in the text of SUB, and it is not unjustified to suspect that Frege did not like to give the formulations we have given because that would have been the same as granting that senses are concepts.

In indirect speech names denote their sense; for instance "the Evening Star" in such a context does not designate the Evening Star but the sense of "the Evening Star", i.e. a particular way in which Venus is given. This is very important for Frege in order to preserve the universality of the Leibnizian principle "eadem sunt, quorum unum potest substitui alteri salva veritate".

Now, there was another important motivation in Frege's thought: unsaturatedness. SUB is referred to several times in BGGE[52] (as a forthcoming paper), and it is in BGGE where Frege's idea of unsaturatedness appears in a most exasperated manner. Moreover, in SUB itself we are given a hint that Frege had in mind the troubles of unsaturatedness, namely, by his otherwise curious decision to exclude from his discussion names of concepts.[53]

According to unsaturatedness, saturated expressions (in particular those beginning with the definite article "the") cannot be considered to be names of unsaturated entities such as are concepts. Thus, "the Evening Star" in indirect speech is the name of a sense, but it cannot be the name of a concept.[54]

Thus if Frege was ever tempted by the possibility of viewing senses as concepts, he had to refrain from such an identification. This is confirmed by the *inedita*.[55]

In all this one may observe the close interdependence between the theory of *Sinn–Bedeutung* and the doctrine on unsaturatedness.[56]

2.25 *Interchangeability of the names of the same entity is not plausible*

The present section is intended to partially correct an interpretation of Frege given in Carnap [1]. There one reads: "his [Frege's] method of semantical analysis is a particular form of what we call the method of the name-relation".[57] And: "the third principle of the name-relation permits replacing a name with another name of the same entity. Although this principle seems quite plausible, it is not always valid".[58]

If names answer to different aspects of the thing, it does not seem plausible that names of a same entity may be interchanged in any context *salva veritate*. To say that names related by "=" may be freely interchanged in any context would be to avow that they do not "make any difference", which is perhaps admissible in the frame of the traditional semantics of names ("ad placitum"), but not in the Fregean one which has been presented in the preceding sections.

Nevertheless, Frege himself has not been faithful to his semantics, and this is why he may be characterized by the third condition of the name relation.

The third principle of Carnap's name-relation is Leibniz's famous formula: "eadem sunt quorum unum potest substitui alteri salva veritate" (leaving aside some unessential confusion of use and mention in Leibniz's formulation).

This principle is assumed without qualification by Frege after BG § 8 (cf. the previous section 2.11). In paragraph 8 of the *Begriffsschrift* of 1879 one may observe (as pointed out above) the collision of the two opposite Fregean approaches; on the one hand Frege stresses the fact that different names answer to different aspects of the designatum (and therefore different names make a difference), but on the other hand he introduces the Leibnizian rule of interchangeability (without mentioning Leibniz).

This rule is explicitly assumed as being due to Leibniz in GRL § 65 (which thus collides with GRL § 67, cf. 2.12). It also appears in the important context of SUB, which is curious because in a sense SUB was written to reconquer for semantics what the rule had lost.

The way in which the Leibnizian principle is introduced in GRL § 65 is most objectionable.

(1) It is *dogmatic*: "Leibniz dixit". It should be remembered that Leibniz was in a sense Frege's model, as is stated in the *Vorwort* of BG.

(2) It is *incoherent*: Frege proposes an analysis of the concept of identity but this reduces to the adoption of Leibniz's principle.

(3) It is *false with respect to Leibniz*. Leibniz *systematically* qualified

his formula "eadem sunt . . .".[59] He did not look at this formula as a plausible universal law whose exceptions are unexpected puzzles *rhapsodically* discovered (as it has happened in post-Fregean philosophy). On the other hand, it is not clear why Frege has adopted precisely the strongest formulation of the Leibnizian principle.[60]

(4) It is of course *inconsistent with respect to Frege's own semantics*, as was already pointed out.[61]

That inconsistency is perhaps concealed by another one. In fact Frege also says that identity means *vollkommene Übereinstimmung*[62], which makes the Leibnizian principle look quite plausible. Apparently, Frege's intention is merely to reject the conception of "=" as equality and as weaker than "full" identity. To this extent, the expression "complete coincidence" would be only a rhetorical emphasis in the context of a polemic against people saying that 4 and 2+2 are "equal but not the same".[63] This is true, and furthermore it must be acknowledged that Frege takes care to add that although the *Bedeutung* is the same, the *Sinne* (the senses) are not the same.[64] Still, the latter is not so much emphasized. *In particular*, it is not even mentioned in the crucial passage (GRL § 65) where Frege decides to adopt the Leibnizian formula (at that time Frege did have the *notions* of *Sinn* and *Bedeutung*; he lacked only the terminology, cf. 2.1). Any reader of GRL § 65 may find a reason for the "plausibility" of the principle in the fact that "identity is full coincidence".[65]

In any case, the third principle of the name relation is accepted by Frege, and in the object language it means for instance that everything truly said of 3+5 is also valid for 8.[66]

To the extent that it is not true (especially in the Fregean perspective) that different senses of names or aspects of things do not make a difference, this mistake will have to be corrected. Any reader of SUB knows how painstaking this correction is.

The Aristotelian procedure seems more natural. Both Aristotle and Frege analyse an entity into its different aspects or ways of being given. A particular human being may be described as *the man who is approaching* or as *Coriscus*. The sophists exploit this ontological situation and affirm that we know and do not know the same thing (in case we know Coriscus but not the man who is approaching). Aristotle emphasizes that there is *no necessity* that things which are only "in a way the same" (*τοῖς ὁπωσοῦν τοῖς αὐτοῖς*) have all their attributes the same.[67] To suppose the contrary is to invite the fallacy of accident, and ultimately to think that the *different* aspects of a thing do *not* make a difference.

The connection between Frege and Aristotle may be established *via* Leibniz, who was aware (since his dissertation) of the subtle traditional distinctions between the different aspects (*rationes*) of an entity, and who used the traditional notion of *reduplication* in order to restrict his "eadem sunt . . .". Reduplication would seem a natural complement to Frege's original insight into a thing and its different ways of being given or, more precisely, to Frege's corresponding semantics of *Sinn* and *Bedeutung*.

2.26 *Pragmatism versus phenomenology in Frege's approach to identity. 'Bedeutung' as 'importance'*

> . . . die Schwierigkeit liegt in den Phaenomenen, ihrer richtigen Beschreibung, Analyse und Deutung . . .
> (Husserl [4], p. 142)

Husserl and intensionalist logicians in general are accused by Frege of psychologism not only because they take into account *Vorstellungen*, but also because they pay attention to the *sense* of words. "Mathematical" logicians on the contrary, says Frege, are interested only in *die Sache selbst*, which is here the *Bedeutung der Worte*.[68]

Now it is perfectly Fregean to say that the sense of words is as objective as its reference; only *Vorstellungen* are banished from objectivity in Frege's ontology.[69] Therefore the above mentioned accusation against Husserl and intensionalist logicians sounds very strange in Frege's works; it is as if Frege were suddenly affirming that sense of words is subjective.

This is not in my view an incidental mistake, but it is related to a particular feature of Frege's thought. There is in Frege some tendency to introduce rapid and efficient criteria of identification, according to which tendency one does not hesitate in "identifying" two entities if they are "equivalent" for some assigned purpose. Such a tendency may be called *pragmatic*.

(1) Already in BG that tendency is manifest; the *Begriffsschrift* is supposed to reflect only *conceptual content*, i.e., what "counts for deduction".[70] For instance, this leads Frege to disregard the difference between the active and the passive voice (*ibid.*).

(2) In BGGE Frege stresses that not every difference in the *sentence* should result in a difference in the *proposition* (*Gedanke*).[71] In the yet unpublished letters to Husserl this will become an almost violent argument: logic cannot multiply distinctions *in infinitum*. To the extent that *Gedanken* are senses for Frege, this involves a disregard of some "senses of senses" (= ways in which senses are given).

(3) In SUB Frege obviously counts as mere "Beleuchtung" aspects which cannot be said to be subjective in the rigorous Fregean sense of "subjective *Vorstellung*".[72] This, again, is a disregard of some "senses of senses".

(4) In GED, published in 1918, Frege's pragmatic tendency definitely becomes explicit; he says: "What is essential depends on our purposes."[73]

Points (1) and (4) might be viewed simply as expressing a general trait of Frege's thought, which could be called his "utilitarian" or "pragmatic" inclination (and which may have fostered his dogmatic adoption of the Leibnizian principle "eadem sunt quorum unum potest alteri substitui salva veritate", or perhaps, inversely, may have been propitiated by the impact of this formula on Frege's mind). On the other hand points (2) and (3) already concern Frege's semantics in a very significant way.

Thereby a limit is placed on the Fregean tendency towards distinguishing different aspects in an entity or different senses in names. Thus the question naturally arises *where* is that limit being drawn by Frege.

The above mentioned Fregean criticism of Husserl and intensionalist logicians shows that at least sometimes that limit was very narrow; narrow to the extent of identifying "Sinn" with "what is unimportant". Accordingly, in the same cases, "Bedeutung" means *importance*.

This means that we have an ambiguity in Frege's terms "Sinn" and "Bedeutung". It is not difficult to associate this with the ordinary ambiguity of the German word "Bedeutung". The complex situation may be described as follows.

Names have sense and reference because entities have aspects, and it may be fascinating to analyse *in infinitum* the different aspects of a *morceau de cire*, or to be pleased by the discovery of the *nuances* distinguishing the road from Thebes to Athens from the road from Athens to Thebes. Similarly, Frege distinguishes *Bestimmungsweisen* or *Arten des Gegebenseins* in a geometrical point (BG, § 8) or in Venus (SUB).

Each aspect becomes the sense of a name of the same thing, which is called then the *Bedeutung* of these various names.

But for many practical reasons both we and Descartes would "identify" two pieces of wax. Analogously, with respect to many contexts (for instance Euclid's Elements) we would "identify", as Leibniz did, the meanings of "triangulum" and "trilaterum".[74] In current German one would say that the two pieces of wax or the two names have the same *Bedeutung*, i.e. the same importance. The ambiguity of "*Sinn*" and "*Bedeutung*" may be employed as a hypothesis explaining some odd fragments of Frege's semantics: sentences and predicate-terms.

The logician's goal is truth.[75] And it happens that concepts having the same extension are interchangeable in many contexts *salva veritate*.[76] Thus the properties *featherless biped* and *rational animal* may be identified, and the names "featherless biped" and "rational animal" may be said to have the same *Bedeutung* – the same importance. *Mutatis mutandis*, this can be applied also to sentences coinciding in their truth-values. Both points will be considered in more detail in subsequent sections.

Kauppi [1][77] rightly points out that Leibniz has formulated his "eadem sunt . . ." also in the following way: "inter ea quorum unum alteri substitui potest salvis calculi legibus, dicetur esse aequipollentiam". This would have been for Frege a means of clarifying the ambiguity hidden in "Bedeutung".

2.3 Sense and reference for sentences

> I think any unprepared reader would be inclined to regard a sentence as a name of a proposition rather than as a name of a truth-value . . . (Carnap [1], § 28).

In SUB a first enigmatic appearance of the possibility of speaking about the *sense of sentences*[78] does not provide too many hints at how this should be understood; it is only later that Frege explicitly asks what is the sense and reference of sentences.[79] To this question the indication is added that sentences *contain* propositions.[80] And then the question becomes: Is the proposition the sense or the reference of the sentence?[81]

It is hard to imagine a reader who would be able to derive a precise meaning from such an abrupt question. In any case he would be presented with two possibilities: (1) to read further and see how the question is resolved, (2) to examine some other texts where Frege eliminates wrong conceptions of sentences, propositions and truth. Let us begin with the latter.

Frege stresses that *true* is not a predicate of a proposition[82], but this does not provide us with much help in searching for an answer to the above question. Nor is the idea of *beurteilbarer Inhalt*[83] – appearing since BG – useful for this purpose.

Frege rejects the traditional doctrine of truth as *adaequatio*[84] (*Übereinstimmung*). "True" is not a dyadic predicator. Further, Frege asks whether the *adaequatio* is supposed to be complete (*vollkommen*) or partial (*in einer gewissen Hinsicht*). In the former case the two things which are said to be "adequate" become one, which result would not be desirable. If the *adaequatio* is not complete, then we would have a "half truth", i.e., non-truth in the final analysis. If we try to say that this non-complete *adaequatio* has to be understood as *Übereinstimmung in einer gewissen Hinsicht*, the question will be: in which *Hinsicht*? Supposing this is fixed, then the *Spiel* would start again, for one should investigate whether that coincidence (in that aspect) is complete or not. Thus, Frege concludes, any attempt to explain truth as *adaequatio* fails. But again, this is merely a negative result and it does not contribute to our making sense of "*Sinn–Bedeutung*" in sentences.

The best approach is to directly see what is Frege's answer to the question about sense and reference in sentences. Frege says that sentences have a sense, namely, the proposition; and a reference, namely, the truth value.[85] Sentences will be proper names, designating the True or the False, *in the same way*[86] in which "the Morning Star" designates Venus.

But although it is natural to see in "Morning Star" a sense (= aspect, way of being given) of Venus, we may wonder which is *the aspect* of Truth expressed by a true sentence. It is a *tour de force* to think that "$2+2 = 4$" and "New York is a large city" express two aspects of anything at all.

This odd thesis can be explained as the result of a clandestine change of perspective. When Frege introduces the question of sense and reference in sentences, the reader keeps thinking in terms of "things and their different aspects", *die Arten des Gegebenseins*, which are associated with *Sinn* at the beginning of SUB. But, according to our hypothesis, Frege has now something different in mind. Frege would not ask about sense and reference of sentences, taking "sense" as "aspect" and "reference" as "substratum", but taking "sense" as *what does not count* and "reference" as *what does count*[87] (for deduction, for truth, or for any other logicians' purpose). If this were clear, no unprepared reader could object to saying that truth values are at least in a large number of cases the reference of sentences.

2.31 *'Proof' that sense and reference for sentences are propositions and truth-values*

Frege knows that his semantics of sentences will appear strange to his readers. Therefore he announces a "better justification" of it[88], which is provided in SUB.[89]

Now the justification of the thesis (the *Begründung*) is even more artificial than the thesis itself. But Frege wants to proceed at any cost as if sense-reference were univocally meant for "proper" proper names and for sentences.

After having asked whether the proposition "contained" by a sentence is the sense or the reference of the sentence, Frege proceeds to suppose that *the proposition* is the reference.[90] *Under this hypothesis* Frege considers the possibility of substituting equireferential terms, say "the Morning Star" and "the Evening Star". His argument is indirect, i.e. he shows that to assume *Gedanke* = reference of sentences, implies a contradiction.

(a) Frege draws the reader's attention to the fact that somebody accepting as true a sentence including "the Evening Star" could take as false the same sentence, once that term is substituted by "the Morning Star". This is trivial. But Frege adds something more: he regards that fact as the reason for affirming that the two sentences contain *different propositions*.

(b) On the other hand, Frege assumes the following thesis: "to interchange equireferential names does not alter the reference of the sentence".[91]

Thus Frege concludes that the proposition cannot be the reference of the sentence.

Let us add some remarks concerning this "argument".

In point (a) we may ask *why* there are *two* propositions under the sentences whose only difference consists in having "Morning Star" instead of "Evening Star". At the time of SUB there was no sharp definition of *Gedanke*, and perhaps it does not exist in the whole Fregean corpus.[92] As for propositions, however, we do know that they may be recognized under different aspects (under different sentences) which is a point much stressed by Frege.[93] It would be natural to say that someone accepting the sentence with "the Morning Star" as true and the sentence with "the Evening Star" as false, simply fails to recognize the same proposition (*Gedanke*) under both presentations, just as he fails to recognize the Morning Star "under" the Evening Star. The latter case does not entail that the Morning Star and the Evening Star are *two* different celestial bodies. If Frege does not proceed in this more natural way, it is probably because he tacitly assumes that the sense of a sentence (if any) is made up of the senses of its parts[94], and further because he already takes for granted what has to be "justified" by the present argument, namely that the sense of a sentence is the proposition (which is of course inconsistent with the provisional hypothesis that the proposition is the reference).

In point (b) we may observe that the formulation of the assumed thesis could also be: ". . . does not alter the *Gedanke* of the sentence". But in this case the sentence would lose some of its apparent obviousness. Now, it should be agreed that Frege's formulation with "*Bedeutung*" instead of "*Gedanke*" either is absolutely meaningless (because in SUB p. 32, line 11 we do not yet know at all what the *Bedeutung* of a sentence is), or else it appears as meaningful and plausible, to the extent that one reads into it the Leibnizian principle "eadem sunt . . ."[95]; i.e., to the extent that one makes "Bedeutung = veritas". But this is to beg the question and is inconsistent with the provisional hypothesis *Bedeutung* = *Gedanke*.

Frege does not only "conclude" in the above argument that the *Gedanke* cannot be the reference of the sentence; but also he positively adds that the *Gedanke* should be conceived rather as *the sense* of the sentence. One may simply assume this without further analysis, as there seems *to be no reason* why the *Gedanke* has to be the sense, in particular because we do not yet know what is the sense of a sentence.

We started by saying that sentences contain propositions (*Gedanke*) and now we find that propositions are the sense of sentences. It would seem that there remains nothing else which could fulfill the role of *Bedeutung*. Frege devotes a dense page of SUB to show the contrary.

There are three main sentences in this argument; let us abbreviate them in the following way: p = we are interested in the *Bedeutung* of the parts of a sentence. $q =$ we are interested in (we ask about, etc.) the truth-value of a sentence. $r =$ we look for the *Bedeutung* of a sentence (i.e., we are not satisfied with the mere *Gedanke* or proposition, which is the sense of the sentence).

First, Frege affirms that r implies p.[96] Secondly, he shows that q implies p.[97] Thirdly, he asserts that p implies r.[98] Fourthly he maintains that p implies q.[99] This is, as far as I am able to understand, the skeleton of the argument. Actually Frege in his final résumé[100] does not mention the first step ($r \supset p$), but this step seems important in order to fully establish the thesis he is looking for, namely that *we ask for the Bedeutung of a sentence if and only if we are interested in the truth-value of a sentence.*

Frege tries only to show that the above mentioned implications among p, q and r are more or less plausible. The desired equivalence ($r \equiv q$) is obtained *via* the semantics of the *parts* of the sentence ($p \equiv q$).

"$p \equiv q$" means that in reading Homer, as far as we do not assume the truth (in some sense) of the *Odyssey*, we do not assign any *Bedeutung* to the name "Odysseus".[101] Nevertheless, Odysseus is an entity about which many non-trivial identity statements are provided; like the geometrical point of BG, § 8, Odysseus may be given under quite different aspects (he is precisely a *polutropos* man[102]). But Frege is not a phenomenologist here, and he is not interested in a general ontology; here sense and reference appear for him within "scientific truth" – a vague designation, but still clearly showing that he intends to *exclude* some other things[103], for instance the *Odyssey*, which thus loses any *Bedeutung* (= importance).

The procedure of arriving at $r \equiv q$ *via* the semantics of the parts of the sentence reflects Frege's desire to retain the distinction sense–reference in the domain of sentences as a particular application of a general distinction for all proper names (sentences becoming, thereby, proper names). This culminates in one's having to view artificially the sense of the sentence (the proposition) as made up of the senses of the parts of the sentence.[104]

In any case Frege passes (without further justification) from the equivalence $r \equiv q$ to the affirmation that one must consider the truth-values as the reference of sentences.

The argument has been *obscurum per obscuriora*; the oddity of both the argument and its conclusion is due to Frege's determination to preserve an artificial univocity of "sense-reference" in sentences and names.

Not only is the reader brought to such an artificial conclusion by such artificial means; but also he is obliged to make of truth-values *objects*[105], which is not trivial because there are *Bedeutungen* which are not objects.[106] But "object" is here associated with the paradox of BGGE[107], and the paradox itself is indeed more puzzling than having truth-values as objects (whatever this may mean). Here, as when he considers sentences as names of truth-values, Frege seems to feel obliged to apologize to the reader.

Two minor inconsistencies in the immediate context contribute to make the whole issue even more questionable. (1) Frege implies that senses (in the case of *Gedanke*) are not objective[108]; (2) he implies that senses are not *objects.*[109] But, contrary to this, we know that *Gedanken* are objective[110] and we know that Frege regarded senses as objects.[111]

Finally, it is clear that the reduction of references of sentences to two objects (the False and the True) is too sweeping and has to be corrected.[112] Whereas in other cases Frege does not seem to assign too much importance to the *sense* of names (actually we know that he considered it as irrelevant), here he is obliged to say that not only the truth-value interests us, but the truth-value plus the *Gedanke.*[113]

In Frege's semantics of sentences we recognize some peculiar traits of philosophical monism; after monism is proclaimed, everything has to be explained as a "manifestation", an epiphenomenon of the chosen fundamental entity.[114]

2.4 Subordinate sentences

Frege's concern with subordinate sentences arises from the necessity of verifying his theory of sentences (conceived as names of truth-values) with respect to the interchangeability of equireferential names.[115] The discussion of subordinate sentences actually occupies the most of SUB. We shall consider three aspects of this discussion.

2.41 *Pseudo-subordinate sentences*

A first remark concerning SUB's long discussion of subordinate sentences is that a significant group of them are not sentences. This is acknowledged by Frege only in later works, where a distinction between *eigentliche* and *uneigentliche* sentences is introduced.[116]

The peculiarity of pseudo-subordinate sentences is nevertheless in SUB clear enough as to avoid any confusion. In fact they are held not to express a *complete Gedanke*; they contain an *indeterminate* element. Frege describes this by means of the adjectives "*(un)vollständig*" and "*(un)selbständig*", or by saying that the sense of these "sentences" is only a part of a *Gedanke*.[117] The indeterminate element need not be explicit[118], and there may be more than one.[119]

It would seem natural to interpret these "incomplete propositions" of SUB as names of functions[120], but this would be inconsistent with Frege's program of dealing only (in SUB) with proper names[121], and on the other hand he himself provides in later works indications which exclude that interpretation.[122] We have here another collision between *sense* and *function*, a problem which is intimately related to unsaturatedness, and therefore does not deserve to be discussed for its own sake.

Of course Frege is not immediately concerned in SUB with discussing the relations of sense and function; but only with excluding pseudo-subordinate sentences from the expressions where the principle of interchangeability of equireferential proper names has to be tested; nevertheless, the very fact that pseudo-subordinate sentences are so excluded from the domain of proper names creates a puzzle about their semantics.

2.42 *Relative subordinate sentences. In perfect languages syntax ensures reference*

There is another sort of so called subordinate sentences where no proposition is expressed and no truth-value is referred to: relative sentences. Frege's example is:

(A) "Der die elliptische Gestalt der Planetenbahnen entdeckte, starb im Elend".[123]

Either taking "der die elliptische Gestalt der Planetenbahnen entdeckte" as a sort of unsaturated expression or as a description of Kepler[124], the point Frege wants to stress is that in this expression *no proposition is contained*, and consequently it is not a candidate for testing the principle of interchangeability of equireferential names (sentences here).

Frege considers the following objection.[125] If the above mentioned phrase is taken as a description of Kepler, then it might be said that to use that phrase implies the assertion that Kepler existed[126], or that the proposition that Kepler existed is contained in (or expressed by) that phrase.

Frege replies in the following manner. If the objection were accepted, then a sentence like "Kepler died in misery" should be expanded into "(Kepler died in misery) & (the name "Kepler" is not reference-less)", and the sentence "Kepler did not die in misery" should be transformed into "(Kepler did not die in misery) & (the name "Kepler" is not reference-less)". Now, the negation of these sentences would be "(Kepler did not die in misery) ∨ (the name "Kepler" is reference-less)" and "(Kepler died in misery) ∨ (the name "Kepler" is reference-less)". Obviously, Frege sees here a menace to the *tertium non datur*.

In natural languages the situation is hopeless, because (1) there may be names having a sense but lacking a reference[127], (2) the existence of a reference depends on the truth of a sentence.[128]

Frege's *Begriffsschrift* is constructed so as to ensure reference if syntax is respected. "Every well-formed name must have a reference".[129] Thus the above mentioned objection becomes "impossible" and the menace to the *tertium non datur* vanishes.[130]

The syntax of natural language is hopeless, not only because it allows reference-less names, but also because it allows *Scheineigennamen*.[131] But this requires another remedy: logical analysis.

2.43 *Indirect sense and reference*

Let us consider the two following well-formed Fregean sentences:

(1) "The Morning Star is the Evening Star"

(2) "$2+2=4$ is (New York is a large city)".

Frege's *Sinn-Bedeutung* originated in his speculations about identity-statements like (1), i.e., those involving "proper" proper names. His interest was to show that there is something different at both sides of the equality sign (the senses of the names, the aspects of the thing), and that therefore such an equality sign was not superfluous. Thereby it was presupposed that there was something identical underlying that diversity.

In case (2) the procedure was quite different. Frege had to prove that there was something identical underlying the two true sentences, and in particular that this was the truth-value.

Indeed, the famous paper SUB seems to have been written exclusively to establish that "proof". To some extent one may say that the preliminary pages on sense and reference for "proper" proper names ("Venus", "the Morning Star") are only a matter of terminology.

The very oddity of the thesis which made of sentences proper names of the truth-values may have stimulated Frege to develop and achieve its "proof".

An essential part of this "proof" would naturally consist in testing interchangeability *salva veritate*. Thereby Frege necessarily encountered such phenomena as indirect speech, where interchangeability seems to fail. (Modalities, as other possible "intensional" contexts, were outside Frege's interest since BG § 4.)

At the end of SUB Frege affirms that he has shown "with sufficient probability" that the cases where a subordinate sentence is not interchangeable *salva veritate* do not contradict his thesis of sentences as names of truth-values because in those cases sentences do *not* refer to their "usual" denotation. In those cases sentences are either pseudo-sentences or they have as reference their "usual" sense (= the proposition) or they behave in some other complicated way (which it is not necessary to analyse here).

It may be conjectured that such a concern for substitutivity of sentences was the reason leading Frege to imagine that interchangeability of "proper" proper names could ever fail. By this conjecture one may understand the otherwise puzzling lack of symmetry in SUB where exceptions to the rule of interchangeability for "proper" proper names are considered in a way only subsidiary to exceptions in the case of sentences, for instance, indirect speech.

That was of course not the right way; Frege ought to have started with the axiom that failures in the interchangeability *salva veritate* are to be expected in any circumstance where a thing (a name) is viewed *qua* having such and such an aspect (sense), or where the aspect (sense) is taken into account rather than the thing.

In any case, some of these circumstances were taken into account by Frege under the pressure of having to deal with substitutivity of sentences. Thereby the paradigmatic case was indirect speech.

In indirect speech one speaks of the *sense* of someone else's words, not about their reference.[132] This is given by Frege as a sort of axiom at the beginning of SUB. As a result, a sentence in indirect speech automatically designates its sense, i.e., "its" proposition.[133] The same applies to other signs, as a further consequence of the above mentioned "axiom" (cf. again SUB, p. 28). Thus names sometimes may have a reference other than their usual one; in such cases their reference is their usual sense.

After the pattern of "indirect" speech, Frege introduces the terminology of "indirect" reference, as opposed to "usual" reference (cf. *ibid.*). In fact, indirect speech exhausts, for him, the possible cases in which a name may refer to its usual sense.

Frege assumes in SUB an equivalence whose two parts are: (a) if signs making up a sentence have a non-customary sense and reference, then the sentence has also a non-customary sense and reference, (b) if a sentence has a non-customary sense and reference, then the signs composing that sentence have also a non-customary sense and reference.

Part (b) is mentioned first[134]; Frege regards it as obvious, but his actual formulations are far from plausible. The same applies to part (a).[135] The above equivalence may be considered as a convention which simply expresses some Fregean views.

The fact that some contexts magically alter the reference of the included names has been viewed as a disadvantageous ambiguity.[136] Nevertheless, this should not be regarded as an unnecessary complication but as mere consequence of a previously chosen ontology, according to which things have different aspects. Fundamentally, the ambiguity is not of "Coriscus" (the name) but of Coriscus (the thing) who on some occasions, as when he is *the man who is approaching*, may fail to be recognized.

Senses can also be the customary *reference* of some names. For instance, "the proposition expressed by the sentence *p*" refers to a sense[137]; "the sense of the expression A" likewise refers to a sense.[138]

Rigorously applying the thesis that every name has sense and reference, these new names as well as "*p*" or "*A*" in indirect contexts will have a *sense* of their own. As an abbreviated description of this situation, one may speak of an iteration of senses or of senses of senses (apart from this intended use such phrases would be of course meaningless).

Iteration of senses is thus a subject to be discussed in Fregean philosophy, although Frege himself has not formulated it. Unfortunately, this problem involves too many unknowns to be appropriately examined in Fregean terms; let us mention three of them.

(1) Even in the case of "proper" proper names, on the one hand Frege could not identify senses with concepts (if he ever wished to do so) because of unsaturatedness, and (2), on the other hand, if he had preferred to say that senses are not concepts, he ought to have widened his ontology in order to include something like "aspects of things". For instance, if senses were concepts, then senses of senses would lie "outside" the initial *Bedeutung* (concepts of concepts are not concepts of the thing), whereas if senses were understood as aspects of things, it would seem natural to consider aspects of aspects of a thing as simple aspects of the thing, and thereby senses of senses would collapse into simple senses, stopping the iteration. (3) The situation becomes even more complicated if one takes into account sentences, or predicate-terms, where, as has been suggested, an ambiguity in the term "Bedeutung" (and "Sinn") seems to be at work.

Against this background, the so called "multiplication of entities"[139] involved in Frege's semantic method is hardly a problem to be meaningfully explored with Fregean help.

In "John thinks that Peter believes that Charles . . . that the Morning Star is the Evening Star", the name "the Morning Star", for instance, would stand for a sense of a sense of . . . a sense ("sense of sense" in the above explained meaning).

Objections to this "infinite" ambiguity[140] ought to consider first the mutual relations or the interdependence among the "infinite" designata flowing from each name. In other words, the ontological aspect of the iteration of senses should be examined. Then the infinite iteration would not be, perhaps, so implausible. In particular, if it happened that "senses of senses . . . of senses" were always "near" to initial senses, in the above example the designatum of "the Morning Star" would not depart greatly from the usual sense of "the Morning Star"; this would minimize, so to speak, the ambiguity.

2.5 Frege's notion of "Vorstellung" and its philosophical implications

2.51 "*Vorstellung*"; *subjective-objective*

Frege wants to eliminate from the philosophical vocabulary the ambiguity of the term "Vorstellung" which is meant both in an objective and in a subjective or psychological sense.[141] In saying "my *Vorstellung* of number 2" I mean the content of my thought, which is objective, at least because of being accessible to others, as well as some private and psychological process taking place in my mind when I think number 2. *Vorstellungen* in the subjective sense are characterized by Frege in a way strikingly similar to the way in which traditional philosophy understood individual accidents; we find again the traditional axiom that there are as many individual accidents as there are individual substances in which they inhere.[142] In opposition to this, if one takes "Vorstellung" in its objective content, then it is clear that there is only one number 2 – in some ideal world – for all the empirical subjects. Frege observes that it would be pointless to maintain the term "Vorstellung" also in the objective sense; there would be no difference between the "objective *Vorstellung*" of number 2 and number 2 itself.[143] This leads Frege to restrict "Vorstellung" to the subjective sense.[144] The significance of this terminological decision can be appreciated only in the wide historical background of traditional philosophy, as we shall see in the next section.

Vorstellung – once restricted to the subjective sense – plays an important, although negative, role in Frege's philosophy. It serves to show what Frege's philosophy is *not* about.[145] Once "Vorstellung" is understood to mean individual accidents inhering in single minds, it becomes trivial to hold that Frege's concern is not *Vorstellung*. Nevertheless, Frege has not kept his use of that term within the strict sense of individual accident. He has also counted as *Vorstellungen* things which could be regarded as belonging to the objective (accessible to all) meaning of words, but which Frege excludes from his logical language.[146] The result is that the distinction of sense–reference on the one hand and *Vorstellung* on the other loses some of its initial sharpness.

"Objective" is used in at least two ways. (1) Objective is that which may be reached by all thinking minds[147]; for instance the concept of *not being self-identical*[148] is objective because it is accessible to several thinkers. (2) Objective is that which exists independently of us[149]; here it might be controversial whether the concept of *not being self-identical* is objective, although it is almost unanimously agreed that, say, the Moon is objective.

Insofar as *subjective* is the complementary class of *objective*, the first sense of *subjective* reduces itself to the domain of *Vorstellungen* as individual accidents; the second sense of *subjective* may include such controversial things as the concept of *not being self-identical* (but Frege did not like to acknowledge this weaker or "transcendental" subjectivity; cf. 10.13).

What is the exact proportional use of the two meanings of "objective" in Frege's works will not be stated here; let us only point out that both *nuances* are, so to speak, coexistent.[150] To realize that there are such degrees in Frege's *objectivity* is important in order to appreciate his theses about classes and numbers as logical objects, i.e., as abstract objects. The latter are characterized as not being *wirklich* but still being objective.[151]

2.52 *A note on the history of semantics*

The distinction between subjective and objective *Vorstellung* is given by Frege without indication of the sources from which it is taken.[152] But there is such a striking similarity between his formulations and the traditional ones (concerning the same subject matter), that the fact that Frege does not explicitly refer to other authors is irrelevant.

There is a certain thread in the history of semantics, starting in a brief Aristotelian text and remaining through the centuries as a source of ambiguity. Aristotle orders, by means of a semantical relation, the following four terms: *written words, spoken words, mental experiences*[153] and *things*. But what are the "mental experiences" here? Two Greek commentators transform the "mental experiences" into a clearly objective terminology: "*noema*".[154] Once this is done, the Stoic *lekton* becomes perhaps superfluous.[155]

The scholastic tradition also stresses the objective interpretation.[156] But in the scholastic tradition there has been another influence: theology. This has perhaps helped to consolidate a *subjective* interpretation in addition to the objective one. When one grasps an objective content, there is a concomitant subjective *verbum* being produced in the mind.[157]

The distinction between the subjective and the objective side of the "mental experiences" is rigorously preserved in the main scholastic tradition; but the point is that thereby the subjective aspect of "ideas" is *also* attributed great importance. We shall quote a text which shows how this was still going on in the 16th century.

> Supponenda est in primis vulgaris distinctio conceptus formalis et obiectivi; conceptus formalis dicitur actus ipse, seu (quod idem est) verbum quo intellectus rem aliquam seu communem rationem concipit; qui dicitur conceptus, quia est veluti proles mentis; formalis autem appellatur, vel quia est ultima forma mentis, vel quia formaliter repraesentat menti rem cognitam, vel quia revera est intrinsecus et formalis terminus conceptionis mentalis, in quo differt a conceptu obiectivo, ut ita dicam. Conceptus obiectivus dicitur res illa, vel ratio, quae proprie et immediate per conceptum formalem cognoscitur seu repraesentatur; ut verbi gratia, cum hominem concipimus, ille actus, quem in mente efficimus ad concipiendum hominem, vocatur conceptus formalis; homo autem cognitus et repraesentatus illo actu dicitur conceptus obiectivus, conceptus quidem per denominationem extrinsecam a conceptu formali, per quem obiectum eius concipi dicitur, et ideo recte dicitur obiectivus, quia non est conceptus ut forma intrinseca terminans conceptionem, sed ut obiectum et materia circa quam versatur formalis conceptio, et ad quam mentis aciem directe tendit, propter quod ab aliquibus, ex Averroe, *intentio intellecta* appellatur; et ab aliis dicitur *ratio obiectiva.* Unde colligitur differentia inter conceptum formalem et obiectivum, quod formalis semper est vera ac positiva res et in creaturis qualitas menti inhaerens, obiectivus vero non semper est vera res positiva; concipimus enim interdum privationes et alia, quae vocantur entia rationis, quia solum habent esse obiective in intellectu. Item conceptus formalis semper est res singularis et individua, quia est res producta per intellectum, eique inhaerens; conceptus autem obiectivus interdum quidem esse potest res singularis et individua, quatenus menti obiici potest, et per actum formalem concipi, saepe vero est res universalis vel confusa et communis, ut est homo, substantia et similia.[158]

Remarks

1. The distinction which Frege demands was qualified as *vulgaris* three centuries before.

2. *Conceptus formalis* has also been called *conceptus subiectivus.*[159]

3. The formal or subjective concept – not the objective one – has a function of *representing . . . Vor-stellen.* This suggests how appropriate Frege's restriction of "Vorstellung" to the subjective sense was.[160]

4. The proper sense of "concept" is the subjective one (= *proles mentis*); the objective content is called "concept" only by extrinsic denomination.[161]

5. Subjective concepts – as Frege's *Vorstellungen* – are concrete and real individuals (individual accidents).

6. Objective concepts (properly: "entities") may be either universal or individual; Frege, similarly, divides *objective Vorstellungen* into *Begriffe* and *Gegenstände*.[162]

7. *Ens rationis* (including e.g. *privatio*) is just an *ob-ject* of the mind, but not a particular quality inhering in the mind. This is essential in order to clarify the much discussed term "Platonism" (cf. next section).

8. Elsewhere, Suarez says: "... scientiae non sunt de nominibus et conceptibus formalibus nostris sed directe de rebus seu conceptibus obiectivis."[163] Subjective concepts are mentioned only in order to be excluded – as are Frege's *Vorstellungen*.

9. Also: "... non enim dicemus esse plures numero species humanas propterea quod humana natura pluribus conceptibus repraesentatur."[164] There is a *Vorstellung* for each *Träger* – for each individual thinker – but the objective content is only one. (Cf. Frege, GED.)

Through *La Fléche* this heavy machinery becomes in Descartes an apparently simple semantical situation, where the following terms are involved: *res*, *idea*, *nomen*. The idea *represents* the thing.[165] In Locke we find an even more simple schema: *words* have just *meaning*, which meaning is the *idea*.[166] Of course "idea" is meant objectively, but nevertheless the term is ambiguous, as Leibniz[167] or Frege[168] will point out.

2.53 *Platonism and "to be in the mind"*

To evaluate Frege's Platonism requires an appreciation of his notion of *objectivity*, but this, as said[169], oscillates between (at least) two variants: *to exist independently of the mind* and *to be accessible to more than one person*. Philosophy had long since introduced ontological qualifications corresponding to Frege's meanings of "objective". Those qualifications are to be found for example in the scholastic tradition and in Kantianism.[170] In the former there has been a fundamental distinction between *esse extra animam* and *esse in anima*. To be in the mind is not at all to be a subjective quality of some particular mind, but simply means to be "in front of" the mind as an *ob-jectum*.[171] Although this terminology lends itself to a "subjectivist" interpretation, this would be a distortion.[172]

The point is that philosophers of previous centuries have been classified as to their being or not being Platonists on the basis of the above distinction, and in such a way that to put universals *extra animam* was Platonism, whereas to put universals *in anima* (objectively) was not Platonism.

According to this, I would say that Frege is not a Platonist as far as his objectivity is described as "capacity of being accessible to many", but that he is a Platonist as far as his objectivity may be described as "existing independently of us".[173] But this is not a problem to be considered separately from another major question, not seen (apparently) by Frege: transcendental subjectivity.[174] The latter, as Averroes saw, was also relevant to earlier discussions on being in the mind (whose mind?).

2.6 Semantics of predicate-terms

2.61 "*Nomina appellativa*" *and* "*nomina propria*"

Frege in BG is not concerned with stressing distinctions between proper and common names. In BG's discussion of identity he may be blamed for blurring the distinction between singular and general terms.[175]

Frege's explicit demand for a sharp distinction of names of concepts and names of objects appears only *after* the BG, simultaneously with his requirement of clearly separating *objects* and *concepts*.[176] It is in GRL where both parallel requirements appear in the form of fundamental methodological principles.[177] In later works, Frege frequently restates either of those requirements.[178]

Now there is something creating a certain *malaise* in speaking of Frege's sharp distinction of concepts and objects: unsaturatedness.[179] If that distinction implies unsaturatedness and its oddities, then it would seem that the distinction disappears as soon as we drop unsaturatedness. But this is not the case. Of course unsaturatedness gives to the distinction of concepts and objects an original rigour in the history of philosophy[180], but I think that this distinction has in Frege an independent source, namely, his basic insight into number as something which concerns concepts, not the individuals falling under the concepts.[181] This is closely related to what we call the "good" criterion for the distinction of concepts and objects.[182] On the other hand, the odd character of unsaturatedness is rather that Frege has been inclined to mix up *two* sorts of unsaturatedness: of the names and of the designata.[183] Each of them, individually taken, is a familiar idea in Western philosophy. The difference between Frege and traditional semantics, here, is that the latter introduces a factor which allows for dealing with unsaturatedness *as if* it did not exist.[184] (This already shows the significance of the famous Fregean notion, which is far from being a curiosity.) As said, even dropping *Ungesättigtheit*, Frege's requirement of a sharp distinction between objects and concepts (and *names* of objects and concepts) remains, for it has an independent source. And it remains as a most important correction to the philosophical tradition, where the distinction was certainly made, but was at the same time obscured by the powerful notion of *essence*.[185]

It is Frege himself who takes care of relating his distinction to the traditional terminology; he identifies *Begriffswort* with *nomen appellativum* and *Eigenname* with *nomen proprium*.[186]

2.62 *Semantics of predicate-terms*

There is already in BG a reference to the semantics of predicators.[187] UWB[188] and GRL[189] provide better references to this subject.

Predicators have a sense and a reference, as do proper names; this is beyond any doubt. Without consulting the *inedita*, the published works of Frege are informative enough on this point.

The reference of a predicate-term is a concept.[190] Frege frees the semantics of universal terms from a traditional confusion culminating in Mill's denotation–connotation[191]; this confusion is closely related to the ambiguities of the ontological square. Aristotle asserts that "white" designates two things: the quality and the subject.[192] But is *the subject* here meant in the line of inherence or in the line of universality–singularity? The fact that *individual whites* cannot exist unless inhering in individual substances has perhaps contributed to magnify the importance of the denotation of "white", i.e., of those things which are white (those substances which are white). Frege reacts against this traditional tendency and he eliminates from the semantics of predicate-terms the individuals falling under the concept. Because of this, he rejects also the terminology according to which predicate-terms are called *general* or *common* (or *universal*) names, as if they were names of *many* things.[193] "Man" is not a name of Hans; when we call Hans a man, we merely say that Hans falls under the concept man.[194] The so-called "common" name "man" has nothing to do *immediately* with the individuals falling under *man*; it has only a *mediate* relation, but one of the relations of this relative product is *not* a semantic one.[195] At most one could say (using one of Frege's terms) that "man" has a relation of *Andeuten*[196] with respect to men.

Does this mean that Frege assigns an *intension* – not an *extension* – as the reference of predicate terms? There are good reasons for a positive answer. First, the fact that unsaturatedness is an essential part of Frege's philosophical system, automatically excludes classes – which are saturated objects – from the semantics of unsaturated names (names of concepts).[197] Secondly, familiarity with Frege's works shows that Frege fundamentally thinks in terms of marks (*Merkmalen*) making up a concept, as stones make up a house, and this is of course an intensional approach.[198] Thirdly, it is a basic insight of Frege that classes have their foundation in concepts, and, better, in the marks of concepts.[199] Fourthly, we have some concrete statements – not necessarily dependent on unsaturatedness – which suggest that the extensions should be excluded from the semantics of predicators.[200]

Nevertheless, as I have already pointed out[201], there is an ambiguity in the theory of *Sinn* and *Bedeutung*; "Bedeutung" should be sometimes translated (in my view) by "importance", without any semantic import. In this sense, it is true that "featherless biped" and "rational animal" are – with respect to many contexts and *salva veritate*[202] – equally "important" terms. Incidentally, I think that this is a reason to be considered in order to understand Frege's attitude against the *Inhaltslogiker*; the sense of "Bedeutung" as synonymous with "importance" is obvious precisely in the context of Frege's attacks upon *Inhaltslogiker*.[203]

2.63 *The "transcendentalia"*

One and *being* are said to be predicates[204], and they are said to be the same *subjecto*, but different *ratione*.[205] It should be observed that this *subjectum* is not necessarily the one "usual" in traditional speculations, namely, an individual substance or *suppositum*, but rather it must be something closer to what we would call, in Fregean terminology, the reference of a predicate-term. Also, the *rationes* by which *one* and *being* differ must be Fregean *senses* of predicate-terms. Thus the traditional problem of the *transcendentalia* provides an important instance of sense and reference for predicate-terms.

Aristotle affirms that *one* and *being* "imply" each other.[206] Without entering into an analysis of this "implication" one can say that it means that *one* and *being* are coextensive predicates. Is the universal class the *subjectum* of *one* and *being*?

2.7 The semantic principle of 'Grundlagen der Arithmetik'

One of the three fundamental principles stated by Frege at the beginning of his research in GRL is the following: "nach der Bedeutung der Wörter muß im Satzzusammenhange, nicht in ihrer Vereinzelung gefragt werden".[207] This principle appears at least four times in GRL, and as far as I know, it does not occur elsewhere.[208]

On the one hand, the principle has enjoyed great fame, having been looked upon as a new approach in semantics.[209] On the other hand, a closer knowledge, both of the text and of Frege, suggests that one can hardly assume it in the sense according to which it has become famous, but rather one should look for a better interpretation. It fortunately happens that there is such a better interpretation.

Frege explains why he has adopted the principle; the reason is to be able to overcome wrong conceptions of number. A wrong conception of number is to make of it a subjective entity; this is pointed out in the first[210] occurrence of the principle. In the fourth occurrence of the principle we see that the principle is supposed to help overcome the false alternative according to which number is either an external (physical, sensible) entity or a subjective (psychological) entity.[211] In the second occurrence[212], we have similar indications.

The context of the second occurrence indicates that if Frege's own evaluation of the principle is accepted we would be faced with an incredible triviality, which of course could hardly have been intended by Frege. In fact, GRL §§ 58–60 would collapse into saying: "If anyone is incapable of refraining from associating concrete mental pictures with names of entities for which such pictures are not adequate, and if he identifies those mental pictures with the designata of the names in question, then he should rather restrict himself to assigning a meaning to contexts (say sentences) and he should not consider the meaning of isolated words."

Moreover, Frege's later anti-Hilbert attitude suggests just the opposite of the principle, namely, that words must have a meaning independent of their contexts.[213] Of course one may object that this does not refer to *Grundlagen der Arithmetik* but to later periods of Frege's life.

As for the semantics of SUB, where names have a customary or an indirect reference according to the context, it should be observed that Frege does not there mention at all his "principle" of GRL. A puzzling detail resulting from the acceptance of Frege's own interpretation of the principle is that it becomes not only trivial, as pointed out, but also unnecessarily strong. If anyone cannot avoid imagining a ball of moderate size when he pronounces the words "the Earth", and if he thinks that he is really experiencing an adequate representation of the Earth, it would be enough to tell him that the *Unvorstellbarkeit des Inhaltes eines Wortes ist kein Grund, ihm jede Bedeutung abzusprechen.*[214] If that person persists in his mistake, one might remind him that *wir werden durch das Denken gar oft über das Vorstellbare hinausgeführt, ohne damit die Unterlage für unsere Schlüsse zu verlieren.*[215] Now, these would be *ad hominem* therapies, not obliging semanticists to deprive the isolated name "the Earth" of its meaning, which is the Earth, *ein so concretes Ding.*[216]

This perplexing situation becomes comprehensible if one looks for another interpretation of the principle, not given by Frege himself, but which is in my view the main reason which led Frege to that principle.

Let us first recall that the second occurrence of the principle takes place in a section whose title is 'Jede einzelne Zahl ist ein selbständiger Gegenstand'.[217] Frege has been compelled by his speculations on natural numbers to think of them as suprasensible individuals, almost *substantiae immateriales* in the mediaeval sense. Certainly a professor of mathematics in Jena in 1884 would hardly have been well received, if, in addition to philosophizing, he had committed himself to a new pythagorean mysticism; and even aside from these social reasons, Frege did, in fact, feel unsure about his theory of numbers as objects.[218]

In GRL § 58, Frege introduces the objection of a not-too-intelligent man, who wonders how it is possible to have a *Vorstellung* of those self-subsistent spiritual individuals which are numbers. Frege replies that not self-subsistence, but the non-sensible character of numbers is the reason for that *Unvorstellbarkeit*. At this point the trivialities begin; they culminate in the above mentioned advice of not identifying the image of an old bearded man with God.

My interpretation consists in regarding these trivialities as (1), a perhaps non-superfluous, common sense advice meant for mathematicians who are incapable of dealing with objects which are neither subjective nor perceptible. To this extent, the principle may be considered as an *ad hominem* semantics. Perhaps Frege has not regarded this as too trivial; the fourth occurrence of the principle suggests that only by means of it, one (every one?) can overcome the dichotomy subjective-physical in the philosophy of number.[219]

But I also look at the above mentioned trivialities as (2), a sort of evasive digression; while the trivialities are being stated, Frege has in mind the embarrassing situation of being obliged to hold that numbers are like angels. Abruptly, the semantic principle appears[220], but it is not directed to the trivial interlude (except to the extent to which it is not an *ad hominem* semantics); rather it is meant as a drastic elimination of the embarrassing spiritual numbers. Thanks to the semantic principle, the self-subsistence of numbers is no longer a problem, because numerals no longer have a meaning to be looked for.

A text immediately following the formulation of the principle reveals Frege's ultimate goal: self-subsistence of numbers does not commit us to look for a spiritual designatum of numerals.[221]

Thus, Frege cannot be accused of a new arithmetical mysticism. (Still, in the next paragraph[222] he clearly indicates that the principle is *not for him*, but for those readers who would dislike mysticism; Frege in fact takes up again the discussion of how the spiritual designata of numerals should be understood, as though the principle had never been formulated.)

The third occurrence of the principle suggests still another interpretation, related to definitions by abstraction. Numbers are grasped not *via* themselves, so to speak, but through statements of equality between numbers.[223] To this extent numerals would have meaning only in context. Nevertheless, if Frege adopts this approach to number (as he does), it is precisely *because* he considers numbers as self-subsistent non-perceptible entities. The definition by abstraction *must* be employed because numbers are beyond intuition or *Vorstellung*[224]; and it *can* be employed because numbers are objects, not concepts.[225]

2.8 Analyticity and a priori

Frege intends to provide an "explication"[226] of Kant's ideas on analyticity and a prrioi, and to use this as a basis for a discussion of Kant's views on mathematics.[227] In BG Frege asserted that statements of identity involving a difference of *senses* (of course Frege did not use *the terminology* "sense-reference"in BG [228]) were synthetic *im Kantischen Sinne.*[229] Definitions as rules of abbreviation were not propositions, but once they became propositions they were analytic[230] – an argument showing Frege's early concern with Kant.[231] Many "synthetic" sentences occur in BG, but they are *not* independently asserted.[232] BG already contains all the elements of Frege's criticism of Kant. Arithmetic is not dependent upon any intuition of time; arithmetical induction is a motionless, timeless fragment of second-order predicate calculus.[233] As soon as Frege is able to define numbers in terms of predicates, the question formulated in the *Vorwort* of BG will be answered: arithmetic is *rein logisch.* Frege rejects Kant's pure form of time because he views this as a *restriction* upon the universal applicability of number.[234] We may not agree with Frege's reading of Kant, but we must understand his argument against Kant. Unfortunately Frege in GRL thought it was necessary to formulate his disagreement with Kant by means of a previous re-definition of the Kantian terminology; this is the "explication" mentioned above.

Frege claims that his "explication" follows the criterion of not considering the "content" of sentences but the reasons justifying their assertion.[235] This formulation is puzzling because one wonders how we shall classify sentences disregarding their meaning. I think that "content" should be expanded into "how we psychologically arrive at the content".[236] Both in BG [237] and GRL [238] Frege says that he is not interested in the genesis of our knowledge. And he does consider the content of sentences both in BG [239] and in his "explication" of the Kantian terms in GRL.[240] Obviously, Frege's distinction of a "good" and a "bad" criterion is irrelevant both to Kant and to Frege's own definitions.[241]

As the *Vorwort* of BG shows, Frege originally had in mind a division of propositions into *two* classes, *à la Leibniz*. The first class included *das reine Denken*, i.e. what is absolutely universal, a priori. The second class included individuals and empirical facts. In GRL this is transformed into a threefold classification by introducing an intermediate case – a *besonderes Wissensgebiet* – between every possible world and the *hic et nunc*. Geometry, for instance, is neither roughly involved with empirical facts nor absolutely universal, as other geometries are conceivable. This is the *tertium* Frege needs in order to have three classes of sentences, *à la Kant*. Thus "synthetic a priori" will mean what applies to some special world only, while "analytic" will become a synonym of "das reine Denken" in BG, i.e. the absolutely universal. "Empirical" will imply the *hic et nunc*, individuals and facts. This Fregean "explication" of the Kantian terminology (1) deviates too much from Kant (cf. "analytic"!), (2) is unimportant (synthetic a priori as a mere "less universal domain"), (3) is artificial within Frege's system (it does not express anything not clearly formulated in some other way), (4) is misleading in that it may allow the reader to think that the Frege-Kant dispute is merely verbal (two senses of "analytic", etc.). The mistake was to try to express a real disagreement with Kant *in Kantian terms* defined *in a non-Kantian way*. Thus, it is advisable to forget Frege's "explication" and only consider the *real* difference between Kant and Frege on the philosophy of arithmetic.

As I have said, Frege rejects pure temporal intuition [242], *because* the latter appears to him to be a restriction upon the transcendental character of number. This is Leibniz's doctrine, as opposed to Kant's [243] and to the traditional aristotelian-scholastic view.[244] *Das Zählbare* is coextensive with *das Denkbare* or with *das reine Denken* [245]; geometry is not.[246] The elimination of time is partially accomplished in the third chapter of BG ("zuerst den Begriff der Anordnung in einer Reihe auf die logische Folge zurückzuführen" [247]). These motionless, non-temporal formulae of second-order predicate calculus are valid for every possible world, even without time; they are analytic in Frege's sense.

The verbal disagreement consists in saying that Frege views the analytic as enlarging knowledge, contrary to Kant.[248] The real disagreement is expressed by saying that for Frege concepts without intuition are not necessarily *leer*. The theorems on the ancestral relation (BG) are a proof of this.[249] Frege asserts that Kant had come upon a more general sense of "analytic".[250] The latter is probably similar to the sense according to which "Fido is black or Fido is not black" may be regarded as analytic [251], i.e. the first of "the two kinds" of analyticity in recent philosophy.[252] Kant only considered the second kind, i.e. subject-predicate analyticity.[253]

Last but not least, Frege's great achievement – as opposed to "philosophical" critics of Kant – is that he actually constructed a *Begriffsschrift* just to detect surreptitious *Anschauungsaxiome* [254] in the course of the proofs, i.e. just to show that Kant was wrong.[255]

2.9 Definitions

The prevailing sense of "definition" in Frege's works is *abbreviation*.[256] According to this, definitions are rules about signs, and therefore outside the object language. The identity statements of the object language corresponding to such definitions will not require a special distinction of *Sinn* and *Bedeutung*, for there is no reason why there should be *two* different senses at each side of the equality sign (given that our purpose was to abbreviate one of the signs in question). This becomes an explicit semantic remark in GRG.[257] In a later paper Frege insists on saying that sentences "resulting" from definitions do not increase knowledge any more than "$a = a$" does.[258] His struggle against "creative definitions" should be understood in the context of these definitions by abbreviation. A definition can "create" in an object only what a name can "create"; i.e., the property of being called in some particular way, quite a "weak" property indeed.[259]

There are also other senses of "definition" in Frege's works. *Definitions by abstraction*, in particular, are illustrated in GRL[260]; they are also explained in a letter to Russell.[261] *Definition of a concept* preserves the traditional sense of "definition"; it consists in setting forth the *marks* of a concept, and it is a way of fulfilling the requirement of *scharfe Begrenzung*.[262] Another sense of "definition" is *definition of an object from a concept under which it falls*. Frege warns against confusing these definite descriptions[263] with the previously mentioned definition of a concept.

REFERENCES

1. BG, §§ 2, 3 *passim*.
2. BG, § 8. Except when other references are given, Frege's texts mentioned in this section belong to BG, § 8.
3. This is the Latin translation of Aristotle's definition of *onoma* at the beginning of *Perihermeneias*. Cf. LNE, p. 73.
4. BG, pp. IV and 3.
5. Cf.: "der Name *B* hat also in diesem Falle denselben Inhalt wie der Name *A*".

6. Cf. GRL, § 51 (quoted in note 177), or HUSS, p. 326, where Frege criticizes Husserl because he suggests that "man" is a name of Hans just as "Hans" is.
7. The metalinguistic approach to identity is emphasized by Frege's stressing that signs are sometimes names standing for things or designata and sometimes standing for themselves. But this reference to "suppositio materialis" is not completed by the deeper distinction between the symbol and its concrete occurrences or tokens. "Suppositio materialis" had been defined with reference to this further distinction: "significatio termini in propositione . . . pro seipso solummodo aut sibi consimili" (Paulus Venetus [2], f. 16a). "Gleichgestaltigkeit" of signs will be discussed by Frege in later works: GRG II, § 99; hints of this are already in UFT, p. 98 top, SUB, p. 26, middle.
8. Frege misses this fundamental point in at least three formulations of his analysis of statements of identity in BG; in the definition proposed before the objection, in the discussion of the geometrical example and in the final definition of the sign of identity.
9. Cf. in particular: ". . . die verschiedenen Namen für denselben Inhalt nicht immer bloß eine gleichgiltige Formsache sind, sondern . . . sie das Wesen der Sache selbst betreffen, wenn sie mit verschiedenen Bestimmungsweisen zusammenhängen."
10. For example SUB, and BGGE, p. 198.
11. GRL, p. 76.
12. GRL, p. 78.
13. In GRL, § 67, Frege opposes: "to introduce an object" and "to assert something about an object", ". . . ein Urteil, das von dem Gegenstande handelt, aber führt ihn nun auch nicht mehr ein . . .". The expression "die Weise wie ein Gegenstand eingeführt ist" appears not only in the text of § 67 but also in the title of this paragraph in the analysis of contents of GRL. Not only is the expression "way in which an object is introduced" misleading (because what is primarily "introduced" is a new sign), but also the expression "definition of an object" (used by Frege in § 67). The latter should not be confounded with "definition of an object from a concept" (cf. Section 2.9) and it should be replaced by "introduction of a new name".
14. This is expressed in GRL, § 67, but already in BG p. 56 it was a clearly formulated view.
15. This sort of superlative "denominatio extrinseca" enjoys in Frege's doctrine the same right to be a property of an object as the essential predicates do (cf. Section 3.5). In fact Frege uses this kind of property in order to have a substitute of existential propositions for individuals; it is not possible to say "there is Julius Caesar" but it is possible to say, instead, "there is an x called Julius Caesar" (cf. BGGE, p. 200).
16. Porphyry [1], p. 12, 1. 19 and p. 13, 1. 1, says that both the *proprium* and the *inseparable accident* may be disregarded in our approach to the thing; i.e., Porphyry implies that the thing may be given under other aspects.
17. UFT, p. 101.
18. Only with such qualifications would I agree with Papst [1], p. 8.
19. In the present section all references (unless otherwise stated) are to SUB, p. 25–26.
20. GRL, §§ 29 and 49, respectively.
21. Frege prefers to use the term "figure" (*Figur*) when the meaning should not be taken into account. Cf. UFT, p. 97, GRG II, p. 107; the situation is clearly

described in KSCH, p. 449, where a figure is said to be able to acquire the property of *serving as a sign*.

22. To use an expression of Quine [3], p. 22; but *then* cf. *ibid.*, p. 9.
23. (i) "Eine Verschiedenheit kann nur dadurch zu Stande kommen, daß der Unterschied des Zeichens einem Unterschiede in der Art des Gegebenseins des Bezeichneten entspricht."
(ii) "Wir haben also verschiedene Bezeichnungen für denselben Punkt, und diese Namen [. . .] deuten zugleich auf die Art des Gegebenseins, und daher ist in dem Satze eine wirkliche Erkenntnis enthalten."
(iii) "Es liegt nun nahe, mit einem Zeichen [. . .] außer dem Bezeichneten, was die Bedeutung des Zeichens heißen möge, noch das verbunden zu denken, was ich den Sinn des Zeichens nennen möchte, worin die Art des Gegebenseins enthalten ist".
Senses as "sides" (*Seiten*) of a thing is an image appearing in SUB, p. 27 and FUB, p. 5. In the latter, the variety of names of a thing is viewed again as grounded on that plurality of "sides". The same in GED.
24. These well-known terminological distinctions are to be found in SUB, p. 26–27, 31.
25. Aristotle [4], 190b, 24. Two examples to be compared with Frege's analysis of identity:
"'To be capable of health' and 'to be capable of illness' are not the same, for if they were there would be no difference between being ill and being well. Yet the subject both of health and of sickness [. . .] is one and the same" (Aristotle [4.1], 201a, 34b, 3).
"This is an identical substratum (whether a point or a stone or something else of this kind), but it has different attributes – as the sophists assume that Coriscus' being in the Lyceum is a different thing from Coriscus' being in the marketplace" (*ibid.*, 219b, 18–22).
There is also the famous distinction between the road from Thebes to Athens and the road from Athens to Thebes (Aristotle [4], 202b, 12).
As for Frege, WIF, pp. 658, 660 may be compared with the Aristotelian or traditional approach.
26. Brentano [1], § 18: "der Name gibt etwas kund".
27. *Ibid.*: "der Name etwas bedeutet, auf einen Begriff hinweist".
28. *Ibid.*: "der Name hat eine Beziehung zum Gegenstand, der möglicherweise der Vorstellung entspricht. In diesem Sinne sagen wir, der Name nennt den Gegenstand".
29. *Ibid.*: "So daß jede [Vorstellung] nur einer gewissen Seite oder einem gewissen Teil eines Dinges entspricht".
30. SUB, p. 27, GED, p. 66.
31. SUB, *ibid.*
32. SUB, p. 28.
33. SUB, p. 27.
34. It should be observed that in SUB, p. 27 Frege is careful to exclude from perfect languages some defects which are typical of natural languages, but he does not explicitly reject the possibility that a sense be given under different names (under . . . different senses). In fact Frege has thought it convenient rather to disregard such different ways of a sense's being given. This is apparent in his reference to propositions being given under many sentences (BGGE, p. 196 note). For proper names the following later text is interesting: "Ob ich das Wort

'Pferd' oder 'Ross' oder 'Gaul' oder 'Märe' gebrauche, macht keinen Unterschied im Gedanken" (GED, p. 63 below). To some extent this is just common sense; nevertheless in the case of Frege there are other implications (cf. 2.26).

35. SUB, p. 26 below, and 31.
36. Carnap [1] § 29: "It is more difficult to see clearly what constitutes the ordinary sense in Frege's method. As mentioned before this is due to the lack of precise explanation and especially of a statement as to the condition of identity of sense." Cf. also Church [1], note 15.
37. Scholz [5], 1, B, but cf. Scholz-Hasenjaeger [1], § 50, 2.5. In the former, the least difference in the sign implies a difference of senses. In the latter, *definiendum* and *definiens*, usually different signs, are allowed to be *gleichsinnig*.
38. I would make a similar objection to the interpretation proposed by Wienpahl [1].
39. "Note Church's ambiguous use of 'meaning'. On the one hand he speaks of denotation as one *aspect* of meaning and of sense as another *kind* of meaning. Either we have two kinds of meaning or only one kind with *two aspects*" (R. M. Martin [1], p. 609, the last italics ours). Such familiar "aspects" of things are all which is involved in Frege's *Sinn*.
40. SUB, p. 27.
41. P. 49.
42. SUB, p. 27.
43. Cf. Section 2.11.
44. SUB, p. 27, especially the note.
45. SUB, p. 28.
46. *Ibid.* and GRL, p. 87 note.
47. According to Frege's dyadic semantics of his earlier works (cf. 2.1), names have a *content*.
48. SUB, p. 27 twice identifies *Bedeutung* and *Gegenstand*; cf. also p. 30. On the other hand, the *Sinn* is said not to be the *Gegenstand selbst* (p. 30).
49. Cf. Section 10.11.
50. Cf. Section 1.46, note 118.
51. SUB, p. 28.
52. BGGE, pp. 195, 198, 203.
53. SUB, p. 27.
54. For the question dealt with in the present section, cf. Jackson [1]; an interesting discussion is in Caton [1].
55. Cf. Bartlett [1], p. 58.
56. Church [1], note 32, rejects unsaturatedness but keeps sense-reference. Cf. also Church [2].
57. § 28.
58. § 31.
59. Cf. Angelelli [2], Buridan [1], p. 49, Bodemann [1], p. 113.
60. A weaker formulation appears *in fine* of *Gedankengefüge*.
61. In comparison with such basic objections, any confusion of use and mention, inherent in the famous Leibnizian principle appears as secondary.
62. GRL, § 65; FUB, p. 2–5; GRG II, p. 71; SCHUB, p. 10.
63. In particular FUB, pp. 2–5.
64. GRG 1, p. IX and FUB, pp. 2–5 are careful to explain that the senses may be different.

65. Incidentally, a further inconsistency in GRL § 65 is that Frege's reduction of *equality* to identity does not seem to respect the meaning of "Eigenschaft" as individual accident, which prevails in some fragments of GRL. Frege says in GRL, § 65 that instead of asserting that two surfaces are equal as to their color, one should say that the color of the two surfaces is the same. But of course it cannot be the same (except specifically) if "color of a surface" means an individual accident inhering in that surface, as is the case for GRL, §§ 21–25 (cf. our 10.11, 1.45 and 1.46).
66. GRG II, p. 111.
67. Aristotle [5], pp. 179a, 36. The quoted Greek formula belongs to Aristotle [4], Γ, 3, 202b, 15. My interpretation of these texts is also intended as a correction of Bocheński [3], 11.46 and [4] *ibid.*
68. Cf. HUSS, p. 319–320 and Bartlett [1], p. 59.
69. SUB, p. 30.
70. BG, pp. IV and 3.
71. P. 196, note.
72. Cf. note 146.
73. GED, p. 64.
74. Leibniz [1], VII, p. 236.
75. "... gemeint ist die Wahrheit, deren Erkenntnis der Wissenschaft als Ziel gesetzt ist" (GED, p. 59). This was written in 1918, but it is in accord with SUB, p. 32–33.
76. Bartlett [1], p. 59 and HUSS, p. 320.
77. Pp. 264–5.
78. SUB, p. 28: "In der ungeraden Rede spricht man von dem Sinne, z.B. der Rede eines Andern."
79. SUB, p. 32: "Wir fragen nun nach Sinn und Bedeutung eines ganzen Behauptungssatzes."
80. "Ein solcher [Behauptungs]satz enthält einen Gedanken" (SUB, p. 32). Frege explains that by "Gedanke" he means the objective content of a sentence which may be the common property of several thinkers (*ibid.*).
81. "Ist dieser Gedanke nun als dessen [of the sentence] Sinn oder als dessen Bedeutung anzusehen?" (*ibid.*)
82. In BG (p. 4) Frege mentions the possibility of making of *assertion* "the only predicate" of his symbolic language. But this is, in my view, a rather ironical way of assigning some function to the term "predicate" (the couple of terms "subject–predicate" having been eliminated in favor of function–argument, cf. Section 6.1). In FUB, p. 22, note, Frege stresses the peculiarity of the assertion sign which is reiterated in GRG I (§ 26).
Frege rejects the unqualified making of the adjective "true" a predicate of propositions or sentences (SUB, pp. 34–35; cf. Bartlett [1], p. 18). The most interesting presentation of this point is to be found in GED, where Frege discusses whether truth is a property, in a way quite similar to GRL's discussion of whether number is a property. In GED (p. 61) as in GRL Frege uses "Eigenschaft" in the sense of individual accident (cf. our 1.46). He assumes that it is meaningful to talk about *sinnlich wahrnehmbare Eigenschaft*, while the normal use of "Eigenschaft" excludes this (properties are abstract entities). Now, even if we provisionally call truth a property, Frege shows that it is quite a peculiar one: (1) to every property of a thing truth is associated as a property of the

proposition which assigns that property to the thing, (2) "*p*" has the same content as "*p* is true" (though – as Frege remarks – they do make a difference for a researcher who has painfully arrived at the second) (GED, p. 61).

83. A particular sub-class of conceptual content (cf. 2.11) is propositional content (*beurteilbarer Inhalt*). Propositional content should be understood as that which counts for deduction, and in this sense the fact that a sentence is given in the active or passive voice does not affect its propositional content (BG, p. 3). The distinction of apodictic and assertoric sentences is rejected on the same grounds (BG, pp. 4–5). The same applies for such "rhetorical" particles as "aber" (BG, p. 13). Nevertheless, it is not clear how far this elimination of elements irrelevant to "deduction" extends. The notion of *beurteilbarer Inhalt* belongs only to the earlier works of Frege; it is afterwards replaced by the well known distinction of *Gedanke* and *truth-value*. In GRG I (p. X) and BGGE (p. 198) Frege says that the propositional content included both the *Gedanke* and the truth-value.
84. GED, pp. 59–60.
85. SUB, p. 32 f.
86. FUB, pp. 13 and 16. Frege says "ebenso". Compare the "ebensogut" in SUB, p. 32, line 10 from the bottom.
87. Cf. Section 2.26.
88. FUB, p. 14.
89. SUB, p. 32f.
90. SUB, p. 32.
91. *Ibid.*
92. At the time of SUB the most that can be attained from Frege as to the nature of *Gedanke* is his footnote to SUB, p. 32 (cf. note 80). But the borderline between objectivity and subjectivity is not clear in Frege. Why are the *Färbung* or *Beleuchtung* of propositions mere subjective elements? Only because they do not concern the logician? (cf. BGGE, p. 196, note; SUB, p. 45). In a later period, Frege suggests a definition of *Gedanken* (in a letter to Husserl, 1906, published recently by Bartlett [1], p. 19). But the criterion set forth therein does not seem to help in deciding whether interchanging non-logical constants (such as "the Morning Star" and "the Evening Star") preserves the same *Gedanke*.
93. BGGE, p. 196, note.
94. Cf. note 104.
95. The Leibnizian principle is actually Frege's source of inspiration, SUB, p. 35.
96. SUB, p. 32, lines 4–9 from the bottom. Actually Frege gives $\sim p \supset \sim r$.
97. *Ibid.*, lines 1–3 from the bottom.
98. SUB, p. 33, lines 10–13.
99. *Ibid.*, lines 15–18.
100. *Ibid.*, below.
101. SUB, p. 32 below, and 33.
102. *Odyssey*, Invocation.
103. "Mit der Frage nach der Wahrheit würden wir den Kunstgenuß verlassen und uns einer wissenschaftlichen Betrachtung zuwenden" (SUB, p. 33). Rivetti Barbò [1] views Frege's semantics in SUB as tacitly related to the principle of contextual meaning of GRL; "Odysseus" has no *Bedeutung* because its context is not true (§ 6). But I think that there was no such principle in Frege's semantics (cf. 2.7) and that "Odysseus" *non supponit* or has no *Bedeutung* because neither it nor the *Odyssey* as a whole have any importance (*Bedeutung*) for Frege (*qua*

philosopher of mathematics), cf. 2.26.

104. SUB, p. 33, lines 8–9: "für den Sinn eines Satzes kann ja nur der Sinn, nicht die Bedeutung dieses Theiles [Frege means a part of the sentence] in Betracht kommen". Cf. Carnap [1], 28.7, and Stegmüller [1], p. 135.
105. SUB, p. 34.
106. Cf. 2.62.
107. As Frege himself suggests (SUB, p. 34, line 16).
108. SUB, p. 34, last line of the first passage.
109. SUB, p. 35, last line of the first passage.
110. SUB, p. 32, note.
111. Cf. Section 2.24.
112. "Wenn nur der Wahrheitswert eines Satzes dessen Bedeutung ist, so haben einerseits alle wahren Sätze dieselbe Bedeutung, andrerseits alle falschen. Wir sehen daraus, dass in der Bedeutung des Satzes alles Einzelne verwischt ist (SUB, p. 35).
113. "Es kann uns also niemals auf die Bedeutung eines Satzes allein ankommen . . ." (*ibid.*).
114. SUB, pp. 35–36.
115. SUB, p. 36.
116. UGG_2 (II), pp. 377 f.; 400; 402.
117. SUB, pp. 36, 39, 42–46, 49.
118. The indetermination is implicit in the following example: "Wenn sich die Sonne im Wendekreise des Krebses befindet, haben wir auf der nördlichen Erdhälfte den längsten Tag" (SUB, pp. 43–44).
Frege understands such a sentence as a formal implication (the "quantifier" applies to the time variable). In formal implications, only the whole has a sense, i.e., expresses a proposition (WIF, p. 659).
119. SUB, p. 44, line 10.
120. This interpretation could be supported by BGGE, p. 205, where Frege says that a *Gedanke* must have at least one unsaturated element in order that its parts can be put together. The same interpretation is likewise favored by considering that pseudo-sentences *become sentences* as soon as a proper name, for example, is put in the "empty" place (SUB, p. 44).
121. SUB, p. 27.
122. UGG_2(II), p. 379; cf. also pp. 400, 402. Frege says that in "If $a^2 = 1$, then $a^4 = 1$", the fragment "$a^2 = 1$" is not the name of a concept until "a" is replaced by a proper variable sign.
123. SUB, p. 39.
124. This ambiguity seems to be present in Frege's analysis of relative subordinate sentences.
125. SUB, p. 39.
126. Against, for example, Aristotle [1], 13b, 16. For Frege's approach, cf. also GRG I, p. XXI.
127. SUB, p. 27–28, 41.
128. SUB, p. 40.
129. GRG I, § 28. Already in UFT (p. 101) there is an indication of the necessity of ensuring reference for the signs being used. The requirement of *scharfe Begrenzung* of functions is closely connected with this; a function which is not defined for some arguments implies that some well formed sentences will be

neither true nor false, a new menace to the *tertium non datur* (GRG II, § 56).
130. SUB, p. 41.
131. KSCH, p. 447. *Scheineigenname* is for instance "nothing"; "nihil", as Paulus Venetus, for example taught, should be expanded into "nulla res" (P. Venetus [2], f. 2a).
132. SUB, p. 28.
133. SUB, p. 36, middle.
134. SUB, p. 28, lines 12–10 from the bottom.
135. SUB, p. 39 (middle), also pp. 37 (line 5, "also"), 46, 48. Cf. for both part (a) and (b), SUB, p. 37, bottom and p. 38, top.
136. Cf. Carnap [1], § 30.
137. SUB, p. 37, top.
138. Cf. SUB, p. 28.
139. Cf. Carnap [1], § 30: "Frege's special form of the method of the name relation involves additional complications. Starting with any ordinary name, it leads to an infinite number of entities . . ."
140. Carnap [1], *ibid.*, and Stegmüller [1], p. 149.
141. GRL, p. X; p. 37 note.
142. Cf. Chapter 1, note 118; also: GRL, p. 37 note, SUB, p. 29, GED.
143. GRL, p. 37, note.
144. For example, GRL, p. X.
145. For example, SUB, p. 31.
146. For instance, the *Färbungen* and *Beleuchtungen* which natural or poetical language adds to the sense and reference of words (SUB, pp. 31, 45). Frege realizes that he is condemning as subjective, things which are not interesting for him *as a logician*; he curiously admits some "accessibility to many thinkers" for *Vorstellungen* ("eine Verwandtschaft des Menschlichen Vorstellens", SUB, p. 31). Other texts where *Vorstellung* is considered are: GRG I, p. XVIII; UTG, p. 160; HUSS; GED, p. 66. In the last mentioned text there is an interesting description of *Vorstellung.*
147. For example, SUB, p. 32, note. Cf. note 150. LNE, p. 74.
148. This is a key concept in Frege's foundations of arithmetic; zero will be the class of concepts equiextensional with *not being self-identical.* To the extent that this concept is sharply defined (i.e., for every object it may be decided whether or not it falls under that concept), it is logically legitimate (GRL, § 74). I take it to be obvious that Frege regards the concept *not being self-identical* as objective.
149. For references, see the next note.
150. HUSS, pp. 317–318: objectivity as *Öffentlichkeit*; HUSS, pp. 331–332: objectivity as *von unserm Denken ganz unabhängig.* In GRG I, p. XVII the sense of *being independent of us* predominates; on p. XVIII the sense *accessible to all* prevails. Predication (*Fallen unter*) in HUSS, p. 317 is described as something independent of us; but is this univocally meant both for the falling of the Moon under *being a satellite* and for the falling of $x \neq x$ under number zero? *Gedanke* (i.e., proposition) is defined in terms of weak objectivity (SUB, p. 32, note) but also as something *previous to me* (GED, pp. 69 note, 77), which suggests the stronger sense of *being independent of me.* By asking further who is the "me" or the "us" we would be compelled to discuss transcendental subjectivity; this is not departing too much from Frege but rather understanding or *clarifying* him as suggested in

our section 10.13.

151. GRG II, p. 86: *Wirklich* is what acts upon the senses ("auf die Sinne wirkt", GRG I, p. XVIII). Since GRL Frege stresses that there is a domain of *unwirkliche* but still objective entities. His supreme category is das *Denkbare* (which for him coincides with *das Zählbare*, GRL, § 14). *Das Denkbare* was in Lotze [1], p. 17 the only supreme concept, and in the second scholastics it was called a *supertranscendental* (Fonseca [1], *lib. primus*, *cap.* 28).
152. A probable source is Eucken [1] (p. 209), where Herbart's distinction *Vorstellung–Begriff* is mentioned. Eucken's book is quoted by Frege in GRL, p. 43.
153. This is the English translation (in Aristotle [3.1]) of the Greek expression παθήματα τῆς ψυχῆς. The text in question is Aristotle [1], 16a, 3–8, i.e., the opening lines of *Perihermeneias*. For Theophrastus, cf. Bocheński [2], p. 39.
154. Ammonius [2], p. 17 and Stephanus Alexandrinus [1], p. 4.
155. *This* would be the opinion of Ammonius [2], and not that assigned to him by Mates [1], p. 12.
156. Aquinas [4] has the four Aristotelian terms in the following version: *scripturae, voces, intellectus conceptiones, res.* The *intellectus conceptiones* are the *locus* of universals and this is enough to suggest that they are (also) *objectively* meant. In Caietanus [1] (p. 19) the objective interpretation is definitely supported: "Nomen autem cum sit nota earum quae sunt objective in anima passionum".
157. Aquinas [5] draws a parallelism between the divine Trinity and human intellectual operations: "Quia semper cum actu intelligitur aliquid, verbum formatur". Human *verbum* is *tanquam speculum in quo res cernitur*. It has nothing to do with the *quidditas* which is grasped through it; the *verbum* is a concrete (accidental) reality, *in continuo fieri*.
158. Suarez [1], II, *sect.* I, 1.
159. For example, Gredt [1], note 7.
160. Eisler [2] (article "Vorstellung") paraphrases our Suarezian text in the following terms: "Die Scholastiker unterscheiden "formale" Vorstellung (Vorstellungsakt) und "objektive" Vorstellung (Vorstellungsinhalt)".
161. Cf. Gredt [1], note 7.
162. GRL, p. 37, note.
163. Suarez [1], VI, *sect.* 2, 1.
164. *Ibid.*, pp. 3, 9.
165. Descartes [1], § 59. That the risk of ambiguity transmitted to modern philosophy was indeed great, may be seen in Pacius' presentation of the Aristotelian semantics: "... Nominibus non significari immediate res ipsas, sed per animi conceptionem. Quodlibet enim nomen significat aliquem mentis conceptum, consequenter significat rem, quae per eum conceptum repraesentatur, ut imago in speculo" (Pacius [3], pp. 60–61).
166. "The meaning of words being only the ideas they are made to stand for by him that uses them ..." (Locke [1], III, Ch. 4, § 6).
167. "Je vois Monsieur que Vous entendez souvent par *idée* la realité objective de l'idée ou la qualité qu'elle represente" (Leibniz [1], V, p. 212).
168. For example, GRG I, p. XVIII. For Russell, cf. Simpson [1], pp. 111–112.
169. Cf. Section 2.51.
170. For the latter, cf. Eisler [1], article "Objektiv".
171. Cf. for instance De Wulf [1], III, p. 223.
172. The tendency to see "to be in the mind" as subjectivism is clear, for instance,

in Goodstein [1], p. 4. Cf. also Russell's suggestion that Leibniz had made of relations subjective entities (Chapter 1, note 83). This tendency is also discernable in Frege, who reads "in the mind" as meaning either "in my mind" or "in your mind" (GRG I, p. 2), but who also is incapable of reading that expression as referring to a transcendental subjectivity (which he, paradoxically and perhaps unconsciously, is compelled to introduce, cf. Section 10.13).

173. It would be necessary to apply the same qualifications to many statements of "platonism", especially in the field of mathematical foundational research (for example: Scholz-Hasenjaeger [1], § 1; Bernays [2]; Bourbaki [1], p. 88, etc.). (For the particular case of H. Scholz, I owe this remark to Prof. I. M. Bocheński). That those qualifications are "pertinent", is indicated by Cantor's distinction of an *inmanente* or *intrasubjektive Realität vs.* a *transsubjektive Realität* (Cantor [1], p. 181); where is Cantor's "paradise"? In terms of traditional philosophy, this would make a difference in one's calling him "platonist".

174. Cf. Section 10.13. For *platonism*, cf. also Mortan [1] and Egidi [1], p. 26.

175. Cf. Section 2.11 (and notes 5 and 6), 5.3 *in fine*.

176. UWB, p. 50. Frege accuses natural language of not being *eindeutig*: "Von vielen Beispielen mag nur eine durchgehende Erscheinung hier erwähnt werden: dasselbe Wort dient zur Bezeichnung eines Begriffes und eines einzelnen unter diesen fallenden Gegenstandes. Überhaupt ist kein Unterschied zwischen Begriff und Einzelnem ausgeprägt. "Das Pferd" kann ein Einzelwesen, es kann auch die Art bezeichnen, wie in dem Satze: "das Pferd ist ein pflanzenfressendes Thier". "Pferd" kann endlich einen Begriff bedeuten wie in dem Satze: "dies ist ein Pferd."
Is it possible to conjecture that Frege has here, already, his later explicitly formulated requirement that concepts be designata of unsaturated expressions? Unsaturatedness would thus not be a mere reaction to Kerry (as we would like to think) but an original insight (cf. Chapter 6). In the last sentence the name of the concept would be "... ist ein Pferd".

177. In GRL Frege states three fundamental principles of research, one of them being "der Unterschied zwischen Begriff und Gegenstand ist im Auge zu behalten" (p. X). The following text shows his requirement of a parallel distinction between *names* of concepts and objects:
"Zunächst ist es unpassend, ein allgemeines Begriffswort Namen eines Dinges zu nennen. Dadurch entsteht der Schein als ob die Zahl Eigenschaft eines Dinges wäre. Ein allgemeines Begriffswort bezeichnet eben einen Begriff. Nur mit dem bestimmten Artikel oder einem Demonstrativpronomen gilt es als Eigenname eines Dinges, hört aber damit auf, als Begriffswort zu gelten. Der Name eines Dinges ist ein Eigenname" (GRL, § 51).
But it is not necessary to see, already, *Ungesättigtheit* in this text. The sharp distinction between concepts and objects is sufficiently supported by what we call "the good" criterion (Section 6.43), which is stated by Frege precisely in the same § 51 of GRL: "Bei einem Begriffe fragt es sich immer, ob etwas und was unter ihn falle. Bei einem Eigennamen sind solche Fragen sinnlos."

178. GRG I, pp. X, XIV, XXIV; GRG II, p. 154 bottom; UBR, p. 9; in the latter text natural language is once again accused: "Doch ist in der Sprache die Schärfe des Unterschiedes etwas verwischt, indem ursprüngliche Eigennamen (z.B. "Mond") Begriffswörter und ursprüngliche Begriffswörter (z.B. "Gott") Eigennamen werden können."

179. Cf. Section 6.7.
180. The traditional passage from *homo* to *humanitas* – from $f(x)$ to $\lambda x(fx)$ – is not allowed by Frege.
181. Once Frege views the concept as the *sachliches Subject* of statements of number, i.e., once he sees a concept like *to be a Jupiter's moon* as the subject of the property of *having four members* (GRL § 57), he is necessarily led to protest against any lack of sharpness in the separation of individuals and universals. Thus, he blames natural language for blurring the true nature of statements of number insofar as it does not show that concepts – not individuals – are the real subjects (GRL, § 52).
182. Cf. Section 6.43.
183. Cf. Section 6.72.
184. The "modus intelligendi", cf. Section 6.75.
185. Cf. Section 4.4.
186. GRG II, § 151. Just before the modern decline of logic and semantics, Fonseca included in his *Dialectica* a thorough discussion on names (Fonseca [1], *Lib.* 1) wherein the chapter 'De nomine communi et singulari' is worth mentioning for our present purposes. Our author defines:

Nomen { *commune seu universale: eadem ratione de pluribus praedicari.*
singulare seu discretum seu individuum: non praedicatur de pluribus.

For comparisons with Fregean terminology, the following remark of Fonseca is interesting: "nomina quidem communia vocari apud Grammaticos appellativa, singularia vero, propria." Fonseca counts definite descriptions (existence and uniqueness) as proper names. See Section 2.9.
187. BG, p. 15.
188. Cf. note 176.
189. Cf. note 177.
190. BGGE – a paper where SUB is announced as a forthcoming publication (pp. 195, 198, 203) – defines concept as *Bedeutung eines grammatischen Prädikats* (p. 193, note). Commenting on the example "dieses Blatt ist grün", Frege says: "Wir sagen dann, daß etwas unter einen Begriff falle, und das grammatische Prädikat bedeutet dabei diesen Begriff. Also diese Worte [i.e., "nichts anderes als Venus"] bedeuten einen Begriff . . ." (BGGE, p. 194). Cf. also pp. 198, 201 (last line of the first passage).

FUB is also written under the semantics of SUB (p. 14, note). Frege analyses the sentence "Caesar eroberte Gallien" into two parts: "Caesar" and "eroberte Gallien". The latter is said to have a function as its reference (FUB, p. 17). It is obvious that Frege would not use the term "Bedeutung" unless he expected the reader to take that term with all its implications within the theory of sense and reference.

Other texts where Frege speaks of the *Bedeutung* of predicate-terms are HUSS, p. 326 below, UGG I, p. 298.

Frege does not seem to speak of the *sense* of predicate-terms; a rare reference would be the following: ". . . der Fehler liegt [. . .] in der Hilbertschen Definition, die der grammatischen Prädikate "ist ein Punkt" weder einen Sinn noch eine Bedeutung verleiht" (UGG_2(I), p. 305).

The *inedita* will show that Husserl at the end of the century did already know what we are now painfully inferring: the reference of a predicate term is a concept (or relation). As for the sense, we (including Husserl) are not further instructed by Frege; but we may trivially say that the sense is that way in which the concept is given.

For this question see also Dummett [2] and [3] and Marschall [1] and [2].

191. Mill [1], I, 2, § 5: "The word 'white' denotes all white things, as snow, paper, the foam of the sea, etc., and implies, or, in the language of the schoolmen, connotes the attribute whiteness". Cf. 3.62, note 85.

192. Aristotle [2], Z, 6, 1031b, 23–25.

193. "Dieser unglückliche Ausdruck 'Gemeinname' [. . .] Dieser sogenannte Gemeinname – besser Begriffswort genannt – hat unmittelbar nichts mit den Gegenständen zu thun, sondern bedeutet einen Begriff, und unter diesen Begriff fallen vielleicht Gegenstände; er kann aber auch leer sein, ohne daß der Begriffswort darum weniger bedeutete" (HUSS, p. 326). Cf. $UGG_2(I)$, p. 308.

194. "Wenn wir Hans einen Mensch nennen, so sagen wir damit, Hans falle unter den Begriff Mensch" (HUSS, p. 326).

195. Cf. text quoted in note 193; also: "Das Wort 'Planet' bezieht sich gar nicht unmittelbar auf die Erde, sondern auf einen Begriffe . . . So ist die Beziehung zur Erde nur eine durch den Begriff vermittelte" (KSCH, p. 454).

196. Cf. GRG I, § 26. (Of course we are here using "Andeuten" in a manner which is not actually Frege's.)

197. Cf. Section 6.7; also Bartlett [1], pp. 58–59. GRG II, p. 254 also stresses that classes are not *unsaturated* or *predicative*.

198. Cf. Chapter 5.

199. Cf. KSCH, and Section 8.3. Frege suggests that classes have their "Bestand" in the marks of concepts.

200. In the same paper, where the text quoted in the preceding note 193 is found, Frege says that in a statement of number (which is actually a statement about a concept) ". . . direkt weder ein Begriffsumfang noch ein Inbegriff bezeichnet ist, sondern nur ein Begriff" (HUSS, p. 322). This would cut any *semantic* relation between the predicate-term and the class.

201. Cf. Section 2.26.

202. As is shown by the texts published by Bartlett [1] (pp. 58–59), it is clear that Frege has in mind an "identification" of equiextensional concepts, in the sense that they "behave" in an equivalent way in many contexts. Cf. also HUSS, p. 320, above.

203. HUSS, p. 319–320; Bartlett [1], p. 59. It is indeed inconsistent that Frege, who has the typical intensionalist insight into concepts as sets of marks (cf. Chapter 5), agressively rejects Husserl's proposal of an identity criterion for concepts, according to which two concepts are identical if their marks are the same (HUSS, *ibid.*). But one should not insist on comparing Frege with extensionalist or intensionalist philosophers of the 19th century; Frege's *class* is "almost" an intension (cf. 8.3), very far removed from the intuitive or traditional notion of class (in spite of Frege's will to preserve the latter in his system). We may say that for Frege a class of stones is a class (now in the intuitive sense) of intensions (cf. *ibid.*). On the other hand, he knows that even if he *says* that he supports "extensionalists", unsaturatedness will ultimately prevent him from falling into the position erroneously attributed to him by Carnap [1], § 29. Against such a background, one should not pay too much attention to Frege's statements about his own attitude with regard to the polemics intensionalism-extensionalism in KSCH (p. 456).

204. *κατηγόρημα* (Aristotle [2], I, 2).
205. Cf. Tricot in Aristotle [2.1], I, p. 179, note 4.
206. *ἀκολουθεῖν ἀλλήλοις* (Aristotle [2], Γ, 2, 1003b, 23.
207. GRL, p. X.
208. GRL, p. X, §§ 60, 62 and 106. Schweitzer in Scholz [5], p. 99 (note 11), views a Fregean phrase in GRG II, § 97 (p. 105, line 6) as a reiteration of the semantical principle of GRL, but the context clearly indicates that this is not Frege's intention.
209. Rivetti Barbó [1] (p. 2) includes many references. Cf. Wittgenstein [2] (p. 24); Quine [3] (p. 39); Geach [2] (p. XI and pp. 25–26); Stegmüller [1] (p. 311); Patzig [1] (p. 139 note). There is some paradox in the fact that in Brentano and his school the idea of *Synsemantika* was indeed a systematically and consciously adopted principle, but has not become proportionally famous. Brentano develops the idea of syncategorematic terms beyond the traditional limits (cf. Brentano [4], II, pp. 214–215; 228–229: "Doch ist es fraglich ob nicht auch Hauptwörter und Adjective manchmal mitbedeutend seien") and Marty makes of that a fundamental notion (cf. Marty [2], p. 47, note). Earlier, the problem of *syncategorematica* was discussed in a most technical and subtle way, cf. Paulus Venetus [2].
210. GRL, p. X.
211. GRL, § 106.
212. GRL, § 60. Actually, the context to be considered begins in § 58; cf. in particular the footnote on page 69.
213. UGG_2(I), pp. 307–308; UGG_1, pp. 319–320, p. 322; UBR, p. 13. Cf. also GRG II, § 66 and p. 255; SUB, p. 41.
214. GRL, § 60.
215. *Ibid.*
216. *Ibid.*
217. GRL, p. 67.
218. Cf. 10.2, at the beginning.
219. Cf. LNE, p. 74, bottom.
220. GRL, p. 71, line 8 from the bottom.
221. GRL, p. 72 top.
222. GRL, § 61.
223. GRL, p. 72 note 1, and also GRL, § 63.
224. GRL, § 62.
225. *Ibid.*
226. Cf. GRL, p. 3, note. For the term "explication", see for instance Carnap [1], p. 8.
227. ". . . außer von Kant noch wenig in dieser Richtung geleistet ist" (COH, p. 324).
228. BG, § 8.
229. Because they enlarge our knowledge, BG, p. 15.
230. BG, p. 56.
231. In the *Vorwort* of BG Frege seems interested only in Leibniz.
232. The sentence "—$c \equiv c$" is asserted as an axiom (proposition 54, in BG). In proposition 55 we have the sentences "—$c \equiv d$" and "—$d \equiv c$"; now these are not separately asserted, but "┬— $d \equiv c$" is asserted; i.e., the commutative law of identity.
     └— $c \equiv d$
233. BG, Chapter III.
234. BG, § 23.
235. GRL, p. 3.

236. *Ibid.*: "wie wir zu dem Inhalte eines Urtheils kommen".
237. BG, *Vorwort.*
238. In particular, GRL, p. 3.
239. In BG, p. III: the question whether a sentence may be proved *rein logisch* depends on the *innern Wesen des betrachteten Satzes.*
240. GRL, § 3. Synthetic propositions are characterized by their being restricted to a *besonderes Wissensgebiet.*
241. Against the foregoing argument it might be observed that in GRL, § 8 (*in fine*) Frege says that there is a sense in which even *Münchhausen*'s tales are empirical or *a posteriori*. This text of GRL could be interpreted as saying that *Münchhausen*'s tales are not *rein a priori* (in Kantian terms, cf. Kant [3], *Einleitung*, I, *in fine*), i.e., that they include *a posteriori concepts.* This would enable us to retain "content" in Frege's formulation of his criterion. Frege would mean that he does not take into account whether some concepts making up a proposition are of empirical origin.
242. BG, p. 55; GRL, §§ 12–14.
243. Cf. Cramer [1], p. III and 74.
244. Cf. Section 10.62.
245. *Reines Denken* is that whose laws the *Begriffsschrift* is supposed to express (cf. the title of BG).
246. GRL, § 13.
247. BG, *Vorwort.*
248. GRL, §§ 17, 87, 88.
249. BG, p. 55; cf. also GRL, § 17 (p. 24).
250. GRL, § 88. Rieffert [1] (p. 123) confirms Frege's view.
251. Carnap [1], p. 222. Cf. GRL, § 17, and especially the note on p. 24.
252. White [1], p. 273, bottom.
253. GRL, § 88.
254. GRL, §§ 90, 91. Also of course BG, *Vorwort.*
255. Frege thinks he has established the plausibility of his *Verbesserung* of Kant's views. Unfortunately, he expresses this by saying that arithmetic is analytic (GRL, § 109). The reason for doing symbolic logic (the *Begriffsschrift* of BG, GRG I and GRG II) was to confirm this view (GRL, § 91).
256. BG, p. 15, GRL, § 67, UFT, p. 98; for a later period: UBR, p. 13; UGG_1, p. 320.
257. GRG I, p. 45.
258. UGG_1, p. 320.
259. GRG I, p. XIII; FUB, p. 4.
260. GRL, § 62 f.
261. Bartlett [1], pp. 55–56. The letter is dated 1902.
262. GRG I, p. XIV, p. 3 (line 15); GRG II, §§ 56, 62; GED, p. 60 (middle).
263. GRL, § 51, § 67, p. 87, p. 89 bottom; UFT, p. 103. Geach [2] (p. IX, 103) suggests that the lack of the article in Latin means that we should not look for a theory of definite descriptions in mediaeval writers. But one of the normal ways of "determining" an individual in traditional logic has been precisely the consideration of existence plus uniqueness; cf., for instance, the following text: "Individuum quadruplex est. Determinatum, ut Socrates. Signatum, ut hic homo. Vagum, ut quidam homo. Ex hypothesi, ut Antonii filius supposito quod Antonius habeat unicum filium" (Gasconius [1], II, 37 v). In Frege, the problem of descriptions and the definite article is so interwoven with the paradoxes of unsaturatedness, that it is better discussed together with *Ungesättigtheit* (Chapter 6).

3. THE SO-CALLED LOGICAL RELATIONS

Summary and general remarks. The relations which Frege would have called *Grundsteine* of his system (GRG I, p. 3) are examined. Why should such relations be called logical rather than, for instance, ontological (3.1)? "Subject–predicate" in Frege has a different meaning from that of traditional logic (3.3); traditional philosophy has taken into account *facts* covered by Frege's UF and UO (3.4). But the most interesting point is what we call *hierarchy of predicates*, about which our contemporary (Fregean) philosophy of logic has not yet provided a clear statement; traditional logic, to the contrary, was somehow "suffocated" by such a hierarchy of predicates (3.5). Some aspects of the relations between Husserl and Frege are next considered. Husserl's *Philosophie der Arithmetik* was still pre-Fregean in matters of predication-theory (3.62), whereas Frege's review of Husserl's book was still pre-Aristotelian, since Frege did not realize that there was a hierarchy of predicates behind Husserl's "psychologism" (3.63).

3.1 Logical or ontological relations?

This chapter deals with some relations which are basic in Frege's system. One of them is, for instance, *das Fallen eines Einzelnen unter einen Begriff*[1] which we shall abbreviate by UF.

There is a strong tradition insisting that these relations be called "logical", where "logical" is opposed to "metaphysical" or "ontological" as *ens rationis* is opposed to real being. Frege himself calls UF *die logische Grundbeziehung*[2], but probably he ignores the above implications of the adjective "logical".

The present research maintains that the incomplete Aristotelian predication theory has served to magnify the traditional separation of logic and ontology.[3] Higher predicates are not easily adjoined to the Aristotelian logic, but traditional philosophers were nevertheless extremely sensitive to them. To add higher predicates to the Aristotelian system required special precautions, because in that system they tend to descend to the individuals producing such absurdities as "Socrates est species". To combat this tendency an ontological abyss was posited between higher predicates and the real things of this world. Second intentions or *logical relations*[4] (cf. also Frege's expression mentioned above), together with logic itself, were thereby relegated to *the mind*, and to deal with them was not to do ontology. To call UF a *logical* relation would be a concession to this questionable tradition.

3.2 Exposition

UF[5] and *Unterordnung*[6] appear in UZBG[7]; Boole is blamed for not expressing in his symbolism the difference between the two relations.[8] Frege, against Schröder's criticism, claims to be able to express both UF and UO in his *Begriffsschrift*.[9]

UF[10] holds between individuals and *Begriffe*.[11] *Socrates* falls under the concept *man*. An individual and a concept should be distinguished even when there is only one individual falling under the concept.[12]

UO holds between *Begriffe*; *man* stands in UO to *animal*. Frege seems to reserve the term "Unterordnung" for denoting a relation between *intensions*[13], although this should not be taken to mean that he sees UO only in the intensional version.[14]

GRL refers frequently to UF. UO is characterized as "objective" and is exemplified by means of familiar universal affirmative sentences[15]; it is already clear that UO does not imply the existence of the individuals of either of the concepts which it relates.[16] But the essentially new fact in GRL is the appearance of higher predicates which is motivated by Frege's insight into number as concerning concepts (not individuals). Frege suggests an extension of UF so that it can be applied between two concepts.[17] The concept *Moon of the Earth* falls under the concept *to have only one individual*. Here again Frege warns against confusing this new UF and UO. GRL also extends UF to predicates of more than one argument.[18] This idea is of course already in BG, but in GRL Frege returns to the terminology "subject-predicate".

BGGE contains a comparison of UF with identity.[19] UF is not *umkehrbar* and Frege stresses that UF is not identity.[20] Nevertheless, identity may be reduced to UF. Frege further holds that any relation between concepts is reducible to UF: *die logische Grundbeziehung*.[21] BGGE introduces a new relation between concepts, or better said, Frege gives a different name to that UF between concepts which he had introduced in GRL. This is due to unsaturatedness. The concept *Moon of the Earth* – says Frege – *fällt in*[22] (falls within) the concept *to have only one individual*; we shall abbreviate this by IF. Frege stresses that IF and UF are "similar".

In GRG I the relation of class-membership is introduced[23]; Frege calls it the *Hineinfallen* of an object in the extension of a concept. Corresponding to Peano's "ε", Frege has "$\cap$".[24] For class-inclusion Frege proposes on one occasion[25] the term "sub" and he protests against the confusion of class-membership and class-inclusion (as he previously did for UF and UO). In later works the term "Subsumption" appears as a designation for UF.[26]

3.3 Subject–predicate and the so-called logical relations

UF may be said to coincide with the traditional relation between singulars and universals.[27] Frege has inherited the idea of a *Begriff* which is one in front of many individuals.[28] This is one of the two sources[29] of his idea of function, and it was this that inspired Frege's insight that number concerns *concepts*.

The fact that Frege in BG rejects the terminology "subject-predicate" may be misleading. This has merely an accidental reason and after BG the powerful term "predicate" is again used.[30] He distinguishes subjects and predicates in a *logical*[31] and a *grammatical*[32] sense. The former is the meaning, the latter the linguistic expression.

Unsaturatedness is also at work here and it is essential to take into account the fact that grammatical predicates must include an empty place where the grammatical subjects are to be inserted.[33] Because of this, Frege cannot allow predicates of predicates, except in what I call an *implicit* way.[34] Traditional logic, since Aristotle, had spoken of predicates of predicates but this meant class-inclusion. In "homo est mortalis" "homo" is the subject and "mortalis" is the predicate.[35] A rare case where Frege maintains this terminology is in GRL, § 88, but it would appear that Frege is merely adopting the vocabulary of his opponent, namely, Kant.

Frege views the four traditional types of sentences (A, I, O, E) as statements about *concepts.*[36] In each of these sentences, predicates of second level are "implicitly" assigned to couples of concepts, The terms "every", "some", etc. are charged with expressing this higher (implicit) predication. Thereby Frege comes into conflict with Schröder, who interpreted "einige Menschen" as the grammatical subject of a particular sentence.[37] Frege's interpretation is closer to Aristotle's[38], but there remains a major difference: the above mentioned fact that in "man is mortal" "man" is (for Aristotle) the subject and "mortal" the predicate. In the "propositiones indefinitae" we have the universal subject in all its purity.[39]

Because of unsaturatedness, no Fregean concept or predicate may be a grammatical subject, nor, consequently, a logical subject.[40] But even without unsaturatedness, Frege's main insights would not allow us to call "subject" the predicate *man* in "man is mortal". Frege's philosophy of number enables him to see that statements of number have concepts as their subjects – as their *sachliches Subject.*[41] And once he acknowledges that *to have n-individuals* is a predicate of the predicate *man*, he can no longer hold that *animal* is a predicate of *man*, nor that *man* is a subject of *animal.*[42]

3.4 UF and UO facts in traditional logic

Although traditional logic lacks a distinction of UF and UO, the facts covered by these relations are of course taken into account. The *Critique of Pure Reason* is structured according to UF and UO, although the distinction is not explicitly made.

As concerns UF, it should be observed that "individual" has in tradition a double meaning, what one would today call both the unit-class and the individual proper.[43] As for an antecedent of the latter, perhaps the notion of *suppositum*[44] is the best equivalent. Also in regard to UF it should be observed that tradition would insist (contrary to Frege) on the identity underlying the situation which Frege calls UF.[45]

The double dimensional character of Aristotelian ontology has also an impact here.[46] Socrates is not an individual of *white*, although Socrates is white. *White* has its own individuals, namely that individual white inhering in Socrates.

These complications are avoided if one restricts oneself to a single category, for instance *substance*, i.e., the tree of Porphyry.[47] The latter is ordered by means of UO, and nothing else. There is a first element: the *species infima*.[48] There are infinite individuals, but a finite number of *species infimae*.[49] The UO-chain has a limit also in the upward direction (*summum genus*) and is finite.[50]

3.5 The hierarchy of predicates in traditional philosophy

> Eine Staubwolke von Distinktionen und Klassifikationen der Prädikate . . . (Kant [4], 2. Ab., p. 232).

The expression "hierarchy of predicates" is used here in a sense different from the Russellian idea of a hierarchy of types. By this expression I mean an order introduced among the predicates of an object *a* according to their cognitive significance in showing[51] what *a* is. There is more knowledge in stating what a thing *is* than in considering what a thing is *not*, and among positive predicates there is more knowledge in that which expresses the essence than in those which express properties progressively more "exterior" to the thing.[52] It is easy to see that such Fregean concepts as *to be a member of the class F but not to be the individual a*[53] are likely to be underestimated in such an essentialist approach.

The first predicate or essence is not provable.[54] It is a limit[55] or, to speak as Locke, a boundary[56] which cannot be trespassed; *essentiae sunt sicut numeri*: the least addition or substraction would make the thing just other, not simply other in quality.[57] Experiments with essence have been called *variations* in different periods of the history of philosophy.[58]

Through the *differentia specifica* one may escape the rigor of essence and enter the hierarchy which – along the two dimensions of traditional ontology – progressively leads into properties less and less significant for what the thing "really is". Starting from the *res* itself we are gradually brought to its *circumstantia* or *denominationes extrinsecae*.[59] In modern philosophy the term "mode"[60] is preferred, and Port-Royal Logic speaks of *modes interieurs* and *modes exterieurs*.[61]

Essence has also been supposed to be a *source* of the other properties of a thing. Accordingly, non-essential predicates have been said to *flow* from essence. The historical sense of Kant's pure intuition seems to be the desire to provide a better foundation for such a *flowing* from the essence.[62]

An example of rejecting a hierarchy of predicates is the mediaeval philosopher Ibn Zaddik: all predicates are equal because all are useless (to reveal the divine essence).[63] An exceptional reference, in Frege's works, to the hierarchy of predicates appears in the later paper GED.[64] But even if the hierarchy of predicates has not been systematically considered in the developments of contemporary philosophy deriving from Frege, we may observe that at least the *feeling* of such a hierarchy has been kept alive.[65]

3.6 Husserl–Frege

3.61 *Frege's review*

Husserl's first book, *Philosophie der Arithmetik*[66], concerns Frege perhaps more than anyone else; although many authors are quoted, the fundamental dialogue is with Frege. As is known, Frege wrote a review of Husserl's book.[67]

Husserl's main motivation in his philosophical approach to arithmetic is similar to Frege's: to vindicate the universal applicability of number.[68] Both thinkers refer to the same Leibnizian text, where the schoolmen are accused of having restricted number to some proper sub-class of reality.[69] But the same thesis has in Husserl some aspects which make it more capable of being easily joined to the philosophical tradition; Husserl has in mind a formal ontology where number (in contrast to the situation in the mediaeval transcendentals[70]) has a place.[71]

It is a defect of Frege's review that it does not consider these important aspects of Husserl's book.[72] Because of not paying attention to those aspects, Frege misses the real motivation of some Husserlian ideas.[73]

In Frege's review I would point out the following positive elements. Frege rightly denounces or questions, (1) the lack of distinction between "*A*" and "die Vorstellung von *A*", (2) the insufficient treatment of identity and definition (as a consequence of only having "Wort-Vorstellung" instead of "Wort–Sinn–Bedeutung"), (3) the treatment of "great numbers".

3.62 *Husserl's 'Philosophie der Arithmetik'*

We shall examine some aspects of Husserl's *Philosophie der Arithmetik*, in order to show that the point of a criticism of that book from a Fregean point of view is not psychologism (as Frege's own review suggests) but a set of more important issues. The following diagram will facilitate our exposition.

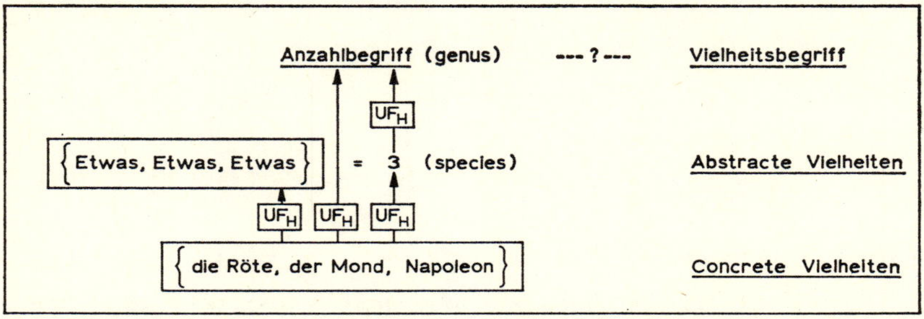

"Vielheit"[74] has as synonyms: "Inbegriff", "Menge", "Aggregat", and "Sammlung".[75]

It should be observed that the opposition *concrete*[76] *Vielheit* and *abstracte Vielheit* is not of individual to property, because *both* are *Vielheiten* and both are individuals of the *Vielheitsbegriff* (which will be one of the confusions, because it will also be possible to say that the *abstracte Vielheiten* are concepts under which fall the *concrete Vielheiten*[77]).

"Concrete" in "concrete Vielheiten" is not meant as a restriction imposed on the notion of multitude. To the contrary, by reason of the universal applicability of number, these concrete multitudes (from which number will be abstracted) may be absolutely arbitrary, for example: {*der Mond, die Röte, Napoleon*}.[78]

Concrete Vielheiten are intended to provide the starting point for the abstraction leading to number. The process of abstraction consists in replacing each element of the given *concrete Vielheit* by the transcendental *Etwas*. From {*der Mond, die Röte, Napoleon*} we obtain {*Etwas, Etwas, Etwas*} and this is at once the number 3, where "is" should be taken as identity or as a mere definition by abbreviation.[79] On the other hand, Husserl says that the number three is a concept under which the initial *concrete Vielheit* falls.[80] (It is not advisable to identify this "falling under a concept" with Frege's UF; Husserl's UF may perhaps include other relations, such as *Unterordnung* of concepts. This is why we provide it with a subindex: UF_H.) Now if between 3 and {*Etwas, Etwas, Etwas*} there is identity, we shall also be able to say that {*Etwas, Etwas, Etwas*} is a concept under which the corresponding *concrete Vielheit* falls.

Textual support for this is not lacking.[81] As already observed, this is a source of confusion, because {*Etwas*, *Etwas*, *Etwas*} is itself a *Vielheit*[82]; moreover, each element of the *concrete Vielheit* behaves as an individual falling under "its" *Etwas*.[83]

Number 3 is also a species with respect to a genus which is the *Anzahlbegriff*; this relation of species to genus is also UF_H.[84] But the *concrete Vielheit* too falls under the *Anzahlbegriff*[85], which would imply that the *concrete Vielheit* {*der Mond*, *Napoleon*, *die Röte*} is itself a number just as 3 is a number.

Abstracte and *concrete Vielheiten* fall under the *Vielheitsbegriff*; the latter is "Eins und Eins u.s.w." (pp. 85, 87). We shall say, in trying to explain Husserl, that the concept of *Vielheit* is "almost identical" with the concept of number. Where the one is, the other also is to be found.[86] As Frege suggests, this would mean some sort of extensional coincidence.[87] The *nuance* is not further explained by Husserl, who leaves the question completely vague. The solution should have been to stress that the *concrete Vielheiten* are *Vielheiten* but are not numbers. But this is not possible so long as the number 3 is considered as a species under the genus *Anzahl* and above the individual *concrete Vielheiten*; the genus descends with the species.

The difficulty of Husserl's *Philosophie der Arithmetik* is not primarily psychologism, as Frege's review suggests, but: (1) obscurity in the notion of predication (which is traditional) and (2) the full acceptance of the Euclidean definition of number (also traditional).

Both mistakes are easily recognized from an acquaintance with Frege. And although Frege's review seems particularly concerned with "psychologism", it also denounces those errors. He points to the absence of the distinction UF-UO[88], and of the distinction *Merkmal-Eigenschaft*[89]; he blames Husserl's equating of predication and identity.[90] When the latter tries to explain 5+5 as the addition of an *abstracte Vielheit* to *another abstracte Vielheit*, Frege asks: *Warum andere?*[91] Husserl also deals with Frege's *aporia* concerning the Euclidean definition of number as set of units.[92] Husserl attempts a solution by distinguishing identity and equality (identity under a given aspect). This is indeed what Frege calls a *psychologischer Waschkessel* or *Magie*[93], due to which the several *Etwas* making up an *abstracte Vielheit* are ambiguously preserved from collapsing into a unique *Etwas*, as would necessarily follow from the absolute lack of determination of each *Etwas*. Here we have an answer to the question mentioned above: *Warum andere?* If there were exactly one *abstracte Vielheit* for number 5, it would be definitely clear that the several *Etwas* should be taken *praecisive*, i.e., disregarding any *differentia*[94]; but then they would collapse into a unique *Etwas*.

3.63 *Husserl and Frege's misunderstanding concerns their diverse appreciation of the hierarchy of predicates*

The thesis supported by Husserl in Chapter IX of *Philosophie der Arithmetik* is: *Die Zahlen sind Prädikaten von Mengen*. This thesis, already hinted at in Mill[95], is offered in opposition to Herbart and Frege, for whom a statement of number contains *eine Aussage von einem Begriffe*.[96] (Husserl's thesis is to be distinguished also from another thesis according to which number is *Prädikat der gezählten Dinge*[97].)

Husserl, as we saw, starts from the transcendental character of number (in the Scholastic sense). This requires that the *concrete Vielheiten* be absolutely indifferent as to the content of their elements; these are only taken into account as far as they are *Etwas*.

Husserl discusses those conceptions which pretend to ground number on some *Gleichheitsrelation* among the elements of the set to be counted. He systematically rejects such conceptions because the fact of requiring that the elements of a set be *gleichartig* is for him a restriction (*Einschränkung*[98]) on the absolute universality of number. But this is due only to the fact that Husserl understands *to be gleichartig* (i.e. to belong to the same class) to imply that there is a "positive" determination, common to the objects which are said to be *gleichartig*. If, on the contrary, one decides to accept as predicates (according to which the things are said to be *gleichartig*) *any* determination, even the most "exterior" to the thing, then Husserl will not object to saying that the things belonging to a set to be counted are *gleichartig*, for instance with respect to the concept *to be an Etwas*.[99] This will contribute to his agreement with Frege's thesis that number-statements are always about a concept.[100] If, on the other hand, Husserl does not choose that approach, then, in order to "unify" the set {*der Mond, die Röte, Napoleon*} he will be obliged to appeal to some "psychological" description, for instance: those three things coincide in the fact of being enumerated by me at this moment.[101] Frege rejects these "psychological" formulations, not seeing their true motivation. On the other hand, what he offers as "common predicate" under which *der Mond, die Röte* and *Napoleon* fall, is indeed too meager[102]: a sort of *räumliche Configuration* which Husserl himself would have accepted[103], had he ever decided to take such "exterior" predicates as predicates at all. Thus the question revolves around whether one decides to take the sentence "paries est visa" as expressing a property of the wall or not, i.e., whether *denominationes extrinsecae*[104] are properties as good as the more "interior" or "essential" ones.

Now, even if Husserl chose to understand "concept" and "predicate" without the requirement of being "interior" to the thing, he would probably not be able to fully accept Frege's view that in statements of number properties of concepts are expressed[105]; for that would presuppose the delicate Fregean distinction of *Merkmal* and *Eigenschaft* which Husserl seems to lack at that time. This would allow a particular application of our thesis that higher predicates are not immediately assimilable to the traditional predication theory.[106]

REFERENCES

1. The falling of an individual under a concept (UZBG, p. 3).
2. Bartlett [1], p. 58.
3. For the following remarks, cf. 7.54.
4. Frege speaks of *die logischen Beziehungen* in UZBG, p. 4.
5. Cf. note 1.
6. We shall abbreviate this by "UO".
7. For instance, pp. 3, 5, 8, 9.
8. *Ibid.*, p. 3.
9. *Ibid.*, p. 8.
10. Cf. note 1.
11. (concepts), UZBG, p. 3.
12. UZBG, p. 2.
13. UZBG, GRG II, §§ 162–164.
14. Cf. GRL, § 9; tyrannicides are said to be *parts* of murder as a whole, and Frege comments: "Hier hat man die logische Unterordnung."
15. GRL, § 47. The example is "alle Wallfische sind Säugethiere".
16. GRG I (p. 24 note) confirms this.
17. GRL, § 53.
18. GRL, § 70.
19. BGGE, p. 194.
20. For example (apart from BGGE, p. 194), WIF, p. 665; HUSS, p. 326. As an example of not distinguishing predication and identity, let us consider the following text (the author would assume that "W. Scott" is predicated about the author of Waverley):

"Cum vero in definitione audis, "de pluribus" [the author means his definition of *nomen universale = quod praedicatur de pluribus*], nomine "Plurium" intellige plura secundum idem nomen. Nam ut nomen aliquod dicatur commune non satis est si praedicetur de iis, quae dicuntur plura secundum aliud nomen, sic nomina singularia, communia esse iudicabuntur. Platonis siquidem nomen una sola ratione acceptum, praedicatur de pluribus attributis Platonis, ut pote de hoc Aristonis filio, de hoc Philosopho, de hoc Aristotelis praeceptore. Nomen etiam Conimbricae praedicatur de pluribus attributis Conimbricae, ut de urbe prope Mondam sita, de hac bonarum artium cultrice..." (Fonseca [1], *Lib. Primus*, Cap. XXVI).

21. Bartlett [1], p. 58.
22. BGGE, p. 201; cf. UGG_1, p. 373.
23. GRG I, p. 240.
24. GRG I, § 34.
25. KSCH, p. 442.
26. UBR, p. 9; UGG_2(III), p. 427 note. In the "inedita" we have "Subordination" for "Unterordnung".
27. This is an *interpretation* which seems correct, although the difficulties implied by the ontological square should be considered. It would be enough to recall Frege's philosophy of number: numbers concern concepts because they say *how many* individuals fall under each concept.
28. Cf., for instance, GRL, § 54.
29. Cf. Section 6.71.
30. GRL associates *Begriff* and *mögliches Prädikat* (§ 66 note), or just *Prädikat* (§ 77). This Kantian terminology also occurs in GRG II (§ 56). In BGGE "predicate" or "predicative" are used to characterize unsaturatedness which indicates the extreme importance those terms have in Frege's system (BGGE, p. 197, note). WIF mentions in several places *subjects of predication* (for example, p. 658). The following text (from a later paper) shows how Frege understands the relation subject–predicate in a sentence: "Nehmen wir den Satz 'Zwei ist eine Primzahl'. Wir unterscheiden hier sprachlich ein Subjekt "Zwei" und einen prädikativen Bestandteil "ist eine Primzahl"" (UGG_1, p. 371).
31. For example SUB, p. 35 (first line).
32. For example UGG_2(I), p. 305, bottom; BGGE, p. 193, note.
33. Cf. 6.7.
34. Cf. Section 6.8.
35. In "Blut ist rot" the subject is "Blut", Sigwart [1], I, p. 117. In "l'homme est un animal", "l'homme" is the subject, "animal" the predicate, Gardeil [1], p. 51, 90. Cf. also Quine [1], § 14 and § 23. Also Geach [2].
36. BGGE, p. 198.
37. Schröder's curious idea (certainly not only his) was that "einige Menschen" denotes a class, but a class consisting of an undetermined number of individuals (KSCH, p. 435, 441 note).
38. Cf. Geach [2]. Aristotle views "every" as giving to the sentence a universal character (Aristotle [1], *Perihermeneias*, 7, 17b, 12).
39. "Indefinita est quae habet subiectum universale sine ulla nota, ut homo est iustus" (Pacius [2], cap. 5, n. 6). Frege has been interested in the vestiges of "propositiones indefinitae", such as "das Pferd ist ein vierbeiniges Thier" (UWB, BGGE, p. 196). He interprets this as a universal affirmative sentence.

Leaving aside whether this interpretation is absolutely valid, let us only refer for this use of the definite article as a universal quantifier, to Sigwart [1] (p. 117) and Reichenbach [2] (p. 25).

40. Cf. Chapter 6.
41. GRL, p. 57.
42. This will be confirmed by the *inedita* (letter to Husserl, Oct. 30, 1906).
43. Petrus Hispanus [1] (2.09) defines: "Individuum est quod de uno solo praedicatur, ut Socrates et Plato", where one would think rather of *individual concepts* or *idées individuelles* (Port-Royal [1], I, Ch. VI) than of individuals proper. Incidentally, Carnap's proposal of speaking of individual concepts (Carnap [1], § 9, p. 41 top) is indeed quite in agreement with the traditional approach. Perhaps Kant's term "Anschauung" reflects the traditional ambiguity of "individuum": (1) without intuitions, concepts are empty, where "intuition" means existent individual, (2) the intuitions "apply" to only one object, while concepts apply to many objects, where "intuition" means individual concept (cf. Eisler [1], "Anschauung"). Frege noticed, in GRL, § 12, an ambiguity in Kant's "Anschauung", which seems to be related to this one. An extensive discussion is to be found in Caietanus [2], p. 62f.
44. Ultimate subject.
45. "Praedicatio enim est quiddam quod completur per actionem intellectus componentis et dividentis, habens fundamentum in re ipsa unitatem eorum quorum unum de altero dicitur" (Aquinas [3], Chap. III). Cf. Ioannes a Sto Thoma [1], p. 470a, top. Frege, on the contrary, says: "Bemerkt sei hierzu noch, daß das gesperrt gedruckte *ist* sowie *sind* als bloße Copula aufzufassen ist, ohne irgend einen besonderen Inhalt, dass also damit keine Identität gemeint ist" (KSCH, p. 442).
46. Cf. Chapter 1.
47. This is actually Porphyry's evasive procedure, to consider only the "substantial" tree, cf. Section 1.41.
48. As for the *species infima* the natural question is *why* there should be at all such a limit in approaching individuals through *Unterordnung* structures. The answer seems to depend on the notion of *matter*; *male* and *female* do not make a new species because they are properties deriving from matter (Aristotle [2], I, 9).
49. Porphyry [1], (*Isagoge*), pp. 6, 12–13.
50. "Now it is clear that if the predications terminate in both the upward and the downward direction (by "upward" I mean the ascent to the more universal, by "downward" the descent to the more particular), the middle terms cannot be infinite in number" (Aristotle [3.1], *Anal. Post.*, A20).
51. Aristotle says that a predicate *δηλοῖ* a thing (Aristotle [1], 2b, 31). Some humanist commentators have translated this Greek word by *declarare* (Pacius [1], Gruchius [1]).
52. Aristotle [2], B2, 996b, 15f.
53. This concept is important in Frege's foundation of arithmetic.
54. Aristotle [3], *An. Post.*, B, 10, 94a, 11.
55. Aristotle [2], Δ, 17, 1022a, 8–10.
56. Locke [1], III, 6, § 2; also § 5.
57. Aquinas [1], 1048. Cf. Porphyry [1], for the notion of *differentia.*
58. Martinus de Dacia [1], n. 34; Husserl [5], § 90.
59. Duns Scotus on Boethius: "Secundo modo accipit Boethius, distinguendo rem

contra modum rei, sicut loquitur libro de Trinitate. "Patet", inquit, "quae sit differentia praedicationum, quia aliae quidem rem mostrant, aliae quidem quasi circumstantiam rei; quia istae praedicantur sic quod secundum se rem aliquam mostrant. Illae vero ut non esse, sed potius extrinsecus aliquid apponunt". Vult ergo distinguere rem contra circumstantiam; et sic, secundum eum, sola tria genera (substantia, qualitas et quantitas) rem mostrant; alia vero rei circumstantias." (In Fernandez–Garcia [1], *distinctio ens-res.*)

60. A Renaissance author (Eust. a Sto. Paulo) shows how the passage from "accident" to "mode" was accomplished: "Quarta conclusio. Essentia accidentis modus quidam est substantiae; omne enim accidens substantiam aliqua ratione modificat" (in Gilson [3], p. 104, "essence").
61. Port-Royal [1], I, Ch. 2.
62. Kant [4], 2. Abs., p. 242. Vaihinger [1] (I, p. 264) clearly explains how *reine Anschauung* is introduced in the sophisticated traditional theory of predication. Locke [1] (II, 31, § 6) had already made it clear that nothing "flows" from the (nominal) essence. Kant nevertheless has to explain the fact of synthetical a priori knowledge.
63. Cf. Kauffmann [1], p. 335. Of course, this is but an example of "negative theology".
64. P. 76 bottom.
65. Carnap [1], § 27. Cf. also Anscombe–Geach [1], p. 34; Quine [3], p. 155. An interesting comparison of both approaches (i.e., with and without hierarchy of predicates) is in Springer [1].
66. Husserl [4]. For Frege–Husserl in general, cf. Føllesdal [1].
67. HUSS.
68. Husserl [4], pp. 11, 91, 92.
69. Frege in GRL, § 24, Husserl in [4], p. 11.
70. Javellus [1] (f. 164) reduces number to a particular category of being (*quantitas*).
71. Husserl [4], Chapter IV *in fine.*
72. Frege mentions only once, briefly and incidentally, Husserl's view of the universality of number (HUSS, p. 315).
73. Which Frege thus easily accuses of psychologism (not using this term). But if Husserl employs a "psychological" terminology, this is motivated by his program of ensuring and respecting the "transcendental" (in the scholastic sense) nature of number and other formal ontological categories (cf. Husserl [4], pp. 86, 91). As we shall see shortly (Section 3.63), Husserl's program plus his traditional approach to the hierarchy of predicates determined that *apparent* psychologism. (For Frege and psychologism, see Papst [1].)
74. Multitude, plurality.
75. Husserl [4], p. 8.
76. For the use of this adjective "concrete", see Husserl [4], pp. 10, 67, 89, 185 (bottom), etc.
77. See below.
78. The example is given in Husserl [4], p. 79; it is also mentioned by Frege in HUSS, pp. 322–323.
79. For example Husserl [4], pp. 87, 88, 164, etc.
80. *Ibid.*, pp. 87, 185.
81. "Die Zahl ist die allgemeine Vielheitsform unter welcher der Inbegriff der Gegenstände *a*, *b*, *c* fällt" (Husserl [4], p. 185). If "allgemeine Vielheitsform" =

"abstracte Vielheit", we may conclude that {*der Mond, die Röte, Napoleon*} falls under {*Etwas, Etwas, Etwas*}. But there is a more explicit text: "Zwei Äpfel, zwei Menschen, ein Apfel und ein Mensch, u.s.w. sind sämmtlich zwei, weil sie concrete Inbegriffe repräsentieren, welche durch das Zählungsverfahren gerade unter die abstracte Mengenform: Eins und Eins, fallen und unter keine andere" (Husserl [4], p. 162).

82. Unless it is explicitly agreed that the concept of *Vielheit* is itself a *Vielheit*, as the concept of *entity* is an entity. But for Husserl the concept *Vielheit* is higher than the *abstracte Vielheiten*; see below.
83. Husserl [4], pp. 90, 158.
84. Cf. the next note. Also, Husserl [4], p. 9.
85. "Bei dem Namen Anzahl compliciert sich die Sache noch dadurch, daß er nicht bloß als allgemeiner Name für irgend welche concrete Mengen, sondern auch als allgemeiner Name für jede unter den Begriff der Anzahl fallenden besonderen Zahlen: Zwei, Drei, Vier . . . dient" (Husserl [4], p. 154).
In this text I assume that "allgemeiner Name für irgend welche concrete Mengen [zu sein]" means that these *Mengen* fall under the concept denoted by that general name. There is justification for this in Husserl himself, some pages previous: "Jeder abstracte Name wird in einer zweifachen Bedeutung gebraucht; das eine Mal dient er als Name für den abstracten Begriff als solchen, das andere Mal als Name für irgend eine unter diesen Begriff fallenden Gegenstand" (Husserl [4], p. 151).
The fact that both *concrete Vielheiten* and *abstracte Vielheiten* (i.e. numbers) fall under the *Anzahlbegriff* had already been suggested by Husserl at the beginning of the book: "Der Anzahlbegriff umfaßt also, obschon erst auf dem Wege über die Umfänge seiner Speciesbegriffe, der Zahlen Zwei, Drei, Vier, . . . dieselben concreten Phänomene wie der Begriff der Vielheit" (Husserl [4], p. 9). Cf. also the example given by Husserl on page 189.
86. Cf. Husserl's text quoted at the end of the preceding note; also Husserl [4], p. 89.
87. HUSS, p. 313.
88. HUSS, p. 313.
89. HUSS, p. 324.
90. HUSS, p. 326. As if "man" were a name of Hans as "Hans" is. Cf. Husserl's semantics of general terms (at the time of Husserl [4]) in note 85 above. Cf. also Section 2.62.
91. HUSS, p. 327.
92. Cf. Chapter 10.
93. HUSS, p. 326.
94. With respect to five concrete stones or five concrete syllogistic modes.
95. Husserl [4], p. 181.
96. *Ibid.*, p. 180.
97. *Ibid.* But of course this is trivially rejected; an apostle is not twelve (p. 181, below).
98. *Ibid.*, p. 164.
99. "Eine leichte Unterscheidung wird zeigen, daß in gewissem Sinne beide Parteien Recht haben. Rechnen wir zum Inhalte einer Vorstellung nur Theilvorstellungen im eigentlichen und strengen Sinne ("innere Merkmale" nannten sie manche Logiker) und betrachten demgemäß Vorstellungen nur dann als vergleichbar,

wenn sie gemeinsame Theilinhalte dieser Art besitzen, dann giebt es unendlich viele disparate und unvergleichbare Vorstellungen, und es ist klar, daß dann die Zählung Vergleichbarkeit (in dieser Bedeutung) nicht verlangt, da vielmehr ganz disparate Dinge zusammengezählt werden können. Meine Seele und ein Dreieck sind zwei, obgleich sie keinerlei gemeinsame innere Merkmale besitzen. Rechnen wir jedoch zum Inhalte einer Vorstellung auch alle ihr zukommenden negativen und relativen Bestimmungen (die "äußeren Merkmale"), dann giebt es überhaupt keine unvergleichbaren Vorstellungen; denn es giebt keine, die nicht mindestens als unter den Begriff Etwas fallende, gleichartig sind. Und gerade diese Subsumption unter den Begriff Etwas müssen wir (nach unserer Theorie) hinsichtlich eines jeden der zu zählenden Gegenstände vollziehen, um die Zahl zu erfassen. Insofern ist also richtig, daß die zu zählenden Dinge unter einen gemeinsamen Gattungsbegriff (dies Wort freilich im äußerlichsten Sinne genommen) gebracht werden müssen" (Husserl [4], p. 158).

100. "Man kann in jedem Falle die gezählten Objecte durch gemeinsame Merkmale (seien es innere oder relative) so genau determinieren, daß der entstehende Gattungsbegriff nur auf die hic et nunc gezählten Objecte päßt und auf keine anderen" (Husserl [4], pp. 187–188). In the following text we notice some irony with respect to considering as concepts predicates which normally would not be so regarded: "Urtheilen wir z.B.: der Wagen des Kaisers wird von vier Pferden gezogen, dann würde der Begriff Pferd dieser Anforderung nicht genügen, denn es giebt auch sonst noch Pferde. Anders wenn wir den Begriff "Pferd, das den Wagen des Kaisers zieht", wählen, insbesondere wenn wir Ort, Raum, Datum und Tageszeit zu notiren nicht vergessen; dieser Begriff päßt nur auf die vier hier concret gegebenen und gezählten Pferde" (Husserl [4], p. 188).

101. "Die vollste Bestätigung für unsere Auffassung bietet wieder die innere Erfahrung. Fragen wir, worin die Verbindung bestehe, wenn wir z.B. eine Mehrheit so disparater Dinge wie die Röte, Napoleon und der Mond denken, so erhalten wir die Antwort, sie bestehe bloß darin, daß wir diese Inhalte zusammen denken, in einem Akte denken" (Husserl [4], p. 79).

102. HUSS, p. 322–323.

103. Husserl [4], p. 184.

104. Signoriello [1].

105. I think that such is the correct interpretation of the following text: "Aber nehmen wir selbst an, es wäre immer so, wie man behauptet, wir colligierten und zählten stets nur Objecte, sofern sie unter einen gemeinsamen Begriff fallen, dann geht aus unserer Betrachtung klar hervor, daß die Zahl in keiner Weise als Bestimmung dieses Begriffes angesehen werden kann" (Husserl [4], p. 185). Perhaps because of this (typically traditional) difficulty of viewing higher predicates (i.e., there are already "higher" predicates: *animal* with respect to *man*!), Husserl finally arrives at the following formulation: "Nur indirect kann man allenfalls sagen, der Begriff hat die Eigenschaft, daß seinem Umfange die Zahl vier zukommt" (Husserl [4], p. 189).

106. Cf. Section 5.32.

4. THE TRADITIONAL LACK OF DISTINCTION BETWEEN UF AND UO

Summary and general remarks. The present chapter is devoted to a consideration of Frege's (or modern logic's) accusation that traditional logic has not distinguished *das Fallen eines Einzelnen unter einem Begriff* from *Unterordnung* of concepts. After formulating the problem (4.1), the previous exposition of the traditional predication theory is completed (4.2). I next try to show that traditional predication theory cannot be viewed as a less fortunate presentation of the Fregean approach, as if it belonged to the same line of development. Indeed traditional predication theory is of *another kind* (4.3). The most important systematic reason responsible for this is next examined (4.4). Finally, some examples are given in which the distinction UF and UO is shown to be intrinsically required by the very traditional doctrines (and not only by our retrospective projections) (4.5). A brief remark on unit-classes in traditional philosophy is added (4.6).

4.1 The problem

Frege often complains that "logicians" do not distinguish UF and UO.[1] Later, *Principia Mathematica* will reiterate the same objection against traditional logic.[2] A similar criticism will also be formulated by H. Scholz.[3]

Frege himself does not refer to earlier logicians but rather to some of his contemporaries, and among these to Boole and Schröder[4], so that strictly speaking he cannot be said to accuse traditional logic proper. Nevertheless, his complaint obviously concerns old logic as a whole, and it is in the light of the philosophical tradition that Frege's protests obtain a greater significance.

Briefly, Frege complains that "Socrates is a man" and "man is mortal" are not regarded as instances of UF and UO, respectively. He also stresses that UF between a first-level concept and a second-level concept[5] should be distinguished from UO between concepts; he does not complain that anyone is confusing higher-level UF (or IF) and UO because – he assumes – nobody knows anything about higher level concepts (which is true for modern philosophy[6]).

Frege's intellectual biography is peculiar in the context of traditional logic. In 1879[7] Frege declares he intends to analyse the concept of number. In 1884[8] he reveals the results of his investigation. Natural numbers are entities appearing *at the second level*, i.e., at the level of properties of properties. One may conjecture that Frege was aware of the traditional predication theory according to which in "Blut ist rot" there is a subject, "Blut", and a predicate, "rot".[9] One may also imagine that he had to make a decision because this way of speaking was incompatible with his own and true insight into higher predicates. *Blood* is a concept which has, for instance, the property that it is difficult to isolate its individuals; how then can one *at the same time* say that blood *is* red? This is the way – I believe – in which Frege was compelled to legislate that "blood is red" is an instance of UO, not of UF (or IF).[10]

The same insight into number with respect to concepts led Frege, in my view, to stress the distinction between universals and singulars. Also, the very nature of the question "How many?" (Frege intends[11] to investigate that number which answers the question "How many?") obliged him to distinguish clearly between the individuals and the subordinate concepts of a concept; "How many animals?" is not duly answered by giving the number of sub-classes ("man", "horse", etc.). Thus, once again, Frege was compelled to legislate on predication theory in a manner which was an improvement over the past, and he stressed that UF (between an individual and a concept) and UO should be carefully distinguished.[12]

The philosophical tradition not only lacked that concrete motivation which Frege had in his approach to number, but it even had a powerful reason working precisely in the opposite direction, namely, the idea of essence.

Of course one may deal with Frege's – or modern logic's – accusation that traditional logic did not distinguish UF and UO by looking for examples disproving such an accusation.[13] But this is not adequate because it presupposes that the absence of distinction between UF and UO was due only to some logical primitivism, which is not the case here. I intend to make it plausible that the absence of that distinction is to be understood in the context of *another* theory of predication where quite peculiar systematic elements are at work (essence).

4.2 Traditional predication theory

4.21 *To assign a name to a substance because of an accident inhering in that substance*[14]

When at the beginning of *Categoriae* Aristotle says that the *name* (not the *logos*) of the accident may be *sometimes* predicated of the substance[15], this should be understood in the sense that *only sometimes* does the Greek language allow us to predicate of the substance the name of the accident *without changing this name*. When the accident *leukón* inheres in a substance, for example in *anthrōpos*, it happens that one may call the substance by the very name "leukón", but this occurs only sometimes. Normally, one must build a "paronymous" term; for instance, when the accident *grammatikḗ* inheres in *anthrōpos*, one cannot call the man "grammatikḗ", but rather "grammatikós".[16] And there are still circumstances when not even a paronymous term is available; then one should build a name in "some other way".[17]

In any case, this predication will be grounded on the actual inherence of an accident in a substance.[18] Calling this predication K, we may define it in the following way:

D7 $K(x, y) =_{\mathrm{df}} (Ez).\ EU(z, y)$ & (x is a name related to a name of z either as homonymous, or as paronymous or in some other way).

"$K(x, y)$" should be read "y is called x". Relata in K may be both first and secondary substances.[19] Referents in K are of course names. (If we ask whether the accidents which inhere in a substance, or which the substance "has", are individual or universal accidents, there is no obvious answer in *Categoriae*[20], apart from the passage on the "ontological square".)

Other passages of *Categoriae* involve still another kind of predication: from accident to accident. For instance *to leukón* is said *polú*.[21]

Thus, on the one hand, there is a strict separation among the categories (the *logos* of accidents is not applied to substances), but on the other hand there is a well organized inter-predicamental predication (of *names*).

4.22 *A change in the terminology of predication theory*

The expression "κάθ' ὑποκειμένου λέγεσθαι"[22] undergoes a radical change in other works of Aristotle; in *Categoriae* it means essential predication, whereas outside *Categoriae* it means (perhaps only) accidental predication[23], i.e. accidents being predicated of substances [24]

As a consequence of the fact that the two ontological dimensions are blurred in the main works of Aristotle, it will be difficult to find an exact formulation of the new sense of "de subiecto dici".

If we call KU_1 this new use of the expression "de subiecto dici", we may give the following definition:

D8 $KU_1(x, y) =_{df}$ (x is an accident[25] of y) & (x is predicated of y).

Here, in opposition to K, the condition that the *logos* of the accident be not said of the substance is not apparent.

Essential predicates (which are perhaps not included among KU_1 referents) seem to have a double sort of subject: *matter*[26], and what we would properly call an *individual.*[27]

Greek language allowed for predicating, (1) a substance of an accident, (2) an accident of a substance, (3) an accident of another accident.[28] Aristotle implies that the three possibilities are equally legitimate (syntactically speaking) but in a particular context he thinks it convenient to eliminate cases (1) and (3), in the sense of reducing them to (2).[29] If one has to legislate, as Aristotle says, then let cases (1) and (3) be predication κατά συμβεβηκὸς and (2) predication ἁπλῶς. Abbreviating the former by KS[30], we obtain a general diagram of Aristotle's predication theory (see p. 111); in comparison to *Categoriae*, essential predication (KU) *within* accidents is not to be found here, i.e., the idea of universality–singularity ceases to be visible within the realm of accidents.[31]

4.23 *The tradition assumes and conciliates the different Aristotelian theories of predication*

Of course the distinction between accidental and essential predication has persisted until the present.[32] Accidental predication became *denomination*, because most of it requires paronymous or denominative terms.[33]

The interesting point of the Aristotelian tradition is that it has combined both versions, *Categoriae* and the main works. This conciliating

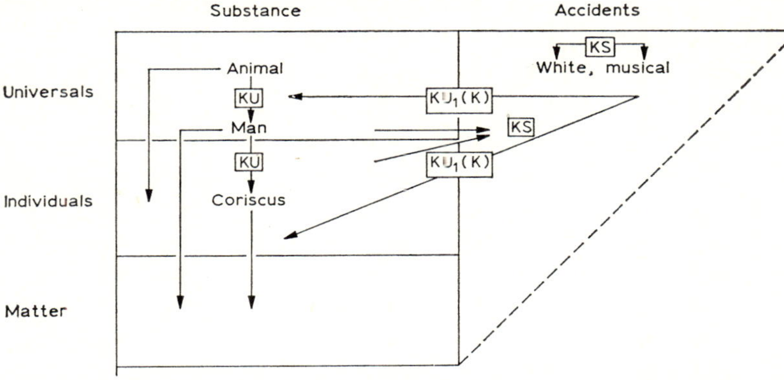

effort reveals itself in a text of Burgersdicius (a 17th-century "very acute writer in logic"[34]) which we shall quote and discuss briefly:

> Vulgo distingui solet inter subjectum *ἐνυπάρξεως καὶ κατηγορίας*, i.e. inhaesionis et praedicationis sive denominationis. Subjectum inhaesionis nihil aliud est quam substantia respectu accidentium sibi inhaerentium; sic nix est subjectum alboris qui sibi inhaeret. Subjectum praedicationis sive denominationis, vel late sumitur, vel stricte. Late sumitur pro qualibet re (sitne substantia an accidens, nihil refert) de qua aliquid dici potest quacumque praedicatione, sive essentiali, sive accidentali; sive interna, sive externa; sive absoluta sive limitata. Atque hoc sensu dici potest, omne subjectum inhaesionis esse subjectum denominationis, quia omne accidens dici potest de subjecto suo: vel voce denominativa, veluti cum nix dicitur alba ab albore sibi inhaerente, vel voce aliunde sumpta, veluti cum quis probus dicitur propter virtutem. At non omne subjectum praedicationis est subjectum inhaesionis. Multa enim dicuntur de subjecto quae non sunt in subjecto. Hoc sensu sumitur subjectum praedicationis in doctrina de praedicabilibus et de enunciatione.
>
> [. . .] Cum subjectum praedicationis sive denominationis stricte sumitur, opponitur subject[o] inhaesionis, idque bifariam. Vel enim sumitur pro eo de quo aliquid praedicatur essentialiter, puta genus, species aut differentia (sic sumitur cap. 2 et 5 lib. Categ., ubi esse in subjecto et dici de subjecto opponuntur) vel etiam sumitur pro eo de quo aliquid praedicatur praedicatione externa aut limitata; ut Miles est armatus, Aethiops est albus, Homo est immortalis. Neque enim armatura inhaeret militi, cum sit substantia; neque albor inhaeret toto Aethiopi, sed dentibus tantum; neque immortalitas toti homini, sed animae solum.[35]

1. This text presupposes the two ontological dimensions: inherence and singularity- universality.

2. The sense of "denomination" is extended to the point of becoming synonymous with "predication".[36]

3. Inherence is defined merely as the relation applying between accident and substance, without further references as to whether the accident (or the substance) is singular or universal.

4. "Predication" may be taken in two senses: (i) The domain of the relation *inherence* is included as a proper sub-class in the domain of the relation *predication*. This is the broad sense of "praedicatio", i.e., that of Aristotle's main works, when K becomes KU_1 (cf. 4.21 and 4.22).[37] (ii) The domain of the relation *inherence* is excluded from the domain of the relation *predication*. This is the restricted meaning of "praedicatio"; accidental predication is only possible in the sense of applying the *name* of the accident to the substance (K, cf. Section 4.21).

5. In the broad sense of "predication", when KU_1 appears, i.e., when accidents are predicable "de subjecto", the expression "de subjecto dici" is still applied to essential predication: "multa enim dicuntur de subjecto quae non sunt in subjecto". As far as our interpretation proposed in Section 4.22 (note 23) is correct, this would be another example of how in the tradition the various versions of Aristotle's theories have been conciliated. The *hupokeimenon* in KU_1 is a *subjectum inhaesionis* (and always is such, according to our above mentioned interpretation); in KU it is a *subjectum* in the sense in which an individual is a subject of its universal (essential) predicates. Burgersdicius uses "de subjecto dici" to cover both KU_1 and KU, where it is of course made clear that "subjectum" has a double meaning. (Cf. the initial clause of the text we are commenting upon and also Chapter 1, note 27.[38])

6. In the strict sense of "predication" we will not consider "external" or "limited" predication; this, in itself, would provide a fruitful point of comparison between traditional and Fregean thought as far as the phenomenon of *reduplicatio* is here concerned, for reduplication is intimately connected with *Sinn* and *Bedeutung*.[39]

Still, in the text of Burgersdicius we do not find that KU *between accidents* which appeared in the ontological square.[40] But the Aristotelian tradition preserved this curious detail, better than Aristotle himself did. In a well known textbook[41] we find, in fact, the doctrine that there is *for accidents* both an essential and an accidental predication; "album est coloratum" is an essential predication (KU between two accidental entities), "homo est albus" is an accidental predication (KU_1 or K).

At this point of our research we should observe that only "praedicatio essentialis" (KU of *Categoriae*) may be used as a pure equivalent of the dimension singularity–universality:

man ↓ Socrates   color ↓ white

The term "predication" may include accidental predication, which is rather a relative product of the two ontological dimensions:

white
↓ (essential predication)
Socrates ← this white[42]
(inherence)

4.3 Traditional predication theory is another theory

4.31 *Predicates of individuals are also predicates of universals*

4.311 An important feature of Aristotelian logic and ontology (*Categoriae*)

The following three diagrams show a significant feature of the three relations of *Categoriae*: KU, K[43], and EU.[44]

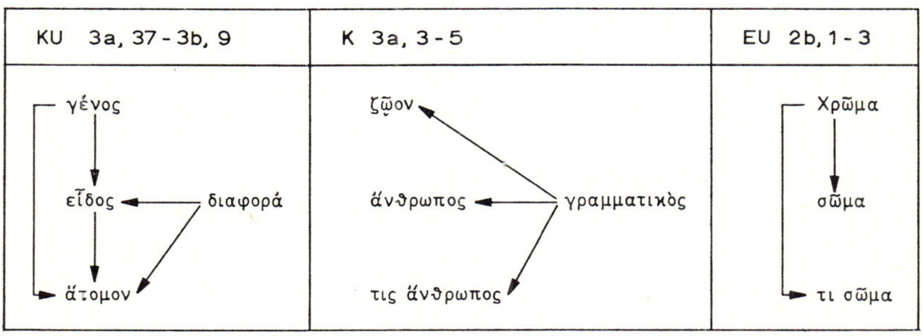

(In schema 1, "*γένος*" must be understood as "that which is a genus", not as "the property of being a genus"; the same holds for the other terms in schema 1.)

There is a trait common to these diagrams: anything which stays in some relation (KU, K, or EU) to an individual also stays in that relation to some universal ("of" that individual). There is only one exception: *eidos*.

This suggests that it is inadequate to say that UF and UO are not distinguished; the author of *Categoriae* had quite another thing in mind. Aristotle's "Weltanschauung", so to speak, and not the mere lack of distinction UF–UO should be investigated.

4.312 Some examples from other Aristotelian works

It is quite surprising to a modern reader to see how one of the anti-platonic arguments in *Metaphysics*[45] is developed. If Ideas are said to be *paradeigmata*, the relation of paradigma will not only apply between Ideas and *aisthetá* but also between two Ideas. A modern reader would understand this in the sense of the Russellian hierarchy of types; Ideas of Ideas would be like *Principia*'s types, or better, functions of functions. But Aristotle proceeds differently; having supposed that the species is a paradigma of sensible individual things, he holds that the genus will be a paradigma of the species. In other words, Aristotle seems to understand the iteration between two Ideas of the initial relation between an Idea and a thing rather in the sense of class inclusion than in the sense of the simple types.[46]

In fact, when he speaks of "upwards" and "downwards" in the world of concepts, he means class inclusion.[47] *Man* is subject with respect to *animal* and predicate with respect to *Callias*.[48] (Of course this situation may be easily "arranged", in order to make comparisons with modern logic, by writing "ι'Callias"; but this is not our method here.[49])

In *Topica* are to be found the following rules: (1) the genus is not predicated of the differentia but of the "inferiors" of which the differentia is predicated.[50] (2) Neither the species nor any "inferior" of the species is predicated of the differentia.[51]

Both rules will play a significant role in the analogy of being.[52] But here it should be observed that Aristotle is perfectly aware of the difference (in these particular cases) between predicating something about a universal and predicating something about an "inferior" of that universal (a subordinated concept or an individual). For a 20th-century reader both rules are puzzling because they presuppose that it is meaningful (although false) in the cases here considered to predicate universals among themselves in the same sense (using the same unqualified term "predication") in which universals are predicated of particulars. The "proof" of the rules is even more puzzling; if the genus *animal* or the species *man* were predicated of the differentia *biped*, then *biped* would become (an?) *animal* or (a?) *man*.[53]

We are indeed in a *different world*, not in a primitive version of the Fregean theory of predication. It is a world where it makes sense to say that if man-itself were not (an?) animal, then a man would not be an animal[54]: a world where accidents are meaningfully predicated of universal substances[55], and where *privation* of a quality is described as the absence of the quality either in the entity in question or in the genus.[56]

4.313 The philosophical tradition since Aristotle

Porphyry's *Isagoge* contains a brief chapter[57] in which the *quinque voces* are concisely examined. They are said to have a common aspect: being predicated of many, i.e., being *universal*. Let us consider the following diagram, where the arrows mean *predicated of*.

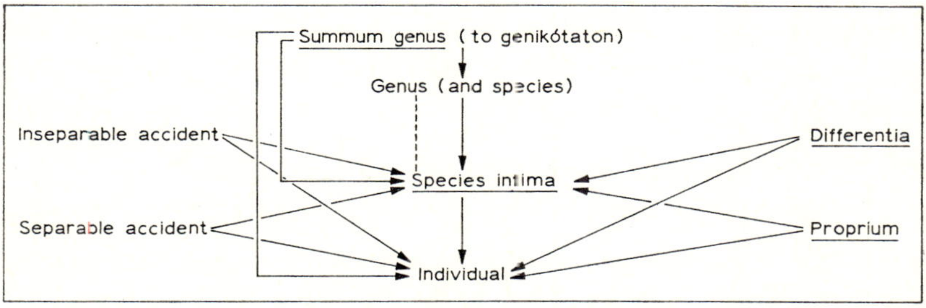

Universals, except *species infima*, are predicated both of other universals and of the individuals. All universals, except the *genikótaton*, the *summum genus*, have *two "faces"*[58]: one toward their "superiors", the other toward their "inferiors". All this is pure *Unterordnung* of concepts, and one may appreciate the difficulty of inserting here authentic higher predication. At the same time it should be observed that this is the image of the world of concepts which has been assumed in the Western philosophical tradition.[59]

4.32 *Available qualifications in the traditional predication theory do not point to a distinction of UF and UO*

We have been brought to acknowledge the validity of modern logic's accusation that traditional logic has not distinguished *the falling under a concept* from the *subordination* between two concepts.

It is true that there are qualifications. Already our diagram representing Porphyry's predication theory should have made it clear that, according to Porphyry, separable accidents are primarily attributed to individuals and only secondarily to species.[60] We may say that *man* is *moving*, but we mean primarily that *this man* is moving. Aristotle would say that *man* is *white* because *Callias* is *white*.[61] Accidents cannot be said without qualifications about *man*; not every man is a musician, or white. By symmetry, essential predicates are primarily attributed to universals.[62] Animal, the genus, *respicit primo* the species man, and *non primo* the individuals.[63] Similar distinctions exist for *proprium*.[64]

These qualifications, however, are neither obvious in traditional textbooks, nor do they point to a distinction of UF and UO. On the contrary, *their effect is precisely to confirm that it makes sense* to say "man (not: this man) is sitting"[65], whereby the fact that the predicate *sitting* applies primarily to *this man* and secondarily to *man*, is irrelevant. This fact is most striking to whoever attempts a comparison of modern and traditional logic. Traditional logic says more about a universal than would be allowed in new logic.[66]

4.33 *The tradition has developed many distinctions about predication: curiously, not that between UF and UO*

In matters of distinctions, traditional predication theory is exuberant: distinctions concerning the degree of information a predicate provides[67] (hierarchy of predicates), distinctions about the correspondence between the order of the grammatical couple *subject–predicate* and the order of things themselves[68] (*substance–accident*; *singular–universal*), distinctions about how predication between two higher predicates should be understood[69], distinctions concerning the full or only partial identity of subject and predicate, or even the case when subject and predicate have no relation at all.[70]

It is significant that something similar to UF–UO has not been developed together with the other foliage of classifications. This strongly suggests that we have *another theory*, not merely a primitive form of a more refined one. Our next step should be to discern the possible reasons underlying that theory.

4.4 Metaphysical background of traditional predication theory

4.41 *Is a thing the same as its essence?*

Aristotle asks whether a thing is the same as its essence[71]; he gives an affirmative answer for things *per se* and a negative one for things *per accidens*. *Anthrōpos* is a thing *per se*, *leukós ánthrōpos* is a thing *per accidens*; *anthrōpos* and *anthrōpos einai* are thus said to be the same.

This would introduce a relation of identity between *a man* and *man*. Not only is there nothing similar in Frege, but, on the contrary, Frege stresses that the relation between *this man* and *man* is not identity. His concern has been to *separate*, not to approach, the concept and its individuals. Apart from this, the identity between an individual and a property leads to the identity of the former with any other individual "falling" under the same property (if identity is to be transitive).

It should be observed, however, that Aristotle does *not* hold that he is identifying individuals and universals; this is *our* interpretation. Chapter 6 of *Metaphysics* Z, stresses above all the opposition substance–accident, and the dimension singular–universal is paid little attention. Now, by agreeing that Aristotle is not here identifying an individual with one of its properties one certainly avoids the previous difficulty, but the result is even more perplexing. If "anthrōpos" is not referring to individuals, to individual men, what does Aristotle's thesis mean in that case? Finally, if "anthrōpos" is not definitely used either as referring to individual men or as involving the universal, then we are passing beyond the Fregean limits of meaningfulness.[72]

Let us see whether our perplexity is removed by some representatives of the main groups of commentators on "il maestro di color che sanno". Alexander is no help to us.[73] Asclepius seems to pose the problem in terms of universals.[74] Averroes, on the contrary, views the question in terms of individuals, but this will lead him to a minor inconsistency.[75] Albertus Magnus follows the Aristotelian text: a predicate is identical with the subject when it provides the essence of the subject.[76] When the predicate is accidental, it has a double meaning (the later connotation–denotation) and therefore it is not true to say that it is identical with its subject(s).[77] But if we ask, *Who* is this subject, is it a singular or a universal?, Albertus Magnus' examples (*homo*, *equus*) will not enlighten us any more than Ross' translation [78] ("hekaston" = "a thing"). Such classical commentators as Aquinas [79] and Suarez [80] do not seem to be concerned by the *mise au point* which a Fregean reader requires.

Javellus' discussion is scrupulous and attractive from a modern point of view; but "the thing" (that thing whose identity with its essence should be decided) is both *Socrates* and *homo*.[81] Fonseca affirms that there is no identity between singular substances and their essences.[82] His commentary and his systematic discussion of the problem are a remarkable exception in the history of *Metaphysics* Z, 6.[83] But, unfortunately, their main contribution to the present question is only negative.

Passing to 19th-century philology, one finds new adherents to the Aristotelian thesis [84], but again this forces us to enter the *terra incognita* of an identity between *this man* and *man*.

Perhaps the most recent scholarly exposition of the Aristotelian text is to be found in Van Auben [1]. This author takes the Aristotelian identification of *man* and *essence of man* as obvious, for reasons similar to those found in Albertus Magnus. Van Auben paraphrases Aristotle's thesis by saying that there is identity between "*un* homme et ce qu'un homme est dit être par soi" (italics mine).[85] The indefinite article indicates that the author has viewed the problem in terms of individuals. But she would protest against the Fregean demand of sharply distinguishing singulars and universals; this distinction "n'a aucune signification métaphysique".[86] In this way, of course, it will be easy to oscillate between *man* and *this man* in order to avoid the difficulties deriving from "Socrates = man & Plato = man".

The result of our brief historical excursion is negative. Consequently, one remains in the problematic alternatives suggested by the Aristotelian text itself. One is compelled to view identity in a peculiar way (questioning, for instance, its transitiveness), or to assume an obscure identity of the universal *man* and its essence, or to depart from the assumption that everything is either particular or universal.

It is important to realize that the classic logic textbook of modern philosophy – Port-Royal logic – includes a metaphysical statement quite similar to the Aristotelian thesis: "l'attribut essentiel, qui est la chose mesme".[87] Now, *la chose* is, for example, *l'homme*; but is "l'homme" an *Eigenname* or a *Begriffswort*?[88], singular or universal?

4.42 *A predicate which "constitutes" the thing is not 'grundverschieden' from the thing*

Leaving aside historical considerations, it seems a priori plausible that once the idea of a hierarchy of predicates is introduced, and once a first privileged predicate (essence) is acknowledged, a strict separation[89] of it and the thing "cuius est quidditas" becomes, to say the least, questionable. This is actually the insight of Western ontology.[90] It is likewise plausible that if our main concern concentrates on this constitutive power of essence, then we will regard the obscurities recorded in the preceding section as *meaningful difficulties*, perhaps *unavoidable*, deriving from the intricacy of the subject.

To borrow a Fregean expression, "what is essential depends on our purposes"[91], and the task of the *zetoumene episteme* was *ousia*.[92] An aspect[93] of *ousia* was *to ti en einai*, essence. This being the primary concern of the author of *Metaphysics*, he was not worried if other insights had to be sacrificed, if, for instance, *ousia* had to become a sort of kaleidoscopic entity, neither universal nor singular, or which is both.[94] Of course, he could not foresee that subsequent to "ousia" there would emerge a series of terms retaining that original ambiguity: "res", "chose", "Gegenstand" or "Ding".[95]

Aristotle's *ousia*, and in particular *essence* has blurred the distinction *singular–universal* which became the center of Frege's philosophy of number. Frege, on the other hand, forces us to purify again the old one–many dimension, but he ignored essence.

Now essence must be either completely ignored or completely assumed. It is not clear why we should speak of a "feeling"[96] with respect to some extrinsic denominations and not with respect to more "interior" predicates. If an order is introduced into a sub-class of the class of predicates of an object *a*, it is necessary to state where this sub-class finishes, and one does not see any necessity for its finishing somewhere before essence.

Western philosophy, in general, has been attracted by the idea of essence, which it has completely assumed. The impact of essence was strong; philosophers were obliged to distinguish between man-in-Callias and man-in-Coriscus[97] (apart from Callias, Coriscus, and *man*), or they had to decree that there cannot be a Coriscus besides Callias, i.e., that there cannot be more than one individual for one essence.[98] Sophisms naturally arose.[99]

4.43 *Impact on predication theory*

The postulated identity between a thing and its essence creates an atmosphere in which "man runs" is as meaningful as "this man runs". This has been explicitly stated for the two ontological dimensions by traditional philosophy.[100] According to this perspective one makes perhaps better sense of the fact that in traditional logic concepts are *subjects* of their own marks rather than of their (second level) properties.[101]

4.431 Brentano's school

Since *Perihermeneias*[102], a sentence obtained by introducing a universal name in ". . . is" has been considered as well-formed: propositions *de secundo adiacente*.

A sort of paroxism of such an approach is to be found in Brentano's school. Brentano admits as well-formed sentences like "A ist"; "A" designates the *Gegenstand*, "ist (nicht)" means that the object is *anerkannt* or *verworfen*.[103] Of course, Brentano, if urged, would decide whether in the place of the variable A an *Eigenname* or a *Begriffswort* should be substituted; and as far as he also thinks that only individuals exist and concepts are fictions, he would probably adopt the first possibility.[104] But this is an extraneous dilemma imposed on Brentano's approach. He does not begin by dividing entities into concepts and objects, universals and particulars. *Universality* is just something "happening" to things when they are thought, and it concerns *our* thinking rather than reality itself.[105] This is traditional philosophy, cf. Avicenna[106] as well as Kant.[107] Existential propositions from such a point of view are not easily analysable into "a concept which is not empty". In Brentano's school, as well as formerly in the case of Hume, existential sentences mean that a kaleidoscopic[108] entity is accepted or rejected.[109]

4.44 *Possible indirect confirmations*

Locke – whose thought on this point may be interpreted as an effort to destroy the kaleidoscopic character of *ousia*[110] – suggests that sentences of the form "man is an animal", "man is rational", "man is white" should be analysed in terms similar to those of modern logic, i.e., by referring to *x*'s which are at the same time animal and men or white and men.[111]

Mill uses "thing" as "individual", not as "species" or "essence". His presentation of the five predicables differs from that of Aristotle precisely in this respect.[112] Although Mill says that *animal* is a genus of *man* or of *John*[113], it is difficult to find in his writings examples where *man* is a subject of predication. This is confirmed by Prior [1].[114]

4.5 Examples and consequences of not distinguishing UF and UO

4.51 *Heidegger on Kant*

There are texts which *cannot* be interpreted without making a distinction of UF and UO. Heidegger [1] maintains that the key to understanding the significance of Kant's theory on analyticity is the Kantian conception of a proposition as implying *three* elements: two concepts (subject, predicate) and the object.[115] Now, the greater the emphasis Heidegger places on the fact that the *Gegenstand* is what makes Kant's theory intelligible, the more it becomes necessary to draw a terminological distinction between the predication of one concept about the other concept and the predication of that same concept about the object. Otherwise, one would not see the point of Kant's achievement. But on the other hand perhaps the distinction would not be welcomed by Heidegger.[116]

4.52 *The notion of class*

Port-Royal's *extension* is ambiguous in the sense that one does not know whether only the individuals proper are meant or also the subordinate concepts.[117] Aristotle distinguishes various kinds of *wholes*, one of which would later be called *totum universale*.[118] *Living* is a whole containing *man*, *horse*, *god*. *Living* is a whole which may be predicated of each of its parts. Assuming traditional predication theory (is *man* or *this man* a part of *living*?[119]) one understands that neither the ancient *totum universale* nor the modern *extension* could be free from the above mentioned ambiguity.

4.53 *The 'totum universale'. Vaihinger and analytic propositions*

One may select the following four theses from traditional philosophy.

1. Parts are not predicated of wholes.[120]
2. Predication means a fundamental *identity* (an identity "in the fundament") of predicate and subject.[121]

3. "Homo est animal" is a predication in which the genus is said of the species.

4. The species *adds* something to the genus: species = genus+differentia. In Fregean terms, the species includes the marks of the genus plus a "differentiating" mark.[122]

One sees that 1 and 4 taken together exclude 3. The solution will consist in qualifying 4, namely, the sense in which the genus is part of the species. The solution is: the species does add something new to the genus but something which already was *implicite* in the genus. Thus, we may say that "potentially" the species does not add anything to the genus, and predicating the genus about the species will not contradict premiss 1.[123]

Vaihinger [1] explains how analytic judgments depend upon a concept A, which is composed of a set of partial concepts a, b, c, d.[124] The analytic judgment does not consist in merely stating this trivial identity $A = (a, b, c, d)$ but in predicating of A each of the partial concepts. This predication is symbolized in Vaihinger [1] not by "=" but by a dash, A–a, A–b, A–c, A–d.

4.531 Locke's general triangle

Locke's famous general triangle may be regarded as an unfortunate consequence of the traditional doctrine concerning the potential indetermination of the genus (cf. preceding section). According to the traditional approach the genus *triangle* contains "implicitly" its differentiae, namely, it is "implicitly" oblique and right-angled, equilateral and scalenon. These opposite differentiae did not come into collision as long as they were hidden under the vagueness of the terminology ("implicitly", "potential indetermination", etc.). Locke seems to have intended to make that terminology more precise; he interprets the potential indetermination of the genus as meaning that the general idea is "at once" "all and none" of its differentiae.[125] Berkeley would protest, of course, against such impossible entities as Locke's triangle or abstract ideas in general.

One may ask whether Locke's way of making more precise the traditional theory is the only possible interpretation, in other words, whether not only Locke's triangle but also the traditional view of the genus as "implicitly" containing its differentiae was an unfortunate doctrine. This question will not be dealt with here; we only mention it as an additional field of comparisons between classical and Fregean predication theory.

4.532 The law of excluded middle

There seems to be no general historical research on the law of excluded middle, particularly concerning the restrictions applied to it down through the centuries. I think, however, that four main groups of restrictions may be distinguished. The problems determining each of these groups are: (1) future events, (2) meaningless statements, (3) predication theory, and, (4) infinite sets. In the present context it is interesting to show how the qualifications due to the third kind of problems are a consequence of those peculiarities by which traditional predication theory is opposed to Fregean predication theory.

In spite of the fact that only the marks of a given predicate can be predicated of the latter in a proper way, traditional logic allows many other predications about a given predicate. They may be divided into two classes: (1) where the predicate is a non-essential first-level property, and, (2) where the predicate is a higher level property. "*Man* is *white*" and "*triangle* is *right-angled*" are examples of the first class; "*man* is *universal*" is an example of the second.

As to the former, the menace to the *tertium non datur* may be easily foreseen, because it also happens that "*man* is *non-white*" and that "*triangle* is *non-right-angled*". We find here once again Locke's *triangle*, but seen in a new light which suggests a restriction to the law of excluded middle.[126] The restriction is not endorsed by all philosophers who depend on traditional predication theory; in fact there were polemics about this.[127] But an examination of Locke's triangle and its presuppositions, for instance, indicates that the most natural decision was to impose exceptions to the *tertium non datur*. On the contrary, for Frege, *right-angled* is predicated only of (some of) those individuals which are triangles (UF), whereas *right-angled* and *triangle* are related by UO, which is not predication at all.

As to higher-level predicates, the situation is different though the results concerning the law of excluded middle turned out to be the same. As will be seen in the next chapter, the traditional tendency was to stress that higher-level predicates are not marks of the first-level properties. (This tendency is intelligible only if one assumes that classical philosophers were under the previous impression that higher-level predicates *are* marks of first-level predicates.) Thus the predicate *man* was said to be neither *universal* nor *non-universal*[128], because for ancient logicians, if F is a mark of M, then F is predicated of M, i.e. M is said to be F (*homo est animal*). The danger was clearly discerned[129]; the mere Avicennian phraseology in matters of higher predication theory directly suggests a restriction to the excluded middle. In Frege's approach the situation is radically different; no Fregean-minded logician would ever come upon the idea that higher-level predicates are marks of first-level predicates; *man* and *animal* are no longer related by predication proper but by UO, which leaves the field open for saying, without fear of fallacies, "*man* is *universal*" and "*animal* is *universal*". New problems arise, of course, concerning the ontological interpretation of properties of properties, but they are not pseudo-problems as in the case of the traditional restriction to the law of excluded middle depending on predication theory.

4.54 *The principle of contradiction in the 'Critique of Pure Reason'*

Kant considers two formulations of the principle of contradiction, as he says, one good and the other bad. The good one is, "Keinem Dinge kommt ein Praedikat zu, welches ihm widerspricht". The bad one is, "Ein Ding $= A$, welches etwas $= B$ ist, kann nicht zu gleicher Zeit non-B sein".[130]

The second formulation is held to be wrong because it introduces *time*, thus making of the principle something synthetic. The reason for introducing time is that *three* elements are considered: two contradictory predicates and one thing.[131] Each predicate by itself is not in contradiction with the thing, but only with the other predicates. Kant's intention is to adopt a formulation wherein only the two mutually exclusive predicates occur. He obviously looks for a pure *Unterordnung* of concepts, and this he finds in the first formulation, where, incidentally, it should be observed that "Ding" *has to* mean *predicate* or *concept*, not *individual*.[132]

4.6 **Unit-classes in traditional philosophy**

Traditional philosophy as a whole could easily reply to Frege that not Callias but ι'Callias is meant.[133] In fact, Porphyry's *individuum* is rather a set of marks defining a unit-class.[134] Duns Scotus' *haecceitas*[135] and Leibniz's *monads*[136] are also in the same line. The individual contains a set of marks, as *man* contains *animal* and *rational*.[137]

These insights come *before* a precise distinction of UF and UO, while *Principia Mathematica*'s $*51.2$[133] comes *after* that distinction. Nevertheless, the situation is much closer to modern logic than Scholz [4][139] misleadingly suggests. The latter accuses traditional logic of working with an undefined notion of "extension of individuals". But thereby Scholz erroneously assumes that traditional *individuals* are Frege's individuals. *Individual* is in traditional logic also a *sextum praedicabile*, i.e., *quod de uno solo praedicatur*[140], and to this extent it coincides with unit-classes.[141]

REFERENCES

1. UZBG; GRL, § 53; BGGE, p. 194 note; GRG I, p. 2; HUSS, p. 313. KSCH is written especially to show "die Notwendigkeit einer Unterscheidung [. . .] die vielen Logikern unbekannt zu sein scheint" (p. 433; cf. also pp. 440, 441, 442 note, 455–456).
2. Whitehead and Russell [1], I, p. 342.
3. Scholz [2], p. 121, where, nevertheless, one finds the error of holding that traditional logic considered predication as *part–whole*; since *Metaphysics* Δ, 26 there is such a notion as *totum universale*.
4. UZBG and KSCH.
5. Or IF, cf. Section 3.2.
6. Cf. Chapter 7.
7. BG.
8. GRL.
9. Cf. Section 3.3, note 35.
10. GRL, § 53.
11. GRL, p. 5 note.
12. Cf. note 1 here.
13. For example, Cornford [1], p. 256: "Plato nowhere implies that [. . .] the Form Man partakes of the Form Animal, in the same way as this man partakes of the Form Man. He uses the same word with his usual disregard for precise terminology, and he nowhere gives an explicit account of either relation. It seems obvious, however, that he cannot have regarded the two relations as the same." One might also point to Ockham's distinction of ε and $\subset$ (cf. Baudry [1], pp. 104, 107).
14. The present section continues Section 1.2.
15. Cf. Section 1.2.
16. "Denominata dicuntur quae ab aliquo ita sumunt appellationem ut terminatione differant; veluti a grammatica, grammaticus. Quod si terminatione non differant, ut a grammatica arte mulier dicitur grammatica, homonymia est, non denominatio" (Pacius [2], cap. 2).
17. For instance, if ἀρετή (virtue) actually inheres in a man, we shall say that this man is σπουδάιος (upright) (Aristotle [1], 10b, 5–9).
18. Aristotle [1], 10a, 27–10b, 11. *Because* it has a quality, a substance will be called by some name related to that quality.

19. Aristotle [1], 3a, 4–6.
20. Cf., nevertheless, 9a, 30–35, where substances are said to receive (to have) *whiteness* (*λευκότης*). 11a, 31–32 would suggest that a substance "has" a singular accident because of the expression "*τά κάθ' ἕκαστα*", but the context beginning in 11a, 20 is not clear as to whether that means individuals or subordinated species.
21. 5b, 2–10. Also 11b, 10–12 (to be completed by 6b, 10–15).
22. To be said of a subject.
23. For "de subiecto dici" as meaning essential predication, cf. note 31 here. For the new sense of that expression, the following references may be given: Aristotle [2], A, 9, 990b, 29–31 (cf. Aristotle [5], *Top.*, 121, a, 11); Aristotle [4], A, 2, 185a, 31–32; A, 3, 186a, 34; A, 4, 188a, 8; A, 7, 190a, 35–36. Aristotle [2], B, 5, 1001b, 31–32; Γ, 4, 1007a, 35; Δ, 8, 1017b, 13–14; Z, 3, 1029a, 7; Z, 13, 1038b, 15. Aristotle [3], A, 22, 83a, 26; *ibid.* 83a, 31; 83b, 20–21 (*Anal. Post.*).
It is perfectly clear that "de subiecto dici" apart from *Categoriae* covers accident–substance predication, and this is enough to justify one's speaking of a "change" in the terminology of predication theory. Another question is whether the new sense of "de subiecto dici" *excludes essential predication*, i.e., whether it excludes the sense of that expression in *Categoriae*. To answer this question we must consider both the original texts and the critics.
The two passages from *Metaph.* Z openly exclude *ousia* from things being said *de subiecto*, but 1038b 15 also excludes *ousia* from the domain of universals (*katholou*), which would still allow for the possibility of having *substantiae secundae* being said *de subiecto*. Nevertheless, this is an exception in our series of texts; Z, 3 and several other passages exclude *ousia* from being said *de subiecto* without further remarks as to whether this concerns singular or universal substance.
On the other hand, Bonitz's *Index* does not enlighten us on this point. Bonitz [1] (p. 798, b, 50–55) states that a genus (an essential predicate) may be said *de subiecto* although not being *in subiecto*, but this is supported only by reference to *Topica* 127, b, 1–3, which is a passage written in *Categoriae*'s terminology. (This is obvious, for the text asserts that if something is *in-a-subject*, it will not be predicated *de subiecto* about the subject in which it inheres.)
A recent study on the two ontological dimensions, Chung-Hwan-Chen [1], affirms that the "new" sense of "*kath'hupokeimenou legesthai*" also involves essential predicates (secondary substances) being said *de subiecto*. But unfortunately the texts referred to (p. 157, note) do not state explicitly that *man* is said *de subiecto* of *Callias* (to take an example), but only affirm that "everything else" is said *de subiecto* of substances.
On these grounds, I believe it is correct to say that "perhaps" the new sense of "de subiecto dici" excludes essential predication. (It is not clear why Simplicius [1], p. 54, 7f. does not pay more attention to the terminological change.)
24. If we look for KU_1 (cf. D8 in the present section) in *Categoriae*, we find a variant of K (cf. Section 4.21, D7) such that the restriction of only predicating *the name* is not apparent (particularly in 12a, 12b). We may perhaps view 3a, 3–6 (where it is said that *all the other things* are predicated of substances) in the same sense, if we follow Chung-Hwan-Chen [1] (p. 153 note 3). This author considers that passage as abandoning the severe restrictive rules at the beginning of *Categoriae* which forbid that the *logos* of accidents be predicated of the sub-

stances. But that passage has been perhaps magnified by Chung-Hwan-Chen, because he has not included *paronymous* predication among the possibilities allowed by the severe rules at the beginning (he only mentions homonymous and synonymous predication). Thanks to paronymous names, it is possible to extend the possibilities of K very far, and if one adds names built "in some other way", then "all other things" will be predicable of substances. Of course, the passage in question should say in addition "*the names*, not *the logoi*", in order to be orthodox with respect to the severe rules.

25. Cf. note 23.
26. Aristotle [2], B, 995b, 35; Z, 3, 1029a, 23; Θ, 7, 1049a, 27–40; A, 9, 992b, 1–3. The second text maintains that *ousia* is predicated of matter; the third that *eidos* is said of matter. Accordingly, *hupokeimenon* now is not only the individual Coriscus or Callias, but also matter. (Aristotle [2], Z, 13, 1038b, 5). Aquinas [1], 1288–9 (commenting on *Metaphysics* Z, 3) calls *praedicatio denominativa* this predication of substance about matter. Concerning *matter* – or *materia prima* – it should be observed that this is perhaps a notion more accessible *today*, considering the increasing interest in logic and ontology, than in the past. Aquinas [1] (1287, also 1308) distinguishes two approaches to matter, one *per viam motus*, the other *per viam praedicationis*; the latter, because of being proper to logic, is more adequate for *Metaphysics*. It is this second approach which today "makes sense" as soon as a hierarchy of predicates (and in particular essence) is introduced.
27. Aristotle [2], Δ, 6, 1015b, 32–35 opposes Coriscus to his two predicates: *man* and *musical*.
28. Cf. note 21.
29. Aristotle [3], A, 22 (*Anal. Post.*).
30. KS should be distinguished from accidental predication. The latter is to predicate an accident of a substance, which is not KS as defined in the text quoted in the preceding note. The Greek commentators have used a more expressive designation for KS (which had also the advantage of avoiding confusions with accidental predication): predication *παρὰ φύσιν* (against nature) (Philoponus [1], 235; Alexander [1], 371, 8–13).
31. Simplicius [1], p. 52, identifies KU (cf. Section 1.2) with essential predication. I assume in the diagram that KU_1 is directed to universal as well as to individual substances; cf. for instance Ross' commentary in Aristotle [3] (p. 579, in the middle), where accidental attributes are said to apply to elements of the essence of an individual subject. Cf. also Aristotle [2], Δ, 6, 1015b, 28. I assume that KS comes *both* from individual *and* universal substances, although I cannot offer textual support for this. For (K) cf. Section 4.21.
32. For example, White [1].
33. Cf. note 16. "Praedicatio denominativa" became synonymous with "accidental predication" (cf. Ioannes a Sto. Thoma [1], p. 476). For a further extension of that term, cf. below, remark 2 to Burgersdicius' text. "Denomination from" is the Lockian translation of the previous "denominatio ab" (Locke [1], II, 7, § 22 *in fine*; II, 25, § 2). In Husserl [1] VI, § 7, one finds an almost literal reproduction of the description of denomination in *Categoriae*: the name "red" is imposed on an object because of a *Rotmoment* appearing in that object. Formerly, denomination was subject to subtle distinctions, one of which is the philosophically important "denominatio extrinseca".

34. Reid [1], *Analysis of Aristotle's Logic*, ch. II.
35. Burgersdicius [1], *Lib.* 1, *cap.* XIX, *theorema* 1 (pp. 59–60).
36. Cf. note 33.
37. "Neither does he [Aristotle] mean that the nine kinds of accidental things may not be predicated concerning substances [. . .]. Isidore, Alcuin and other wise men tell us that all the remaining categories are predicated of primary substances" (John of Salisbury [1], III, 3 = p. 160).
38. Aquinas [1], n. 1576, makes an interesting contribution to the present question. The author holds that essential predicates may be viewed as being predicated *de subjecto* only from the logician's point of view, not from the point of view of the *philosophus primus*; by means of this distinction *Categoriae* and *Metaphysics* are conciliated. But we should observe that this is possible because the dimension singular–universal (the logician's concern) is actually underestimated; it is "our" intervention in things (cf. Section 1.44).
39. Cf. Section 2.25 *in fine*.
40. Cf. Section 1.2.
41. Gredt [1], n. 139.
42. Caietanus [2], p. 63, shows that even individual accidents, for example *this white*, have been considered as predicable of their substances: ". . . individuis accidentium tantum, quae praedicantur de subiectis suis denominative, ut cum dicitur: 'Sortes est hoc album'." (This is Averroes' view, reported by Caietanus.)
43. Or KU_1, cf. note 24. (The text of *Categoriae* is that of Aristotle [1].) "In demselben Sinne, wie von dem einzelnen Menschen das Prädikat sprachkundig ausgesagt wird, kann es auch von dem Menschen überhaupt ausgesagt werden" (Trendelenburg [1], p. 59).
44. An example of how seriously the tradition has assumed the possibility of *universal* accidents inhering in substances is given by Boethius: "Probatur quoque particulare album in subjecto esse hoc modo, nam color quod genus est albi vel cujusdam albi in corpore est, et est in subjecto. Quare cujus genus in subjecto est, ipsum quoque in subjecto est" (Boethius [1], p. 172, A–B).
45. Aristotle [2], A, 9, 991a, 29–32 (also: M, 5, 1079b, 32–35).
46. Ross' analysis of the text: "Not only will the species be the pattern of the individuals, but the genus will be the pattern of its species, so that the same thing will be pattern and copy" (in Aristotle [2], I, p. 188).
47. Aristotle [3], *Anal. Priora*, I, 27; *Analyt. Post.*, I, 19–23.
48. *Ibid. Anal. Priora*, I, 27.
49. Cf. Section 4.1 *in fine*.
50. Aristotle [5], *Topica*, Z, 6, 144a, 32–33.
51. *Ibid.*, 144b, 4–5.
52. For example Aristotle [2], B, 3, 998b, 22–27. Cf. Tricot in Aristotle [2.1], I, p. 140 and 141. Aquinas [1], n. 433.
53. Consider the Oxford translation: "Moreover, the differentiae will be all either species or individuals, if they are animals; for every animal is either a species or an individual" (Aristotle [3.1], 144b).
    If the species is predicated of the differentia, then *δῆλον ὅτι ἡ διαφορὰ ἄνθρωπος ἐστιν,* which Pacius translates in the following way: "manifestum est, differentiam esse hominem" (Pacius [1], p. 716). The Oxford translation seems to surround this text with some ambiguity: "the differentia is clearly the human race" (Aristotle [3.1], *ibid.*).

54. Aristotle [6], P, 133 (*On Ideas*).
55. Aristotle [2], Δ, 6, 1015b, 28.
56. *Ibid.*, 22, 1022b, 25.
57. Porphyry [1], p. 13.
58. *Ibid.*, p. 5, 1.7.
59. A second-scholastics commentary:
"Cum enim perpetuo superiora de inferioribus praedicentur, species quidem de individuis praedicabitur; genus autem de specie et individuis; genus vero supremum de genere vel generibus (si in ea recta serie plura sint genera et species subalternae) atque etiam de specie, et individuis praedicatur. Genus namque supremum de omnibus generibus, speciebus et individuis dicitur. Genus autem quod collocatur ante speciem infimam, de omnibus speciebus infimis sub se contentis et individuis effertur. Species infima tantummodo praedicatur de omnibus individuis; at vero individuum de uno solo particulari" (Gasconius [1], II, 28a).
"Ex iis quae dicta sunt colligo duo. Alterum est, quod genus de speciebus sub se contentis et individuis illarum specierum dicitur, species tantummodo de individuis, differentia vero, proprium et accidens de specie cuius sunt talia et de individuis sub illa specie contentis praedicantur. Alterum est [. . .] Species namque est essentia individuorum, quae sub ea in categoria continentur. Genus autem, et differentia de speciebus et de individuis earum specierum essentialiter praedicantur" (*ibid.*, I, 2b–3a).
Pacius' presentation of the same subject-matter:
"Secundo, cum ait 'genus quidem', tradit primam regulam: Superiora inferioribus attribuuntur, non contra superioribus inferiora. Intellige superiora et inferiora in eadem Categoria. Tertio cum ait 'Oportet enim' datam regulam ex eo confirmat, quod vel attribuuntur aequalia aequalibus, vel maiora minoribus, non minora maioribus in singulis [enim?] Categoriis" (Pacius [3], in the commentary on *Isagoge*).
In the 17th century:
"Quum in inferiori sit superius, [. . .] est in individuo species, genus infimum, subalterna, summum, in specie genera, in genere infimo et subalterno superiora, in inferioribus omnibus summum" (Baumgarten [1], § 153).
"Determinationes generis summi sunt in inferioribus eius [. . .] i.e. generibus subalternis, infimo, speciebus et individuis; determinationes generis subalterni sunt in inferioribus eius generibus, speciebus, et individuis; determinationes generis infimi sunt in speciebus et individuis; determinationes speciei sunt in individuis [. ..] i.e. *determinationes superioris sunt in eius inferiori, seu positivae fuerint seu negative* [. . .] *Haec propositio dicitur dictum de O*[*mni*] *et N*[*ullo*]" (*Ibid.*, § 154, italics of the author).
Reid's exposition:
"Every genus, and every species of things may be either the subject or the predicate of a proposition, nay of innumerable propositions; for every attribute common to the genus or species may be affirmed of it; and the genus may be affirmed of every species, and both genus and species of every individual to which it extends" (Reid [1], Essay V, ch. 1, 7).
It should be observed that Reid had, shortly before, stated the possibility of *attributes of attributes* in a sense "corresponding" to our contemporary use of this expression. I say only "corresponding" because Reid's *attributes of at-*

tributes are Reichenbach's individual accidents (cf. Chapter 1, note 108) rather than predicates of predicates. Nevertheless, it is clear that Reid's insight into attributes of attributes conflicts with his Aristotelian view of *animal* as an attribute of the attribute *man* (cf. Section 5.32).

60. Porphyry [1], p. 13, 1. 20.

61. Aristotle [2], I, 9, 1058b, 10–13; Δ, 9, 1018a, 1.
"Convenit enim idem esse album et nigrum. Sed diversimode. Quia si illud quod dicitur album et nigrum sit aliquod universale, simul est album et nigrum quantum ad diversos. Sicut simul verum est dicere quod homo est albus propter Socratem et niger propter Platonem. Si vero fuerit aliquid singularium, non erit simul album et nigrum" (Aquinas [1], n. 2138).
"Substantiae vero secundae, id est genera et species, substant solis accidentibus. Et hoc etiam non habent nisi ratione primarum. Homo enim est albus in quantum hic homo est albus" (*Ibid.*, n. 1274).
"Accidens commune inest magis individuis, quam universalibus. Teste Aristot. 9 Met. cap. 9, ubi ait: homo est albus, quia Callias est albus, i.e. albedo speciei inest propter individua; huius rei ratio est, quia communia non fluunt ab essentia subiecti, sed ab existentia potius, quae est singularium" (Keckermann [1], Liber I, cap. XXI).

62. "Quia vero huiusmodi praedicata per accidens prius praedicantur de singularibus, et per posterius de universalibus, cum tamen e converso sit de praedicatis per se..." (Aquinas [1], n. 845).

63. Gasconius [1], after having explained the Porphyrian doctrine that a genus is predicated both of the subordinate species and of the individuals, considers the question whether "genus respectu solius speciei genus sit, an vero respectu quoque individuorum, ita ut haec oratio 'Socrates est animal' sit praedicatio generis, non minus quam haec 'homo est animal'" (II, 20b). It should be observed that the distinction *praedicatio per se–praedicatio per accidens* (notes 61 and 62) is not sufficient to qualify the two statements "Socrates est animal" and "homo est animal", because both are essential predications. Thus, a further distinction is required, namely, the genus belongs *per se primo* to the species, and *per se non primo* to the individual. Still, our author thinks that some opponent would reply that even under such a qualification it happens that a genus has *duo correlata*, which *absurdissimum est*. The answer consists in simply repeating the distinction already made: "genus enim non habet duo correlata ad quae ex aequo ordinem dicat" (*ibid.*).
Also: "Aliter enim individuum et aliter species ponitur sub genere" (Caietanus [2], p. 35).

64. Signoriello [1], p. 250.

65. How the above mentioned qualifications may disappoint anyone hoping to find there an equivalent of UF–UO distinctions is shown by the following text: "Accidens vero ante praedicatur de individuis et postea de speciebus. Nam si quis dicat, homo sedet, quod est accidens separabile, cum quicumque singulum hominem, id est individuum, sedere viderit, tunc id et de specie praedicat, ut dicat: quoniam Cicero sedet, Cicero autem homo est, homo sedet" (Boethius [2], p. 103).
Certainly, this may be "arranged" by writing "(Ex) x is a man and x is sitting down". This procedure is adopted for instance by A. Church (in Runes [1], "supposition"). But, did Boethius think in that way? Such an interpretation

would appear as false if applied to traditional texts which depend on the predication theory presented by Aquinas (cf. the text quoted in the next note).

66. "Est autem considerandum quod de universali aliquid enunciatur quattuor modis.

(A) Nam universale potest *uno modo* considerari quasi separatum a singularibus, sive per se subsistens, ut Plato posuit, sive secundum sententiam Aristotelis, secundum esse quod habet in intellectu. Et sic potest ei aliquid attribui dupliciter. Quandoque enim attribuitur ei sic considerato aliquid, quod pertinet ad solam considerationem intellectus, ut si dicatur quod *homo est praedicabile de multis*, sive universale, sive species. Huiusmodi enim intentiones format intellectus attribuens eas naturae intellectae, secundum quod comparat ipsam ad res, quae sunt extra animam.

Quandoque vero attribuitur aliquid universali sic considerato, quod scilicet apprehenditur ab intellectu ut unum, tamen id quod attribuitur ei non pertinet ad actum intellectus, sed ad esse, quod habet natura apprehensa in rebus, quae sunt extra animam, puta si dicatur quod homo est dignissima creaturarum. Hoc enim convenit naturae humanae etiam secundum quod est in singularibus. Nam quilibet homo singularis dignior est omnibus creaturis irrationalibus; sed tamen omnes homines singulares non sunt unus homo extra animam, sed solum in acceptione intellectus; et per hunc modum attribuitur ei praedicatum, scilicet ut uni rei.

(B) Alio autem modo attribuitur universali, prout est in singularibus, et hoc dupliciter.

Quandoque quidem ratione ipsius naturae universalis, puta cum attribuitur ei aliquid quod ad essentiam eius pertinet, vel quod consequitur principia essentialia; ut cum dicitur *homo est animal*, vel *homo est risibilis*.

Quandoque autem attribuitur ei aliquid ratione singularis in quo invenitur, puta cum attribuitur ei aliquid quod pertinet ad actionem individui; ut cum dicitur *homo ambulat*.

Singulari autem attribuitur aliquid *tripliciter*: uno modo, secundum quod cadit in apprehensione, ut cum dicitur *Socrates est singulare*, vel *praedicabile de uno solo*. Quandoque autem, ratione naturae communis; ut cum dicitur *Socrates est animal*. Quandoque autem, ratione sui ipsius, ut cum dicitur, *Socrates ambulat*. De singulari autem quamvis aliquid diversa ratione praedicetur, ut supra dictum est, tamen totum refertur ad singularitatem ipsius, quia etiam natura universalis in ipso singulari individuatur; ut ideo nihil refert quantum ad naturam singularitatis, utrum aliquid praedicetur de eo ratione universalis naturae, ut cum dicitur *Socrates est homo*, vel conveniat ei ratione singularitatis" (Aquinas [4], *In Per.*, n. 126f.).

The content of this important text of predication theory may be summarized by means of the schema placed on p. 132.

The last passage of the quoted text indicates that cases 3 and 2a, for instance, may be different, as far as the universal "concerned" in each of them is either a universal "proper" or a universal which is "individuated".

I have not found a clear enough interpretation of case 2 (an interpretation in Fregean terms). Is *to be the dignissima creatura* a mark of the concept man, or is it a property of the concept man? It cannot be the former, because it would follow that Socrates is the *dignissima* among creatures; nor can it be the latter, for this would be outside of the author's intention.

Statements about		*Examples*
A universal	1. Abstracted from the individuals (either in Plato's or Aristotle's interpretation)	"Homo est species"
	2. . . .?	"Homo est dignissima creaturarum"
	3. Considered in the individuals; but the predicate "concerns" rather the universal	"Homo est animal"
	4. Considered in the individuals; but the predicate "concerns" rather the individual	"Homo ambulat"
A particular	1a. . . .?	
	2a. The predicate "concerns" rather the universal (essence)	"Socrates est animal"
	3a. The predicate "concerns" rather the individual	"Socrates ambulat"

Case 3 should not be misunderstood, as if the statement "homo est animal" implied that individual men exist (cf. Aquinas [3], cap. 4: "Omnis autem essentia vel quiditas potest intelligi sine hoc quod aliquid intelligatur de esse suo; possum enim intelligere quid est homo vel fenix et tamen ignorare an esse habeat in rerum natura"). The universal in case 3 is considered *qua* being capable of existing *extra animam.*

Case 1a involves a reference to second intentions and the phrase "cadit in apprehensione" does not have any unusual meaning in this context. (I am grateful to Prof. M. D. Philippe for valuable remarks on this point.) Nevertheless, I have preferred not to attempt a precise formulation of this case.

The point I wish to stress here is that such sentences as "homo ambulat" are not adequately interpreted by writing, "there is an *x* such that it is a man and it walks". "Homo ambulat" involves a true predication about a universal (universal-in-the-thing).

Frege's distinction of *Merkmal-Eigenschaft* (cf. Chapter 5) is a most remarkable clarification of case 3 (and case 1), but his "logical" relations (UF, UO, IF . . .) are not sufficient to absorb cases 2, 4, and the *nuance* between 2a and 3a.

67. Cf. Section 3.5.

68. Genus about species, differentia about species, accident about substance, are *praedicatio directa*; species about genus, etc. is *praedicatio indirecta.* Also a

superior (concept) about an inferior is *praedicatio ordinata*; otherwise: *praedicatio inordinata* (Signoriello [1], "praedicatio").

69. This problem appears with *second intentions* (cf. Chapter 7). A very rare modern account is to be found in Świeżawski [1]; a thorough discussion in Sanchez Sedeño [1]. The problem for tradition was how to insert higher predication in the Aristotelian system.
70. The Greek Antisthenes is a well known instance. Subsequently, predications or propositions where the subject has "no relation" with the predicate were called *disparatae*. These, together with *propositiones identicae* (tautological, $a = a$) were considered as useless for science; only an intermediate kind (*nec disparatae nec identicae*) appeared as having a cognitive value (Gasconius [1], II, 13b–14a). Cf. Bocheński [1], 29.02, and, of course, Frege's SUB.
71. Aristotle [2], Z, 6. In Greek terms, the question is whether *ἕκαστον* is *ταὐτὸν* as its *τὸ τί ἦν εἶναι*. For the translation, we follow Ross, *ibid.*
72. This is an opportunity to consider one aspect of Frege's requirement of a sharp distinction between individuals and predicates, namely his stressing that there are no "intermediate" entities between an object and a concept. In our case, *anthrōpos* must be either a particular or a universal man: *tertium non datur*. Both in traditional and modern logic one finds several vague entities between individuals and predicates; in traditional logic the *individuum vagum*, in Russell the "denoting" expressions. Caietanus [2] contains an interesting discussion on *individuum vagum* (*aliquis homo, aliquis bos, et huiusmodi*) and *individuum signatum* (*hic homo, hic bos*, etc.; *Sortes*, etc.). Cf. also Geach [2]. Frege rejected such "vague individuals":
"Das Wort 'Wallfisch' benennt aber kein Einzelwesen. Wenn man erwidert, allerdings sei nicht von einem einzelnen, bestimmten Gegenstande die Rede, wohl aber von einem unbestimmten, so meine ich, daß "unbestimmter Gegenstand" nur ein andrer Ausdruck für "Begriff" ist, und zwar ein schlechter, widerspruchsvoller" (GRL, p. 60).
Frege reacted against Schröder's assumption that "some men" is the name of an (indeterminate) class (cf. KSCH, p. 441 note).
Frege's reasons for rejecting "variable" signs are similar to those against "indeterminate objects" (cf. for instance, JOURD, p. 238).
73. Alexander [1], p. 479.
74. Asclepius [1], p. 391.
75. Averroes [1], vol. VIII. The Latin text of Averroes asks: "utrum ista substantia, quae est quidditas, et substantia singularis, sive individuum substantiae, sint idem". In other words: whether individual and universal substances are identical. Averroes' answer is affirmative: "Socrates enim nihil aliud est quam animalitas et rationalitas, quae sunt quidditates eius." Once Averroes has said that Socrates is nothing else than his essence, he also gives the converse, namely, that Socrates' essence (i.e. *animalitas* plus *rationalitas*) is nothing else than Socrates . . ., which of course is wrong, and Averroes must add, "and Plato". "Nec animalitas et rationalitas sunt quidditates nisi Socratis et Platonis."
76. Albertus Magnus [1], lib. VII, tract. II, cap. III (pp. 434–435). "Et ideo praedicatum de subjecto aliquando secundum quidditatem idem est subjecto, et aliquando non est idem cum ipso."
77. *Ibid.*: "Ideo non est verum dicere de illis, quod idem sit quid esse ipsorum et id subjectum de quo praedicantur".

78. Ross in Aristotle [2], II, p. 175f.
79. Aquinas [1], n. 1356–1380.
80. Suarez [1], 34, sect. 3, 18.
81. Javellus [2], f. 320: "res autem cuius est quidditas, ut Socrates et homo".
82. Fonseca [2], *tomus* III, p. 231–239.
83. There is first an "explanatio" of the chapter 6 of Book Z, *with the Greek text*. This occupies almost 7 pages. Afterwards there is a systematic *quaestio*: "Num quod quid est sit idem cum eo, cuius est?"
84. Schwegler [1], p. 68: "Ist das Einzelding identisch mit seinem begrifflichen Wesen (seinem ti en einai)? Ja – wie im Verlaufe bewiesen wird". Cf. also: "Aus der eben nachgewiesenen Identität des ti en einai mit den daseienden Einzeldingen . . ." (p. 71).
    Bonitz [2], p. 318: "His igitur ex causis idem per se sunt substantiae singulares earumque ta ti en einai".
85. P. 373.
86. P. 376.
87. Port-Royal [1], I, Ch. II. An 18th-century Latin translation reads: "et tunc essentiale attributum, quod ipsissima res est" (Port-Royal [2], p. 12). Joffre [1], an "ars syllogistica" written *more geometrico*, includes the following ontological proposition: ". . . nam homo et humanitas [. . .] sunt unum et idem . . ." (Lib. I, cap. 1, artic. 1, definitio VII). Also: "Nota attributum distingui a modo: quod attributum sit ita rei essentiale, ut sine illo res nec esse nec concipi possit" (*ibid.*, *art.* 2, *defin.* II).
88. GRG II, § 151 (the title, in the analysis of contents).
89. Frege would say "Grundverschiedenheit" (GRG I, p. 37, *passim*), which does not necessarily imply unsaturatedness in the Fregean form. Here one might say that Frege is a platonist; Chapter 6 of *Metaphysics Z* is directed precisely against Plato (cf. Tricot in Aristotle [2.1], I, p. 378, note 1).
90. For example, Albertus Magnus [1]: ". . . quia hoc quidem erat quid esse quod *constituit* rem in eo quod est, oportet unum esse cum re, hoc est, non separatum ab ipsa" (lib. VII, tract. II, cap. III = p. 436; italics ours).
91. GED, p. 64.
92. Aristotle [2], Z, 1, 1028b, 4.
93. *Ibid.*, 3, 1028b 33.
94. Cf. Ross in Aristotle [2], *ad* Z, 1. Aristotle [3.1] *ad* 83b. Zeller as quoted by Owens [1], p. 13. Tricot in Aristotle [2.1], I, p. 22. But especially Book Z itself (*Metaph.*) should be considered; and Owens [1], p. 242.
95. For "res", cf. Chapter 1, note 96 and this chapter note 81; for "Ding", cf. Section 4.54; for "Gegenstand" cf. Chapter 1, note 96; for "chose", Section 4.41 *in fine*.
96. "Utraque forma est idem secundum speciem" (Aquinas [1], n. 1435). Cf. Tricot in Aristotle [2.1], I, p. 381, note 1.
97. Cf. Chapter 3, note 65.
98. Spinoza [1], I, *prop.* 5; also, Locke [1], III, 6, § 8.
99. "Si Socrates est idem cum sua quiditate, ergo est idem cum animali rationali. Sed animal rationale est duo, ergo Socrates est duo [. . .] Item si homo est sua quiditas, ergo est incorruptibilis, quia rerum quiditates sunt incorruptibiles, cum sint universales et ut sic abstrahant ab hic et nunc" (Javellus [2], f. 320).
100. Accidents inhere in *universal* substances as well as in individual ones (cf. Section

1.2; this chapter, notes 44 and 61). And of course *animal* is predicated both of *man* and *Socrates*.

101. It is quite clear that once a universal has the power of *sub-stare*, it becomes the subject of the properties of the individual, in particular of those properties which depend on essence (cf. Aquinas' text quoted in note 66). Springer [1] has clearly detected these peculiarities in predication theory deriving from metaphysics (pp. 21, 22 etc.). How else could the predication theory of a logical textbook be which, like Mercier [1], makes essence = *res*, and takes essence to be the subject (of inherence) of accidents (p. 77, note)? If *white* inheres in *man* as well as in *Socrates*, we shall say "man is white" as well as "Socrates is white".

102. In Aristotle [1], *Perihermeneias* 10, 19b, 5: *ἔστιν ἄνθρωπος*, "homo est". Cf. Bocheński [1], 29.01.

103. Brentano [1], § 27 (p. 101). Brentano intends to show that propositions are not necessarily *zweigliedrig*, i.e., they do not always contain a subject and a predicate.

104. "Wenn er aber mit Recht sagt, ein Lebewesen, ein Mensch, ein Mann *sei*, so muß das Ding, wovon diese Aussagen richtig sind, natürlich ein vollkommen bestimmtes Individuum sein" (Brentano [1], § 17, p. 41).

105. "Das universell und individuell (oder besser weniger universell) bezieht sich also nur auf das Vorstellen" (Brentano [1], p. 50). "Kein Gegenstand wird also mit allen seinen individuellen Merkmalen, sondern in einer gewissen (größeren oder geringeren) Allgemeinheit vorgestellt" (*ibid.*, p. 43).
If we compare these texts with that quoted in the preceding note, we have: things in themselves are individuals, universality–singularity is an irrelevant dimension due to *our* dealing with things. In Hillebrand [1] there is a disagreement with Sigwart about existential propositions. Sigwart demands a sharper distinction between a "content" and the "instances" (particulars) of that content (p. 36). But Hillebrand does not care about this; within a single page he uses the expressions "einen Thaler", "Thaler", "der Thaler", "der Thaler selbst", and all these variants are different names for (the). . . *Gegenstand* (which he opposes to the subjective *vorgestellte Thaler*). In Kastil [1], as well as in Brentano's works, the variable "*A*" appears many times in order to facilitate the discussion. But shall we introduce concept-words or proper names into that empty place? Or rather: is this very question meaningful at all (for Brentano)?

106. Cf. Chapter 5.

107. Chapter 1, notes 96 and 97.

108. Section 4.42, in particular note 94.

109. For Brentano's sympathetic approach to Hume's notion of existence, cf. Brentano [3]. Also Marty [1], pp. 189, 200. All this indicates that we are faced with *another theory*, and not with a mere obscure version of the same theory, as Scholz's evaluation of Brentano's doctrines suggests: "Nach Brentano ist das "ist" in "homo est" nicht als Prädikat aufzufassen – darin stimmen wir mit ihm überein – sondern als Anerkennung der eingliedrigen Urteilsmaterie "Mensch" (Was ist das?) (Scholz [2], p. 116). Scholz [2] translates the propositions *de secundo adiacente* by "(*Ex*). *x* ist ein Mensch", which would be accepted as correct by traditional philosophers as far as "aliquis homo est" and "homo est" are equivalent, i.e. *quodammodo eamden vim habent* (Aquinas [4], n. 210). But the point of traditional predication theory is that *homo* is as good a subject of *being* or *running* as is Socrates. For Brentano, concepts or universals are fictions; nevertheless, his predication theory regards them as subjects (of predication) of their

own marks: "Wir machen den Menschen, den Wasserstoff usw. zum Subjekt von Aussagen", Brentano [1], § 17 = p. 44.

110. "So that of substance, we have no idea of what it is, but only a confused, obscure one of what it does" (Locke [1], II, 13, § 19).
111. "All our affirmations then are only in concrete, which is the affirming, not one abstract idea to be another, but one abstract idea to be joined to another" (Locke [1], III, 8, § 1). The context supports my interpretation.
112. Mill [1], 1, 8, § 2.
113. *Ibid.*
114. p. 164.
115. Heidegger [1], pp. 119f.
116. This is suggested by Heidegger's remark concerning two different formulations of the principle of contradiction in Kant's works, one of them deals with *Ding, das worauf der Subjektbegriff bezogen ist*, the other concerns the *Subjektbegriff selbst*. Now, Heidegger says that "beide Fassungen unterscheiden sich nicht wesentlich" (*ibid.*, p. 134).
117. Cf. Kneale [1], p. 318.
118. Aristotle (2), Δ, 26, 1023b, 26–32.
119. Cf. Section 4.313.
120. Aristotle [5], *Topica*, Δ, 5, 126a, 27.
121. Cf. Chapter 3, note 45.
122. *το ζῷον θνητὸν ἐξίσαζει τῷ ἀνθρώπῳ* (Asclepius [1], p. 383, 1.27).
123. "Constat quidem genus continere sub se tum species cum differentias sibi subjectas, saltem potestate: hoc enim videtur pertinere ad rationem totius potentialis seu universalis, alioquin non potest intelligi quomodo aptum sit de illis praedicari" (Eust. a Sto. Paulo, *Summa Philos.*, quoted by Gilson [3], p. 134).
124. Vaihinger [1], I, pp. 253f.
125. Cf. Aaron [1], pp. 60, 65.
126. "Jedes Ding der Wirklichkeit ist so beschaffen, daß ihm jede beliebige Bestimmung (gemäß dem Satze vom ausgeschlossenen Dritten) entweder zukommt oder nicht zukommt, *indes etwa* jeder Begriffsgegenstand, z.B., "das" Dreieck, unendlich viele Bestimmungen (wie Gleichseitigkeit, Rechtwinkligkeit) weder an sich hat noch nicht an sich hat (daher insofern dem Satze vom ausgeschlossenen Dritten nicht untersteht)" (Meinong [1], p. 16).
127. Fries [1], p. X contains a very interesting discussion. Cf. also Bolzano [1], § 45.
128. "Non multa, non unum" (Henry of Ghent, quoted by De Wulf [2], p. 207, note 2).
129. Ioannes a Sto. Thoma [1], p. 315: "Dicimus enim, quod natura secundum se neque est una nec plures, nec est alba nec est non alba [. . .] Nec tamen inde inferas verificari duas contradictorias de natura secundum se; hoc enim numquam est possibile, sed semper altera est vera, altera falsa".
130. Kant [3], p. 141.
131. "Der Mißverstand kommt bloß daher, daß man ein Prädicat eines Dinges zuvörderst von dem Begriff desselben absondert und nachher sein Gegentheil mit diesem Prädicate verknüpft, welches niemals einen Widerspruch mit dem Subjecte, sondern nur mit dessen Prädicate, welches mit jenem synthetisch verbunden worden, abgiebt, und zwar nur dann, wenn das erste und zweite Prädicat zu gleicher Zeit gesetzt werden" (*ibid.*).
132. In *Categoriae's* terminology "Ding" must mean *deutera ousia*. In the "bad" formulation "Ding" means *prōte ousia*.

133. But Frege would not say that *man* is predicated (UF) of ι'Callias.
134. Porphyry [1], p. 7, bottom.
135. Cf. Gilson [3], p. 456, *passim*.
136. Heimsoeth [1], p. 263; Kneale [1], p. 324.
137. "... praedicatum continetur in subjecto [...] Superiores gradus includuntur cum suis proprietatibus [...] in Petro" (Goudin [1], p. 168).
138. $x\varepsilon a \equiv \iota' x \subset a$. Cf. also Scholz [2], p. 151.
139. P. 40, especially note 21.
140. P. Hispanus [1], 2.09.
141. "Theorema 8, Propositio 17.
Propositio singularis est universalis, seu species propositionis universalis.
Demonstratio. Ex demonstratis illa propositio est universalis, cujus subjectum sumitur pro tota sua extensione. Atqui, subjectum propositionis singularis sumitur pro tota sua extensione: illius enim subjectum est unum individuum, quod non aliam habet extensionem, quam ipsum; et consequenter, non potest sumi, nisi secundum totam suam extensionem. Ergo propositio singularis est universalis. Quod erat probandum" (Joffre [1], p. 68).

5. *MERKMAL–EIGENSCHAFT*

Summary and general remarks. After a brief reference to Frege's distinction between *Merkmal* (mark) and *Eigenschaft* (property) of a concept (5.1), the philosophical significance of this distinction is pointed out, first, in general (5.2) and secondly, in the particular cases of the first antepredicamental rule (5.3) and the so-called "triplex status naturae" (5.4). Higher predicates could not be added easily to the standard Aristotelian predication theory (5.32) and they seem to have had a tendency to "descend" to the first-level predicates (5.5).

5.1 Exposition

Frege's distinction of *Merkmal* and *Eigenschaft*[1] is as simple as its applications in traditional philosophy are extraordinary. The doctrine appears in GRL[2], and its main motivation is Frege's insight into concepts as the *real* subjects of statements of number. According to this insight, it would be unnecessarily confusing to maintain the traditional predication theory. In fact, against such a predication theory, Frege holds that *animal* is not a property of *man*, but a mark of it; a property of *man*, for instance, is *to have n individuals. Animal* and *man* are properties of Socrates.

The distinction mark-property is *intensional*: *animal* is a part of *man.* Marks "make up" concepts as stones make up houses.[3]

5.2 The general philosophical significance of Frege's distinction

Before considering some particularly fruitful applications of Frege's distinction, it is well to observe that important chapters of the philosophical tradition are centered around the analysis of concepts as composed of marks. This is actually the way in which ideal being has been analysed since Plato.[4] Kant, although condemning concepts to be *leer*, although depriving them of *Bedeutung*, *Sinn* and *Inhalt*[5] unless an intuition was provided, permanently disects concepts into marks and thereby suggests that his concepts are quite complex structures. The well known distinctions of modern philosophy – clear, obscure, distinct or confused ideas – are elaborated according to the analysis of concepts into their marks.[6]

Leibniz says, "la définition nominale explique le nom par les marques de la chose"[7], and Kant affirms that the marks of a concept provide a partial knowledge of the thing.[8] It should be remembered that these basic terms of ontology (*chose*, *Ding*) are rather indifferent with respect to universality and singularity. *La chose* may be *man*, and *this man* too. This already indicates that it will be difficult to find a sharp distinction between the double function of being a mark of a concept and of being a property of an individual falling under the concept.[9]

The distinction between a mark of a concept and a property of the concept does not seem to have existed at all before Frege.[10] As will be seen in the next sections, traditional philosophy was compelled to introduce devices equivalent to Frege's distinction.

5.3 The first antepredicamental rule

5.31 *Formulation*

At the beginning of *Categoriae*, Aristotle gives the following rule: "Whenever one thing is predicated of another as of a subject, all things said of what is predicated will be said of the subject also."[11] A few pages after, the rule is formulated once more: "For everything said of what is predicated will be said of the subject also."[12]

The example immediately given by Aristotle shows that the meaning of the rule is what today would be called class-inclusion.[13] The Greek commentators stress that the rule is to be understood as applying only to essential predication[14], so that in the terminology of *Categoriae*[15] the rule should be formulated in the following way:

$$\frac{\mathrm{KU}(x, y)\ \&\ \mathrm{KU}(z, x)}{\mathrm{KU}(z, y).}$$

5.32 *Traditional predication theory cannot immediately be enriched with predicates of predicates in the modern sense*

This is obvious if one recalls that *animal* is a predicate of the predicate *man*.[16] To say that *genus* is a predicate of *animal*, or *species* a predicate of *man*, would lead to absurdities unless special qualifications are introduced. Both traditional philosophy and Frege had to deal with higher predicates, but the qualifications they introduced were different.[17]

5.33 *Aristotle's meager report on predicates of predicates*

The Aristotelian corpus seems to lack clear references about predicates of predicates. Hints are to be found mostly within contexts concerning Plato. Let us consider some texts.

1. *Topica* E, 7, 137b, 3–10.[18] The discussion is concerned with when a *proprium* may be recognized. The author suggests that one examine the Idea of the subject of the statement; thus it will be possible to decide whether a given property is a *proprium* or not. The name of the Idea is obtained by prefixing "αὐτὸ" to, for example, "ἄνθρωπος".[19] Aristotle explains that man-himself may have properties which do not belong to *man*, for instance *being motionless*. A classification of predicates results: (1) those belonging to man-himself *qua* Idea, (2) those belonging to man-himself *qua* man. It is important to observe the "reduplicative" approach, in contrast to Frege's distinction between properties of a concept and marks of a concept.[20]

2. *Metaphysics*, M, 4, 1079b, 3–11.[21] This is an anti-Plato argument appearing in book M but not in book A. Here predicates of predicates in the modern sense are clearly visible to the extent that Aristotle mentions a property like *to be an Idea*. The Idea of circle contains all the marks making up the essence of circle, *plus* the property *being an Idea of*. According to Bonitz[22], the aim of the argument is that this property cannot be placed on a level with the marks of the Idea of circle. We may observe that from Frege's point of view this requires the distinction of *Merkmal* and *Eigenschaft*.

3. *Metaphysics* A, 9, 990b, 29-34.[23] We are led to *double-itself*, and from this to *eternalness*. Without entering into the difficulties of the argument (whose aim is to show that there cannot be Ideas of things other than substances) it is worth noting that Aristotle suggests that higher predicates are "accidentally" shared by (said of) individuals.[24]

5.34 *The Greek commentators*

In this section the Greek commentaries on the antepredicamental rule will be considered in detail; some concluding remarks will be added.

Porphyry [1] comments on *Categoriae*[25] in the form of a dialogue. Once the rule is stated, the disciple asks: "But how may this be true?" The disciple observes that not only *animal*, but also *species* is predicated of *man*; nevertheless, Socrates is not a species, and this is the difficulty. The master replies by pointing to the phrase "as of a subject" in the formulation of the rule, and he observes that *to be a species* is rather an accident of *man*.

Simplicius [1][26], after presenting the rule and identifying it with *Barbara*, introduces the same objection. It is important to note that the objection is regarded as being made by "some people".[27] These "people" observe that *genus* being said of *animal*, and *animal* of *man*, would give rise to the false conclusion that man is a genus. Simplicius replies that *genus* is not said "as of a subject" of *animal*, and therefore the rule does not apply.

Dexippus [1][28] reiterates the same difficulties, but his response seems more complex. First, he employs the expression *τὰ ἀνωτέρω* to designate higher predicates, while "upwards" is normally meant in the line of class-inclusion (UO). Secondly, he states a sort of general rule for these higher predicates; they do not communicate their *logos* to their subjects, but only their names. Thirdly, he says that the other predicates (first-level predicates) may be submitted to the *dictum de omni* while this is not possible in the case of *being a genus* and *being a species*. Finally, Dexippus decides to approach the problem in metalinguistic terms; he says that higher predicates are rather names of names, whose function consists in indicating the universal application of other names.

Ammonius [1][29] formulates the same objection and replies in the same way: *genus* is not a predicate *de subjecto* of *animal*. Positively, Ammonius says that *genus* is predicated of *animal κατὰ συμβεβηκὸς καὶ κατὰ σχέσιν*; the first part of this phrase means that higher predication is accidental and the second part seems to refer to a metalinguistic approach, as in Dexippus.

Elias [1][30] develops a refined analysis of all the possibilities in which one may consider the premisses of the rule, but, curiously, he does not examine higher predicates. Similarly, Philoponus [2][31] does not consider higher predicates but only sophisms concerning metalanguage.

Finally, the Anonymous[32] maintains that the rule requires predication "of a subject", which avoids absurdities.

Let us conclude with the following remarks.

1. The problem of predicates of predicates is quite alive in the tradition of the Greek commentators.

2. The first antepredicamental rule suggests an interpretation in the modern sense of predicates of predicates, *not only* to us, but *also* to the Greek readers of Aristotle. But then, *why* do the *Categoriae* give such a misleading formulation of such a simple rule?

3. The commentators reply to the objections in two steps: one, negative, consists in drawing the reader's attention to the fact that the phrase "as of a subject" has not been respected; another, positive, consists in calling "accidental" that predication which applies between second-level and first-level concepts. In fact the *fallacia accidentis* will be a *locus* for higher predicates in the philosophical tradition.[33] This vague reference to the already much-employed "accidental predication" should be compared with Frege's clear distinction between marks of a concept and properties of a concept.

4. The notion of *mode* is (with respect to Aristotle's ontology) an extension quite similar to that of higher predicates. The former applies in the dimension substance-accident. It is interesting to consider that there is some parallel between the traditional efforts to add the notion of mode to the Aristotelian system, and those concerning higher predicates.[34]

5.35 *A critical history of the rule: A 'desideratum'. 'Dictum de omni', 'nota notae'. 'Sein ist gelten'.*

A critical and exhaustive history of the first antepredicamental rule would provide an insight into the various reactions of traditional philosophers to higher predication, down to the present. Commentators range from Barthélemy de St. Hilaire, who says, "cette règle est evidente"[35], to authors extensively discussing *utrum regula sit bona*.[36]

In the scholastic tradition the rule has been associated with second intentions.[37] There are interpreters who directly view the rule as identical with the *dictum de omni* and others who do not.[38] This obviously depends on the above mentioned sensitivity to higher predicates.

The same distinction applies to the principle *nota notae est nota rei*. If a philosopher like Husserl does not accept this formulation[39], it is because he is sensitive to the subtleties of predication. On the contrary, the easy acceptance of that principle, as in Kant[40], indicates that there is a lack of interest on his part in predicates of higher level.[41]

Lask [1] is an example of how these subtleties are not mere commentaries on Aristotle. Lask [1] argues against the confusion of *Sein* and *Gelten*, which confusion would depend on a fallacy quite similar to those wrongly suggested by the Aristotelian rule.[42]

5.4 The 'triplex status naturae'

5.41 *Presentation*

De Wulf [1] presents Avicenna's theory of the "triplex respectus essentiae" as a solution to the problem of universals which has been considered by all the great philosophers of the 13th century.[43]

Avicenna holds that we may consider a predicate as existing in the things (in the individuals), or as existing in the mind, *or as independent of any sort of existence.*[44]

5.42 *A probable reason for the doctrine*

Nizolius' clear mind confesses not to understand why there is a consideration of essence *in itself* apart from essence in the individuals and essence in the mind.[45]

The reason (or at least a reason) may be found in the following text of Avicenna.

> Animal est in se quiddam, et idem est utrum sit sensibile aut intellectum in anima. In se autem [. . .] nec est universale nec est singulare. Si enim in se esset universale, ita quod animalitas, ex hoc quod est animalitas, es[se]t universale, oporteret nullum animal esse singulare, sed omne animal esset universale.[46]

In the first part of this text one can observe Avicenna's general tendency to *isolate* predicates from anything which is not one of their own marks, and in particular from higher-level predicates.[47]

It may be assumed that thinkers influenced by the Aristotelian predication theory[48], and who are anxious to introduce higher predicates into their system, have the natural tendency to count higher predicates as marks of concepts (not as properties of concepts).[49] Under this assumption, Avicenna's opposite tendency (to separate those higher predicates from the marks of the concepts to which they apply) becomes meaningful.

Avicenna expresses this isolation of the higher-level predicates by means of a qualification: marks are predicated of essence-in-itself, higher properties are predicated of essence-in-the-mind. *Praedicari de praedicato contingit dupliciter*, will say Caietanus many centuries after.[50] If *universal* were said of *animal* . . . in-itself, then every animal would be a universal.[51] This conditional statement is, in my view, the key for understanding the mediaeval doctrine.

We may conclude that the doctrine on the "triplex respectus essentiae" is due (at least partially) to a peculiar situation in predication theory, and that it is intended (aside from other possible reasons) to overcome that situation.

5.43 *Misinterpretations of the doctrine*

To inquire about the sort of existence or about the ontological status of the essence taken in itself, would be, in my view, to miss the real significance of the doctrine in question. Only misleading requirements of symmetry could motivate this inquiry because in traditional ontology there is not a third possibility apart from being in the mind and being *in rerum natura*. As Suarez indicates, questions about the kind of existence of essences "in themselves" would lead to a *fourth* distinction.[52]

There is a remarkable text showing that the sense of the doctrine is primarily logical (predication theory): even "in the mind" the property *universal* does not belong to *man*.[53] Of course, even taking *man* as being "in the mind", universality is not a mark of it.

5.44 *The 'triplex status' and Frege's 'Merkmal-Eigenschaft': two alternative approaches*

In a recent exposition of the doctrine on the *triplex status*, given by Tonquedec [1], it may be corroborated that the *triplex status* is an alternative approach to higher predication. Tonquedec [1] accepts *à la lettre* the formulation of the first antepredicamental rule[54]; he assumes therefore that to say something about a predicate is to assign one of its marks to it. To this extent, one may not really say that *universality* is a predicate of *man*; and the Avicennian distinction of man-in-the-mind and man-in-itself (the "isolated" set of marks) appears as a means of still being able to have higher predicates without their descending to the individuals.

But this goal *could* be attained in another way, namely in Frege's way, and Tonquedec [1] actually undertakes this, although incidentally and perhaps unintentionally.[55] This other approach is indeed more elegant; one has simply to assume that predicates of *man* are not necessarily marks of *man*. But in a sense it is – it was – a more difficult way; it required substituting the theory of predication of the *Organon* by that of *Grundlagen der Arithmetik*.

5.5 The fear of the 'descensus' of higher predicates

Traditional logic may be characterized as being obliged to deal with higher predicates in a negative way: universality *non intrat* in the concept of man, i.e., it is not a mark of *man*. (Positively, it would be said, for instance, that universality belongs to *man qua* known.) The concern of traditional philosophers is to ensure that a predicate of higher level does not fall down to individuals.[56] In contemporary logic, perhaps thanks to Frege, such a logical fear is not present.

REFERENCES

1. "Mark" and "property"; for the translation, "Merkmal" = "mark" cf. my note in Birjukov [1], glossary.
2. § 53. In addition BGGE, p. 201; UBR, p. 9. The distinction is also mentioned in GRL, § 88, SUB, 42, GRG I, p. XIV (where "psychologism" – the word is not used – is said to be a reason why logicians did not make Frege's distinction); cf. following note.
3. "Ich vergleiche die einzelnen Merkmale eines Begriffes den Steinen, aus denen ein Haus besteht . . ." (UBR, p. 9).
   "Ich kann eine Vorstellung von einem schweren Geschoße haben. Diese enthält dann als Teilvorstellung die der Geschwindigkeit. Diese Teilvorstellung ist aber nicht Eigenschaft der Gesamtvorstellung, ebenso wenig wie Deutschland Eigenschaft Europas ist" (GED, p. 70).
   Of course, Frege says that marks are "logische Teile" (UGG, p. 373). But it should be observed how persistent Frege is in speaking of marks as *composing* concepts. Cf. GRL, § 53, GRG I, p. 3, 24.
4. Cf. Becker [1] (first *Unters.*); Cornford [1] (the structure of the world of forms), etc.
5. Kant [3], pp. 204, 205.
6. In the 16th century Caietanus gives careful definitions combining the analysis of a concept into its marks with the subordination (UO) of concepts. Caietanus [1], *proe.*
7. Leibniz [1], V, p. 18.
8. Kant [2], *Einleitung*, VIII.
9. A traditional textbook (19th century) says: ". . . L'idée inadequate nous present

l'objet au moyen de caractères qui ne suffisent pas à nous le faire distinguer de toute *autre* ... par example si je me represente *le poisson* comme un animal qui nage" (Mercier [1], p. 83, italics ours).
It may be presumed that *le poisson* or *l'objet* are those *natures*, typical of traditional philosophy, which are neutral with respect to singularity and universality.
I would not assert, however, that Frege was exactly the first in introducing the distinction mark (of a concept)-property (of an individual falling under that concept). Höfler [1], 15, 21 (first ed., 1890) introduces practically the same distinction, without indicating his sources. Eisler [2] article "Merkmal", gives as the central meaning something close to Frege's distinction; the same applies with respect to some of the other reported meanings (Külpe, Honecker).
In the '90's a disciple of Brentano said: "Im übrigen ist der Terminus "Merkmal" einer von denjenigen, über dessen Anwendung eine Einigung unter den Logikern noch herbeizuführen ist ..." (Marty [1], p. 214).

10. Cf., for instance, Trendelenburg [1], pp. 72–73 (in particular note 2). Commenting on Aristotle, Trendelenburg says: "Der Theil des ganzen Begriffes ist das Merkmal." But, at the very most, this implies the Fregean distinction between being a mark of a concept and being a property of the individual falling under that concept, not the distinction between a mark of a concept and a property of the concept. Trendelenburg, in agreement with traditional standards, holds in fact that a mark of a concept is a property of the concept: ". . . das Merkmal als ein Begriff des Begriffes ..." (p. 73). "Und jedes Merkmal eines Begriffs darf von ihm ausgesagt werden" (Mauthner [1], III, p. 360).
A similar distinction is that of "praedicatio intrinseca" and "extrinseca", an example of the latter being "animal est genus" (Signoriello [1], "praedicatio"). Of course, there may be incidental or isolated distinctions coinciding with that of Frege (cf. Section 5.44).
11. Aristotle [1.1], 1b, 10. It should be observed that Aristotle [3.1] does not translate the *essential* phrase "as of a subject".
12. Aristotle [1.1], 3b, 4.
13. *Man* predicated of *this man* and *animal* of *man*; therefore, *animal* is predicated of *this man*.
14. Cf. Section 5.34.
15. Cf. Section 1.2.
16. Cf. Section 4.3.
17. Cf. Section 5.4.
18. Aristotle [5].
19. "Man-himself" (Aristotle [3.1]) or "ipse homo" (Pacius [1]).
20. Pacius sums up the Aristotelian text in the following way: "Rei proprium convenire debet etiam ideae, non quatenus est idea simpliciter, sed quatenus illius rei est idea. Hinc refutatur proprium, si ideae non convenit. Confirmatur, si ideae convenit, quatenus est illius rei, cui proprium attribuitur, idea" (Pacius [1], p. 685).
21. Aristotle [2].
22. Cf. Tricot's interesting note in Aristotle [2.1], II, p. 737. Bonitz's commentary is partially quoted there; it is interesting because it uses the Latin term "nota" to designate those "elements" which make up an Idea (*biped*, *animal* in the case of *man*). Frege's "Merkmal" is the exactly corresponding word in German.
23. Aristotle [2].

24. I follow Ross in Aristotle [2], II, p. 197.
25. Pp. 80–81.
26. Pp. 51f.
27. τινες δὲ ἀποροῦσι (*ibid.*, p. 52, 1.9).
28. P. 26.
29. P. 30.
30. P. 153.
31. P. 38.
32. Anonymous [1], p. 7.
33. Petrus Hispanus [1], 7.45; also 6.06.
34. Alcorta [1], p. 14.
35. Aristotle [3.2], I, p. 57 note.
36. Duns Scotus [2].
37. "Ubi notandum, quod haec regula habet veritatem quando est praedicatio essentialis superioris de inferiori. Et hoc notatur per illud quod dicitur "ut de subiecto". Et ideo si arguatur: Sortes est homo, homo est species, ergo sortes est species, non valet, quia cum species sit secunda intentio et ens rationis non praedicatur essentialiter de homine" (Nicolaus Dorbelli [1]).
38. Tonquedec [1] (p. 546 below): "Dire: "Si *A* est attribut de tout *B*, et *B* attribut de tout *Γ*, *A* est attribut de tout *Γ*" [. . .] c'est dire équivalemment: "Tout ce qui s'affirme de l'attribut devra s'affirmer du sujet"."
    Joseph [1], on the contrary, affirms that the antepredicamental rule is not the *dictum de omni* (p. 50). Of course, these are but two examples.
39. Husserl [1], I, § 41.
40. Kant [2], § 63.
41. Cf. Section 7.56.
42. Lask [1], (p. 120): "Dann kommt man immer, wie jetzt rekapituliert werden mag, zu folgenden Substitutionen: Sein ist Kategorie, Kategorie gilt, also Kategorie ist ein Gelten, folglich ist auch Sein ein Gelten."
43. De Wulf [1], I, n. 187.
44. "Essentiae vero rerum aut sunt in ipsis rebus, aut sunt in intellectu; unde habent tres respectus: unus respectus essentiae est secundum quod ipsa est non relata ad aliquid tertium esse, nec ad id quod sequitur eam secundum quod ipsa est sic. Alius respectus est secundum quod est in his singularibus. Et alius secundum quod est in intellectu" (Avicenna [1], *Logica*, f. 2b).
45. "At enim inquiunt, hominem, et caetera huiusmodi, tribus modis esse posse, et tria quodammodo esse habere, unum in mente et cognitione nostra, quod nuncupant esse mentale, sive esse cognitum; alterum in singularibus et individuis suis, quod vocant esse existentiae, sive esse fundamentale; tertium, ut ipsi loquuntur, in se et in natura, sive essentia sive quidditate sua, quod appellant esse essentiae, sive esse quidditatis . . .
    . . . Nam ego quidem probe intelligo quid sit esse in mente et cognitione nostra, et quid sit esse in singularibus et individuis, sed quid sit esse in se, et in natura sive essentia sive quidditate sua prorsus non intelligo; ac nec eos quidem qui hunc tertium essendi modum finxerunt, satis arbitror intellexisse, quid comminiscerentur . . ." (Nizolius [1], Lib. 1, cap. VII).
46. Avicenna [1], *Logica*, f. 12a, below.
47. For example: "Diffinitio enim equinitatis est praeter diffinitionem universalitatis. Nec universalitas continetur in diffinitione equinitatis. Equinitas etenim habet

diffinitionem que non eget universalitate. Sed est cui accidit universalitas. Unde ipsa equinitas non est aliquid nisi equinitas tantum. Ipsa enim ex se nec est multa nec unum nec est existens in his sensibilibus nec in anima, nec est aliquid horum potentia vel effectu, ita ut hoc contineatur intra essentiam equinitatis" (Avicenna [1], *Metaphysics*, f. 86c, below).

48. Where *animal* is a predicate of *man*, and the latter a predicate of *Socrates*, i.e., where *animal* is a predicate of a predicate (cf. Section 4.3).
49. Caietanus [1], n. 75 (pp. 117–118), is a remarkable text for showing how all these historical motivations are at work, and actually come into conflict. An Aristotelian logician, who already employs the expression "predicate of predicate" for class-inclusion, and who also has some interest in higher predicates in the true sense, begins by *having to remove* an objection. As Caietanus says (commenting on Aquinas [3]): "In hac parte tertia capituli huius talem obiectionem ex supradictis excludere intendit: quia quod praedicatur de praedicato praedicatur et de subjecto; sed species praedicatur de homine, quod est praedicatum respectu Sortis: ergo species praedicatur de Sorte . . ."
50. *Ibid.*
51. This argument will be repeated down through the centuries; to appreciate its influence, it suffices to remember that it appears in Aquinas [3], p. 27 (cap. III): ". . . si enim communitas esset de intellectu hominis, tunc in quolibet inveniretur humanitas inveniretur communitas, et hoc falsum est quia in Socrate non invenitur communitas aliqua . . ." Perhaps already Alfarabi [1], p. 111.
   De Wulf [2] (Chap. III, sect. III, § 5: "La théorie des universaux et le problème de l'individuation") includes rich references to the "triplex respectus", and in particular that the Avicennian argument "is an idea expressed many times in the *Summa* and *Quodlibeta* of Henry of Ghent." Cf. Gomez Caffarena [1].
52. Suarez [1], VI, sect. III, 6. Cf. De Wulf, [2] p. 207.
53. We give Gilson's paraphrase: "Or non seulement il est indifférent à la nature qu'elle existe dans l'intellect ou dans un être particulier, donc qu'elle soit universelle ou singulière, mais même si on la prend telle qu'elle existe dans l'intellect, elle ne possède pas immédiatement et de soi l'universalité. Sans doute l'universalité lui appartient alors en vertu de notre manière de la concevoir, mais l'universalité ne fait pas pour cela partie de son concept premier; . . ." (Gilson [2], p. 450).
54. For instance, p. 154. Cf. note 38.
55. P. 163 note: "L'essence humaine est affirmable de plusieurs individus, mais cette propriété ne convient qu'à elle, et non aux individus où elle se réalise. On affirme des individus l'essence, et non l'affirmabilité".
   This is "Merkmal-Eigenschaft".
56. Speaking of properties (essences), Albertus Magnus says: "Accipitur enim aliquando secundum quod est absoluta per intellectum a suis appellatis, sicut quando dicitur, homo praedicatur de pluribus: nihil enim est in appellatis ipsis quod de pluribus praedicetur; *tale enim praedicatum contingit formae, ita quod non contingit appellatis* (Albertus Magnus [1], Lib. 7, tract. 2, cap. 1, italics ours).
   Why is it necessary to stress that a higher property is not a mark? See also Suarez [1], VI, sect. 2, 10. "Unitas universalis" and "unitas formalis" are characterized by the fact that the former does not "pass" to the individuals, while the latter does. Cf. *ibid.*, VI, 3, 1. Leibniz [1], IV, p. 120 ("Defensio Trinitatis . . .") regards the *suppositiones* as a device for avoiding the "falling down" of higher predicates: "Hoc principio adhibito, Scholasticorum taediosis circa suppositiones praeceptis

carere possumus. V.g. "animal est genus, Petrus est animal, ergo Petrus est genus". Respondeo; majorem non esse universalem, *neque enim is qui est animal est genus*" (italics ours). Again, *genus* is not a mark of *animal.*

Incidentally, also the "suppositio naturalis" (cf. Petrus Hispanus [1], 6.04) should be understood within the context of the *triplex respectus*; otherwise it certainly appears unclear (cf. A. Church, in Runes [1], "suppositio personalis").

6. FUNCTION

Summary and general remarks. The present chapter begins with the notion of function as found in the *Begriffsschrift* of 1879 and some related questions (6.1–6.3). The distinction function–argument is first considered from the point of view of its being preferred by Frege to the traditional subject–predicate (6.1). Frege's intention is to introduce a symbolism for relational propositions, which satisfies an old logical *desideratum* (6.11). In this context, there is occasion to mention Frege's relation with a member of Brentano's school, A. Marty (6.2). Finally, the notion of function in BG is presented (6.3).

The principle of sharply distinguishing concepts and objects was considered in 2.61; it is again discussed in the present chapter because concepts are the paradigmatic case of functions. The tendency of the present research is to distinguish that principle as much as possible from the puzzling Fregean idea of unsaturatedness (6.41 and 6.42). I point out the "good" criterion for distinguishing concepts and objects, independent of oddities of unsaturatedness (6.43), and I stress that Frege had a good grasp at what older philosophers would call *unitas formalis* (*ibid.*).

There follows a discussion of Kerry's criticism, to which I assign special importance, a maieutic significance in Frege's intellectual evolution (6.5).

I try to show that Kerry's interpretation of GRL and UFT is inadequate, but at the same time one must acknowledge that Frege fully accepts Kerry's criticism, as if it were perfectly adequate (6.6). One may escape this embarrassing situation by suggesting that Frege happens to have "now", at the time of BGGE, the ideas previously assigned to him by Kerry. If Frege had these ideas already in GRL and UFT, that was not duly expressed in these works. In any case, about 1890 Frege does have *Ungesättigtheit*, and this fundamental notion of his philosophy has to be examined (6.7).

First it is pointed out that there is no opposition between the mathematical *mapping* and the philosophical *Begriff* which Frege tried to unify under the heading "function" (6.71). Unsaturatedness applies to both names of functions and to functions themselves (6.72), but functions are . . . the designata of unsaturated names (6.73). Frege's paradox is mentioned (6.74) and it is observed that his semantics lacks a factor which older semanticists used to consider (6.75). The oddities of unsaturatedness are perhaps due to an ambiguity in the word "function" (6.76). It is easy to find unsaturatedness of concepts or of names in the philosophical tradition before (6.771–2) or after Frege (6.773).

Finally, Frege's idea of *levels* is considered: how it was influenced by unsaturatedness (6.81) and how Frege managed to combine levels and unsaturatedness (6.82–6.83).

6.1 Function–argument versus subject–object (rather than versus subject–predicate)

In the very prologue to the BG Frege announces to logicians that a noteworthy improvement in his symbolic language with respect to traditional logic is the substitution of the distinction subject–predicate by a new one, function–argument.[1]

It should first be observed that Frege is not attacking here the traditional doctrine according to which universal terms are subjects of first-level properties (*man* is *mortal*). Secondly, it must be remembered that in BG "function" applies to linguistic entities[2]; this is important because Frege rejects "subject–predicate" on the ground that this distinction is too closely dependent on grammar and language, which could suggest that "function–argument" is intended to stress a non-linguistic approach.

The *Begriffsschrift* (Frege's symbolic logic) is not supposed to record rhetorical aspects of language, but only *conceptual content*, i.e., "what counts for deduction".[3] In the sentence "The Greeks defeated the Persians", there is a subject ("the Greeks"), and an "object"[4] ("the Persians"). If we say "the Persians were defeated by the Greeks" we have still the same conceptual content (Frege says), but we want to stress the importance of the Persians, making of them the "subject".[5] Frege the mathematician is well trained for viewing Persians and Greeks as terms of equal importance, standing in a certain relation. Moreover, what grammar calls "object" tends to be absorbed by the whole predicate.[6] In order to both prevent relational propositions from collapsing into subject–predicate ones, and to express the "equality of importance" of so-called subjects and objects, there was no better means than introducing the terminology "function–argument".[7] The latter is thus opposed rather to "subject–object" than to "subject–predicate". In fact, Frege has little to say about "predicate" in BG; he trivially finishes by identifying it with "assertion".[8] Only afterwards will this term be resurrected and become essential in Frege's philosophy.[9]

6.11 *The analysis function–argument satisfies an old logical 'desideratum'*

Without considering earlier periods of the history of logic, where relational statements had already been an object of research, it is interesting to analyse the way in which Port-Royal deals with this kind of statements. In Port-Royal Logic relational propositions are concealed under the designation of "propositions complexes" (or "composées"). A particular case of them are those considered by Frege in BG, namely, such as contain a "subject" and an "object".[10] The authors of 'The Art of Thinking' show high esteem for so-called complex propositions and complex syllogisms.[11] They wonder why these syllogisms have not been sufficiently studied, while the useless "syllogismes simples" absorb the attention of logicians.[12] Still, Port-Royal does not make the decision of viewing relational propositions as being built by the introduction of proper names in the $n(n \geqq 2)$ argument-places of a (name of a) function. Port-Royal remains in the area of monadic predicates, and a sentence like "Brutus a tué un tyran" is expanded into "Brutus a tué quelqu'un et celui qu'il a tué etait un tyran."[13]

6.2 **Frege and Marty**

Frege, like *L'art de penser*, does not make of negation an opposite of assertion, but counts it as an element of the proposition to be asserted.[14] Marty's strongest criticism concerns precisely this treatment of negation.[15] He applauds Frege's "purification" of the term "Urteil", restricting it to mean the act of acceptance of a given proposition, but Marty further distinguishes two species of assertion (*Urteil*): *Anerkennung* and *Verwerfung* (this is of course Brentano's school).

Marty attacks Frege's distinction of *beurteilbarer* and *unbeurteilbarer*

Inhalt. For Marty, it is irrelevant whether the content to be rejected or accepted is a simple or a complex one.[16] Without entering into the discussion of how a simple content like *Haus*[17] can be at all the subject-matter of an *Urteil*, I shall only refer to my previous section 4.431.

Marty does not seem to appreciate the real meaning of Frege's rejection of subject–predicate (i.e., that it is actually a rejection of subject–object[18]); he thinks that Frege's reference to the "unique predicate"[19] is made in seriousness (in which case, of course, Marty has to criticize Frege for demanding a subject–predicate structure for every sentence).[20]

6.3 Function–argument in 'Begriffsschrift'

In BG Frege affirms that one may imagine some symbols of a given sentence as replaceable by others, while the rest of the sentence is supposed to be fixed.[21] The former are then called the *argument(s)* and the latter the *function*. Function and argument are officially defined as linguistic entities.[22] Although the first examples given by Frege respect the "natural" order of individuals and properties, this is not at all necessary.[23]

"The number 20 can be represented as the sum of four squares" and "every positive integer can be represented as the sum of four squares" may *not* be considered as being derived from one function[24] (i.e., "being representable as the sum of four squares") by means of two successive arguments ("the number 20" and "every positive integer"). Actually "every positive integer" is *not* an argument but rather the indication that for *any* argument of a given sort (positive integers) a true sentence will result. One may somehow say that the argument is *indeterminate*, although this indetermination should be carefully distinguished from the later unsaturatedness. In BG, indetermination means universal quantification ("any").[25] Frege affirms that the distinction function–argument does not concern *conceptual content* as long as both function and argument are completely determined; if the argument (or the function) becomes indeterminate, then that distinction does concern content.[26] I understand this in the following way: a given sentence may be arranged in different ways according to what is argument and what is function, and thereby "what counts for deduction" remains the same. But this is not guaranteed if a name, in that sentence, is replaced by a universally quantified variable.

In his discussion of the sentences, "the number 20 can be represented as the sum of four squares" and "every positive integer can be represented as the sum of four squares", Frege introduces a distinction which may be considered as a prelude to his later notion of *levels*. He says that *the number 20* and *every positive integer* are not concepts of the same rank (*Rang*).[27] *The number 20* is a *selbständige Vorstellung*, while "every positive integer" acquires a meaning only in the context of a sentence. Incidentally, this shows that we have not yet arrived at the sharp distinction of objects and concepts (required five years later in GRL). Frege, here, calls *the number 20* a concept; also in BG he says that "hydrogen" designates an object[28]; we have already mentioned similar confusions in the treatment of identity.[29]

6.4 Concept–object in 'Grundlagen der Arithmetik'

6.41 *An immediate reason for the distinction of concepts and objects. No need for paradoxes*

We have already referred to the clear Fregean distinction of concepts and objects (or of names of concepts and objects).[30] We said that its main motivation was the basic Fregean insight into number as concerns concepts, not objects (falling under those concepts). Also, we stressed that the sharp distinction should not necessarily be identified with the extreme form it has received later in Frege's works, namely, unsaturatedness. We shall now consider what Frege himself suggests as a more particular motivation which led him to the distinction of concepts and objects.

After stating in GRL the principle of clearly separating *Begriff* and *Gegenstand*, Frege provides a justification of it:

> Was den dritten Punkt betrifft, so ist es nur Schein, wenn man meint, einen Begriff zum Gegenstande machen zu können, ohne ihn zu verändern. Von hieraus ergiebt sich die Unhaltbarkeit einer verbreiteten formalen Theorie der Brüche, negativen Zahlen u.s.w.[31]

In this text the critical phrase is "einen Begriff zum Gegenstand zu machen". In view of the later polemics with Kerry (BGGE) this might be understood as referring to the difficulties of *Ungesättigtheit*. But I deliberately prefer to read GRL under the assumption that unsaturatedness and its paradoxes do not yet exist; this approach does not try to force the text, but seeks any sound interpretation which enables us to avoid accepting unsaturatedness as belonging to Frege's early periods. Now, the expression "to make of a concept an object" may be assigned enough meaning in GRL without having to appeal to unsaturatedness. One "transforms" a concept into an object when one prefixes the definite article to the name of the concept.[32] Unless existence and uniqueness are ensured, the definite article may lead to meaningless statements.[33] This is precisely one of the mistakes of the "formalists" (the proponents of the "formale Theorie" of arithmetic) who uncritically pass from the concept *to be a square root of —1* to the object, *the square root of —1*.[34] Frege's above quoted text, and in general his requirement of sharply distinguishing concepts and objects, may be interpreted as a warning against this confusion, without implying the problems of unsaturatedness (BGGE). When Meinong thought of "the" round square, he was probably involved in a similar confusion.[35]

6.42 *A problematic definition of concept and object in 'Grundlagen der Arithmetik'*

Frege considers the following sentence: "die Richtung von *a* ist gleich der Richtung von *b*" and he says that *die Richtung von a* appears here as an object. This statement is immediately justified by the following footnote:

> Der bestimmte Artikel deutet dies an. Begriff ist für mich ein mögliches Prädicat eines singularen beurtheilbaren Inhalts, Gegenstand ein mögliches Subject eines solchen. Wenn wir in dem Satze: "Die Richtung der Fernrohraxe ist gleich der Richtung der Erdaxe", die Richtung der Fernrohraxe als Subject ansehen, so ist das Prädicat "gleich der Richtung der Erdaxe". Dies ist ein Begriff. Aber die Richtung der Erdaxe ist nur ein Teil des Prädicates; sie ist ein Gegenstand, da sie auch zum Subjecte gemacht werden kann.[36]

In this text one should not demand a rigorous distinction of name and designatum, i.e., whether or not a concept or a predicate are signs; this is not the point here.[37]

Is it possible to understand this text without already seeing in it the ideas of BGGE? Frege seems to clearly imply that something (*die Richtung der Erdaxe*) is an object and not a concept, because it may become *a* or *the*[38] subject of .... At this point we must pause to ask how our account of Frege's thought should be completed: "of *the given* (*a given*) sentence" or "of *any* sentence"? The latter would mean that concepts cannot be subjects of sentences[39], or that they cannot be objects. This is probably how Kerry has understood our text; in fact, he replies that concepts may also be objects (man is a species). But Frege's text does *not* at all indicate which of the two alternative readings should be adopted. He is indeed speaking of *a given* sentence: "die Richtung der Fernrohraxe ist gleich der Richtung der Erdaxe", and the last phrase of our text – without exegetical *tour de force* – may be expanded into "da sie auch zum Subjecte *dieses Satzes* gemacht werden kann". This interpretation is not only possible but also finds positive support in the context. The context indicates that Frege wishes to prove that in the given sentence one entity is recognized under two different guises ("to be a direction of *a*" and "to be a direction of *b*"). Having said that *die Richtung von a* is an object, he now warns against taking *die Richtung von b* as the predicate of the given sentence.[40] The given sentence may be analysed in at least three ways: (1) "... gleich der Richtung der Erdaxe", (2) "die Richtung der Fernrohraxe ist gleich ...", (3) "... gleich ...".[41] In the footnote on page 77 of GRL Frege stresses – I believe – that not only (1) but also (2) or (3) are to be considered. Taking this fact into account, we are justified in reading "zum Subjecte *dieses Satzes*" without the danger of assigning to Frege superfluous or meaningless words. The point is that this interpretation does not already involve us in the oddities of BGGE, i.e., it does not exclude the possibility of having the predicate (concept) "gleich der Richtung der Erdaxe" as subject of *some other sentence*, for instance, "*gleich der Richtung der Erdaxe* is a non-empty concept". This would be a singular[42] *beurtheilbarer Inhalt*, a singular statement with a universal term in *suppositio simplex*. In these sentences concepts would be objects, just as Kerry insisted.

Of course we also have to consider the first clause of the quoted text: "der bestimmte Artikel deutet dies an", i.e., the definite article indicates that an object is the designatum of the expression which it introduces. Is this supposed *to exclude* that designatum from being simultaneously a concept? In other words, does GRL already imply that "the concept F" is not the name of a concept? Kerry was able to give an affirmative answer to this question; I cannot provide either a positive or a negative answer.

6.43 *The 'good' criterion for distinguishing concepts and objects. Concept as 'unitas formalis'*[43]

When *concept* in GRL is opposed to *Ding*[44] or when it is characterized as *mögliches Prädicat*[45], the Kantian language of Frege becomes evident.[46] The same Kantian influence is found in the first appearance of unsaturatedness in the Fregean corpus, where concepts are described as entities which in themselves lack *einen Sinn*.[47] This should be taken into account lest one be tempted to interpret what in GRL is merely Kant's or traditional unsaturatedness, as Frege's unsaturatedness.

In my view the best formula in GRL for characterizing concepts and objects (names of concepts and names of objects) is the following: "Bei einem Begriffe fragt es sich immer, ob etwas und was etwa unter ihn falle. Bei einem Eigennamen sind solche Fragen sinnlos."[48] This means that there are entities which may only be referents in the fundamental logical relation (UF), i.e., that there are ultimate subjects of predication. But the quoted criterion, which is obviously but a restatement of traditional, well-known doctrines does not exclude concepts from being referents in that relation.

While the Aristotelian tradition, as well as Kant, had considered concepts as unsaturated entities (in a sense partially identical to Frege's *Ungesättigtheit*[49]), the fact that concepts or universals are well-determined entities had also been stressed. Of course, the "individuality" of concepts was regarded as weaker than the individuality of real things, as a *unitas formalis* and not as a *unitas numerica*; still, it was a *unitas*. This "positive" aspect of universals is also visible in GRL. Indeed, it is much more apparent than the brief and ambiguous references to unsaturatedness which Kerry will exploit in anticipated complicity with Frege. Not only are Frege's concepts "solid" entities, as far as they have a complicated structure of marks, but they are also the key for solving the difficulties inherent in the Euclidean definition of number in a way which presupposes that concepts are ideal *Einheiten* in front – above – the individuals.[50] Also, Frege's account of abstraction presupposes that concepts are ideal *Einheiten*; in direct proportion to the way in which Frege rejects Cantor's "impossible abstractions"[51], he ought to stress the "unity", the "individuality", of concepts. From two cats one does not arrive at a set of *Einsen* (of one's) but to one concept, *cat*.[52] It is due to concepts that one may introduce order into *heaps*, making of them *classes*[53]; concepts have a "determining", "defining" power which Frege proudly proclaims to be superior to the unifying power of synthetic apperception.[54] On such grounds a reader of GRL (who does not yet know the later works, in particular BGGE) would think that Frege allows the viewing of concepts as possible subjects of higher-level concepts in a more open way than the later "implicit" higher predication.[55] Concepts in GRL appear as entities so well defined that expressions of the form "the concept *F*" seem quite adequate for expressing the "saturated" aspect of concepts, and are more than mere "explanatory language".[56]

But the later Frege – helped by his reviewer Kerry – will proceed as if none of this had been said in GRL.

Before entering the analysis of Kerry's criticism, let us complete the presentation of the notion of concept in GRL by observing that concepts are objective[57] and are not necessarily the result of a process of abstraction; they may be empty.[58] Further, concepts may have exactly one individual, in which case they should still be distinguished from it.[59] Inconsistency among the marks of a concept is not a reason for banishing this concept from logic; all that logic asks from a concept is its *scharfe Begrenzung*, namely, that one may decide for every object, whether it falls under the concept.[60] Strictly speaking, one can show only that a concept is "consistent" by pointing to an individual falling under it.[61] Even if a concept looks "consistent", there is still no guarantee as to the existence of individuals.[62]

6.5 Kerry's criticism

6.51 *Presentation*

Kerry [1] is devoted to an examination of Frege's works up to UFT (published in 1885). In Kerry [1] Frege is considered as representing a view opposed to Kant's philosophy of arithmetic. After an expository section, Kerry begins his criticism by saying that he would first like to clear up a general question, namely, the Fregean distinction of objects and concepts.[63] Kerry observes that he himself has already described that distinction as something ultimate, but he has not thereby implied that the properties *to be a concept* and *to be an object* would exclude each other. The latter does not follow from the former, just as from the fact that the relation between father and son is something ultimate, it does not follow that someone cannot be a father and a son at the same time. Kerry affirms that Frege – the author of GRL – does maintain such an extreme view as regards concepts and objects, namely, that *to be a concept* and *to be an object* are mutually exclusive properties. But let us quote Kerry's own presentation of this, which we shall have to examine in detail.

> Frege hingegen verficht, wie wir gesehen haben, den Satz, daß ein Begriff nicht zum Gegenstande und ein Gegenstand nicht zum Begriffe gemacht werden könne, ohne daß Begriff oder Gegenstand verändert würden; er behandelt also die Differenz zwischen Begriff und Gegenstand nicht als relative, sondern als absolut. Demgemäß definirt er: "Begriff ist für mich ein mögliches Prädikat eines singulären beurtheilbaren Inhalts, Gegenstand ein mögliches Subject eines solchen", und als ein Kriterium, durch welches ganz allgemein Gegenstände und Begriffe sollen unterschieden werden können, gibt er an: "die Namen der Gegenstände werden mit dem bestimmten Artikel, diejenigen der Begriffe mit dem unbestimmten Artikel, gebraucht" (GRL, p. 80 Anm.). Definition und Kriterium sind unzutreffend.[64]

It should be first observed that the more qualified the reviewers, the less exact seems to be their understanding of the object of their criticism. Neither Cantor nor Marty[65] understood Frege, and Kerry is still another case. Kerry expresses his surprise that Frege in GRL defines *concept* and *object* by means of *subject* and *predicate*, while these notions had already been dismissed by the author of BG and substituted by *function-argument*.[66] This simply means that Kerry – like Marty – has not grasped the real motivation of the terminological change undertaken by the author of BG.[67] Further, Kerry feels much concerned with the "identification" of *Begriff* and *Begriffsumfang* suggested by GRL p. 80, note.[68] This is a serious misunderstanding of the whole context of GRL, for in this work Frege was not, in fact, looking for an essential definition of number, but rather for a "characterization" of number; consequently, the fact that he used two different characterizations (once with *concept*, another time with *extension of a concept*) does not imply that he identifies these two characterizations. Thus, one should not be surprised that Kerry is mistaken in some other ways, which we shall consider next.

6.52 *The 'absolute' separation of concepts and objects*

Let us examine, in Kerry's text quoted in the preceding section, the phrase "wie wir gesehen haben". Kerry refers to his previous expository section and I believe that he means the following passage:

> Die objectiven Vorstellungen werden eingeteilt in "Gegenstände und Begriffe": einen Begriff kann man nicht zum Gegenstande machen, ohne ihn zu verändern[5] und Gegenstände darf man nicht als Begriffe auffassen[6].[69]

In the footnote corresponding to "5)", Kerry refers to GRL, p. X; in that corresponding to "6)" he refers to GRL, p. 72 (§ 60) and p. 116.

Let us begin with the second part: objects cannot be transformed into concepts. Of course this is as old as Greek philosophy, and it actually means that there are ultimate subjects of predication, say *Callias* (to use Aristotle's example[70]). The only non-trivial detail is that Kerry seems to establish a connection that is not obvious[71] between two distant phrases of GRL; in fact the text of GRL, p. 72 (referred to by Kerry) says that the self-subsistence of numbers is only intended to exclude its use as predicate or attribute, *wodurch seine Bedeutung etwas verändert wird*. I would not commit myself to an exact interpretation of the latter phrase, but in any case I think Frege means that numbers are ultimate subjects of predication (like Callias), so that to treat them as predicates or concepts, as universals, would be the same as to treat Callias as a predicate. Obviously, Callias' significance would be thereby *etwas verändert*. "Verändern" here means to falsely treat an entity as something which it is not. The other text (GRL, p. 116) referred to by Kerry[72] suggests that he has been very impressed by this "Verändern" which falsifies objects into concepts. Now Kerry seems to connect this "verändert" (which concerns the "transformation" of objects into concepts) with a previous occurrence of the same verb, where the "transformation" takes place in the inverse direction: from concepts to objects: *es ist nur Schein, wenn man meint, einen Begriff zum Gegenstande machen zu können, ohne ihn zu verändern.*[73] We have seen[74] that *this* "verändern" might be understood in the sense that it is impossible to pass from $\varphi(x)$ to $(\imath x)\varphi x$ without "transforming" the concept denoted by "$\varphi(x)$". This latter "transformation" is quite different from the former one, but perhaps Kerry was inclined to regard both cases in terms of symmetry;

to treat a concept as an object is to "falsify" its nature just as it is to treat Callias as a universal. In any case Kerry reads the second "verändern" as if it established the impossibility of having a concept playing the role of object (with respect to a higher concept). Curiously enough, Kerry happens to be right, at least with respect to the author of BGGE, if not with respect to the author of GRL. One wonders how Kerry was able to foresee the future doctrines of Frege simply on the basis of the texts of GRL which he quotes.

6.53 *Consequences of the 'absolute' separation of concepts and objects*

Next, Kerry writes (in the text quoted in Section 6.51) that according (*demgemäß*) to the premiss of the "absolute" separation of concepts and objects, Frege gives a *definition* of "concept" and "object" and a *criterion* with which to distinguish them from one another.

6.531 The 'definition'

Kerry could neither justify his statement that Frege in GRL supported an "absolute" separation of concepts and objects, nor can he now justify his statement that Frege "defines" concepts and objects in GRL according (*demgemäß*) to that "absolute" separation. Obviously the fragment of GRL, p. 77, footnote, quoted by Kerry [75] does not entail such a separation (that *to be a concept* and *to be an object* are mutually exclusive properties). For this, the text should be completed by some explicit premiss, for example, that an entity which can appear as a predicate cannot appear as a subject (plus some explanations about "predicate" and "subject" in order to make more precise that impossibility). But nothing like this is to be found in GRL; on the contrary, GRL forces the imagination of a traditional (after Port-Royal) reader, who has not been trained to think of levels of concepts, and demands from him the capacity to distinguish UO and UF between two concepts. A reader of GRL is asked to think of entities given under quite different guises: a number may be hidden under Julius Caesar [76] or a geometrical direction under England.[77] Thus the reader does not see why the same entity could not be hidden at one time under the form of *subject* and another time under the form of *predicate*. The reference to unsaturatedness in GRL [78] may be regarded as an echo of traditional ideas (where unsaturatedness did not lead to paradoxes thanks to a semantic factor lacking in Frege [79]). And we have seen how a problematic text could be interpreted in still another way.[80]

6.532 The 'criterion'. The definite article in *Grundlagen der Arithmetik*

Kerry sees in the definite article the criterion of GRL for distinguishing concepts and objects. In order to determine whether this view is justified, let us enumerate those Fregean texts up to UFT where the virtues of the definite article are mentioned. Our list ist perhaps exhaustive.

1. GRL, p. 1 (*Einleitung*):

> "... der Satz "die Zahl Eins ist ein Ding" keine Definition ist, weil auf der einen Seite der bestimmte Artikel, auf der andern der unbestimmte steht..."

2. GRL, p. 30:

> "Hier ist zunächst der bestimmte Artikel in dem Ausdrucke "die charakteristische Weise" ein Fehler; denn es giebt sehr verschiedene Weisen . . ."

3. GRL, p. 49:

> "Man sagt "die Zahl Eins" und deutet mit dem bestimmten Artikel einen bestimmten, einzelnen Gegenstand der wissenschaftlichen Forschung an. Es giebt nicht verschiedene Zahlen Eins, sondern nur Eine."

4. GRL, pp. 63–64:

> "Ein allgemeines Begriffswort bezeichnet eben einen Begriff. Nur mit dem bestimmten Artikel oder einen Demonstrativpronomen gilt es als Eigenname eines Dinges, hört aber damit auf, als Begriffswort zu gelten[. . .] Sobald ein Wort mit dem unbestimmten Artikel oder im Plural ohne Artikel gebraucht wird, ist es Begriffswort."

5. GRL, p. 68:

> "Wir können ferner mit Hilfe unserer Erklärungsversuche nicht beweisen, daß $a = b$ sein muß, wenn dem Begriff F die Zahl a zukommt, und wenn demselben die Zahl b zukommt. Der Ausdruck "*die* Zahl, welche dem Begriffe F zukommt" wäre also nicht zu rechtfertigen..."

6. *Ibid.*:

"... daß man "die 1" sagt und durch den bestimmten Artikel 1 als Gegenstand hinstellt."

7. GRL, p. 77:

"Der bestimmte Artikel deutet dies an..." [namely, that "the direction of *a*" is the name of an object].

8. GRL, p. 80:

"... daß die einzelne Zahl ein Gegenstand sei, was durch den bestimmten Artikel in Ausdrücken wie "die Zwei" und durch die Unmöglichkeit, von Einsen, Zweien, u.s.w. im Plural zu sprechen, angedeutet werde..."

9. UFT, p. 104:

"... sondern ½ wird als bestimmter, einzelner Gegenstand behandelt, wie aus dem Ausdruck "die Zahl ½" hervorgeht..."

10. GRL, p. 87:

"Ganz davon verschieden ist die Definition eines Gegenstandes aus einem Begriffe, unter den er fällt. Der Ausdruck "der größte ächte Bruch" hat z.B. keinen Inhalt, weil der bestimmte Artikel den Anspruch erhebt, auf einen bestimmten Gegenstand hinzuweisen. Dagegen ist der Begriff "Bruch, der kleiner als 1, und so beschaffen ist, daß kein Bruch, der kleiner als 1 ist, ihn an Größe übertrifft" ganz unbedenklich, und um beweisen zu können, daß es keinen solchen Bruch gebe, braucht man sogar diesen Begriff, obgleich er einen Widerspruch enthält. Wenn man aber durch diesen Begriff einen Gegenstand bestimmen wollte, der unter ihn fällt, wäre es allerdings nöthig, zweierlei vorher zu zeigen:
(1) daß unter diesen Begriff ein Gegenstand falle;
(2) daß nur ein einziger Gegenstand unter ihn falle.
Da nun schon der erste dieser Sätze falsch ist, so ist der Ausdruck "der größte ächte Bruch" sinnlos."

11. UFT, p. 103:

"Es liegt hier offenbar eine Schwierigkeit vor, und diese besteht in der Definition von Gegenständen, während man sonst nur mit Definitionen von Begriffen zu thun hat..."

12. GRL, p. 89:

> "... weil zur Rechtfertigung des bestimmten Artikels erst zwei Sätze bewiesen werden müßten." [a footnote refers to the two conditions stated in 10 above].

13. GRL, p. 108:

> "Daß dieser Fehler so leicht begangen wird, liegt wohl an einer mangelhaften Unterscheidung der Begriffe von den Gegenständen. Nichts hindert uns, den Begriff "Quadratwurzel aus -1" zu gebrauchen; aber wir sind nicht ohne Weiteres berechtigt, den bestimmten Artikel davor zu setzen und den Ausdruck "die Quadratwurzel aus -1" als einen sinnvollen anzusehen."

14. UFT, p. 100:

> "Es würde ein logischer Fehler sein, nun sogleich den bestimmten Artikel zu gebrauchen und zu sagen: "*die* Zahl, welche mit sich multiplicirt 2 giebt"[...] solange man nicht bewiesen hat, daß es etwas derart giebt und zwar nur eins."

15. GRL, p. 109:

> "Man darf nicht auf der einen Seite einer Definitionsgleichung den unbestimmten und auf der andern den bestimmten Artikel gebrauchen. Dann sagt Hankel ohne Weiteres: "der Modul der Operation", ohne bewiesen zu haben, daß es einen und nur einen giebt."

16. GRL p. 114:

> "... aber trotzdem ist 1000^{1000} ein Gegenstand [...] Man überzeugt sich davon, indem man bei der Einführung des Zeichens a^n für die Potenz zeigt, daß immer eine und nur eine positive ganze Zahl dadurch ausgedrückt wird, wenn a und n positive ganze Zahlen sind."

It is obvious that the majority of texts refer to the definite article as implying existence and uniqueness. This is particularly explicit in text (10): also in (2), (5), (12), (13), (14), (16). Texts (1) and (15) seem to point at the same requirement with respect to the definite article. Text (4) describes a "transformation" of concepts into objects. As already mentioned[81], this may be correctly interpreted without appealing to Kerry's reading. Text (6) could be understood as having suggested Kerry's interpretation, but this text is preceded by the words: "Ich habe schon darauf aufmerksam gemacht . . .", and there is no possible *locus*, as reference, other than our text (3). Now, text (3) poses the question in a slightly different way; it "expands" text (6) by adding: "Es giebt nicht verschiedene Zahlen Eins, sondern nur Eine." Here again one sees that the point is uniqueness (plus existence).

It is one of Frege's major concerns to show that numbers are not concepts, but objects, better, that they are ultimate subjects of predication as is the Aristotelian Callias. Frege substantiates this sufficiently by means *independent of the definite article*; he affirms that it does not make sense to speak of *a two*, *two's*, or *three's* (which would make sense if numbers were universals, if *two* were like *man*). I believe that Frege's recourse to the definite article (i.e., to the fact that we say "die Zwei") is only a step towards proving that numbers are ultimate subjects of predication, namely, only in so far as the possibility of speaking of *two's* or *three's* is thereby excluded. Once this quite traditional way of speaking is eliminated, much ground is gained towards showing that numbers are objects and not concepts. But the goal is not yet attained. It is still necessary (unless one adopts the ideas of BGGE) to show that *die Zwei* is not a concept, which can only be done by pointing out, as Frege did, that it does not make sense to speak even of one individual falling under *two*. This recourse to what "makes sense (or not)" is nothing else than an appeal to what we have called the "good" criterion for distinguishing concepts and objects, which is independent of the definite article.

We have tried to avoid Kerry's interpretation of text (6) by referring it to text (3), where it is clear that the effect of the definite article (in the philosophy of number) is only the partial result that there are no *two's* or *three's*, as had been thought in tradition.

We may avoid Kerry's interpretation of text (8) in a similar way. Here the author of GRL would regard the use of the definite article only as a partial step leading to the thesis that numbers are not concepts. Text (8) should be completed with: ". . . daß die einzelne Zahl ein *einzelner* Gegenstand sei . . .". In any case, if this interpretation of (8) is not plausible, it should be observed that an interpretation *à la Kerry* is not any more justified (to the extent, of course, that the future ideas of

BGGE are not surrepticiously introduced). Kerry would have to appeal to text (7), which is indeed favourable to his cause, but he could not find support in any other text.

In text (9) Frege draws from the use of the definite article ("die $\frac{1}{2}$") the conclusion that $\frac{1}{2}$ is a *bestimmter, einzelner Gegenstand.* I am inclined to stress the idea expressed by "bestimmter, einzelner" rather than the *Gegenstand.* The same pair of adjectives appears in text (3) where it is definitely clear that the article serves to indicate that "there is only one" (uniqueness). In the context immediately preceding text (9) Frege had already proved that $\frac{1}{2}$ *ist als Gegenstand aufzufassen* (UFT, p. 103 below), but he did this through recourse to the good criterion (i.e., it does not make sense to speak of individuals falling under $\frac{1}{2}$). Subsequently he appeals to the fact that one says "die Zahl $\frac{1}{2}$", but this is to show that $\frac{1}{2}$ is a *bestimmter, einzelner* entity, as is indicated by any expression of the form "the . . .".

Text (7) is, as mentioned above, the text which could have provided best support or inspiration for Kerry's interpretation.

Thus, in favour of Kerry there is only text (7), and – not necessarily – text (8), which texts are but a minor detail in the whole Fregean concern with the definite article. Nevertheless, Kerry enlarges this into the solemn form of a fundamental principle of research. He does not even quote text (7) in order to support his interpretation; he quotes only text (8).

On the other hand, Kerry's formulation of the "criterion" concerns also the uses of the definite article before names of higher-level concepts ("the concept . . ."). He attacks Frege because the criterion in such cases would result in saying that "der Begriff F" is not the name of a concept. Of course, such rules concerning the definite article are not to be found at all in GRL or UFT. On the contrary, in the very context of our text (8) above (quoted by Kerry), it is possible to observe that Frege had no well defined ideas in GRL about the denotation of such expressions as "der Begriff F". He proposes to replace the phrase "Umfang des Begriffes" by "Begriff" (in his famous definition of number). He says that this could be objected to on the ground that it would contradict the thesis that numbers are objects, not concepts (whereby it is supposed that extensions of concepts are objects). If Frege had had ideas in GRL as clear as those in BGGE about the virtues of the definite article, he would have directly expressed them; he would have openly stated that the objection fails because "der Begriff" (instead of "der Umfang des Begriffes") is the name of an object, not the name of a concept. Frege only provides an enigmatic remark[82], which of course *from* the standpoint of BGGE may be retrospectively interpreted in that sense, but which no normal reader of GRL (except Kerry) could interpret as meaning that the expression "der Begriff F" does not designate a concept. On the contrary, everything in GRL contributes to create the impression that "der Begriff F" does designate a concept – as it is supposed to do. Frege makes frequent use of that kind of expression, and nowhere in GRL does he stop to indicate to his readers that he is not speaking of concepts. Actually, readers of GRL receive the impression that concepts are most "solid" entities whose *Einheit*[83] has sufficient personality to stand in front of its individuals; the concept *Jupitersmond* stands in front of the four moons of Jupiter almost as Jupiter itself does.[84] Actually, if this were not the case, Frege's philosophy of number would collapse.

Kerry not only foresees the results of BGGE, he also polemizes against this yet unpublished paper. Against the view that "der Begriff F" is not the name of a concept, Kerry states two reasons. The first consists in observing that it is illegitimate to base logic on linguistic differences.[85] The second objection is not trivial, and it consists in providing counterexamples; when one says "the concept about which I am talking right now is an individual concept", he clearly means a concept, in spite of the definite article.[86]

6.54 *Kerry's own view. Conclusion*

After having developed a negative criticism of Frege, Kerry goes on to show positively that concepts may at the same time be objects.[87] He again proceeds by providing an example: in the sentence "der Begriff 'Pferd' ist ein leicht gewinnbarer Begriff" the concept "Pferd" is an object falling under the concept "leicht gewinnbarer Begriff". He points out that under some of the concepts mentioned by Frege, for example, "gleichzahlig dem Begriffe F", *other concepts* only may fall.

Kerry is further interested in showing, contrary to Frege, that numbers are also conceivable as *concepts*. We will not here enter into the analysis of Kerry's doctrine, but this point should be mentioned as a factor which perhaps influenced his general interpretation of Frege. In Kerry's presentation, the "absolute" separation of concepts and objects has two parts:

(1) concepts cannot be transformed into (or regarded as) objects, (2) objects cannot be considered as concepts. A reader of Frege, especially if he knows BGGE, is particularly sensitive to the first part. This is precisely the "trouble" created by unsaturatedness. As to the second part, one would normally assume that, if the objects are meant as ultimate subjects of predication, then, in agreement with the philosophical tradition, there would be no reason to object to such a view. But the particular point of numbers considered by Frege as ultimate subjects of predication provokes a special reaction in Kerry. The latter does not simply say, "Frege's conception of numbers as ultimate subjects of predication is wrong", but he protests that numbers are (in some sense) *also concepts*. One of the results of his showing that concepts (like *Pferd*) may be objects to other higher concepts (like *leicht gewinnbarer Begriff*) is precisely the correction of Frege's thesis that numbers are objects, the correction being that numbers are also concepts.[88] Kerry thus has a peculiar reason for viewing the "transformation" (*verändern*) of GRL, p. X[89] as a situation symmetrical to the other "transformation" of objects (in particular, numbers) into concepts. In this way he was perhaps led to understand the fundamental principle of distinguishing concepts and objects (GRL, p. X) as implying the exclusion of concepts from the class of objects. Furthermore, the same reasons perhaps led him to interpret some subtle hints (such as our text (7) in the preceding section) as clearly formulated theses, which curiously turned out to be the theses of BGGE.

As a general conclusion, it may be said that Kerry's criticism is *inadequate* with respect *to the Fregean works known to him*. We would not say that Kerry's criticism is inadequate with respect *to Frege's ideas at the time of GRL*, and this for two reasons: (1) because there *are* actually some hints (text (7) and perhaps (8) of our preceding section) or some ambiguous statements (the last phrase of GRL, p. 77, footnote) which may be counted in favour of Kerry. Moreover, there are enigmatic Fregean phrases which could be retrospectively interpreted in the manner of Kerry (GRL, p. 80, note, *in fine*), and (2) because Frege himself in BGGE did not say that Kerry was wrong . . .; indeed, one may assume that BGGE, *qua* answer to Kerry, definitely implies that Kerry's criticism *is adequate*.

The reason why we stress here the fact that Kerry's criticism is not correct (with respect to what readers could know about Frege in 1885) is that we are seeking an understanding of the puzzling and fundamental feature of Frege's philosophy: unsaturatedness. And one way of doing this is to see how long the appearance of *Ungesättigtheit* in the Fregean corpus *may* be delayed. In addition we do not exclude the possibility that Kerry's criticism had a pernicious influence on Frege's thought, namely, by forcing Frege into the muddle of unsaturatedness. If such is the case, one can blame the author of BGGE for allowing the reader to think that Kerry's interpretation is adequate.

6.6 Frege's reply to Kerry. 'The concept horse' is not the name of a concept

6.61 *To be a concept and to be an object*

In BGGE – a paper especially devoted to Kerry's criticism – Frege begins with a misleading statement. After referring to the different ways of understanding the term "Begriff" (psychological, logical, or an unclear mixture of both), he chooses to adopt the purely logical sense. This statement is misleading in that it approaches the problem, or better, the polemic with Kerry, as if Frege were representing "logic" and Kerry "psychologism", which in fact is not at all the point of the disagreements between them.

The discussion proper begins with the following assertion: "Kerry möchte den Unterschied zwischen Begriff und Gegenstand nicht als absoluten gelten lassen."[90] Frege shows that he agrees with Kerry as to the meaning of "absolut": the mutually exclusive character of the properties *to be a concept* and *to be an object*. First, Frege defends the thesis that there are ultimate subjects of predication, i.e., objects which are not concepts. He curiously remarks that even in the example of the relation of *paternity* (proposed by Kerry) one would find that those particular entities which are fathers but not sons would be of quite a different kind (*ganz andrer Art*) than all those men who are sons. The admission that objects may become (be considered as) concepts is for Frege a consequence of not distinguishing the "is" of identity and the "is" of UF. This certainly applies to tradition[91], but Frege fails to consider what is apparently the real motivation leading Kerry to stress the possibility of regarding numbers *also* as concepts[92] (while Frege restricts them to being objects). Frege comes close to seeing this real motivation in another passage of BGGE[93] – but in any case without realizing its significance in the present issue.

As to Kerry's thesis that concepts may be treated as objects (objects falling under higher concepts), and that in the sentence "der Begriff 'Pferd' ist ein leicht gewinnbarer Begriff", the concept *Pferd* is an object falling under the concept *leicht gewinnbarer Begriff*, Frege replies: "Yes! the three words "the concept 'horse'" designate an object, *but precisely for this reason they do not designate a concept*, in the way I understand this term."[94]

With this ready answer Frege makes it definitely clear that he fully accepts the "absolute" separation of concepts and objects. For us, former readers of GRL, there is no choice other than to accept this, even if we are not quite convinced of its retrospective validity for GRL.

6.62 *Frege's interpretation of the definite article*

Inmediately after his reply to Kerry, Frege adds that it agrees completely with the criterion given by him (Frege), according to which the definite article in the singular always means that an object is in question. In support of this, Frege refers to three texts of GRL. They are our items (4), (7) and (8).[95] For those who are reluctant to accept Kerry's interpretation, this is embarrassing. Nevertheless, I still venture to maintain that it is not sure that Frege in 1884 (GRL) had exactly the same ideas as those exposed later in BGGE. In fact, it is curious that Frege does not feel obliged to provide an explanation concerning his having supported in GRL the ideas which Kerry assigns to him. For, again, these ideas are almost invisible there.[96]

Kerry had found Frege's criterion *unzutreffend.* To this, Frege replies that if Kerry understands that "der Begriff F" is the name of a concept, then he is taking the word "concept" in a sense different from that of Frege's.[97] But Frege should acknowledge that the peculiar way in which he takes "concept" in BGGE is not manifest in his previous works. Kerry cannot be expected to know the sense of "Begriff" at the time of BGGE.

Frege acknowledges that his interpretation of the definite article involves some difficulties. It is indeed difficult to accept that the concept horse is not a concept, while the city of Berlin is a city.[98] Frege describes this situation as a *Zwangslage*[99] of language.

In BGGE he frequently employs expressions of the form "der Begriff ...". He acknowledges this, observing that this is a case where what one means by a name is not what the name names[100], which brings to mind Hegel.[101]

6.63 *Then what does the expression 'the concept horse' designate?*

The concept F (not what these three words name but what we mean in saying them[102]) fails to be designated by "the concept F"; the latter expression designates an object. Frege does not specify what this object is, but by grouping together some passages of BGGE we may obtain a sort of implicit definition of it. In this paper Frege accepts as meaningful the following sentences.

(1) "Der Begriff Mensch ist nicht leer."[103]
(2) "Jesus fällt unter den Begriff Mensch."[104]
(3) "Der Begriff Säugethier ist untergeordnet dem Begriffe Landbewohner."[105]
(4) "Der Begriff Quadratwurzel aus 4 ist erfüllt."[106]
(5) "Die Zahl 4 hat die Eigenschaft, daß es etwas gibt, dessen Quadrat sie ist."[107]
(6) "Die Zahl 2 fällt unter den Begriff Primzahl."[108]
(7) "Es gibt mindestens eine Quadratwurzel aus 4."[109]

To say that all these sentences are accepted and meaningful is not trivial because in BGGE – as in GRG I – there is the clear statement of a rule of "types" according to which some sentences are rejected as *sinnlos*.[110]

Now, if one substitutes "Julius Caesar" in the place of "der Begriff Quadratwurzel aus 4" in (4), one obtains a meaningful, but *false*, sentence because non-emptiness is a property which can truly be said only of objects of a quite peculiar kind, namely those objects designated by proper names of the form "the concept F".[111] We obtain thus a characteristic property of the yet unknown designata of "der Begriff F": non-emptiness. It is clear that these enigmatic objects cannot be other than the *classes* corresponding to the concepts. Classes are objects, although concepts are not.[112] Thus, if we agree that "der Begriff F" designates a class, the result is that our naming does not depart so far from our meaning, and we may allow concepts to be "represented"[113] by classes everytime we wish to speak about them ... as if they were objects.[114]

6.7 Unsaturatedness

We have seen that Frege (1) affirms the "absolute" separation of concepts and objects, (2) considers the definite article to be a good criterion for revealing the presence of an object which object is not (because of 1) a concept. Kerry had already attributed this to Frege, but we did not believe him; now we must believe Frege.

The Frege of the early 1890's assumes not only points (1) and (2) above. These are, in fact, but special cases of a general theory centered around the term "Ungesättigtheit". Concepts are a particular instance of functions. Points (1) and (2) become the "absolute" separation of objects and functions, which means that functions (and their names) are unsaturated while objects (and their names) are saturated. This leads to the paradoxes of Frege's unsaturatedness.

6.71 *Functions and concepts: two convergent traditions*

FUB generalizes and reinforces the distinction concept–object. The generalization consists in viewing concepts as functions; the reinforcement consists in strictly decreeing the *Ungesättigtheit* of functions.

Until FUB, Frege had not used the mathematical notion of function (mapping). The idea, of course, was familiar to Frege, the professor of mathematics. In his dissertation, this idea appears under the name "Operation"[115] and in BG under the term "Verfahren".[116] As we have seen[117], the term "function" in BG is a response primarily to another motivation, namely, that of allowing the consideration of n-adic predicates. In GRL the powerful term "predicate" reappears.[118] Up to FUB it is the traditional opposition one-many of concepts and objects which plays the important role in Frege's thought, not the mathematical notion of function. This was due, in fact, to Frege's philosophical analysis of number.

A major aim of FUB is to show that the *Begriff* of the philosophical tradition and the notion of *mapping* are convergent ideas. In so doing, Frege exerts no *tour de force* on the traditional *Begriff*: I do not think there is a collision involved here of exemplification with mapping.[119] If there be any victim at all, it is the concept of mathematical function, because *this* concept is generalized in order to embrace traditional *Begriffe*, and not *vice versa*. In this way, Frege intends to bring to its ultimate stage an evolution, already quite advanced, of the notion of mathematical function. The latter is expanded in the domain of arguments as well as in the domain of values of the function.[120] Frege extends this generalization to its maximum: truth-values are admitted as possible values of functions[121], which thus include what will later be called logical or propositional functions. Frege calls them "concepts" (or "relations", in the case of two arguments). Concerning the domain of arguments, *Gegenstände überhaupt* are admitted. Here we enter ontology, where the terminology "mathematical function" becomes completely out of place. Frege's philosophical logicism is at work.

6.72 *Unsaturatedness of names and unsaturatedness of designata*

FUB begins with a semantical *mise au point* of the necessity of distinguishing names and designata, in this case functions and the names of functions. This is vehemently stated, and it is clear (in opposition to the previous mathematical tradition) that functions are *not* signs. Such a semantic distinction provides a more precise basis for the discussion of unsaturatedness.[122]

What does "unsaturatedness" mean and "what" is unsaturated? The clearest sense of "unsaturatedness" is that which applies to *linguistic expressions.* A sign is unsaturated if and only if it contains at least one empty place where it is possible to introduce another sign which has the effect of "completing" the given initial expression.[123] It is not possible to provide a less vague description.

But also *functions* are unsaturated.[124] What does this mean? If we restrict ourselves to the paradigmatic case of concepts, it seems obvious that unsaturatedness coincides with that tenacious traditional view according to which concepts (predicates, universals, etc.) include an essential reference to their "inferiors" (individuals, etc.). This is Aristotle and Kant[125], and in fact the first occurrence of unsaturatedness in the Fregean corpus reminds us of Kant.[126]

For other cases (apart from concepts), for instance for "2(   )"[127] or "the capital of . . .", one may still imagine that the designatum of these expressions is something "indeterminate" (as the expressions themselves are). Frege himself provides, to represent functions, the image of mathematical open intervals which require closed intervals (at least one point) to be "completed".[128] "Complete" or saturated entities are called "objects".[129] To such an extent, there are unsaturated and saturated *names*, unsaturated and saturated *designata*. In such a semantic "expansion" the adjective "(un)saturated" may claim only a sort of analogical meaning; but Frege does not go into this.[130]

6.73 *Functions are defined as the reference of unsaturated expressions*

Fregean ontology divides the world into objects and functions, which division is *absolute* in the sense proposed by Kerry and accepted by Frege. The class of functions and the class of objects are mutually exclusive.

To consider again the special case of concepts, let us observe that Frege defines concepts as the reference of grammatical predicates.[131] Unsaturatedness is perhaps not always visible in the grammatical predicates of natural languages where a symbolism of "empty places" for receiving names of arguments is not usual. But Frege obliges us to "see" empty argument-places in each grammatical predicate.[132] *Predicability* is in the special case of concepts (or propositional functions with any number of arguments) what unsaturatedness is for functions in general.[133]

Frege's definition of "object" shows that not only objects are defined as the reference of saturated expressions, but also that functions are defined as the reference of unsaturated expressions.[134]

This obviously tends to make superfluous the distinction of functions and their names (or objects and their names). Frege nevertheless poses this distinction, not only because he respects the opposition signs–designata, but also because he seems to think that the priority – in matters of unsaturatedness – corresponds to *functions* rather than to their names.[135]

Names of unsaturated names must be unsaturated; names of saturated names must be saturated.[136] As a result, we have the following general diagram (see p. 175).

6.74 *The paradox of unsaturatedness*

The paradox of BGGE has two forms:

(1) "the concept horse" is not the name of a concept[137],

(2) the concept horse is not a concept.[138] The idea underlying form (1)

	Unsaturated	Saturated
Entities	functions	objects
Names	names of functions	names of objects
Names of names	names of names of functions	names of names of objects
Names of names of names . . .	. . .	. . .

is that there are entities which are defined as the reference of unsaturated expressions. Frege regards the prefixing of "the" as saturating the expressions which follow. As for (2), it follows from (1). The paradox derives from the fact that for Frege it is not possible to call some entities by some names or descriptions which ordinary language does accept as correct designations of those entities.

A rare text in which point (1) above occurs as a conclusion of an argument, is GRG I, p. 8, note. Let us consider the following expressions:

(a) The truth-value of the proposition that Socrates falls under the concept (ξ) *is mortal*;

(b) The truth-value of the proposition that ( ) falls under the concept (ξ) *is mortal*;

(c) (Socrates) is mortal;

(d) ( ) is mortal; and

(e) The concept (ξ) *is mortal.*

(a) and (c) are names of the object Truth. (d) is the name of a function (concept). (b) is also the name of a function which is at least extensionally identical with the former. Frege establishes a "correspondence" between (b) and (d); he states that (d) "entspricht" to (b) and not to (e), which is a part of (b). Consequently, he concludes ("also") that (e) is not the name of a concept.

The argument seems to hinge on the tacit step that (d) *cannot* "correspond" (cannot have the same meaning, at least extensionally) to both (b) and (e) at the same time. Without entering into this question, it is puzzling to observe that Frege distinguishes the empty place of (e) from the empty places of (d) and (b) (with the exception of the occurrence of (e) in (b)).

Names of unsaturated entities are also unsaturated ("analogically", cf. Section 6.72 *in fine*), and, again, names of unsaturated names must be unsaturated. This infinite self-mirroring of unsaturatedness involves an infinite reiteration of the paradox[139], which is, indeed, unsolvable.[140]

6.75 *Martinus de Dacia*: '*modus intelligendi*'

In traditional semantics there is a factor which Frege does not seem to take into account: the *modus intelligendi*. In Martinus de Dacia [1] we find two applications of this. (1) At the level of *modus essendi* there are only individuals, and universals are not to be found there. Universals appear, first of all, in the other extreme, namely, in the *modus significandi* (in the names). But what or how we *signify* (*modus significandi*) is not only "caused" by reality (*modus essendi*) but also depends, as on its *causa immediata*, on our *modus intelligendi*. "Quidquid enim contingit intelligere, contingit et significare."[141] Our power of abstraction – *modus intelligendi* – precipitates the actual appearance of universals, and consequently universal names appear in language.[142] (2) The *modus intelligendi* serves also to justify the passage from an unsaturated name to a saturated name of the same thing; from *homo* to *humanitas*. Martinus de Dacia considers an objector who presents the following argument:

(1) "Homo" means the same as "humanitas";
(2) "Humanitas" is not predicated of Socrates,
(3) Therefore "homo" is not predicated of Socrates either.[143]

Our author accepts (1), but with a qualification. Both terms mean the same, but in different ways, this being due to the different *modus intelligendi*. "Homo" has a *modus significandi concretive respectu eius de quo praedicatur*, which amounts to saying that it has an empty argument place, or that it is unsaturated. The designatum of "homo" is also unsaturated, but it has an element of determination, of "saturatedness" too, as the Frege of GRL would readily admit. We may concentrate upon this saturated part, and we may pass from *homo* to *humanitas*.[144]

Frege is perhaps the only semanticist who has denied the possibility of such a passage; the latter was admitted both before him (for instance, Martinus de Dacia) and after him (for instance, Hilbert-Ackermann[145]).

6.76 *Hypothesis: the ultimate ambiguity lies in the term "function" rather than in "unsaturatedness"*

Frege's views on unsaturatedness have been presented. Especially if these views are considered in the paradigmatic case of concepts, they appear as remarkably peculiar in a history of philosophy made up of "footnotes to Plato".

We have observed that "unsaturatedness" is used in two senses: for functions and for names of functions. The point was that it is not possible to designate an unsaturated entity (i.e. a function) by means of a saturated name. Functions are defined as the reference of unsaturated expressions.

It is surprising how an author, who clearly distinguishes signs and designata, devotes so much time discussing how the name of an entity should look.[146] This stands in contrast to Frege's anti-formalism, as well as to other Fregean insights, for instance, the much stressed possibility of having the same entity under the most different "aspects". Actually, Frege is committing the same mistake as those who would define *a direction* in the way criticized in GRL § 67.[147]

Why does Frege not admit the possibility of saturated names for unsaturated entities? Why would he not admit the traditional (and new logic's) passage from *homo* to *humanitas*?

The reason is perhaps that Frege, in spite of his distinction of signs and designata, has continued to view functions *also* as linguistic expressions.

"Function" would thus have two meanings: (1) what Frege himself calls *function*, and, (2) what Frege calls the *name* of the function.[148] Functions are unsaturated; this is why names of functions, which would also be functions, must be unsaturated (in the manner in which names can be unsaturated, namely, by having empty places for arguments).

6.77 *Unsaturatedness in the history of philosophy*

Unless otherwise stated, I mean here unsaturatedness of entities or of names, but not necessarily the Fregean thesis that unsaturated entities can be named only by unsaturated names.

6.771 Unsaturatedness in the two ontological dimensions

The idea of unsaturatedness is trivial in the philosophical tradition.[149] Classical ontology had two dimensions, in both of which the phenomenon of unsaturatedness appears, as a mediaeval treatise on semantics states.[150] Both kinds of unsaturatedness may be called by "abstract", or saturated, names: *albedo* or *humanitas* are accepted designations because *abstrahentium non est mendacium.*[151] Leaving aside this last point, the fact that Frege has only UF should be taken into account, but as far as UF may be identified with singularity–universality, comparisons are justified in some cases, for instance, Kant.[152]

6.772 Unsaturatedness and modes

In speaking of unsaturatedness, Frege seems to have in mind the mathematical image of closed and open intervals as capable of "completing" or "saturating" each other.[153] If the intervals have to be joined, at least one of them must have an open extreme; if sentences have to be formed, at least one of the parts of each sentence must be unsaturated or predicative.[154] Otherwise, there is no *Bindemittel.* But the *Bindemittel* itself cannot be thought of as a new entity. "The relation UF" is not the name of UF.[155] The name of UF is "$\varphi(\xi)$".[156] This is strikingly similar to the scholastic theory of modes[157], which are for inherence what second intentions are for predication. Modes are even weaker entities than accidents; accidents inhere in substances, but modes do not inhere in accidents (or substances). As far as *inherence* itself is a mode, it may be said that inherence does not inhere. Thus, Frege's symbol" $\varphi(\xi)$" could also be a good designation of *inhaerentia.*[158]

6.773 Unsaturatedness and *Principia Mathematica*

Unsaturatedness in symbolic languages prior to the *Begriffsschrift* is a worthwhile object of research.[159] Since Frege, unsaturatedness has been explicitly mentioned by the most important treatises on logic.[160]

In *Principia*, when types are introduced, two reasons are provided, the so-called vicious circle principle and the nature of propositional functions.[161] The nature of propositional functions is described in terms of "ambiguity". Now it should be observed that "ambiguity" is an ambiguous word in *Principia*; the senses assigned to it in Sections II and IV[162] do not seem to be the same. Ambiguity$_1$ is a relation which might be called "ambiguously denoting" and which applies between the function and its values or some "indeterminate" value.[163] Ambiguity$_2$ is, so to speak, more intrinsic to functions: "a function is essentially an ambiguity . . ." and "a function . . . is a mere ambiguity awaiting determination".[164] Ambiguity$_1$ plus the vicious circle principle is enough to exclude as an argument of a function anything "involving" the given function, or a fortiori, the function itself. Ambiguity$_2$ seems to fulfil the particular task of extending the former restriction to any other function or anything "involving" it. Ambiguity$_2$ fulfils this task without the help of the vicious circle principle, and at the same time it accomplishes what was demanded of ambiguity$_1$.

Ambiguity$_2$ is obviously in the line of Frege's unsaturatedness. Not only the above given characterizations, but also and especially the consequences *Principia* draws from such an ambiguity$_2$, are strikingly similar to some consequences Frege derives from *Ungesättigtheit*.[165] It seems that the effect ambiguity$_2$ is intended to have requires its identification with Frege's unsaturatedness. If ambiguity$_2$ concerned only designata, then the argument for the justification of types would fail. If, however, it concerns also *names*, then there will no longer be explicit function of functions (cf. Section 6.83) to be arranged in types.

Aside from this particular argument, the idea of unsaturatedness is not considered by *Principia*.[166] It has also been rejected afterwards, in a more explicit way, by A. Church.[167] Still, how it is possible to reject *Ungesättigtheit* without revising the whole system of Frege should be considered.[168]

6.8 Levels ('Stufen')

6.81 *The impact of unsaturatedness on higher predicates*

The analysis of statements of number led Frege to the idea of levels in concepts because numbers *appear at a second level* with respect to the individuals making up the sets to be counted.

In BG there was a vague reference to a *Rang* of concepts[169], but levels really appear in GRL, i.e., in conjunction with Frege's philosophy of number.[170] In GRL Frege distinguishes concepts of first and second *Ordnung*. One would normally understand that concepts of second order are predicated of concepts of first order, *in the same way* in which the latter are predicated of objects. But we already know that this was better understood by Kerry[171], and the Frege of BGGE and later works presents a fundamental difficulty to that interpretation. In fact, the "absolute" separation of concepts and objects means, in particular, that concepts cannot be also objects with respect to higher concepts. In general, if "*f*( )" is the name of a function, no other name of a function, say "*g*( )", will have the capacity of completely filling the empty argument place in the former, and we shall not obtain a sentence, i.e., the saturated name of a saturated object (here: truth-values).[172] For example, as far as Frege obliges us to "see" empty-argument places in predicates of natural language[173] (which is certainly in agreement with traditional interpretations), we may say that the function whose name is "( ) is a species" cannot be saturated by the function whose name is "( ) is a man". "(( ) is a man) is a species" is not yet a saturated name of a truth-value.

To make sense of all this amounts to understanding Frege's doctrine on unsaturatedness. *If* one accepts the insights and images (open and closed intervals, etc.) making up Frege's notion of *Ungesättigtheit*, *then* it is obvious that one cannot have "homo est species". Traditional strategies, such as passing from *homo* to *humanitas* or to *suppositio simplex*, will not be feasible here. Any of those devices, in fact, "kills" unsaturatedness.

Still, Frege does admit higher predicates, and this in two peculiar ways.

6.82 *The 'Ersatz' approach*

The first way of preserving higher predicates may be called the *Ersatz* approach. As we have seen[174], it is meaningful to say "the concept man is a species", although "the concept man" is not the name of a concept. "The concept man" is still the name of an object, which object can be interpreted as the *class* (here, class of men). There are many things common to concepts and classes: (non-)emptiness, subordination or inclusion, etc. For *these* things, our *saying* will not depart too much from our *meaning*, and one will not be disappointed if, while one *means* that the concept man is a species, one *says* that the class of men is a species (thereby allowing "species" to adapt its meaning to the new extensional context). Of course, for those higher predicates which involve the idea of unsaturatedness, such as *to be a concept* or *to be a function* or *to be unsaturated*, there will be no *Ersatz* solution; one cannot say that the concept man is a concept.

6.83 *Implicit higher predication*

The second way of preserving higher predicates consists in what I call *implicit*[175] higher predication. The grammatical subjects of sentences of this sort do not designate concepts or functions about which we wish to speak. For instance, if one really wants to say that the concept *square root of 4* is non-empty, and if one is not satisfied with the *Ersatz* solution, then one may simply say: "there is a square root of 4".[176] The skeleton of this sentence is actually "(Ex) x is a square root of 4", which is obtained from the name "( ) is a square root of 4" *via* existential quantification. Though one is not able to "say" *explicitly* that the concept is not empty, one speaks *implicitly* of it "showing" that it is not empty.[177]

Again, many things about concepts can be "shown" in this way. The distinguishing trait of implicit higher predication is that the predicative (unsaturated) nature of concepts is preserved. To use a famous Hegelian expression, we may say that unsaturatedness is not thereby eliminated, but that it is *aufgehoben*. Martinus de Dacia or Hilbert-Ackermann eliminate predicability; the former gives us a reason: *modus intelligendi*.[178]

Once we have "$(Ex)fx$" we may think of "$f($ $)$" as variable (the function itself as variable). But we shall not be able to substitute "$f($ $)$" by "( )"; the result would be "$(Ex)($ $)$". The reference to the variable which is bound by the existential quantifier has to be preserved.[179] Frege settles this by writing "$(Ex)\varphi(x)$"[180], where the purpose of "φ" is merely to indicate that any name of a function with one argument may be introduced. "$(Ex)\varphi(x)$" is a name of non-emptiness (for concepts). Any concept (or name of concept) of the first level, may be introduced in the argument-place of that expression. The result, perhaps, will be false, but in any case *meaningful*. Thus, in "$(Ex)\varphi(x)$" one really has a property of properties: it is a function whose arguments are properties. Similarly, the property of being a property of number 2 will be written "$\varphi(2)$".[181] To avoid misunderstandings *à la Kerry*, Frege decided to designate by a special name the relation between a (first-level) property of number 2 and the property of being a property of number 2; number 2 *falls under* (UF) being odd, but being odd *falls within* being a property of number 2 (IF).[182] The relation itself of *falling under a concept* (UF), which is doubly unsaturated (as any relation), cannot of course be designated by a saturated name (say, "the relation UF") but can only be "shown" in the following way: "$\varphi(\xi)$"[183], where "φ" is a variable for a function and "ξ" is a variable for an object. It is difficult to find, in the entire history of philosophy, a more suggestive version of *methexis.*

Frege has provided examples of second-level functions and also of third-level[184] ones, always of course in the implicit approach. The law of construction is always the same: the ultimate subjects of predication (the variables for objects) must also be there. One may ask whether higher levels than the third are attained or attainable in Frege's system, but this question has not been dealt with by Frege.[185] Actually, he built an infinite pyramid of classes of classes, but for him classes of classes were *on a same level* with classes and individuals.[186] Because of this illusion, he perhaps thought he could dispense with levels of functions higher than the second or third.[187]

Frege's logic contains exactly as many rules of types as unsaturatedness dictates. In the *Ersatz* approach unsaturatedness is eliminated; hence, there are no "types" for classes. In the implicit approach, unsaturatedness fixes the limits of meaningfulness, and here some equivalents of later rules of types are to be found.[188]

REFERENCES

1. Frege explains his new terminology in BG, §§ 3, 9 (*in fine*).
2. Cf. Section 6.3.
3. Cf. BG, p. IV, § 3.
4. "Objekt, grammatisch res obiecta, das Ziel der Thätigkeit" (Grimm [1], "Objekt"). For the English equivalent, cf. Nesfield [1], § 136: "the word or words denoting that person or thing, to which the action of the verb is directed, are called the object of the verb". For the present section, cf. also Reichenbach [2], p. 24.
5. BG, p. 3.
6. Cf. Grimm [1], or again Nesfield [1], § 2: "the word or words which say something about the person or thing denoted by the subject [. . .] are called the predicate".
7. Of course "subject–object" could be maintained, but only with the meaning of "referent–relatum".
8. BG, § 3, *in fine*.
9. Cf. Sections 6.42, 6.73, and notes 44 and 45.
10. "Mais il faut particulièrement remarquer ici que toutes les propositions composées de verbes actifs et de leur régime peuvent être appelées complexes, et qu'elles contiennent en quelque manière deux propositions" (Port-Royal [1], Partie II, chap. 5).
11. Port-Royal [1], Partie III, chap. 9.
12. A non-trivial syllogism is one involving relational propositions:
    "La loi divine commande d'honnorer les rois;
    Louis XIV est roi;

Donc la loi divine commande d'honnorer Louis XIV".
(Port-Royal [1], Partie III, chap. 9).

13. Port-Royal [1], Partie II, chap. 2. In reference to the syllogism quoted in the preceding note, Port-Royal asks what "les rois" is; since it is not an attribute (because it is not said about anything), the authors agree that "il est le sujet d'une autre proposition, enveloppée dans celle-là" (Port-Royal [1], Partie III, Chap. 9).
14. BG, §§ 4, 7; GRG I; VERN, *in fine*; UZBG, p. 10. Cf. Port-Royal [1], Partie II, chap. 2.
15. Marty [1], p. 56.
16. *Ibid.*, p. 55.
17. *Ibid.*, p. 57, note 2. Frege gives *Haus* as an example of "unbeurtheilbarer Inhalt" in BG, p. 2, note.
18. Nevertheless, Marty realizes that relational propositions are a strong motivation in Frege's philosophy (p. 57, note 2).
19. BG, § 3, *in fine*.
20. I am grateful to Professor O. Funke (University of Bern) for having informed me (in a letter dated January 22, 1961) that he did not recall having seen Frege's name in the *Nachlass* of A. Marty.
21. BG, p. 16.
22. This applies to the definition in BG, p. 16, but it does not apply, of course, when Frege says that we may regard in several different ways the same conceptual *content* as a function of some argument (BG, p. 17).
23. In BG, p. 15, a sentence like "oxygen is lighter than carbon dioxide" is analysed into a function "being lighter than" and two arguments, "oxygen" and "carbon dioxide", which is a "natural" order. But in BG, § 10 it is said that functions may be viewed as arguments.
24. BG, p. 17.
25. BG, § 1 (unsaturatedness might be seen as incidentally appearing in BG, p. 14, cf. 2.11).
26. BG, p. 17.
27. *Ibid.*
28. BG, p. 15.
29. Cf. Section 2.11.
30. Cf. Section 2.61.
31. GRL, p. X.
32. Prefixing the definite article is indeed a "transformation". The concept "ceases to be" a concept; cf. text (4) quoted in Section 6.532.
33. Cf. text (10) quoted in Section 6.532.
34. GRL, § 94f; GRL, p. 119; UFT, p. 97f. In a paragraph of GRL whose title is *Begriffe sind von Gegenständen zu unterscheiden*, it is obvious that Frege associates his principle of the sharp distinction of concepts and objects with the mistake of building definite descriptions where uniqueness and existence are not guaranteed. Cf. text (13) in 6.532.
35. "Round square" is not an empty name, but the name of an empty concept ... Frege says in KSCH (p. 454). For Frege, to use "the round square" implies that "there is an *x* such that it is round and it is a square and it is the only entity fulfilling this condition" (cf. 6.532), i.e.. "the round square" is an empty name. But there is another use of the definite article in the philosophical

tradition according to which "the round square" means rather the empty Fregean concept. This other use of the definite article might be called *Meinong's beard.*

36. GRL, p. 77.
37. In BGGE, p. 198, line 12, Frege would correct this.
38. "zum Subjecte". In GRL (p. 82 bottom) Frege speaks of the *two* subjects of a relation.
39. This could be held consistently along with the main thesis of GRL (i.e. concepts as subjects of statements of number); it would suffice to consider implicit higher predication (cf. 6.83).
40. Such warning is not trivial with respect to traditional predication theory. Cf. 3.2, note 20.
41. Cf. BG, chapter on function; GRL, p. 82.
42. With regard to the restriction to singular *beurtheilbaren Inhalt*, I think this is done in order to avoid having "whales" as object and "mammals" as concept in such sentences as "all whales are mammals". Cf. GRL, pp. 60 and 100 above.
43. For this expression, well known in traditional philosophy, cf. for instance Gredt [1], I, 123, 1: "carentia divisionis ex parte principiorum formalium, quae constituunt quidditatem"; in Fregean terms: the set of marks making up a concept. Frege also sees in the concept an *Einheit* (GRL, p. 66).
44. GRL, §§ 51, 52.
45. Cf. text quoted at the beginning of the preceding section; also, GRG II, § 56.
46. Kant [3], quoted in note 152.
47. Cf. Chapter 5, note 5. (Of course, "Sinn" here has no relation with Frege's technical term).
48. GRL, p. 64; also: "Plural ist nur von Begriffswörtern möglich" (GRL, p. 49).
49. Traditional unsaturated entities did not require unsaturated names; cf. Section 6.77.
50. GRL, p. 66.
51. CANT, p. 270.
52. GRL, § 34: "Der Begriff Katze [. . .] ist aber eben dadurch nur Einer."
53. GRL, § 54.
54. GRL, § 48.
55. Cf. Section 6.83.
56. To use an expression of Bernays-Fraenkel [1], p. 58.
57. But this is the weak objectivity (cf. Section 2.51); Frege asks from concepts only that they not be subjective in the sense of empirical subjectivity (in modern terms) or in the sense of not being "conceptus subiectivus" (in earlier terminology). But then Frege's demand is trivial.
58. GRL, § 49.
59. For instance, GRL, § 51.
60. For instance, GRL, p. 87. The idea of *scharfe Begrenzung* had already appeared in Frege's dissertation (*venia docendi*): "Wenn wir in jedem Falle beurtheilen können, wann Gegenstände in einer Eigenschaft übereinstimmen, so haben wir offenbar den richtigen Begriff der Eigenschaft" ($DISS_2$, p. 2). Any function (in particular, logical functions) must render a well determined value for *every* object; cf. GRG II, § 56.
61. GRL, § 95.
62. GRL, § 94; also § 95, third line, § 96 *in fine* and p. 119.
63. Kerry [1], p. 272.

64. *Ibid.*
65. For Cantor, cf. Cantor [1], p. 440–442. For Marty, cf. Section 6.2.
66. Kerry [1], p. 273 note.
67. Cf. Section 6.1.
68. Kerry [1], p. 281f.
69. Kerry [1], p. 265.
70. Aristotle [3], (*Anal. Priora*) A, 27.
71. For some explanation of this, cf. Section 6.54.
72. "Es zeigte sich, dass die Zahl, mit der sich die Arithmetik beschäftigt, nicht als ein unselbständiges Attribut, sondern substantivisch gefaßt werden muß" (GRL, p. 116).
73. GRL, p. X; this is the text referred to by Kerry in order to support the first part of the thesis that Frege introduced in GRL an "absolute" separation of concepts and objects.
74. Section 6.41.
75. Cf. Kerry's text in Section 6.51. I quote the passage of GRL in Section 6.42.
76. GRL, p. 68.
77. GRL, § 66.
78. GRL, p. 82.
79. Cf. Section 6.75.
80. Section 6.42. I mean not necessarily in Kerry's way.
81. Section 6.41.
82. "Ich bin nun zwar der Meinung, daß beide Einwände gehoben werden können; aber das möchte hier zu weit führen" (GRL, p. 80 note).
83. Our text (3) should be compared with GRL, § 34, where it is stressed that the process of abstraction leads to *nur Einer* (concept).
84. GRL, § 54.
85. Kerry [1], p. 273.
86. *Ibid*: ". . . so z.B. bedeutet in dem Satze "der Begriff, von dem ich jetzt eben spreche, ist ein Individualbegriff", der aus den ersten acht Wörtern bestehende Name, wiewohl er mit dem bestimmten Artikel versehen ist ("der Begriff"), sicherlich einen Begriff und – falls ein Begriff nicht zugleich auch Gegenstand sein kann – keinen Gegenstand."
87. "Man kann nämlich auch positiv zeigen daß Begriffe zugleich Gegenstände – und hierin liegt ja auch das Umgekehrte involvirt – sein können. Betrachtet man auch den Fall des Begriffes von einem Begriffe [. . .] und den Fall einander subordinirter Begriffe als verschieden von den Verhältnissen, wie es zwischen Begriff und Gegenstand besteht, und läßt sie darum hier nicht in Frage kommen, so muß doch, um gleich ein Beispiel zu geben, eingeräumt werden, daß vermöge des Urteiles: "Der Begriff 'Pferd' ist ein leicht gewinnbarer Begriff" der Begriff "Pferd" auch Gegenstand ist und zwar einer der Gegenstände, die unter den Begriff "leicht gewinnbarer Begriff" fallen. Ebenso fallen unter Begriffe, wie der von Frege in seiner Darlegung [. . .] benutzte: "gleichzahlig dem Begriffe F" einer ist, lauter Begriffe als Gegenstände" (Kerry [1], p. 274).
88. "Wenn daher Frege nicht müde wird zu betonen, daß die 0, die 1, u.s.w. nur als Gegenstände anzusehen seien – Begriffe seien sie jedenfalls nicht – so wäre dem gegenüber vorerst das Resultat der obigen Ausführungen: daß Gegenständlichkeit und Begrifflichkeit einander nicht ausschließen, geltend zu machen . . ." (Kerry [1], p. 274).

89. Cf. Section 6.41.
90. BGGE, p. 193.
91. Cf. Chapter 3, note 20.
92. Cf. note 88.
93. BGGE, pp. 202–204.
94. BGGE, p. 195.
95. Cf. 6.531.
96. Moreover, it should be observed:
    (a) References to the definite article continue to concern primarily the passage from $\varphi(x)$ to $(\imath x)(\varphi x)$ and not the magic creation of non-concepts out of concepts. Cf. FUB, p. 5; BGGE, p. 204, 1.10–13.
    (b) Frege's references (in BGGE) to his previous works are quite questionable. They are: (b1) p. 195, note 2, (b2) p. 197, note 1, (b3) p. 199. The first concerns the "criterion" of the definite article; as we mention in the present section, Frege refers to texts (4), (7) and (8) of our list in 6.532. Frege should at least have taken into account the fact that these texts hardly provide a clear criterion in the sense of BGGE. The second reference to GRL (b2) amounts to saying that the idea of a "transformation" (*verändern*) of concepts into objects in GRL, p. X was exactly what Kerry understood it to be. The third reference (b3) concerns GRL, p. 80, note; the same remarks apply here as in the case of (b1).
97. BGGE, p. 196.
98. BGGE, pp. 196–197.
99. *Ibid.*
100. BGGE, p. 204: "indem ein Gegenstand genannt wird, wo ein Begriff gemeint ist". Cf. BGGE, p. 197, note 3.
101. "Die Sprache aber ist, wie wir sehen, das Wahrhaftere; in ihr widerlegen wir selbst unmittelbar unsere Meinung . . ." (Hegel [1], A, 1).
102. If it is at all possible to say that what we mean by "the concept F" is a concept.
103. BGGE, p. 197.
104. *Ibid.*
105. BGGE, p. 198.
106. BGGE, p. 199.
107. *Ibid.*
108. BGGE, p. 205.
109. BGGE, p. 199.
110. BGGE, p. 200–201. It is important to observe that sentences (4), (5) and (7) are said to express the same *Gedanke* (BGGE, p. 196 note).
111. *Ibid.*, p. 201.
112. FUB, p. 19; GRG 1, p. 7 (at the end of § 2).
113. Frege says "vertreten", BGGE, p. 197.
114. For the present section cf. Wells [1], p. 550.
115. $DISS_2$, p. 2; also $DISS_1$, introduction, "eindeutige Zuordnung".
116. BG, pp. 18, 57.
117. Cf. Section 6.1.
118. Cf. for instance Section 6.42. "Predicability" is the name for unsaturatedness in the paradigmatic case of concepts; BGGE, p. 197, note.
119. To this extent I am inclined to disagree with Prof. Bergmann's interesting argument (Bergmann [2]). As to the opposition of concept and function in Cassirer [1], there seems to be some misunderstanding and unclearness in-

volved. For instance, on page 28 of Cassirer's book the "advantage" of functions consists in that they (their names!) have *variables*, and that thereby the *Inbegriff*, the class of entities falling under the concept, is somehow preserved. This is what enables Cassirer to hold that in the new approach abstraction does not lead to ever more impoverished contents, in fact, the poorer the concept, the wider the class. Cassirer seems to oppose one-place to many-place predicates, rather than exemplification to mapping. In any case the Fregean synthesis of the latter appears not to be reached by Cassirer's argument.

120. FUB, p. 28f; also GRG I, § 72.
121. As possible antecedents, there is perhaps the conception of concepts as rules (Gassendi, Kant); cf. Aaron [1], pp. 112, 93.
122. GRL's reference to unsaturatedness, on the contrary, is not preceded by that semantic distinction (GRL, § 70).
123. Examples are abundant in Frege's works. The first (apart from GRL, § 70) are to be found in FUB, pp. 17, 18, 19, 27.
124. This is also a constantly recurring theme in Frege's works. Apart from GRL, § 70, the first references appear in FUB, pp. 6, 7–8.
125. Cf. below, Section 6.771.
126. Cf. *ibid.*, note 4.
127. Frege would prefer this symbolism rather than "2*x*", in order to express the function "the double of a number *x*". The reason is that "*x*" is used *also* in order to express universality ("any").
128. FUB, p. 7–8. The image of open and closed intervals seems to have played a dominant role in Frege's insight into unsaturatedness; see the last page of BGGE.
129. This is again a frequently recurring theme in Frege's works, after FUB.
130. This is the most which Frege's published or unpublished works may allow one to say; the term "analogy" is mine. Cf. note 135 below. Also, Stenius [1], p. 138.
131. BGGE, p. 193 note; for "grammatical predicate" cf. 3.3. Carnap [2], § 38 erroneously associates "incomplete symbols" with unsaturated symbols.
132. This *a priori* follows from the fact that grammatical predicates in ordinary language are viewed as names of functions (names of concepts), and *therefore* they must include empty argument places. And Frege, in fact, stresses that the unsaturatedness should be expressed either by empty brackets (not "sin *x*" but, better, "sin( )", WIF, p. 664), or by points ("...", VERN, p. 155) or by a special letter ("ξ", GRG II, § 63). This for natural language or mathematics; for the description of his *Begriffsschrift* Frege uses a special symbolism for unsaturatedness.
133. BGGE, p. 197, note 3; also UBR, p. 9.
134. "Gegenstand ist Alles, was nicht Function ist, dessen Ausdruck also keine leere Stelle mit sich führt" (FUB, p. 18). Apart from the peculiar Fregean view that objects are characterized by their names, this definition may be compared with a definition of individual (*Gegenstand*) given by Hering [1]: "... Alles, ausgenommen die Wesenheit und ihre Dienerin die Washaftigkeit" (p. 510, n. 3). Cf. GRG I, §§ 1, 2, 4.
135. Cf. GRG II, p. 148, note 2; also a letter to Russell, dated 1904, in Bartlett [1], p. 56; or VERN, p. 155, where it is said that names should "reflect" the unsaturatedness of entities. But I would not affirm that Frege always thought

in this way. In the *Nachwort* (GRG II) both kinds of unsaturatedness appear, but is it clear which is the first? Or in WIF (p. 665) is not the unsaturatedness of names perhaps the prior one?

136. BGGE, p. 196, note 2.
137. BGGE, pp. 195, 196 (and note), 198 (bottom), 204, 205.
138. *Ibid.*, p. 196.
139. BGGE, p. 196, note 2. We cannot name grammatical predicates unless by means of unsaturated signs. This is why Carnap's solution (cf. Geach [1], p. 146), consisting in recourse to language about language, cannot be accepted.
140. Professor Geach points out two ways of escaping the paradox. These seem to be intended to preserve Frege's system. The first (Geach [1], p. 156) is to be found also in the *Nachlaß* ("was ..." = "what ..."), but it seems to be a concession which could be only momentarily taken into account. In fact, the proposed expression would have no passport enabling it to enter Frege's world, where it is asked: *Begriffswort oder Eigenname*? (GRG II, p. XII, top; the "oder" is exclusive). If concept-word, the expression must have an empty place; if proper name it must have *no* empty place. The "*was*" solution is an *ad hoc* solution, resorted to in order to formulate in ordinary language a criterion of identity of meaning for concept words (cf. Bartlett [1], p. 50). Frege could not consistently assume it; and on the other hand he gives only a tentative and hesitating formulation, *en passant* and *ad hoc*. The criterion of identity for concepts is qualified in such a way that Frege is obliged to speak of an *uneigentlichen Gebrauch des Wortes "dasselbe"*, and one wonders whether this is not the same as saying that the two "*was* ..." expressions at both sides of "=" are not capable of *ausfüllen* (GRG I, p. 37) the two gaps of the function ( ) *dasselbe* ( ). I think that the second solution proposed by Professor Geach fails because of the same reasons.
    Dummett [1] mentions "two ways of escape" (from the paradox). Unfortunately, the second does not seem to be quite clear. As to the first, I think that it is in agreement with Frege's *implicit* higher predication (cf. Section 6.8), but I believe that no Fregean name of concept can fill the empty place of "the concept '( )' is realized".
    In my view, there is no way out of the paradox, if one wishes to stay *within* Frege's system. *Outside* Frege's system solutions have been available for many centuries.
    Frege himself clearly indicates that there is no real way out. In *Über Logik und Mathematik* (Dated 1914. I am grateful to the Library of the University of Münster for having provided a microfilm of this long unpublished text), Frege continues to maintain, as in BGGE (p. 204 bottom) that one has to take such expressions as "the function ..." *cum grano salis*. "*Cum grano salis*" indicates that we should take into account what we *mean* and not what we *say*. Is this perhaps the simplest way out?
141. Martinus de Dacia [1], *Modi significandi*, n. 3. Cf. Tomas de Erfurt [1].
142. *Ibid.*, n. 32.
143. *Ibid.*, *Quaest. sup. lib. Porph.*, q. 19 (p. 144). Frege would say that "homo" and "humanitas" have different reference because they are not meaningfully interchangeable (BGGE, p. 201, top).
144. "Humanitas autem, licet significat illud idem [as "homo"] cum tamen non eodem modo, sed de suo modo intelligendi habet modum significandi in ab-

stractione, quasi absolvendo hanc formam, quae est humanitas, ab omni materia ..." (Martinus de Dacia [1], *Quaest. sup. lib. Porph.*, q. 19).

145. Hilbert-Ackermann [1], p. 114; also p. 50. Russell [4], § 49 is a quite "traditional" reply to Frege's *Ungesättigtheit*: properties of concepts are called "external relations" and the marks of concepts are described as the "intrinsic nature" of concepts. Russell (*ibid.*) tries to show that unsaturatedness leads to contradictions, but Frege will say that these are *scheinbare Widersprüche* (UGG_1, p. 372). One of the three points of disagreement between Russell and Frege is precisely that Russell rejects the Fregean unsaturatedness (*ibid.*, § 475). But there seems to be a grave misunderstanding involved in Russell's consideration of unsaturatedness; § 481 seems to read BGGE, pp. 195 and 197 (not 196!) as if "the concept F" were the name of a name, rather than the name of an object as Frege holds. Russell [4] (§ 481) is obscure on this point, but I presume that the author was misled by the reference to inverted commas in BGGE, p. 197, or perhaps also by a letter of Frege dated 1902, where the latter apparently suggests that the paradoxes of unsaturatedness do not pass into metalanguage (against our Section 6.74 *in fine*). In any case, "Frege's theory" (on unsaturatedness) is *not* the one found in Russell [4] (§ 483).
For a recent criticism of Frege's doctrine, cf. Kneale [1], especially p. 586 (also: pp. 621, 622, 667, 671).

146. When Frege talks about *das Wesen der Function*, this seems to concern only designata, not signs (FUB, p. 3, GRG I, § 1). Still, in a letter to Russell (edited by Bartlett [1], p. 57), Frege declares: "Die Isolierung des Funktionszeichens widerspricht dem Wesen der Funktion." Does the essence of a function consist in being named in some particular way? In the present section I suggest that the answer is trivially affirmative, for functions are also names (perhaps) for Frege. In any case, his stress upon the distinction between signs and designata (for instance: GRL, p. 107; UFT, p. 97 last line; FUB, p. 4 top; GRG II, p. 72) is hardly compatible with someone so concerned with names, unless one grants that for him *names themselves are the object of research.*

147. Cf. Section 2.12.

148. Cf. Carnap [3], *Introduction to Semantics*, p. 233.

149. Aristotle [2], Z, 1, 1028a, 20–27. Also Aristotle [3], (*An. Post.* A, 22) 83b, 17–23; the idea of *prosthesis*, for instance, points to a similar fact (cf. Ross in Aristotle [3], p. 582). These ideas have been developed by the philosophical tradition. Cf. Aquinas [1], n. 1255; Caietanus [1], p. 244f. Pacius [2] will say that an accident *connotat subiectum.*

150. Martinus de Dacia [1], *Modi significandi*, n. 41 and 43, and *Quaest. sup. lib. Porph.*, q. 19 (p. 144). Our author uses the term *indeterminatio*, which seems to be reserved for the dimension singularity–universality.

151. Aristotle [4], B, 2, 193b, 35. Frege, on the contrary, will say that concepts can be *unterschieden*, but not *abgeschieden* from their relation to objects (UGG_1, p. 372).

152. As Scholz [5] (pp. 15–16) has pointed out. Cf. the following passage: "Begriffe aber beziehen sich, als Prädicate möglicher Urteile, auf irgend eine Vorstellung von einem noch unbestimmten Gegenstand" (Kant [3], p. 86).

153. FUB, p. 7.

154. BGGE, *in fine.*

155. Is not the name of what we *mean* by saying "UF". For, again, "UF" (if taken

as a saturated name) would fail to designate a relation.

156. GRG I, p. 39.
157. As presented, for instance, by Suarez [1], VII, sect. 1, n. 18, 19, etc.
158. But we find, again, in classical ontology, the individuality of accidents, and even modes: "haec inhaerentia numero" (*ibid.*).
159. For example Maimon [1], p. 56: "Ein allgemeiner Begriff wird als etwas auf mehr als einerlei Art Bestimmbares gedacht. Er muß daher durch zwei mit einander verbundene Zeichen ausgedrückt werden. Ein Zeichen für das (gegebene) Bestimmbare, und das andere für die unbestimmte Bestimmung. Er kann also durch ax bezeichnet werden, a bedeutet (so wie in der Algebra) das gegebene Bestimmbare, und x eine jede mögliche Bestimmung desselben."
160. Church [1], note 32; Scholz–Hasenjaeger [1], p. 127.
161. Whitehead–Russell [1], Introd. 1st. ed., Ch. II.
162. *Ibid.*
163. "When we say that "φx" ambiguously denotes φa, φb, φc, etc., we mean that "φx" means one of the objects φa, φb, φc, etc., though not a definite one, but an undetermined one" (p. 39). "We may regard the function itself as that which ambiguously denotes, while an undetermined value of the function is that which is ambiguously denoted" (p. 40). "The function itself, $\varphi \hat{x}$, is the single thing which ambiguously denotes its many values; while φx, where x is not specified, is one of the denoted objects, with the ambiguity belonging to the manner of denoting" (p. 40).
164. P. 47.
165. "This [the formulation of the rules of types] arises from the fact that a function is essentially an ambiguity, and that, if it is to occur in a definite proposition, it must occur in such a way that the ambiguity has disappeared and a wholly unambiguous statement has resulted" (p. 47). "But it is obvious that we cannot substitute for the function something which is not a function" (p. 47).
"... when a function can occur significantly as argument, something which is not a function cannot occur significantly as argument. But conversely, when something which is not a function can occur significantly as argument, a function cannot occur significantly ..." (p. 48).
"... a function is a mere ambiguity awaiting determination ... and in order that it may occur significantly it must receive the necessary determination, which it obviously does not receive if it is merely substituted for something determinate in a proposition" (p. 48).
Finally, p. 48, note, there is a reference to a rule according to which "the elimination of the functional ambiguity is necessary to significance".
All this should be compared with Frege's statement:
"... erkennen wir daß ein Functionsname niemals die Stelle eines Eigennamens einnehmen kann, weil er leere Stellen entsprechend der Ungesättigtheit der Function mit sich führt ... Als Argument der Function $X(\ )$ kann also niemals selbst wieder eine Function auftreten, wohl aber der Wert einer Function für ein Argument ..." (GRG I, § 21).
166. Cf., for instance, p. 49, note.
167. Cf. note 160.
168. This would especially concern the distinction *Sinn–Bedeutung*. Cf. Section 2.23.
169. BG, p. 17. UGG_1, p. 371 note 2 would confirm that "Rang" in BG anticipates the later *Stufen*.

170. GRL, p. 65 bottom.
171. But Frege kindly admits that one could have interpreted GRL in a sense other than Kerry's. BGGE, p. 199.
172. Perhaps the best Fregean page for this is GRG I, p. 37; some passages have been quoted in note 165.
173. Cf. note 132.
174. Section 6.6.3.
175. Cf. for instance Fitch [1], 17.1, attributes implicitly or explicitly assigned. This is a terminology familiar in mathematics.
176. BGGE, p. 199.
177. Cf. 6.771, note 151.
178. Cf. 6.75, note 145.
179. Frege's symbolism for existential quantification is of course different. Cf. FUB, p. 26.
180. Implicit higher predication may have been suggested to Frege by mathematical analysis; in integrals, for instance, there is a reference to the variable of the integrated function. Cf. FUB, *in fine*, GRG I, pp. 38–39; JOURD, p. 266.
181. GRG I, § 22.
182. BGGE, p. 201.
183. GRG I, p. 39.
184. GRG I, § 24.
185. Cf. Sluga [1], p. 197.
186. With respect to being saturated, see below in this section.
187. Cf. FUB, *in fine*.
188. GRG I, p. 41. Cf. Sluga [1]. Frege should be defended against Carnap [2], § 38, where it is overlooked that Frege did classify expressions into meaningless and meaningful (the latter being either true or false); cf. for instance BGGE, p. 200.

7. THE IDEA OF LEVELS (*STUFEN*) IN THE PHILOSOPHICAL TRADITION

> Hier kommt meine Unterscheidung von Begriffen erster und zweiter Stufe in Betracht – ich sage "meine", weil mir nicht bekannt ist, daß sie vor mir in hinreichender Schärfe gemacht ist. (Frege, UBR, p. 23)

Summary and general remarks. In the present chapter those elements of the philosophical tradition which may be said to involve a *structure of levels* are examined (7.1). The analysis begins with some miscellaneous remarks about several doctrines which seem to be of this kind (7.2–7.4). As for second intentions (the most suitable theme for comparison with Frege's and contemporary logic's levels), little research has been done which could serve as a starting point. After examining three important cases (Aquinas, Scotus, Ockham: 7.51–7.53), I propose some general considerations about the usual manner of presenting second intentions in traditional textbooks (7.54). Although Nizolius' contribution to second intentions seems to be unimportant, he is the only (known) "extensionalist" thinker of the philosophical tradition, and to this extent it was necessary to inquire whether he had classes of classes (7.55). In modern philosophy, second intentions and predicates of predicates no longer attract the attention of philosophers (7.56). Finally, Brentano's views (7.57) are examined and the chapter is completed by a brief reference to Platonism and levels (7.58).

7.1 Introduction

Frege's idea of *Stufen* (levels) suggests one's asking whether the philosophical tradition had considered anything similar. This question may be reduced to seeing whether the following schema had been taken into account in philosophy before Frege. Accordingly, the particular Fregean interpretation of levels (implicit higher predicates[1]) will not be stressed but rather we shall focus upon Frege's previous insight as it appears in

GRL, which might also have developed in the direction of explicit[2] higher predication. The traditional ambiguity concerning "accident" and "predicate" makes it necessary to take also into account possible speculations on "levels" in the domain of accidents.

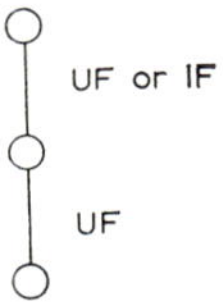

Speaking of "levels", we do not imply "rules of types", sanctioning certain expressions as meaningless, but simply the fact of a structure wherein the relation of predication (singularity–universality) is, so to speak, iterated.[3] There must be an entity which is a predicate of a predicate of an individual. As a counterexample, it is worth noting that the Aristotelian structure of secondary and primary substance does *not* fulfil our requirements.[4]

Finally, it is important to remember that traditional terminology is quite misleading on this point, because class inclusion (subordination of concepts) is *also* predicates of predicates. The famous principle "nota notae est nota rei" may erroneously suggest that "true" higher predicates are meant.[5]

7.2 Accidents of accidents

> Porro hoc quoque addam, quod accidens quoque dicatur saepe accidentis subiectum, sed modo quodam imperfecto. Sicut enim accidens est ens imperfectum, ita etiam est subiectum; imo proprie loquendo accidenti nihil accidit, qua accidens est, ne detur progressus in infinitum; id quod philosophus docuit 4. Metaph. text. 14 cum inquit: [. . .] id est accidens non est accidentis accidens, nisi quatenus ambo inhaerent subiecto uni, scilicet perfecte dicto, seu substantiae. Et certum est quando accidenti aliquid tribuitur, seu inesse dicitur, id plerumque esse nudam relationem; ut cum duabus qualitatibus tribuitur similitudo; quantitatibus aequalitas; lineis anguli; numeris proportio; peccato gravitas vel levitas.[6]

1. Even in an author like Keckermann, who is quite aware of the two ontological dimensions[7], the treatment of accidents of accidents shows

how vague the borderlines are between this and the parallel question of predicates of predicates.

2. Keckermann takes a position against authors maintaining that there are accidents of accidents.[8] Agreeing with some main lines of traditional ontology, he admits such a view, but with the reservation that an accident is accident of another accident only in so far as they both inhere in a "true" subject. This is strikingly similar to Frege's *implicit* higher predication.[9]

3. Finally, our author takes advantage of the fact that relations are deprived of a "strong" ontological status in order to place many interesting properties (accidents? predicates?) of accidents under the heading of "mere relations".

7.3 Self-predication

The class of men is not a man, nor has the concept *being number two* the property of being the half of four.[10] In Frege's published works there is no reference to self-predication, which is naturally excluded by the Fregean doctrine on unsaturatedness.[11]

The theme is Platonic[12] and has received particular attention in certain areas of traditional philosophy. The better known scholastic formal logicians do not seem to have shown much concern for self-predication[13], as is indirectly suggested by the fact that semantic paradoxes rather than logical ones are discussed by them.[14] Still, there are authors, perhaps more philosophers of logic than logicians, who have seriously considered that the property of being universal is universal, while the property of being a man is not a man.[15] Of course, to say that the class of *universalia* contains itself is dangerous, unless logical frameworks ensuring consistency are provided.[16]

7.4 Duns Scotus: 'modus intrinsecus'

In *albedo intensa* we do not have a concept with two marks.[17] "Intense" qualifies whiteness, and is a property of the latter rather than another mark of the concept. The same applies to "infinite".[18] Traditional philosophers, faced with these higher properties, were destined to begin by affirming that they are *not* marks, or that they do not belong to the essence, or that they only "happen", extrinsically, to the essence[19]; all this because by Aristotelian standards properties of properties were above all concepts related by UO. Duns Scotus' *modus intrinsecus* is precisely an example of this.[20]

7.5 Second intentions

Second intentions is a subject which still lacks a comprehensive presentation. In the present section I aim only at: (1) discussing some research already done, (2) suggesting some new approaches, either historical or of interpretation.

7.51 *Świeżawski on Duns Scotus*

Świeżawski [1] is a rare example of research on second intentions. The author concentrates on Duns Scotus and the earlier commentators. The paper is divided into a first expository part[21] and a second part dealing with second intentions in their relations to the categories, to universals and to predication theory.[22] There is a rich quotation of sources, which makes this paper a valuable anthology as well.

A Fregean reader who looks for objective contents and not for *Vorstellungen*, would be irritated by a first misleading definition of second intentions.[23] Nevertheless, this is corrected later in such a way that the intention in the strict sense of the word may be identified with *conceptus obiectivus*.[24] We are interested in objective intentions, not in the subjective acts "tending in" the object. The former are simply things themselves[25], and they may be divided into first and second intentions.[26] A first intention is *homo*; a second intention is *species*. These are intentions *in concreto* or *ut modus* (unsaturated). *In abstracto* or *ut quid* they become *humanitas* or *specialitas*.[27]

With Socrates–homo–species we already have the minimal structure required in the present chapter. But a further problem is whether there are *third* intentions, or *n*-intentions. Church [3], in establishing a comparison between simple types and second intentions, remarks that "no 'third' intentions were separated out or distinguished from second". But the term "second" seems to mean not a position in the series of predication, but the fact that a property is assigned to a thing as a consequence of our previous – "first" – knowledge of that thing.[28] For in spite of there not being "third" intentions, the series of predication goes upwards as exhuberantly as one may wish. While accidents of accidents are stopped ("nisi ratione subiecti"), there is no obstacle for an infinite *construction* of predicates of predicates.[29] Philosophers did not refrain from constructing such sentences as "universale est secunda intentio", "secunda intentio praedicatur de universale".[30]

In Świeżawski [1] we have many examples of the traditional periphrasis for describing phenomena of higher predication; properties of properties are, first of all, said to lie *outside* the properties to which they apply.[31]

7.52 *Hayen on Aquinas*

Hayen [1], after having presented a series of texts where Aquinas mentions second intentions, makes the following statement:

> Les rapports que nous avons relevés entre *conceptio*, *ratio*, *intentio*, etc. nous invitent à poser l'équation suivante: *intentio rei, sive verbum a mente conceptum* = *ratio sive definitio rei* + *intentio quam intellectus adinvenit.*
> Pour donner un sens à cette équation, il faudrait préciser la nature de l'*intentio quam intellectus adinvenit.*[32]

The most common trait of the texts presented by Hayen [1] is (what in modern language may be called) the attribution of a second-level property to a concept. It is clear that in Aquinas we find the structure which we require here, for instance, *genus–animal–asinus.*[33] I think that what should first be clarified is the sign "+" in the above text. The *intentio quam intellectus adinvenit* is simply a property of the *ratio sive definitio rei,* since the latter is a property of some individual or *suppositum.* Unfortunately, traditional predication theory teaches that marks of the *ratio sive definitio rei* are also properties of it. Frege would say that "+" *here* is IF (or UF, leaving aside his peculiar approach due to unsaturatedness). On the other hand, it is difficult to see exactly the point of some images proposed by Hayen [1] with respect to the sign "+".[34]

7.53 *Ockham*

Bocheński [1][35] considers two different conceptions of second intentions. The first is represented by Aquinas, the second by Ockham. Now,

Ockham's doctrine is rather puzzling, and one may wonder whether *there is* such a doctrine at all. For Ockham, second intentions (1) are concepts and, (2) are "predicated of" first intentions. But what does "concept" mean? If it means the same as "objective concept" then there is nothing peculiar in Ockham's doctrine. If it means *subjective* concept, then it is unintelligible, for, to use Frege's language, there is no possible sense for saying that "a *Vorstellung* is predicated of another *Vorstellung*". There are indications that one should understand Ockham in this subjective sense.[36] In Bocheński [1][37] it is suggested that ockhamist second intentions concern metalanguage, but this seems hardly conceivable if one considers that *just before dealing with second intentions* Ockham [1] discusses *names of names*, and both things seem to be given as quite different.[38] Thus, we seem to be obliged to view Ockham's second intentions according to the unintelligible sense of subjective concepts being predicated of subjective concepts. Perhaps the solution to this puzzle is that Ockham was not at all interested in the distinction subjective–objective (as applied to concepts[39]), which would involve his treatment of second intentions in an ambiguity equally irrelevant for him.

7.54 *Impact of traditional predication theory on a main interpretation of second intentions*

The famous small book *De Ente et Essentia* has as one of its main purposes the clarification of the relation between first-level predicates and those predicates such as *genus* or *species* which are not to be found among the things *in rerum natura*.[40] Not of course Frege's *Merkmal–Eigenschaft* but Avicenna's *triplex respectus* is applied in the treatment of higher predicates. Neither the platonic idea of animal, nor *animalitas* may be instances of the predicate *genus*; not *animalitas*, for people do not say "Socrates est animalitas"[41], and the assumption is that that thing which is an instance of *genus* is predicated of *Socrates*. Is then *animal* a genus? Following Avicenna, the *animal* of "Socrates est animal" may be taken in three ways: (1) in itself, (2) in the mind, (3) in the individuals. Thus one may say that animal in case (2) is, in fact, a genus. If *animal* in case (1) were a genus, then every animal would be a genus.

Second intentions, according to a usual account, are not located on the second floor of the logical building; second and first intentions are assigned different rooms on the same floor. To be a second intention a property must be shown to hold of an individual (or, more generally, a *res*) *qua known*; to be of the class of first intentions a property must be shown to hold of the individual *qua existing* independently of our knowledge. Thus, higher predicates give the appearance of being a special sort of first-level predicates. Thus, also, they came to be included in the little known *eleventh* category[42], one more class of entities. The following structure,

species
|
(1) *man*
|
Socrates,

may be conceived to be a traditional insight, neglected by Aristotle, who stressed rather a structure based on class-inclusion,

animal
|
(2) *man*
|
Socrates.

Now, (1) and (2) are not compatible insofar as "predication" is not qualified. The Avicennian qualification consists in transforming (1) into

species
|
(3) *man-in-the-mind* *man-in-itself*
|
Socrates.

We also know that the notion of *essence* led to the establishment of a sort of identity between *man* and *this man*, and led rather to the introduction of a neutral entity (*ousia*, *res*) which is neither universal nor singular (nor both). Schema (3) is *Categoriae* rather than *Metaphysics*. The *res* is the Avicennian *natura* isolated from its universal or individual existence. Thus (3) becomes, properly:

second intentions ↘ ↙ *first intentions*

(4) *res*

qua known, in the mind | *qua* being capable of existing independently of the mind

I suggest that the frequent presence of schema (4) in traditional textbooks[43] should not lead us to overlook the fact that the basic structure (1) is also there.

7.55 *Nizolius*

Nizolius [1] is the only known serious extensional approach in the history of philosophy.[44] Universals are substituted by *multitudines*. The universal *species* should be replaced by a class of classes, according to his program, but unfortunately Nizolius does not seem concerned with this. He says only that there is a maximal set, the *multitudo* of *entia* or *res*.[45] This invalidates his otherwise interesting attack on second intentions.[46]

7.56 *Modern philosophy*

About 1550 at the university of Evora public discussions were held on philosophy. But there was an especially solemn day, when, in the presence of higher authorities, the question of first and second intentions was the object of heated dispute.[47] This festive assembly was perhaps the closing episode in the history of second intentions because some years later Port-Royal joyously declared that "personne, Dieu mercy, ne prend interest à l'Universel a parte rei, à l'être de raison *ny aux secondes intentions*" (italic ours).[48] In fact, Port-Royal [1] contributed very little to second intentions[49], which began to fade out[50] until philosophers like Frege rediscovered them.

7.57 *Brentano*

Brentano [2] comes upon the traditional *locus* for higher predication: the "praedicabilia". As any other traditional philosopher, Brentano has to "find a place" for higher predicates, and this he does in that sphere of being which Aristotle calls *ens tanquam verum*.[51] From entities belonging to this class, true propositions are made, but these entities do not have any existence outside the mind. This prepares the way for Brentano's later view that names of higher predicates have only contextual meaning, not even designating *entia rationis*.[52] He extends traditional syncategoremata to include also those names or adjectives denoting *entia rationis*, in particular higher predicates.[53] The point here is to find sentences, (1) equivalent to those containing syncategoremata but where, (2) the syncategoremata have – to a certain extent – disappeared.[54] In mentioning this desideratum Brentano refers to Leibniz[55] and obviously the method dates from earlier times (Paulus Venetus [2], the largest work on formal logic before *Principia* in the Western tradition, has as *the* main task that of providing for any obscure construction of ordinary Latin an "if and only if" equivalent, which is mostly a conjunction of more perspicuous sentences). Brentano's elimination of fictitious names is based upon conceiving of them as denoting what a real, *hic et nunc* human being has in mind intentionally.[56] Thereby, the fictitious name is not absolutely eliminated from the sentence, but the new sentence no longer contains it in the privileged position of a grammatical subject.[57] Second intentions are thus only "obliquely" seen.[58] There is certainly a great similarity between this and Frege's allowing only implicit[59] higher predicates. The difference would consist in the fact that Brentano confines higher predicates not to the domain of paradoxes ("the concept F" is not the name of a concept), but to a domain very close to Frege's indirect speech.

7.58 *Levels and platonism*

The traditional approach to higher predicates has had the obvious effect of having contributed to the opening of an abyss[60] between second intentions and the real world. Without this abyss between *homo*-in-the-mind and *homo*-in-itself or *homo*-in-the-individuals[61] higher predicates would have become mere predicates of individuals. Once Frege's new logic provides a better theory of predication, it is no longer requisite to separate in that way *species* from *man*. Now, this is not necessarily to commit oneself to platonism[62]; it is, merely, to have a more adequate language.

REFERENCES

1. Cf. Section 6.8.
2. *Ibid.*
3. Cf. Fitch [1].

4. Cf. Beth [1], p. 498, and Fraenkel-Bar-Hillel [1], p. 168 n. 3.
5. Another example of pseudo-levels: "quality of quality" in Trendelenburg [1], pp. 225–226.
6. Keckermann [1], Liber 1, cap. XX, *in fine*.
7. Keckermann's treatises on logic are to a great extent ontology, insofar as they follow the contents of the *Organon*. Cf. Chapter 1, notes 62 and 63.
8. "Un accident peut être le sujet d'un autre accident", will say later Descartes, quoted in Gilson [3], p. 4.
9. Cf. Section 6.8.
10. GRG II, p. 253; UFT, p. 100.
11. This is confirmed by Sluga [1], pp. 198–199. But Frege's version of self-predication proposed therein is unintelligible, because it depends on unsaturatedness and on what a class really is.
12. Cf. for instance Kent Sprague [1], pp. 26–28, Moravcsik [1].
13. This is apparent in Bocheński [1].
14. Prior [2], p. 286 points out that Buridan erroneously deals with a true case of self-predication as if it were to be solved by mere semantic means.
15. "Objicies secundo: si universale genus esset horum universalium colligeretur aperte, non esse quinque universalia, consequens absurdum videtur, ergo et antecedens. Maior probatur hoc modo: genus est species universalis, igitur genus et species erunt unicum universale. Dicendum est, speciem non praedicari de genere, ea ratione qua species est: haec enim propositio falsa est, secunda notio generis est species universalis, hoc est denominatur a secunda notione speciei: siquidem potest praedicari de pluribus differentibus numero in eo quod quid. Neque hoc est aliquod inconveniens: nam quemadmodum homo, et albedo sunt duae species, quarum una albedo videlicet denominat hominem, ita etiam secunda notio generis et speciei sunt duae species, quarum altera, hoc est secunda notio speciei denominat secundam notionem generis hac denominatione, quod sit species. Neque hoc solum fieri poterit, sed etiam ut, *aliqua notio seipsam denominet*: quemadmodum universalitas denominat seipsam universalem, atque secunda notio speciei seipsam speciem denominat, ex accidenti tamen. Nam cum proprium sit secundae notionis speciei rem illam afficere, quae de pluribus differentibus numero praedicari potest in eo quod quid, atque contingat ipsammet notionem de pluribus secundis notionibus in quaestione quid est praedicari, ideo seipsam denominat speciem. *Eodem modo de universalitate, et aliquibus aliis secundis notionibus* loquendum est. Hinc ortum habuit illud, quod de Dialectica dicitur, nimirum ipsam non solum deseruire aliis scientiis, sed etiam sibi: *reflectuntur enim secundae notiones interdum in seipsas*, atque ita praecepta quibus aliae scientiae utuntur, in Logica ipsa exerceri possunt" (Gasconius [1], f. 13, italics ours).

    It is interesting to observe how cumbersome the Aristotelian predication theory was for dealing with these subtle phenomena of higher predicates. Higher predicates are submitted to the preliminary remark that they do not belong to . . . the set of marks (of essences). They are in a sense equated with accidental *properties of individuals*, which is true because neither *white* nor *universal* belong to the set of marks of the concept *man*. Unfortunately, this seems to be all that Aristotelian logic can say about higher predicates: they apply to other predicates, they apply even to themselves . . . *ex accidenti tamen*.
16. Cf. Fitch [1].

17. Gilson [2], p. 53 note.
18. "L'infinité n'est de la raison d'aucun attribut comme tel. Si elle l'était, elle serait incluse dans la définition de chacun d'eux et il n'y aurait alors de sagesse ou de bonté qu'infinies, ce qui est manifestement faux." (Gilson [2], p. 248). We find here a variant of the argument mentioned in Section 5.42.
19. ". . . l'infinité n'est à proprement parler un attribut de Dieu, mais le mode propre de l'essence divine" (*ibid.*).
20. ". . . et non intrare quidditatem rei sed ipsam circumstare." In such terms a later scotist, Mastrius de Meldula, describes the "modus intrinsecus" (quoted by Alcorta [1], p. 160).
21. Pp. 205–241.
22. Pp. 242–244, 244–252, 252–261, respectively.
23. A relation "entre la raison et l'objet de son acte comparatif" (p. 211). Of course, "intentio" had also, perhaps primarily, a subjective sense, but this is not the point of the discussions on second intentions in traditional philosophy.
24. "l'objet de l'acte raisonnable" (pp. 221–223).
25. P. 221, note.
26. *Ibid.*
27. P. 241.
28. Ioannes a Sto. Thoma [1], p. 292 (I owe this reference to Prof. A. Moreno). For Duns Scotus' school, cf: "secunda intentio [potest] cognosci ab intellectu et in quantum obiectum cognitum [est . . .] prima intentio" (Sarnanus, quoted by Świeżawski [1], p. 211, note 3). The same idea in Piaget.
29. Texts quoted and the author's own conclusion (p. 227) confirm that a *processus in infinitum* is allowed. The so-to-speak "constructive" character of these predicates of predicates is clear in Ioannes a Sto Thoma's text referred to in the preceding note.
30. Quoted from Sarnanus, in Świeżawski [1], p. 247, note.
31. Pp. 232, 234, 239 (note 2), 240. At the same time, the author mentions the Avicennian doctrine of the *triplex respectus* without discussing its intimate relation to higher predicates (pp. 244–252), in the sense in which, I think, that should be done (cf. our Chapter 5). Moreover, it is regrettable that the author has not discussed such important questions as self-predication or quantification of higher predicates. Nevertheless, Świeżawski [1] is not only a remarkable contribution, but it is worth noting that it is a work done with acquaintance with modern logic, an exception indeed in the early thirties.
32. P. 216.
33. P. 217.
34. "La difficulté, pensons nous, serait sans issue, si l'*intentio* n'était qu'une forme inerte et bien decoupée, colleé comme une étiquette a la *natura cui attribuitur*" (p. 217, above).
35. Pp. 176–179.
36. Baudry [1] "intentio", shows that intentions should be understood as acts of the mind, and he quotes: "tam intentiones primae quam secundae sunt vere entia realia quia sunt vere qualitates existentes subjective in intellectu". Cf. also De Wulf [1], §§ 380, 472.
37. Pp. 176–179.
38. Cf. also Baudry [1], "impositio". But certainly second intentions and names of names are closely related.

39. De Wulf [1], § 380.
40. Aquinas [3], Chapter 3.
41. "Animal" is opposed to "animalitas" because "animal" signifies the same thing *per modum totius*, not *per modum partis* as does the abstract term "animalitas". Frege says that "the concept F" is only *a part* of the grammatical predicate, i.e., of the name of the concept in question (BGGE, p. 197). "Animal" is unsaturated, as "... is an animal" in Frege's system; it involves, though *implicite et indistincte, totum quod in individuo est.* Would Frege have admitted that "the concept F" is a name of a concept *per modum partis*?
42. The eleventh category is meticulously described in, for instance, Gasconius [1].
43. Authors presenting schema (4) are Caietanus [2], pp. 18–19; Eust. a Sto-Paulo, quoted by Gilson [3], p. 107; Signoriello [1], "intentio"; Fonseca [1], lib. primus, cap. 32; Ioannes a Sto. Thoma [1], p. 291, bottom; and of course many others. Recently, cf. Gardeil [1], p. 52.
44. Cf. Angelelli [1].
45. "... supra quod nullum est genus ..." (Nizolius [1], Lib. II, cap. IX).
46. Cf. the index of Nizolius [1]: "Intentiones primae et secundae in philosophiam introductae fuerunt propter ignorationem sermonum propriorum et figuratorum", which is precisely Nixolius' point in semantics.
47. Pereira Gomez [1], p. 17.
48. Port-Royal [1], *Premier Discours.*
49. "Que si ces mots sont tiréz de quelque manière dont on conçoit les choses, on les appelle secondes intentions" (Port-Royal [1], Part. I, Ch. II). *To be a subject* and *to be a predicate* are examples of second intentions (*ibid.*).
50. Kant [3], pp. 280–281 speaks of "die logischen Functionen des Subjekts und Praedikats" (cf. preceding note). A rare reference is given in Spinoza [1], II, prop. 40, schol. 1. Kauppi [1], p. 48 suggests that Leibniz's *abstracta abstractorum* are in the line of "logical types", but the fact that Leibniz expresses them by means of adverbs (Couturat [1], (pp. 437–38) casts some doubt on this interpretation; adverbs in higher predication mean accidents rather than predicates (cf. Section 1.45, in particular note 108).
51. Brentano [2], Chapter V, § 8 (p. 113).
52. This is an important change in Brentano's thought; cf. Stegmüller [2], p. 16, note and p. 63, note.
53. Brentano [4], II, pp. 214–215; 231, *passim.*
54. "Daß man für jeden Satz, der etwas von dem Erwähnten zum Subjekt oder Prädikat zu haben scheint, einen äquivalenten bilden kann, bei welchem Subjekt und Prädikat durch Reales ersetzt sind" (Brentano [4], "Von den wahren und fiktiven Objekten", p. 163).
55. Brentano [1], p. 40.
56. "Wir können oft von solchen, was wir denkend zum Gegenstand haben, nichts prädizieren, weil er gar nicht ist und weil nur, was ist *in recto* mit etwas identifiziert werden kann. Gleichwohl haben wir es zum Objekt und nichts hindert, daß wir unser Denken seinem Gegenstande nach beschreiben" (Brentano [1], p. 43).
57. The expressions "ein den allgemeinen Begriff von etwas Denkender" or "ein etwas universell Denkender" are *echte Namen.* "Aber die darin verwendeten Worte "Begriff", "Gattung", "Spezies" sind es nicht, sie fungieren nur synsemantisch" (Brentano [1], p. 43).
58. I am grateful to Prof. F. Mayer-Hillebrand for generous information about

Brentano. On the basis of such information we may confirm that Brentano was not especially concerned with second intentions (in the sense of predicates of predicates, i.e., in the objective sense of "intentio"). A rare reference is to be found in Brentano [1], p. 57. Second intentions are absorbed by contextual meaning.

59. Cf. Section 6.8.
60. Cf. Clauberg's phrase quoted in Chapter 1, note 13. Cf. Bocheński [1], p. 179, or Aquinas [1], n. 574 and 1308, where we see how there is a parallelism between logic and metaphysics consisting in the fact that the former deals with *ens rationis*, while the second deals with "real" being.
61. Cf. Section 7.54.
62. As perhaps Brentano would say ([4], II, p. 275). Cf. also De Muralt [1], who refers to Husserl's platonism. But Husserl was rid of traditional predication theory (cf. in particular the text referred to in Chapter 5 note 39), and to this extent he was not obliged to drive away second intentions from his ontology in the sense of opening a Clauberg's abyss between them and real things.

8. *WERTVERLAUF*

Summary and general remarks. Frege's notion of *Begriffsumfang* (which preceded the introduction of *Wertverlauf*) is considered first (8.1). The notion of *Wertverlauf* was certainly *intended* to preserve the traditional *Begriffsumfang* as an interpretation of the "something common" which is yielded by definitions by abstraction. But at the same time Frege wishes to keep his *Wertverläufe* as unintuitive and semantically undetermined as possible (8.21). Thus it is necessary to consider two Fregean approaches to the notion of class. The first may be called *formal*; Frege views *Wertverläufe* simply as a result of definitions by abstraction (8.22). The second approach is that according to which the *Wertverlauf* signs are *intended* to denote the traditional extensions and then one may ask Frege what he means by "class".

Frege's statements about what classes really are must be carefully analysed, since some "class mythology" seems to have developed from it. I think that Frege should have interpreted classes in terms of *Sinn* and *Bedeutung* (8.31), but he decided to project classes into the platonic heaven (8.32). The conclusion is rather paradoxical with respect to the traditional *Begriffsumfang* (8.33).

Finally, it is indicated that the famous Axiom V was a hybrid result of the above mentioned approaches (8.4).

8.1 Frege's notion of extension of a concept before 'Wertverlauf'

Frege first mentions "Umfang des Begriffs" in a context dealing with Boole's logic.[1] In GRL Frege employs this expression many times. It is important to observe that he assumes that his readers are well acquainted with the meaning of the phrase "extension of a concept".[2]

At the time of GRL or UFT Frege does not seem to use the expressions "empty concept" or "empty class"; nevertheless, the former expression could be added to the text of those works without altering Frege's thought (the same does not apply to the latter expression, in my view). The insight into the nature of numbers led Frege to understand the number zero as an entity concerning concepts which do not have instances.[3]

In GRL and UFT there is a curious way of understanding the term "Menge". Frege assumes the meaning of this word as (1) excluding empty sets and unit-sets, (2) implying a sort of "juxtaposition in space".[4] Other related words are understood in a similar way.[5] Frege thereby ignores the respectable tradition of some of these terms.[6] In any case, it is because of such an interpretation of "Menge" that Frege prefers "Begriff" to "Menge".[7]

8.2 'Wertverlauf'

8.21 *Frege's intention with regard to "Wertverlauf"* (*of propositional functions*) *and extensions of concepts is twofold: both to preserve and to ignore their identity*

In the period from UFT (1885) to FUB[8] (1891) Frege conceived the notion of *Wertverlauf einer Funktion.*[9]

Frege had at least three motivations for introducing this notion. (1) *Wertverläufe* are objects, i.e. saturated entities, actually the only objects to be found in the domain of pure logic apart from the two truth-values; thus they appear to be very important for Frege's simultaneous assertion that numbers are objects and that arithmetic is logic.[10] (2) *Wertverläufe* allow him to dispense with unsaturatedness, i.e. with the corresponding unsaturated functions.[11] (3) In the particular case of *classes*, equi-extensional concepts have the same (non-semantic) *Bedeutung*: what "counts" is the class.[12]

Frege adopts two approaches to *Wertverläufe* in the particular case of extensions of concepts. One of them is based upon the traditional, familiar notion of *Begriffsumfang*, which Frege in GRL assumes to be known by his readers[13]; let us call this the *intuitive* approach. According to this, Frege could have associated with each sign "$\varepsilon\phi(\varepsilon)$" a well-known, familiar entity. There is also what may be called the *formal* approach; this is based on the "definitions by abstraction", which Frege extensively commented upon in GRL. One may think of $\varepsilon\phi(\varepsilon)$ as an entity determined by the equivalence-relation which applies between propositional functions when they yield the same truth-value for the same argument. Frege tries to prove that there is at least one and at most one such entity, but this is all we know about it.

In fact, although on the one hand Frege is very explicit in stating his desire to preserve traditional extensions under his *Wertverläufe*[14] (which does not imply that he achieved such a program, as will be seen), on the other hand he curiously clouds in mystery the designata of his *Wertverlauf*-signs. "Officially" *Wertverläufe* are introduced in the *Begriffsschrift* as an *etwas Gemeinsames*[15] which is possessed by two propositional functions when they are formally equivalent (in *Principia*'s language), but this "something common" is an entity about which we know only that it is . . . common (to some functions). Frege devotes one of his most difficult chapters (GRG, I, § 10) to eliminating such an indeterminate character in the meaning of the *Wertverlauf*-signs (namely, to show that they have only one designatum), and the most difficult part of his proof of "semantic completeness" (GRG I, § 31) is the proof that *Wertverlauf*-signs do always denote something. But the *Begriffsschrift* goes on as if we did not know at all what sort of things *Wertverläufe* are. Moreover, the uniqueness-existence assertion is provisional, i.e. relative to the functions we have introduced up to a certain point. Thus, those who play the game of the *Begriffsschrift* can pretend that they will never know exactly what a class is (so Frege in GRG I, § 10, *in fine*).

This attitude might be determined by his intention to weaken as much as possible the assumptions of the system, but I am inclined to believe that the decisive reason lies elsewhere, namely, in Frege's main goal of "grasping" numbers by means of his *Wertverläufe*. Ultimately, any commitment as to the real nature of classes would have been a commitment as to the real nature of numbers. Now, since GRL it was no longer a question of asking or saying what numbers really are. Frege only tried to "grasp" numbers by means of some device, for instance his famous "definition"; concepts (functions) were less useful for that than classes because of unsaturatedness. For the sake of the logical purity of his foundations of arithmetic, he thought it convenient to reduce the meaning of his *Wertverlauf*-signs to a minimum: *etwas Gemeinsames*. This is of course my interpretation, but *some* interpretation is needed here, not only to explain Frege's reluctance to combine his intuitive and formal approaches, but also to free him from the accusation of abusing definition by abstraction, as if the *etwas Gemeinsames* were some mysterious entity distinct from the mere partition of a set.[16]

We shall first examine Frege's formal approach; subsequently, the intricacies of Frege's intuitive statements about classes will be considered. The main victim of this unclear situation will be the famous Axiom V.

8.22 *Formal introduction of 'Wertverläufe'*

> Wie es auch immer sei, die durch Abstraktion erlangten Definitionen sind offenbar sehr unvollständig und unvollkommen, denn sie determinieren nicht den bestimmten Gegenstand und beweisen nicht seine Existenz.
>
> (Couturat, 'Die Prinzipien der Logik', *Enc. d. ph. W.*, I, p. 181)

Some steps or aspects in Frege's formal introduction of *Wertverläufe* into his *Begriffsschrift* will be considered.

(1) The words "the function $\Phi(\xi)$ has the same *Wertverlauf* as the function $\Psi(\xi)$" are synonymous (*gleichbedeutend*) with the words "the functions $\Phi(\xi)$ and $\Psi(\xi)$ yield the same value for any argument."[17] We shall not enter into the question whether "gleichbedeutend" means equality of *Bedeutung* only, or also *Sinn*. We have already seen that if a set of signs is introduced as an abbreviation of another, there is no reason to think that a different *Sinn* is involved.[18]

(2) Frege insists on the necessity of viewing as a logical law the passing from the formal equivalence of two functions (to use *Principia*'s language) to the identity of their *Wertverläufe*, and *vice versa*.[19] This "vice versa" will be dropped in the *Nachwort* of GRG II, as a possible way out of the contradiction.

(3) Frege says[20]: "es bedeute "$\grave{\varepsilon}\Phi(\varepsilon)$" *den* Wertverlauf der Function $\Phi(\xi)$" (italics ours).

(4) At this point Frege is obliged to deal with some inconsistency between (3) and (1). In (3) it seems to be assumed that there is such a thing as "the" *Wertverlauf* of a function, while in (1) there is no hint as to what is the "isolated" meaning of the signs of the form "$\grave{\varepsilon}\Phi(\varepsilon)$". Actually there are two questions: (1) Is there a *Wertverlauf* for any given function? (2) Is there *exactly one Wertverlauf* for any given function? Frege proves in GRG I, § 31 that (1) has an affirmative answer. Bartlett [1] has shown that Frege's proof is defective. As to (2) Frege tries to

ensure uniqueness in GRG I, § 10. This is one of the most difficult paragraphs[21] in Frege's works, which I do not pretend to analyse exhaustively, but only to clarify in some of its aspects.

If $\chi(\xi)$ is a function of which one requires that it never yield the same value for different arguments, *then* $\grave{\varepsilon}\Phi(\varepsilon) = \alpha\Psi(\alpha)$ iff $\chi(\grave{\varepsilon}\Phi(\varepsilon)) = \chi(\grave{\alpha}\Psi(\alpha))$. If, moreover, $\chi(\xi)$ never yields the argument for *Wertverläufe* as argument, one has here *two other* candidates for *Wertverläufe* of our functions: $\chi(\grave{\varepsilon}\Phi(\varepsilon))$ and $\chi(\grave{\alpha}\Psi(\alpha))$.

Obviously, if there were an infinite number of functions in the system, then it would be impossible to decide whether or not each of them is like our hypothetical function $\chi(\xi)$, i.e., such as to generate *other* ranges of values (*Wertverläufe*) from a given *Wertverlauf* of a given function. Not only is the number of functions finite, there are "bisher"[22] only *three* functions and only *two kinds of objects*.[23] Moreover, Frege remarks that for the present purpose it is sufficient to consider $\xi = \zeta$. Therefore, our particular situation at this point of the construction of the *Begriffsschrift* is quite simple; one need only see what are the values of $\xi = \zeta$ for *Wertverläufe* as arguments.

Case (a). The two sides of "=" are occupied by names of the form "$\grave{\varepsilon}\Phi(\varepsilon)$", i.e., one must decide the identity of *Wertverläufe* given as *Wertverläufe*. This case is easy; we have only to consider the associated functions and to see whether these are formally equivalent.

Case (b). One side of "=" is occupied by a name of the form "$\grave{\varepsilon}\Phi(\varepsilon)$" and the other side by the name of a truth-value (there are no other possible objects at this point of the *Begriffsschrift*). Let us abbreviate "F" = "False", "T" = "True"; then the sentences to be decided are:

(i) $\grave{\varepsilon}\Phi(\varepsilon) = \mathrm{F}$,

(ii) $\grave{\varepsilon}\Phi(\varepsilon) = \mathrm{T}$.

To decide these sentences one either proceeds conventionally or appeals to some intuitive knowledge about *Wertverläufe*, in particular about *Begriffsumfänge* (that knowledge which Frege presupposes in the readers of GRL). Here the intended interpretation teaches that T and F are actually the members of the unit-classes determined by the functions $-\xi$ and $\xi = \top\!\!\smile^{\mathfrak{a}}\!\!- \mathfrak{a} = \mathfrak{a}$. Frege identifies T with $\grave{\varepsilon}(-\varepsilon)$ and F with $\grave{\varepsilon}(\varepsilon = \top\!\!\smile^{\mathfrak{a}}\!\!- \mathfrak{a} = \mathfrak{a})$. Then the sentences (i) and (ii) are decidable, because they are reduced to case (a). As pointed out by T. M. Simpson, it is puzzling to see

Frege identifying T and F with their unit-classes, an identification which Frege himself rejects *in general* (cf. 5)). But the puzzle disappears as soon as one considers that x and $\iota' x$ may be viewed as two aspects of the same entity, similarly to *Venus* and *the Morningstar*. Frege did *not* attempt to view x and $\iota' x$ in this way, but such would have been the natural development of his insights.

Frege develops a particular argument to show that the fact of making T and F the *Wertverläufe* of any arbitrary function does not contradict the "definition by abstraction" of *Wertverläufe*. (This argument will not be analysed here.)

The objection is now met, but, of course, only with respect to the functions and objects we have "until now" introduced in the construction of the *Begriffsschrift*. Frege expresses this by saying that we have *determined* the ranges of values *as far as possible*. Still, there remains a task: in the future any new function should be introduced together with an indication of its values for *Wertverläufe* as arguments. This will not only be a progressive determination of the concept *to be a Wertverlauf*, but also a determination of the newly introduced function. So there is at least one concept (*to be a range of values*) whose *scharfe Begrenzung* is being drawn *sur la route*. The point is extremely valuable for a philosophical appreciation of Frege (platonism – constructivism).

In my presentation of the objection and its solution I have omitted a passage where Frege formulates this sort of relative "ignorance" about *Wertverläufe* in terms perhaps more general.[24] The content of this passage seems to me equivalent to the immediately following discussion (concerning the example $\chi(\xi)$) which we have analysed. Frege says that in so far as we depend on our "definition by abstraction", we ignore:

(i) whether an object not given as *Wertverlauf* (not named by a name of the form "$\grave{\varepsilon}\Phi(\varepsilon)$") is a *Wertverlauf*,

(ii) whether a *Wertverlauf* has a given property, unless this property is connected (*verbunden*) with some property of the associated function.

Obviously, point (i) means that the concept, *to be a Wertverlauf*, is not yet sharply defined. And point (ii) means that there are properties not yet sharply defined, as a consequence of the "definition by abstraction" of *Wertverläufe*. Without pretending to go deeper into this, let us only observe that (i) and (ii) correspond to case (b) above, while the clause "unless . . ." in (ii) corresponds to case (a). Our "ignorance" about classes must be compensated by successive *Festsetzungen* such as the one which helped us to decide case (b).

(5) Frege considers the possibility of identifying any object with the *Wertverlauf* of a concept under which only that object falls. He rejects this hypothesis by showing that it lacks logical truth.[25]

(6) Frege introduces the function $\xi \frown \zeta$[26], class-membership. He calls it the *Hineinfallen eines Gegenstandes in einen Begriffsumfang*.[27] This function has an extraordinary significance in Frege's *Begriffsschrift* because it allows him to "reduce"[28] the level of concepts, but of course this is possible because Frege does not introduce rules of types into the domain of *Wertverläufe*: classes of classes are as saturated objects as classes are.[29]

(7) Frege introduces *Doppelwertverlauf*, i.e., the extension of relations.[30]

(8) The definition of number in GRL identified each number with a set of concepts. In view of Frege's unsaturatedness, a set of concepts is likely, rather, to be unsaturated. It is perhaps due to this that, beginning with GRG I, *Wertverläufe* of higher-level concepts will no longer occur. Frege restricts himself to *rechte Wertverläufe* which were defined as *Wertverläufe* of first-level functions.[31]

8.3 Philosophy of class

> In short, a class may be thought of as an aggregate or collection or combination of objects just so long as 'aggregate' or 'collection' or 'combination' is understood strictly in the sense of 'class'. (Quine [4], p. 1)

8.31 *The non-developed possibility of viewing classes from the point of view of "Sinn" and "Bedeutung"*

Although Frege's *intention* is to preserve the "traditional" notion of *Begriffsumfang*[32], he does not provide much on how to understand that notion.

The *term* "class" appears with the humanist logicians[33]; the word "extension" is famous since Port Royal. But the *notion* of extension of a concept is already implicit in the classical idea of the one and the many.[34]

From the standpoint of contemporary philosophy one may pose the following two provocative questions: (1) Did the traditional notion of extension involve the possibility of empty classes?, (2) Were traditional extensions concrete or abstract entities?

As to the former question, it should be observed that empty as well as unit properties were commonplace in the philosophical tradition.[35] The idea of empty concepts was easily transmitted to Frege *via* Kantian philosophy and from the beginning the author of the *Begriffsschrift* struggled in favor of such an idea.[36] But the fact that one allows empty concepts and that one has a notion of the extension of a concept does not yet yield the result that empty concepts have empty extensions. The creator of set theory is witness to this.[37]

As to the second point, it is difficult to find an answer in traditional discussions of extensions of concepts. Certainly, classical ontology had trouble with *sets* of entities; sets of substances or accidents are not substances and if the property *to be a set* is conceived as an accident, the awkward result will be that ubiquity becomes a natural phenomenon. Sets, therefore, as well as numbers, relations, and other collective entities tend to be at least partially located "in the mind", in whose shadows they could elude the dichotomy substance–accident. Brentano's view of *Begriffsumfänge* as pseudo-objects is probably not unrelated to such a tradition. But it does not seem valid to compare this traditional approach with our contemporary doctrine of classes as abstract entities. The latter presumably originated in Frege, and we shall see that the probable reasons for it have nothing to do with the traditional ones mentioned above. Had contemporary philosophy considered classes abstract entities as a consequence of those traditional difficulties, it would not have been able either to deal with relations in a way which opposes contemporary to traditional thought. This applies in particular to Frege, who both viewed classes as abstract entities and introduced relations in logic.

Apart from the difficulties created by the ontological status of sets, an answer to question (2) above should consider the implicit or explicit views in the rare extensional doctrines of the past as well as in the many authors who, particularly during the 19th century, have discussed *Begriffsumfänge*.[38]

Returning to Frege, it should be observed that his philosophy of GRL enables one to sketch an interpretation of classes which has been overlooked both by Frege and by post-Fregean thinkers, and which provides an "intuitive" understanding of classes more acceptable than the current "agnosticism" as to what classes really are, or than the obscure doctrine of classes as abstract objects. This interpretation is so to speak "confirmed" by a hint provided by Frege himself (cf. the end of the present section).

The Frege of GRL views concepts as introducing a sort of *structure* into the world of things. The same heap may be "organized" or "arranged" in different ways by different concepts.[39] Classes are, in such an approach, the different ways in which a heap is given (to use Fregean terminology). Classes are different from, and identical with, "their" heaps, similar to the way in which the Morning Star is both identical with and different from Venus. To employ classical terms, classes "concerning the same heap" are *fundamentaliter* identical though *formaliter* different. This ontological situation can be expressed by the so-called "reduplicative" sentences (a device not chosen by Frege). Names of classes concerning the same heap refer to the same *Bedeutung* but express different *Sinne*.

Despite the fact that Frege did not develop this very Fregean approach to classes, there is some evidence that he was not unaware of it. Let us consider the following brief text: "Der *Sinn* der Worte "Umfang des Begriffes Marsmond" ist ein andrer, als der *Sinn* der Worte "Deimos und Phobos" ". This was published in 1894[40] when Frege was already using "Sinn" and "Bedeutung" in their technical sense.[41] *Deimos und Phobos* (which is meant by Frege as an *Inbegriff*, i.e. as opposed to *Begriffsumfang*, as heap is opposed to class) and *Umfang des Begriffes Marsmond* involve different senses; why does not Frege *complete* this statement by saying that these two senses concern the same *Bedeutung*; in other words, that the reference of a class-name is the heap, while its sense is a peculiar *Art des Gegebenseins* of the heap (given as a class of . . .)?

8.32 *For Frege, classes are abstract entities*

Frege did not follow the natural evolution of considering classes in terms of *Sinn* and *Bedeutung*, or in terms of aspects of heaps. Frege stated that classes are *logische Gegenstände*, which in his vocabulary amounts to saying that they are abstract, not concrete, entities.[42] One does not properly "see" or "eat" a certain class of biscuits.[43] All the classes determining or structuring the heap which underlies our initial class of biscuits are projected by Frege into the platonic heaven. We only eat the *Ganze* (heap, whole). Why did Frege do this?

First, there is a curious point of comparison. When Frege describes identity as *völliges Zusammenfallen* he certainly is inconsistent with his own view that the coincidence applies only to the *Bedeutung*.[44] This may be understood as a rhetorical exaggeration in reply to those authors who sought to interpret the "=" as a mere equality. Now Frege, following one of his basic insights, is supposed to have seen that many different classes have a "partial coincidence" in as much as they concern the same *Ganze*.[45] These classes are like the coexisting senses around the same *Bedeutung*, or more closely, they are like the different numbers coexisting around the same "heap", each number depending on a particular *Abgrenzung* of the heap. In spite of having definitely *seen*[46] this, Frege (in contrast to his former behaviour concerning sense and reference) now suppresses the coincidence (the *Bedeutung*) and focuses only on the differences (the *Sinne*); in other words, Frege now exaggerates in the opposite direction. While the Morning Star and the Evening Star, in spite of their differences, were said to be the same, the class of featherless bipeds and the class of human cells, in spite of being *fundamentaliter* the same, are now said to be *two classes*. These two classes are projected into the world of abstractions. With equal justification one could say that the Morning Star and the Evening Star are two abstract (stars), invisible to the human eye or to telescopes.

One *motivation* for such a projection of classes into the world of ideas seems to be the need of assigning a status to the empty class, equal to that of the other classes. "The empty class" here means the result of Frege's formal approach to classes when applied to empty concepts.[47] All empty concepts have "something in common"; this is their *Wertverlauf*. Now such an empty class seems to be essentially abstract in any possible intuitive interpretation.[48] Thus a non-abstract interpretation of the other classes would destroy symmetry. This lack of proportion may be one reason which led Frege to absolutely separate classes and *Ganze* (wholes, heaps).[49] For the sake of the empty class let all classes be abstract.

But the most important motivation for the abstract interpretation of classes is perhaps that Frege was obliged to view classes as abstract entities as a consequence of having identified numbers with (some) classes. This may be asserted for two reasons.

(1) The following text expresses in my view a basic insight of Frege:

> Wenn wir die Zahl durch Zusammenfassung von verschiedenen Gegenständen entstehen lassen wollen, so erhalten wir eine Anhäufung, in der die Gegenstände mit eben den Eigenschaften enthalten sind, durch die sie sich unterscheiden, und *das ist nicht die Zahl.* (GRL § 39, italics ours).

Unless a class (of concepts or of stones) is interpreted as an abstract, "geometrical", colourless point, the Fregean "definition" of numbers (as classes of classes or of concepts) would make of number a plurality, and then Frege would say: *und das ist nicht die Zahl.* In the particular case of number 3, he would say: *so sieht jeder leicht ein, daß das nicht die Zahl 3 ist* (GRL, *ibid.*). The result of the phenomenological analysis of number in GRL is negative: numbers cannot be *seen* anywhere, they have no place in any of the departments of Frege's ontology. When Frege, after this intuitive failure, tries to "grasp" (*erfassen*) numbers in terms of classes, it will be convenient to deprive classes of any intuitive content, in the first place of any connotation of *plurality*, *many*, and so on, which would collide with Frege's insight: *das ist nicht die Zahl.*

(2) Unless classes are radically separated from their elements, numbers conceived as classes (of classes) would not be sufficiently independent of the concrete world.[50]

In any case we must follow Frege's own line of thought, and pay attention to his requirements that classes are logical objects. But then we may and should seek more information about these logical objects.

First, it should be observed that an important Fregean insight prevents retaining in our abstract classes any trace of that idea of "many" or "plurality" which we commonly associate with "class". The class of biscuits is not something to be eaten, but neither is it a set of transcendental or abstract biscuits. This would be Cantor's mistake about impossible abstractions.[51] The dialectic of GRL would reappear in order to banish these impossible "abstract sets".[52]

Secondly, Frege's plan is that the "definition by abstraction" (i.e., the formal introduction of *Wertverlauf*) be very uninformative as to the nature of classes. Classes are an *etwas Gemeinsames* (cf. 8.21) to formally equivalent propositional functions. One may "constructively" reach the result that names of the form "$\grave{\varepsilon}\Phi(\varepsilon)$" have a unique meaning, but even then this meaning is not determined in its content[53]; the sole advantage is that one may speak of "the" *etwas Gemeinsames*.

Thirdly, we may consider what Frege explicitly says classes are *not*. His adversaries[54] on the subject of classes fall (according to him) into the common error of saying that classes are made up of their individuals. This is the same mistake as to say that a work of art is *only* its raw material. Frege observes that this view excludes empty classes, and prevents distinguishing a unit class from its unique element.[55]

Fourthly, it is necessary to consider what Frege *positively* affirms about classes. After his many criticisms of the wrong conception of class some positive statement should appear. Nevertheless, Frege's positive assertions are either curiously irrelevant or unsymmetrical with respect to his rejection of the wrong views.[56] Perhaps Frege had in mind a strange interpretation of classes as made up (*bestehend aus*) of concepts.[57]

8.33 *A class of chairs is a class of concepts*

In conclusion, either we content ourselves with the meager information provided by definitions by abstraction, or we try to examine some Fregean insights or hints which Frege himself did not develop.

A Fregean insight is that which suggests the view of classes in terms of *Sinn* and *Bedeutung*. This is an interesting approach, in agreement with the Frege of GRL and deeply rooted in the philosophical tradition. To draw a sharp distinction between abstract and concrete entities is, of course, correct, and it has appeared as a fruitful procedure in dealing with predication theory.[58] But with respect to the philosophical tradition such a dichotomy appears to be naive, as well. Aristotelian hylemorphism or Hegelian concrete universals are but instances of a classic concern with the possible partial association of the abstract and the concrete (ideal, real). From this point of view, it is philosophically naive to remain in the pre-Aristotelian simple dichotomy of singulars and universals. Thus, it is similarly inadequate to deal with classes under the alternative *aut* concrete *aut* abstract.[59] Classes are heaps *qua* structured[60] by one or another concept. This is a Fregean insight, but Frege did not go this way. Leśniewski did exactly the contrary.

As far as the development of the above mentioned Fregean insight is barred by Frege's own statement that classes are logical (= abstract) objects, there is no other choice than to accept his hint that classes are made up of concepts. And indeed, once classes are projected into Plato's heaven, what other choice could there be?

But then it would be apparent that Frege's departure from the usual sense of "Begriffsumfang" had occurred before, and independently of, the Russellian discovery, i.e. before the *Nachwort.*[61] In the *Nachwort* Frege says that his new axiom implies a departure from the traditional notion of *Begriffsumfang*, in the sense that some objects falling under a concept *F* are not counted now as members of the extension of *F*. This means that Frege believed that before the *Nachwort* he had viewed classes as somehow determined by all the objects falling under a concept: if one object is eliminated, the class *im hergebrachten Sinne des Wortes* [*ist*] *eigentlich aufgehoben.* But this is self-contradictory, because Frege before the *Nachwort* (for instance in his criticism of Schröder) had rejected any "determination" of the class by means of its individuals. Frege had stressed that even when all the individuals disappear the class is still there, is not *aufgehoben*. Curiously, in the *Nachwort* the elimination of one member is enough to destroy the class. This inconsistency is but an indication of the lack of clarity in Frege's notion of class. The solution would lie in the development of some previous insight of Frege himself, such as the distinction between an individual as member of a class and as anything else. In any case, in spite of the self-contradiction, Frege did think before the *Nachwort* that the class is somehow determined by all the objects falling under a concept. For this "determination" Frege provided a technical term: *Hineinfallen*, and a logical symbol: "$\frown$" (not primitive). Now, if we take into account the only intuitive interpretation of classes which Frege has perhaps admitted, namely that of classes as made up of concepts, then the way in which the members "determine" the class, i.e. the *Hineinfallen*, must be conceived as a strange relation between (for example) the actual chairs of the class of my chairs and the concepts making up the class of my chairs. If we abbreviate "class $_F$" for the Fregean notion of class, and "class $_T$" for the traditional[62] notion of class, then we may say that a class $_F$ of chairs is a class $_T$ of concepts.[63] Such oddity appears to be the only possible intuitive background of the *Wertverlauf*-signs and related axioms in Frege's *Grundgesetze der Arithmetik*. It is better to assume that Frege had no intuitive support at all in this respect, namely that he just did not know what is the nature of classes. As we have seen, this "intuitive ignorance" must be taken as total: even the minimal knowledge about classes, namely that there are things which are their members, makes the class dependent on its elements, which is inconsistent with other Fregean assertions (especially his criticism of Schröder).

8.4 On Frege's 'way in'

Sobociński [1] formulates, in accordance with Leśniewski, the only philosophically acceptable manner of planning a "way out" of the antinomies, and in particular of the antinomy which appeared in Frege's system. Such a "way out" is an analysis of the different conditions which made the antinomy possible, especially of the presuppositions which were initially taken as *true*. Thus, it is more appropriate to speak of an analysis of the "way in".

The investigation of the conditions which made possible the appearance of the contradiction in Frege's system is not yet complete, in spite of some brilliant analysis.[64]

In my view it has not yet been sufficiently pointed out that Axiom V is a statement whose ambiguity is greater than that attributed to it by Leśniewski. But not only are there more than two ways of understanding the term "class", there is simply a complete lack of clarity about what classes really are; the nature of classes, or *Wertverläufe* in general, is likely to have been a lifelong interrogation for Frege, as our preceding considerations suggest. Axiom V – the axiom of classes – seems to lack any clear intuitive background in Frege. After examining Frege's philosophy of class, Vb becomes unintelligible. From this point of view, it is easy to agree that he did not have the right to affirm Axiom V (for Frege axioms must be *true*[65]). But then the system could not have been built, and Russell would not have had the possibility of pointing out an antinomy.

Frege could hide the intuitive difficulties of his *Wertverläufe* (in particular, classes) by introducing them according to what has been called "the complicated way".[66] By so doing he was not obliged to commit himself to this or that intuitive interpretation of his *Wertverlauf*-signs. But then, to borrow a very Fregean term, Frege becomes a "formalist", against his vocation.

In either case Axiom V is untenable from a Fregean point of view. This accounts for the otherwise inexplicable apprehension which Frege reveals in reference to that axiom[67]; if Axiom V were really for Frege only an explicit formulation of a truth already used by generations of logicians, as he claims[68], then he would have accepted it without hesitation. (Frege was writing on these questions at about 1890.)

REFERENCES

1. UZBG.
2. GRL, § 68 note, § 107.
3. GRL, p. 59, § 74.
4. GRL, § 28; UFT, pp. 96–97.
5. "Vielheit", "Mehrheit" (*ibid.*).
6. "... les unités sont à part et l'entendement les prend ensemble quelques dispersées qu'elles soyent" (Leibniz [1], V, p. 132 (= *Nouv. Ess.* 2, XII).
   "Quis autem credat unitatem, quae est in India, uniri per se cum unitate, quae est in Hispania, ut constituat binarium vel aliquem alium numerum?" Answer: "... dicitur, quod unitates inter se distantes ad rationem numeri eodem modo uniuntur atque indistantes, quia cum supponantur divisae et separatae, perinde est, quod multum vel parum distent" (Ioannes a Sto Thoma [1], I, p. 562–563). Frege's objection against the term "Menge", or rather the notion of *Menge* as a definition of number (i.e., the Euclidean definition), is partially based on his conception of "set" as implying "räumliches Zusammensein". Frege rejects as well Mill's "physical" conception of number (i.e, a number is a concrete perceptible phenomenon), by pointing out that it would imply that a horse in Germany and another horse in America would not make two (horses) (GRL, § 25).
7. UFT, pp. 96–97.
8. FUB, pp. 16–17.
9. Literally: "range of values of a function".
10. JOURD, p. 251; letter to Russell in Sluga [1], p. 199.
11. JOURD, *ibid.*: "because by that many simplifications could be reached". Cf. Section 8.22, point 6.
12. This is, of course, my interpretation; cf. 2.26 and 2.62.
13. Cf. note 2.
14. Of course, since GRL Frege's system imposes some qualifications upon the traditional notion, in particular that the *Begriffsumfang* should not ambiguously include both subordinate concepts and individuals (this is a consequence of the distinction UF–UO, made, for instance, in UZBG, p. 3). But this is a minor correction, occurring *within* the familiar notion of the extension of a concept. Frege has often suggested that he intended to identify traditional *Begriffsumfänge* with his *Wertverläufe* of logical functions (FUB, p. 16; GRG I, p. VII (bottom), p. X top; § 3, § 9 (p. 14), p. 18, note 1, second line; etc.) JOURD, p. 251 (dated 1910) shows that Frege wished to use the notion of "extent of a concept" in the way in which that notion had "for a long time been spoken of in logic". Frege's later adoption of the term "Klasse" (as synonymous with "Begriffsumfang" and therefore with "Wertverlauf" of a logical function) also indicates that the set of arguments satisfying the propositional function is the intended interpretation. (For instance, *Nachwort* to GRG II, also GRG II, § 161; at the same time he

introduces "Relation" to designate the extension of a *Beziehung*, *ibid.*, § 162.) If Frege had changed the meaning of the term "Begriffsumfang" (by identifying it with some other possible "something in common" provided by the definitions by abstraction), he would have remembered that in GRL he had taken "Begriffsumfang" in the sense of "his readers" and he would have explicitly explained the new terminology. In fact, in the *Nachwort* to GRG II Frege shows regret that his "way out" of the contradiction discovered by Russell is a departure from the "traditional" (p. 260 bottom) or the "usual" (p. 257 second column) sense of "Begriffsumfang". The same text corroborates the fact that Frege *had intended* to fix in his Axiom V that traditional and usual sense (*ibid.*, pp. 260–261). For all of this see Sluga [1], where some fragments of the Frege–Russell correspondence are published (especially pp. 201–202). When the *Wertverlauf* is not assigned to a propositional or logical function, it must be interpreted in some other way, for example, as graph of a curve (FUB, pp. 8–9; GRG I, p. 36).

15. GRG II, § 146.
16. Hausdorff [1] (III, § 1 and *Anhang*, p. 453) points out some confusion in the use of definitions by abstraction which would apply to Frege unless our proposed interpretation is adopted. As for the term "formal" in "formal approach", I follow Hausdorff [1], p. 47.
17. GRG I, § 3. Also FUB, pp. 9–10, 16.
18. Materials for this: GRG I, p. 16 note 1; FUB, p. 11 above. Definitions imply equality of *Bedeutung* and *Sinn* (GRG I, § 27), but the statement identifying the meaning of the two phrases in question here is not a definition but a *Festsetzung* (GRG II, § 146). On the other hand, this *Festsetzung* becomes, in the object language, Axiom V.
19. GRG I, p. VII, § 9, etc. Also FUB.
20. GRG I, § 9.
21. The content of this paragraph (GRG I, § 10) is not invalidated by the *Nachwort* (GRG II, p. 263).
22. GRG I, p. 16, line 11 from the bottom, p. 17, line 5.
23. Our *Wertverläufe* and the two truth-values.
24. GRG I, p. 16, lines 6–11.
25. GRG I, p. 18 note 1. Cf. Whitehead–Russell [1] *51. These authors refer to KSCH (pp. 444–446); cf. also GRG I, p. 2 (middle).
26. GRG I, § 34.
27. GRG I, p. 240.
28. GRG I, § 35.
29. GRG II, p. 254.
30. GRG I, § 36.
31. GRG I, p. 49.
32. Cf. Section 8.21.
33. Melanchton, Hospinianus.
34. Which means that it is a Socratic discovery. Scholz has suggested that the threefold analysis of sentences (S–is–P) should be correlated with a class-interpretation of the predicate symbols, while the twofold analysis (*nomen* + *verbum*) corresponds to the predicate calculus. Cf. for instance Scholz-Hasenjaeger [1], p. 125, note, Scholz [2], p. 144, Scholz [3], p. 88, note 3. (I owe this reference to Prof. A. R. Raggio.) But this is meaningless if intended as a criterion for detecting the notion of class in the philosophical past. The notion of class can

exist independently of one or another analysis of sentences. "Qui quidem notionis complexus et ambitus iam ab Aristotele discernuntur in *Analyt. Post.* I, 4, quamvis non peculiari nomine" (Trendelenburg [2], § 58). For instance, Olympiodorus [1], p. 49, distinguishes the *βάθος* and the *πλάτος* of predicates. Cf. also Chapter 4, note 3.

35. That certain forms of ordinary Latin did imply existence is *another* question (for instance, sentences beginning with "omnes").
"Omnis autem essentia vel quidditas potest intelligi sine hoc quod aliquid intelligatur de esse suo; possum enim intelligere quid est homo vel fenix et tamen ignorare an esse habeat in rerum natura" (Aquinas [3], cap. IV).
"Omnis sol lucet, igitur iste sol lucet", is valid because there is only one sun (Paulus Venetus [2], f. 111). "Quia quaedam universalia sunt, quae non continent sub se nisi singulare, sicut sol et luna" (Aquinas [1], quoted in Gredt [1], ad 115).
36. Cf. Section 6.43.
37. Cantor [1], p. 146: "Es ist ferner zweckmässig, ein Zeichen zu haben, welches die Abwesenheit von Punkten ausdrückt, wir wählen dazu den Buchstaben O; $P \equiv O$ bedeutet also, das die Menge P *keinen einzigen* Punkt enthält, also streng genommen *als solche gar nicht vorhanden ist.*" Hausdorff [1], I, § 1, betrays a certain artificiality in his introduction of the idea of empty class. After having described what happens when the elements of a *Menge* disappear by saying that *die Menge . . . verschwindet,* he tries to qualify this revealing expression in a footnote, unsuccessfully I think.
38. Mauthner [1], III, p. 282: ". . . der Begriffsumfang oder der Assoziationsbereich des Begriffs ist immer konkret. Und mit diesem einzig Wirklichen am Begriff . . ." *Ibid.*, p. 323: "Die Satzbildung oder das Urteilen braucht aber nicht immer vom Inhalt des Begriffs auszugehen; der Ausgangspunkt kann auch der Umfang des Begriffs sein, also etwas, was der Wirklichkeit näher liegt."
Cantor [1], p. 379: "Jede Menge wohlunterschiedener Dinge kann als ein einheitliches Ding für sich angesehen werden, *in welchem jene Dinge Bestandteile oder konstitutive Elemente sind*" (italics ours).
39. For instance, GRL, §§ 22, 48, 54.
40. HUSS, p. 322.
41. HUSS, p. 320 note.
42. GRG II (p. 86) divides objects into *logical* and *physical* ones according to their capacity of being perceived by our senses. Classes are explicitly defined as logical objects (and are excluded from physical objects) in a text published by Bartlett [1], p. 44. Cf. Quine [2], § 22, Bernays-Fraenkel [1], p. 56, Carnap [5], § 37.
43. Only a *whole* (*Ganze*) of material things is itself material. Frege says that he is not sitting upon the class of atoms of his chair (*Ibid.*, as in note 42).
44. Cf. Section 2.25.
45. Cf. GRL, §§ 22, 48, 54.
46. Cf., for instance, GRL § 54.
47. In KSCH, p. 451, Frege states that all empty concepts have the same extension. For relations, cf. GRG II, p. 160. Frege uses "leere Klasse" perhaps for the first time GRG I, *Einleitung*. (There he also uses "leerer Begriff", which is perhaps the first occurrence of such a *phrase*, but of course the *notion* of empty concepts was most familiar to the author of GRL.)
48. But in Frege there are no indications as to how the empty class should be viewed intuitively.

49. On the contrary, Frege wants to preserve a "proportion" between the empty class and the other classes. Cf. the following text: "Ein Begriff, unter welchen nur ein Gegenstand fällt, hat *ebenso* einen bestimmten Umfang, wie ein Begriff, unter welchen kein Gegenstand fällt, oder ein Begriff, unter welchen unendlich viele Gegenstände fallen, in welchen Fällen es nach Herrn Husserl gar keinen Inbegriff giebt" (HUSS, p. 322).
50. GRG II (p. 86, § 147, p. 253, p. 265) include numbers among logical objects. And of course numbers are, since GRL, non-perceptible entities. In GRL numbers were classes of concepts; in GRG they are classes of classes. Thus, *in GRG*, if a class of two stones were "stony", number 2 would be somehow contaminated. Cf. Carnap [5], § 40 (Carnap works with the "*aut* abstract *aut* concrete", "*aut* class *aut* whole").
51. CANT, p. 270.
52. Cf. Section 10.3.
53. Cf. Section 8.22.
54. Dedekind, Schröder in GRG I, *Einleitung*, Schröder particularly in KSCH.
55. If the work of art = its raw material, the "idea" (*causa formalis, causa exemplaris*) vanishes. Then the *leere Klasse* has to be an *Erdichtung* (GRG I, p. 2–3). Frege wishes to control *die Grenzen dieser Erdichtungswillkür* (*ibid.*) and I understand that he achieves this by the formal introduction of *Wertverläufe*: "Dann hat es kein Bedenken, von der Klasse der Gegenstände die *b* sind, auch zu sprechen, wenn es kein *b* giebt" (KSCH, p. 451).
56. After discussing Dedekind's contention that classes are made up of their individuals, and when it is time for giving his own view, Frege says that "die Merkmale den Bestand des Begriffes ausmachen, nicht die unter den Begriff fallende Gegenstände" (GRG I, p. 3). Is this not curiously *irrelevant* as a rejection of Dedekind's view? In opposition to the view that classes *bestehen aus* individuals, Frege affirms that classes do not have their *Bestand* in the individuals but in the concepts (KSCH, 451). Apparently this means that classes have their *Halt* (*ibid.*, p. 455) in the concepts, which is of course not satisfactory as a negation of the thesis that classes *bestehen aus* individuals.
57. "Dagegen sind das, was den Bestand des Begriffes – *oder seines Umfanges* [italics ours] – ausmacht, nicht die Gegenstände, die unter ihn fallen, sondern seine Merkmale . . ." (GRG II, § 150).
Here "Bestand" would be used not as "Halt" but in the sense of "der Bestand von meiner Kaß ist nicht des zählens werth" (Lessing, quoted in Grimm [1], article "Bestand") or of "der Bestand der Bibliothek beträgt 10.000 Bände". For this ambiguity of "Bestand" cf. Grimm [1], *ibid.*
58. Cf. Chapter 4.
59. For instance, Słupecki [1], *in fine.*
60. Frege would use, for example, the term *Abgrenzung* (CANT, p. 270).
61. GRG II, p. 260.
62. ". . . der Begriffsumfang im hergebrachten Sinne . . ." (GRG II, p. 260 bottom).
63. For an ambiguity in the term "class" similar to class_F–class_T, cf. Professor Geach's interesting remark about Russell's use of that term (Geach [1], p. 157).
64. Quine [5], Geach [3], Resnik [1], etc. Leśniewski's analysis, in Sobociński [1], is *sui generis.*
65. For Frege's texts on the nature of axioms, cf. Steiner [1], p. 182.
66. Scholz–Schweitzer [5], *Anhang* 1.

67. "Ein Streit kann hierbei, soviel ich sehe, nur um mein Grundgesetz der Werte verläufe (V) entbrennen, das von den Logikern vielleicht noch nicht eigens ausgesprochen ist, obwohl man danach denkt, z.B. wenn man von Begriffsumfängen redet. Ich halte es für rein logisch. Jedenfalls ist hiermit die Stelle bezeichnet, wo die Entscheidung fallen muß" (GRG I, p. VII).
This presentation offers some similarities with the way in which Cantor introduces the *Wohlordnungssatz* (Cantor ([1], p. 169).
68. GRG I, § 9.

9. EXISTENCE

Summary and general remarks. Frege's concept of existence as *non-emptiness* is first presented (9.1). Next, it is shown that such an approach to existence is but a clarification of what Gilson calls the "Avicennian" or "essentialist" tendency in western metaphysics (9.2). The chapter concludes with a brief reference to the place of *being* in the world of concepts (9.3).

9.1 Exposition

In BG Frege does not understand particular affirmative sentences as implying existence. Such sentences are read not only "Some M's are P's" but also "It is possible that an M be a P".[1] But perhaps because in the realm of extra-temporal things (Frege's concern) there is no difference between possibility and being[2], he later dropped that difference, and he understood particular affirmative sentences as implying existence[3] ("there is at least one . . .").

Concerning universal affirmative sentences, Frege in BG and GRL[4] had already practically implied that they do not entail existence. This is formally stated afterwards in GRG I[5] and is subsequently justified in a letter to Husserl.[6]

In his earlier writings Frege maintains that the logical symbolism should express existence; thus in UZBG Frege objects to Boole's lack of *Existentialurteile.* In his earlier writings Frege has a philosophy of existence. In GRL as well, Frege's ideas on existence are characterized by the two following traits. (1) Existence is a predicate of predicates[7] (a second intention), i.e., existence is the fact that a concept "has" at least one individual; existence is non-emptiness of predicates. (2) The lack of contradiction does not imply existence.[8]

Frege's ideas on unsaturatedness will oblige him to understand point (1) in a very special sense. According to him, it may be *shown,* but not *said*, that a first-level property has the property of not being empty.[9]

In a later period he coins a good neologism to designate the kind of existence to which he is referring, "Esgiebtexistenz".[10] It is the existence expressed by sentences of the form "there is a . . .", where the name of a concept should be introduced.[11]

9.2 Gilson's history of ontology and Frege's concept of existence

Thinkers from other provinces of the philosophical world will probably protest against Frege's viewing existence as a predicate of predicates, as a second intention which belongs only to the realm of *ens rationis*. But actually little is new in Frege's conception of existence, and one may show that it enjoys a most respectable metaphysical past.

Gilson stresses that there have been two metaphysics or two ontological traditions, one, of *essence*, the other, of *actus essendi*.[12] Gilson's meaning is correctly rendered – in my view – if one says that his dualism corresponds (is correlated) to the fact that for him the data (taken into account here) are *two*: essence and existence.

But perhaps this is a bad starting point, for one may ask *where* the dimension singularity–universality is to be found in that pair of concepts (essence and existence). Probably it will be found that "essence" (*ousia*, *res*, . . .) is still ambiguous concerning that dimension.

It would be more adequate to add a third factor to Gilson's essence and existence, namely, the *suppositum*.[13] Even without considering the relation between existence and each of the other two terms, one may at least affirm that the latter are located at different levels of Porphyry's tree (UO). This will facilitate the understanding of the "dualism" pointed out by Gilson in the ontological tradition, for it will appear that Gilson's characterization of both metaphysical tendencies cannot be sufficiently appreciated *unless* the dimension singularity–universality is taken into account.

In fact, while Gilson's presentation of the views stressing the *actus essendi* may be easily grasped[14], this is not the case with respect to his presentation of the opposite trend.[15] But the latter suddenly becomes as clear as the former if one remembers Frege's concept of existence. Frege's view on existence requires a distinction of concepts and objects clearer than is usually the case in Aristotelian metaphysics.[16]

According to Gilson the origin of the "essentialist" tradition can be traced back to the Avicennian formula *esse accidit essentiae*.[17] Here "accidit" has that peculiar sense which the Aristotelian tradition was obliged to introduce in order to deal with those higher predicates about which Aristotle himself gave no information. "x accidit y" means that x is not a mark of the property y, but a property of it.[18] This "accidit" has a primarily negative sense: to exclude from the set of marks (of a given concept) such higher predicates as *esse*, *universale*, and so on.[19] Gilson himself commends the "triplex respectus essentiae" as a means of better understanding the Avicennian formula "esse accidit essentiae".[20] And the whole "essentialist" tradition is but a reiteration of that exclusion of higher predicates: *existence is not a predicate*[21] (i.e., existence is not a mark of a first-level predicate).

Thus, it becomes plausible that the "essentialist" tradition considered by Gilson has viewed *esse* as a higher predicate. Here one should recognize the importance of the introduction of the dimension singularity–universality into our basic data. What Avicenna or Duns Scotus have in mind is that there is an x such that x falls under the concept F; they mean that "it happens" (*accidit*) to the concept F to have an individual. This is, in our interpretation, the meaning of *esse accidit essentiae*: existence as non-emptiness. This is also, of course, existence as a *second intention*, *Esgiebtexistenz*.[22] Such a view of existence is also familiar to Gilson himself[23], although it may be presumed that he is not inclined to appreciate as "ontologically relevant" this sort of existence. What metaphysical relevancy may a second intention have? Is there not an "infinite abyss"[24] between first- and second-level predicates? But these questions, in my view, could be spared if Frege's – instead of Avicenna's[25] – theory of predication were assumed.

Incidentally, to think of existence as a property of properties, is not necessarily platonism, as Brentano's impressive anti-platonism manifesto would suggest.[26] In reply to this manifesto (as was already pointed out[27]), one should observe that some anti-platonisms are mere victims of traditional predication theory.

Whereas Gilson is inclined to consider the "essentialist" tradition as a sort of decadence[28], Carnap sees an "Überwindung der Metaphysik"[29] in something which is, at most, a better formulation of that "essentialist" tradition.

Anscombe-Geach [1] is a remarkable contribution "towards reunion in philosophy" in so far as they point to the possibility of complementing Frege's *Esgiebtsein* with the *actus essendi.*[30] Ontology, as Gilson teaches, has had *both* views for a long time: Frege has contributed to the clarification of one of them, clarifying thereby their mutual relation as well.[31]

Finally, let us consider an important example. Both Kant and Frege[32] reject the ontological argument, the former because existence is not a predicate and the latter because it *is* a second-level predicate. Now, these two reasons are not so different if one considers that Kant actually means that existence is not a *first-level* predicate.[33] As was mentioned, levels of predicates were banished from modern philosophy.[34]

9.3 'Utrum ens sit summum genus'

On the basis of Gilson's research plus Frege's clarification of the Avicennian approach, other subjects could be investigated, for instance the problem of existential import.[35]

Frege's predication theory allows one to make an interesting analysis of traditional problems, such as the question serving as title to the present section. In fact, in Aristotelian standards this question seems to be reduced to asking whether in the UO order there is a unique last element, because what other ordering relation (for concepts) could be found in those standards? If philosophers actually had in mind other relations (say, *praedicatio notionalis*[36]), these relations were necessarily isolated from UO as belonging to another world (the world of *ens rationis*). Only in Frege's approach may these relations be fearlessly dealt with, and in a way which does not necessitate committing oneself either to platonism or to anti-platonism.[37] Now it is obvious that in Frege's approach the question "utrum ens sit summum genus" becomes ambiguous with respect to the term "summum", because more than one relation between two concepts is available. To think of *being* as "the most general concept" was, already in 1884, not a *Vorurteil*[38] but a meaningless question, for it was not duly specified in which sense "most" was to be understood.

REFERENCES

1. BG, p. 24.
2. Aristotle [4], Γ, 203,b, 30. Cf. also Maritain [1], § 84, p. 272; Bocheński [1], p. 257.
3. GRG I, p. 24 note 2.

4. BG, p. 23; GRL, for example, § 47.
5. GRG I, p. 24 note 2.
6. Published by Bartlett [1], p. 11. The letter is dated 1906.
7. GRL, § 53.
8. Cf. Section 6.43, *in fine*.
9. Cf. Section 6.83.
10. UBR, p. 10.
11. KSCH, p. 453.
12. Particularly Gilson [1]. For the special case Aquinas–Duns Scotus (as two representatives of both tendencies), cf. Gilson [2].
13. This is, as far as I know, the best designation for *individual* in the Western philosophical tradition. The necessity of having a threefold schema (instead of the much repeated essence–existence or *Sosein–Dasein*), clearly follows from some texts of Gilson [2], for example, p. 205 (in particular the footnotes). The discussion reproduced there between Aquinas and Duns Scotus shows that there are *three* factors. It likewise becomes apparent that only in terms of three such factors may the disagreement between both philosophers be formulated. For Scotus "nec valet, habet duo esse, igitur est duo entia", while for Aquinas speaking of two *esse*'s implies two individuals. It is correct to say that the disagreement concerns the insight into *esse* (Gilson [2], pp. 347–348, 378), but this, in turn, requires the taking into account of the dimension singularity–universality as well.
14. Aquinas' *esse*: "Pour Thomas d'Aquin [...] chaque être a son *esse* propre, en vertu duquel precisément il est un être, et qui est en lui ce qu'il a de plus intime: *illud quod est magis intimum cuilibet et quod profundius omnibus inest*" (Gilson [2], *ibid.*, as in the preceding note). It is clear, at least, that this existence has nothing to do with second intentions, i.e., with non-emptiness of predicates. Here existence is, so to speak, a property of the first level ... of course a most exceptional one, because it cannot be conceived as other properties (i.e., of an "already existing" entity). According to some critics, Aquinas' *esse* is today represented by Heidegger's *Sein* (cf. for instance Echauri [1]).
15. "... le terme 'esse' ne connote plus d'abord l'acte d'exister mais plutôt l'être de la substance définie par sa quiddité" (Gilson [2], p. 378). "Chez Duns Scot, il n'y a pas d'*esse* par lequel une essence soit un être; le mot *esse* désigne alors simplement la substance elle-même prise dans sa réalité actuelle hors de sa cause et de l'intellect" (*ibid.*, p. 486). "Dès que l'*esse* ne signifie plus l'acte d'être mais la réalité de l'essence posée hors de sa cause ..." (*ibid.*, p. 486, note 2).
16. Because it will be necessary to stress that existence does not concern individuals, but properties.
    Kaufmann [1] describes existence, one, many, number (i.e. the higher predicates of his Avicennian philosophers) as being accidents of *the things* (pp. 422, 424, 343 etc.). What are these things? Frequently they are ... sets of marks, i.e., concepts. Thus, to say that existence is an accident (p. 422) is not to say that existence is an entity which may be absent from Peter (while Peter continues to exist), but that existence is not a mark of *man*.
17. Cf. Gilson [1], Ch. IV.
18. "Accidens accipitur dupliciter, uno modo proprie, alio modo pro extraneo; quando Avicenna inquit quod existentia accidit essentiae, ly *accidit* accipitur pro extraneo, non alio modo, id est non est de quidditate essentiae" (a text of a

later Scotist, quoted by Gilson [1], p. 134). Gilson [1], p. 126, note 1, removes any doubt about whether the original text of Avicenna's doctrine is duly respected by the Latin versions.

19. Cf. the following decisive text: "et sic loquitur Avicenna de quidditate V *Metaph.*, cap. 1, ubi dicit omne tale esse accidens essentiae, quod non est de formali conceptu ejus, et quidditatem ad omne hujusmodi esse in potentia, ut ad unum et multum et caetera hujusmodi" (Duns Scotus, quoted by Gilson [2], p. 203).
20. Gilson [1], p. 123.
21. Gilson [1] as a whole might be quoted.
22. Whitehead–Russell [1], *24.03, Russell [5], V.
23. "on ne peut pas démontrer qu'un être existe parce qu'il est nécessaire, ou infini, ou suprême; tout au contraire, on saura que la nécessité ou l'infinité existe lorsqu'on aura prouvé l'existence d'une essence [read: "suppositum"] qui les possède" (Gilson [2], p. 124, commenting on Duns Scotus).
24. Cf. Chapter 1, note 13.
25. Cf. Section 5.44.
26. Chapter 7, note 62.
27. *Ibid.*
28. As it follows from Gilson [1].
29. Carnap [6], p. 234. Springer [1] could have seen a perfect agreement between Maimonides and Carnap. For Maimonides, cf. Kaufmann [1], p. 389, note 48.
30. Although these authors do not employ my terms, I think that this is what Anscombe–Geach [1] (pp. 90–91) mean.
31. The result is that Gilson's suggestion: *il faut choisir* (Gilson [2], p. 205) is no longer meaningful.
32. For instance, FUB, p. 27, note.
33. It is curious to observe that Kant [1], (*Erste Abt.*, *erste Bet.*, 1) begins by viewing the problem in terms of higher predication: "Es ist aber das Daseyn in denen Fällen da es im gemeinen Redegebrauch als ein Prädikat vorkommt, nicht sowohl ein Prädikat von dem Dinge selbst, als vielmehr von dem Gedanken den man davon hat." (We quote the text of the edition Königsberg 1783.)
As Wolff [1], § 243 indicates, "realitas" also means *quidditas* and *real* predicates are those which belong to the set of *marks* of a *quidditas*. (Cf. Heidegger [1], p. 164f, p. 184f.; Heidegger [2], p. 10.) Instead of developing the idea of existence as predicate *von dem Gedanken*, Kant will content himself with saying that existence is not a "real" (first level) predicate. (Cf. Eisler [1], "Existenz", *in fine*.)
Heidegger, commenting on Kant, seems interested in pointing out the *positive* side of that negative statement. (Cf. Heidegger [1], p. 184; Heidegger [2], pp. 8, 14, 26), and he even suggests (as does Kant) that existence is some sort of predicate, for instance: "Weil Sein kein reales Prädikat, *aber gleichwohl Prädikat ist*, mithin dem Objekt zugesprochen und doch nicht dem Sachgehalt des Objekts entnehmbar ist . . ." (Heidegger [2], p. 26). But when it is time to say more precisely what sort of predicate existence is, we see that existence is related to *subjectivity* (*ibid.*).
Brentano is perhaps the only coherent philosopher in matters of whether existence is a predicate; he definitely considers existential sentences as *eingliedrig* ("*A* ist") and the possibility does not even remain for asking what sort of predicate existence is. (For instance, Brentano [1], 27, *in fine*, cf. Brentano [3], for example, p. 106.) But behind Brentano's "*A*", the dimension singularity–universality *is hidden* as

it is concealed behind Gilson's incomplete dichotomy essence–existence.
Aristotelian metaphysics of *ousia* and Aristotelian predication theory together have contributed to create the illusion that such pairs of terms as essence–existence, *Sosein–Dasein*, etc. are exhaustive.
"La chose", "res", "Ding" – *ousia's* inheritors –, ambiguously cover both universals and singulars. Such is the ambiguity covered by "essence" or "Sosein".

34. Section 7.56.
35. "Les Scholastiques on fort disputé *de constantia subiecti*, comme ils l'appelloient, c'est à dire, comment la proposition faite sur un sujet peut avoir une verité réelle, si ce sujet n'existe pas" (Leibniz [1], p. 429). What is that *subject*? Is it a singular or a universal? If that term corresponds to "res", then we may realize how ambiguous was the problem *de constantia subiecti*.
36. Keckermann [1] (Liber II, Sectio Posterior, cap. I) distinguishes "praedicatio notionalis" and "praedicatio realis"; the former occurs when a *secunda notio de prima praedicatur*. (This is of course but one example.)
37. Cf. Section 7.58.
38. Heidegger [3], § 1.

10. NUMBER

Summary and general remarks. The analysis of the concept of number is indeed the ultimate goal of Frege's scientific program, already stated in the *Vorwort* of the *Begriffsschrift.* We begin by considering Frege's negative statements about numbers; numbers are neither external things nor subjective entities. This is an opportunity to see an interesting limitation in Frege's system of concepts: he is not clear about *subjective.* This is why the dichotomy mentioned above (external thing-subjective) is not capable of covering all past philosophies of number. Something like transcendental subjectivity should be taken into account (10.1).

Next, we consider the most difficult point in Frege's philosophy of number: numbers are not universals, they are individuals, like the Aristotelian *Callias.* But unlike Callias, numbers are non-perceptible entities (10.2).

Frege's brilliant attack on the Euclidean definition is examined (10.3) and, finally, Frege's own positive statement about numbers and his device of viewing numbers as classes of classes (10.4).

To appreciate Frege's philosophy of number it is necessary to take into account the traditional distinction of concrete and abstract numbers (i.e., numbers and their *instances*) and of course the Euclidean definition. The latter had an interesting impact on metaphysics (10.5).

Frege's so-called logicism appears as a non-trivial thesis in the context of the philosophical tradition (10.6).

10.1 Frege approaches past philosophies of number by means of an inadequate dichotomy

10.11 *Number is not an "external" entity. 'Eigenschaft' as 'accident'*

It would be erroneous to think that the long section of GRL[1] devoted to "whether number is a property of external things" has anything to do with the question whether numbers are properties or objects.

It seems necessary to interpret Frege's use of "Eigenschaft" in that section as meaning rather *accident*, and more precisely, *individual accident*, because *here* Frege presupposes the following axiom: if F is a property of an external (physical, sensible) thing, then F itself is external (physical, sensible) too. *Eigenschaften* are concepts, and indeed it is not in agreement with Frege's views on concepts[2] to think that the concept *to be a stone* is more "sensible" or more "physical" than the concept *to be a square root of 2*. Now if this normal way of understanding properties were meant here, it would not be possible to understand Frege's argument that numbers cannot be properties of sensible things because they apply also to non-sensible things.[3] To understand this argument, it is necessary to assume the above mentioned axiom.[4] But then the general question "Ist die Anzahl eine Eigenschaft der äusseren Dinge?" should be properly reworded as: "Is number an external (physical, sensible) thing?"[5] In addition, there are some references concerning the possible question as to whether numbers are properties (concepts) or objects in the "logical" sense, but these references are incidental.[6]

10.12 *Number is not subjective*

A next question concerning number is: "Ist die Zahl etwas Subjectives?"[7] This is a natural complement to the previous problem once the latter is reworded as "Is number an external entity?"

By "subjective" as a qualification of views on numbers, Frege seems, at the least, to mean (in GRL) the following: (1) the psychological investigation pretends to substitute arithmetical investigation[8], (2) number is a *Vorstellung*.[9]

In the introduction to GRL, Frege stated the principle of separating logic and psychology, subjective and objective.[10] This principle, as the context indicates, was intended to be a reaction against tendencies reducing foundational research on arithmetic to psychology or biology (point (1) above). Frege also says that, in order to respect the principle, he has decided to use "Vorstellung" only in a psychological sense (this concerns point (2) above). But it is indeed difficult to imagine that, once "Vorstellung" is so understood, anyone would claim that numbers are *Vorstellungen*. Thus, the non-trivial part is only point (1). Now, with regard to this, Frege says very little, apart from protesting against the "imperialism" of biology and psychology toward arithmetic and logic. And in his protest, some *nuances* are distinguishable. It is one thing to state that a psychological description of number cannot substitute a logical *Begriffsbestimmung*[11], and quite another to absolutely reject psychology as a contributing tool in foundational research.[12]

To conclude, let us say that to the extent that the question "Is number something subjective?" involves the two points above, Frege's answer is certainly negative.

10.13 *'Being in the mind' and transcendental subjectivity coincide with Frege's realm of non-sensible but objective entities, where he locates number*

But Frege's anti-subjectivism raises another, more subtle question. We may call this the question of "being in the mind". In some passages of GRL Frege seems to suspect that phrase of subjectivism. Having concluded the discussion on Mill's "physical" conception of number (i.e., external things), Frege begins[13] by contrasting it with Leibniz's thesis that numbers exist "only in the mind". "To be in the mind" may be understood as being in the mind objectively, but it seems that Frege would like to count Leibniz among the subjectivists for at least two reasons. (1) Throughout GRL Frege treats a basic dichotomy, physical (external)–subjective, as being the two equally erroneous poles in philosophy of number, and the introductory phrase of GRL § 25[14] suggests that Leibniz, who does not belong to the first class, belongs to the second. (2) Hankel's thesis that numbers are no longer "outside the subject" is explicitly condemned as subjectivism.[15] On the other hand, the introductory phrase of § 26[16] indicates that Leibniz (together with Locke and Berkeley) is not completely classified as a subjectivist. And Frege is quite right in hesitating here. Subjectivism (in the philosophy of number) is described in GRL by the two conditions mentioned in our preceding section. Now Leibniz neither pretends to replace arithmetic by psychology nor does he mean that numbers are *Vorstellungen* (i.e., *conceptus subiectivus*) when he declares that numbers are "in the mind".[17]

We have distinguished[18] two senses of Frege's term "objective". The strong one implies existence outside the mind, or existence independent of us. The weak sense requires only "being accessible to many thinkers" as is the concept *non-self-identical*, i.e., transcendental objectivity or "being in the mind". Now, in the term "subjective" I would analogously distinguish two senses: a strong one, where "to be subjective" means *to be a Vorstellung* (*conceptus subiectivus*), and a weak sense, where "subjective" implies some reference to a subject, but not to an individual subject. The weak sense of "subjective" would embrace the so-called transcendental subjectivity. The latter coincides with transcendental objectivity (cf. note 22), and it is not difficult to attain it starting from "being in the mind" if one asks – like Frege[19] – *in whose mind?* Averroes did something similar.

These sophisticated terminological distinctions are necessary in order to understand Frege in such matters as philosophy of number and platonism.

It can be seen that whereas Frege clearly has two senses of "objective" (though he does not introduce two names for them), he has only one meaning of "subjective" – the strong one.[20] In this meaning numbers are not subjective, i.e., they are not *Vorstellungen*, and this is trivial.

Still, Frege gives some hints of weak or transcendental subjectivity. This may be observed in the following two ways. (1) Frege "feels" that there is a weak sense in the case of Leibniz; consequently, he hesitates in classifying him among "subjectivists", and he leaves him outside the dichotomy physical–subjective. (2) Frege himself, in the final analysis, assigns to numbers this sort of subjectivity.[21] But of course, he gives only some slight indications of such a transcendental subjectivity. Or one may say that he actually thinks of this but under another terminology; the typical Fregean realm of entities which are not sensible but are objective (not implying strong objectivity) could perhaps be described *also*[22] as a realm of transcendental subjectivity, or of "being in the mind" ("the mind" of no one in particular).

10.14 *Conclusion*

That Frege has not been able to clarify his terminology (assigning different terms for his two senses of "objective" and extending "subjective" also to transcendental subjectivity) is perhaps the reason why the dichotomy "physical(external)–subjective", so much stressed in GRL[23], appears as incapable of absorbing the case of Leibniz, whom Frege cannot classify at all.

On the other hand the dichotomy of GRL does not reflect the real issue involved in the historical evolution of philosophy of number. This issue (which belongs to history of metaphysics, not to that of mathematics[24]) revolves around the Euclidean definition. Frege himself brilliantly discusses this definition in GRL, and he is perhaps the first in the history of metaphysics to reject it.[25] Here let us only observe that Leibniz's "numbers in the mind" becomes meaningful when seen within the context of the Euclidean definition[26] *and* classical ontology.

The significance of the dichotomy of GRL consists rather in that (1), it is very important for an understanding of the actual structure of GRL, and (2), it is associated with such aspects of Frege's thought as (i), the two senses of "Eigenschaft", (ii), his half-way anti-subjectivism, and (iii) the "semantical principle of GRL".[27]

10.2 Number is an object, not a concept

The best way of seeing what Frege's conception of number is *not*, is to consider an authoritative presentation of a view which one might be inclined to ascribe to Frege. Hilbert–Ackermann [1] asserts that number is not assigned to the individuals but is a property of the predicate under which these individuals fall.[28] Frege, of course, would have agreed with the first part of this, but he would have rejected the second. In fact, he explicitly denied that number is a property at all, and in particular a property of concepts. Numbers according to him are *objects*, which means for him that they are ultimate subjects of predication, as Callias was for Aristotle.[29] Wittgenstein asked Frege whether his view of numbers as objects did not create any difficulty; Frege's answer was: "Sometimes I *seem* to see a difficulty, but then again I *do not* see it."[30] Let us try to analyse Frege's doctrine on this point.

The task of GRL is to determine whether number may be defined.[31] Frege concentrates above all on those numbers answering to the question "how many?".[32]

At least three times[33] in GRL he affirms that numbers are not *Begriffe*. In the context where "Eigenschaft" means *individual accident* he takes the occasion to remind us that numbers are not properties in the "logical" sense.[34] In view of the Aristotelian classification of "all entities" into things like *Callias* (ultimate subjects of predication) and *predicates*, or, similarly, of the Kantian background of a classification of *Vorstellungen* (objective sense) into *Anschauungen* and their *Begriffe*, there would not seem to be any other possibility for Frege than to make of numbers individuals like Callias. It could be replied that Frege has a richer world of concepts than Aristotle or Kant, because Frege's world of concepts is not exclusively made up of predicates of Callias (Porphyry's tree), but, in addition, of true predicates of predicates. Now Frege also explicitly rejects this possibility that numbers are predicates or concepts of a higher level.[35] By UO alone we do not attain numbers (cf. GRL, p. 57: numbers are nowhere in Porphyry's tree). Frege's insight is that not even by means of UO plus IF can we attain numbers (although this will be possible by means of the "definition"); starting from the moon we attain the concept *moon of the Earth* (*via* UF), which falls under (UF) or within (IF) the concept *to have only one individual*; in the latter one finds, as a mark, *Einzigkeit*, but Frege *does not say that this is the number one* (GRL, § 53).

It could be replied that Frege in GRL had already his ideas of unsaturatedness (though unexpressed) and therefore his doctrine that numbers are not concepts has no significance apart from his doctrine that "the concept F" is not the name of a concept[36] or, in particular, that "die Eins" cannot designate a concept.

But this is not valid. First, because the hypothesis that in GRL Frege was perfectly aware of unsaturatedness, is not demonstrable. Such texts as GRL, § 12 (*in fine*) or § 89, where Frege maintains, contrary to Kant, that numbers are not *allgemeine Begriffe*, seem to be independent of unsaturatedness, and rather similar to the text of UFT quoted in note 40.

Secondly, even granting that Frege in GRL had clear ideas on unsaturatedness, it is easy to show that the thesis that numbers are no concepts is not necessarily dependent on *Ungesättigtheit*. For this we may appeal to what we have called the good criterion for distinguishing concepts and objects.[37] This is also Frege's criterion, although he assigns a primary importance to unsaturatedness and definite article. "Humanitas" is not predicated of Socrates, whereas "homo" is. But apart from this, both the tradition and Frege acknowledge that *humanitas* is a universal under which individuals (may) fall; even under the *régime* of unsaturatedness and Frege's paradox, "the concept *man*" (the saturated "humanitas") is still an object of which it is meaningful and true to say that it is not empty.[38] The point is that apart from the fact that due to the *modus intelligendi*[39] one may choose between an abstract (saturated) and a concrete (unsaturated) approach to universals, universals are entities capable of standing in a relation of predication or of "One *versus* Many" with respect to other entities called their individuals. Now, *for numbers, this is excluded by Frege.*

Numbers are not concepts (predicates, properties, universals) for it does not make sense to say "this is an instance of 2", "this is a two" (much less to speak of *some* or *all* two's). It makes sense to say "this is 2" only in the way in which we say "this is Peter" ("is" as identity).[40]

It is not sufficient to reply that, *qua* arithmetician, Frege makes of numbers fictitious individuals. In GRL Frege is not an arithmetician (in the usual sense) but an ontologist.

I assume that according to Frege there is nothing to which we might apply the supposed property *two*.[41] To what extent this insight was preserved by the famous "definition" is another matter. However, there is no conflict, because the "definition" is not meant as an essential definition, but as a way of "grasping" numbers.[42]

The idea that numbers are not universals is not at all trivial, and it is a point which can be appreciated only by contrast with the philosophical past.[43] We stress the need of assigning this a primary place in Frege's philosophy of number, more important than the so-called "definition".[44]

10.3 Numbers are not sets: criticism of the Euclidean definition

In GRL § 28, Frege attacks the view of number as *set*. "Set" is meant in a very broad sense, embracing the following possibilities[45]:

(1) "Set" means spatial juxtaposition of things (units[46]).

(2) "Set" means something *more general, unbestimmter*, than number. This is the Euclidean definition. Number is defined as a set of *Einheiten*, where, (2a) "Einheit" = "number one"[47] (therefore, "Einheiten" = "several number one's"), (2b) "Einheit" = "to have unity" (to be *indivisum*), (2c) "Einheit" = "unit" (i.e., "any object", because any object may be regarded as a unit to be counted).

Frege rejects (1) which, as we have mentioned, is trivial.[48] His rejection of (1) should be understood rather as a rejection of the thesis that numbers are physical entities, similar to his rejection of numbers as "properties of external things".[49] Neither "property" nor "set" are the targets here, but rather "spatial juxtaposition" or "physical".

In (2) Frege touches upon a minor tenacious fragment of the philosophical tradition, already found in Aristotle: number as a species of the genus *plurality*.[50] This appears in Suarez's account of *quantitas discreta*[51] and is still to be found in Husserl's *Philosophie der Arithmetik*.[52]

It should be observed that Frege rejects under (2) the equation *Zahl* = *Menge von Dingen oder Gegenständen*.[53] *Ding* or *Gegenstand* is perhaps meant to exclude *Begriff*.[54] If such is the case, one can guess that Frege purposively avoids considering *Menge von Begriffen* which will be, *cum grano salis*, his own definition of number in GRL.[55]

(2a) is rejected on the ground that if we say "one and one and one"[56] in the sense in which we say "Peter and John" we may not equate that expression with "three", but just with "one", as if we said "Peter and Peter", because an object is not found more than once (*kommt nicht wiederholt vor*[57]). Cornford [2][58] relates that in Antiquity, as long as the notion of *monad* was conceived in such a way that there could be only *one* monad, the expression "*πλῆθος μονάδων*" did not impose itself. What Frege means belongs to the rudiments of contemporary set-theory.[59] To obtain 3 we need $1+1+1$; "and" and "+" are not the same.

(2b) is rejected on the grounds that there is not such a property of being *one* (*indivisum*). The content of this concept vanishes, because the extension is universal.[60]

With (2c) we come upon the interesting case: number defined as a set of *units*, i.e., objects, or things in general, which may be counted. Frege begins discussing this in GRL, § 34. He continues to employ the term "Einheit", but now this is a superfluous synonym of "Ding" or "Gegenstand". He utilizes that term probably in order to adapt himself to the terminology of the authors under discussion who take advantage precisely of the ambiguities of "Einheit": abstract unit, unit, unity. Frege attacks (2c) by asking: "Are the objects to be counted (the "units" making up number) identical or different?"[61] If the objects are identical, they do not "make number" (supposing we want numbers greater than 1[62]). In other words, the units collapse into a unique unit: *so fließt dies immerfort in eins zusammen*.[63] As for the case where the objects are different, Frege's reply is partially inconsistent with his own "definition" of number. He takes for granted that a set in which the objects are included with all their properties (in particular those distinguishing them) *is not number.*[64] This thesis certainly expresses some basic Fregean insight into numbers, but unfortunately I am not able to trace this insight. In any case, then, one wonders how a set of (different of course) *concepts* or *classes* can be a number at all. One solution apparently consists in taking into account the fact that Frege's "definition" is not meant to express his insight into what numbers really are, but only to provide a means of "grasping" them. Another solution consists in destroying the intuitive notion of a class, replacing it by a notion of class according to which classes are abstract, ideal points, completely independent from the variety and multitude of their elements.

Moreover, Frege could reject, without being inconsistent with his "definition", the alternative that the objects are different, by merely observing that such an alternative would result in having *two's* and *three's*, indeed, as many of these as there are couples or triplets in the world.[65]

Frege thus reduces the Euclidean definition to an *impasse*.[66] His own way out, nevertheless, consists in introducing a distinction in this definition rather than in seeking some other approach.

10.4 Frege's own solution: Numbers 'concern' concepts, and there is a way of 'grasping' numbers

> Mais le nombre *Deux* n'est ni une pluralité particulière de cette sorte ni le symbole d'une telle pluralité. *Peut-être on se rapprocherait plus de la vérité* en disant que c'est l'espèce ou la classe des pluralités formées d'une unité adjointe à une autre unité.
>
> (Frege, LNE, p. 77, italics ours)

> Two, for instance, denotes all pairs of things, and twelve all dozens of things, connoting what makes them pairs or dozens. (Mill [1], Book III, ch. XXIV, § 5)

Frege approaches the "solution of the difficulty"[67] not by pretending to give another definition of number, but rather by indicating how sentences, in which we assign numbers, are made. In such sentences (1), there is a *concept*, and (2), we state how many individuals fall under that concept. This analysis preserves both the difference and the identity which in the Euclidean definition were mixed together in the "units". But now the individuals are responsible for the difference, and the concept is responsible for the identity.[68] Frege had said that a *Gegenstand kommt nicht wiederholt vor*[69], but he had added: *mehre Gegenstände fallen unter einen Begriff.*[70] The former was the reason why the "unum et unum et unum" did not render three; now (with respect to the unity *to be a Jupiter's moon*) there is no difficulty in equating "one moon and one moon and one moon and one moon" with "four moons". Each moon is different from the other three, but they are *formaliter* the same; *qua moons of Jupiter* they are identical.[71] At this point we may observe that Frege's insights may sometimes be formulated in terms of reduplication, although he himself does not seem to have considered this sort of formulation. Frege had indeed an equivalent formulation, namely his *Sinn–Bedeutung* doctrine, but he did not apply it to the investigation of the relations among the elements of a concept or class.[72]

After this analysis one knows only that numbers "appear" at the second level[73] of "logical" entities; number concerns concepts because numbers indicate *how many* individuals fall under a concept. But what does "concerns" mean?

Frege stresses that numbers are self-subsistent entities.[74] Leaving aside the vague implications of "substance" in this phrase, let us simply recall what (in our interpretation) is perfectly clear in this phrase: numbers are ultimate subjects of predication, like the Aristotelian *Callias*. They are neither predicates, nor predicates of predicates (in Frege's or modern logic's sense); they are subjects of other predicates but they themselves are not predicated of anything. There is not a two, as there is not a Peter (if "Peter" is used as a proper name and not as *sextum praedicabile*). On the other hand, numbers are not like Callias because Callias is a visible (physical, sensible) entity whereas 2 cannot be seen *in rerum natura*. They are not sets of units, as the Euclidean definition has falsely taught during two thousand years. What are they?

Frege does not know. He could have found some analogy between his numbers and mediaeval *substantiae separatae*, but precisely to stop this or similar speculations he launched his semantic principle that names do not have meaning in isolation.[75] Such *ad hoc* semantics, along with some other references to numbers being *directly given to the Vernunft*[76] is all that Frege offers as to the real nature of numbers.

After this failure[77], Frege tries a new approach to the invisible numbers. As in other quite distant fields of contemporary philosophy, where a *coffret* may be an "equivalent" or "representative" of a dead person[78], Frege too considers the possibility of "retaining" numbers by means of a (later famous) "definition": numbers are classes of concepts whose individuals may be correlated one–one. Or also, numbers are second-level concepts applying to concepts whose individuals may be correlated one–one.[79] GRL § 7 shows that this comes from Mill.

Thereby other views of Frege are threatened: his rejection of the Euclidean definition (now number continues to be a *multitudo . . . conceptuum*[80]), or his idea that numbers are not universals.[81]

The former difficulty has been already considered in the preceding section. Frege mentions the latter difficulty only as being a consequence of choosing the formulation with "concept" instead of "class of concepts".[82] He enigmatically says that the objection might be solved: Does he already mean unsaturatedness? And to what extent does unsaturatedness help to meet that difficulty?

But these problems do not seem to concern Frege because, we think, he did not expect his "definition" to be more than merely a way of "grasping"[83] numbers once the true philosophical analysis had failed or had led to a sort of 'angelology'. Russell's contradiction, on the other hand, will present a real difficulty because it will question the very legitimacy of that way of grasping numbers. This will be a second failure in Frege's assault upon natural numbers.

10.5 Historical excursus

10.51 *Abstract and concrete numbers*

There was already in Greek philosophy a distinction between abstract and concrete numbers.[84] In the 16th century, the Conimbricenses reiterated that for Peripateticians number is divided into concrete and abstract. *Binarium* or *ternarium* are abstract numbers, *binarium lapidum* or *ternarium leonum* are concrete numbers; the former are abstracted "from" the things, the latter are concrete "with" the things.[85]

What exactly is the relation between abstract and concrete numbers? Are abstract numbers to be found somewhere in the UO-series, starting from Callias? It seems that the philosophical tradition has been generally silent about this. Perhaps the best clarification was reached by Husserl's *Philosophie der Arithmetik*.[86] Frege of course opened a radically new approach, but after the failure of his properly philosophical examination of the notion of number the "definition" perhaps obliged him to keep silent about some of his previous insights.[87]

Still, in the philosophical tradition one finds some awareness of the peculiarity of the relation between number and its "instances" or "individuals". It is observed[88], for example, that the species *binarium* is not only predicated of its individuals, but also of couples of its individuals:

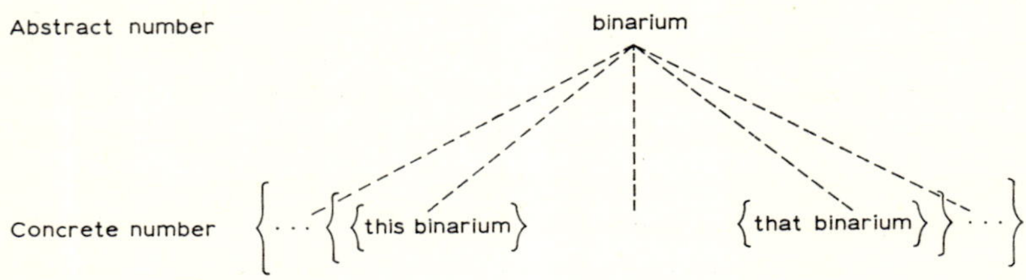

10.52 *The Euclidean definition*

Jamblichus assigns to Thales the definition of number as a "system of monads" and Thales is supposed to have inherited it from the Egyptians.[89] From such legendary origins, passing through Aristotle, Euclid, the Middle Ages and modern philosophy, this definition reaches Frege's GRL.

The Euclidean definition of number does not seem to have had any significance in the history of mathematics[90], but to the contrary, it makes an interesting chapter in the history of metaphysics. Book Z of Aristotle's *Metaphysics* mentions the definition in a way which makes for an interesting comparison with Frege. To this definition Aristotle objects that if two is a collection of units, then two will not be one entity, and if two is one entity, it will not be a collection of units.[91]

In Bortolotti [1] and [2], there is an extensive review of definitions of number, from the Greeks up to the 20th century. Number as a set of units is an impressive continuing theme in this history. Although many reactions have arisen against that definition (for instance Newton[92]) the author concludes his research by pointing out that the history of number begins and finishes with the Euclidean definition.

But the Euclidean definition only encourages difficult problems within metaphysics. Authors such as Aquinas[93] and Scotus[94] adopted it and the definition was a source of dispute.[95]

What is the ontological status of collections of entities in classical ontology? Are they substances or accidents? Accidents (contrary to what is normally thought about universal properties) are real entities, just as individual as the individual substances in which they inhere. One accident cannot be in more than one subject, unless ubiquity is assumed. Now, number being a set of entities, the question was what degree of unity does a set of entities have, independent of our minds.[96] *Two* seems to be the property unifying these two chairs into a (concrete[97]) number. No one would object to this in so far as that property and its unifying power are rather our own mental intervention, i.e., in so far as number belongs to *ens rationis*. Aristotle in *Categoriae* considers number to be a species of quantity, which is a class[98] of real entities. This would imply thinking of *two* as an accident inhering in a set of two things, *in more than one subject*. Thus a conflict emerges in the Aristotelian tradition and its occasion is the Euclidean definition.

Keckermann [1][99] begins his exposition on number with a richly documented presentation of the Euclidean definition. Afterwards he remarks that once such a definition is given, it is no wonder that some philosophers conclude that number is not a real being.[100] Our author does not enter into the discussion; he contents himself with referring us to other authors, *imprimis Fonsecam ad 5. Metaphysicorum.*

In Fonseca's exposition we find the interesting point that classical ontology seems to have *progressively assumed* a subjectivist interpretation of number, which was more and more reduced to an *ens rationis*.[101] Thus, modern philosophers will find such textbooks as Suarez's *Disputationes*, where number is relegated to being in the mind.[102] Frege finds this in Leibniz, but he is unable to "absorb" it.[103]

The reasons behind the doctrine "being in the mind" are the same as those which led to the subjectivism of relations.[104] For classical ontology the dilemma was either to grant ubiquity or to put relations (numbers, etc.) in the mind. Some philosophers imagined that the solution consisted in introducing so-called *formae discretae*[105]; but it is obvious that this could not be a way out.[106]

10.6 Number as a transcendental

10.61 *Frege's philosophical logicism*

By "philosophical logicism" I mean the view that a science dealing with natural numbers must necessarily be something quite close to logic or ontology for the reason that number is a transcendental.

Frege distinguishes two senses of "formal theory": (1) meaning that only signs are taken into account, (2) meaning that a theory deals with the most general features of reality. Arithmetic is a formal theory in the second sense for Frege.[107]

Not only has Frege frequently stressed the transcendental character of number[108], but he has also explicitly said that the logical nature of arithmetic (not geometry) is a conclusion drawn from that metaphysical significance of number.[109]

10.62 *The universal applicability of number in the philosophical tradition*

Whether number is a "transcendental" was a much disputed question in the philosophical past. One of the richest accounts is perhaps to be found in Suarez's *Disputationes*.[110] The critical point was whether the "three" of "three stones" had the same meaning as the "three" of any three supra-sensible entities. This depended on whether the particular nature of the "units" constituting number (under the assumption of the Euclidean definition) was or was not significant for number as such.[111] If the units constituting number must be thought of as resulting from "a division of continuous quantity", then there will be no number proper in the realm of supra-sensible entities; number proper will be that of stones or material entities in general. Indeed, there will be a special sort of number for non-sensible entities: a number made up of transcendental units, but this is not "number proper".[112] Had traditional philosophers[113] decided to identify number with these sets of transcendental units (as Husserl did[114]), they would have *ipso facto* assigned to number that metaphysical status required originally by some important thinkers or schools[115] and subsequently by such philosophers as Leibniz[116], Husserl and Frege.[117]

REFERENCES

1. GRL, §§ 21–25.
2. Concepts are for the author of GRL *etwas Unsinnliches* (GRL, p. 31 below; cf. also GRL, §§ 48, 87, 92; for later works: GRG II, p. 110).
3. This argument is given in § 24 and especially on page 31. Cf. a rather similar argument in Klemke [1], p. 511: "In other words, an object has properties. Hence, if the object has the right to be called an existent, then surely its properties are existent, too".
4. That Frege is thinking of individual accidents, is clear from the following lines: "Wenn wir eine blaue Fläche sehen, so haben wir einen eigenthümlichen Eindruck, der dem Worte "blau" entspricht; und diesen erkennen wir wieder, wenn wir eine andere blaue Fläche erblicken" (GRL, p. 31).
   Also GRL, p. 34 below, implies that properties of external things (for instance *Farbe*) are *sinnlich wahrnehmbar*. Cf. GRL, § 87: "denn in der Außenwelt [. . .] giebt es keine Begriffe, keine *Eigenschaften von Begriffen*", as if "Eigenschaften von Dingen" were not excluded from the "external world".
5. Actually Frege gives this "good" formulation in the title of § 24 (in the analysis of contents of GRL): "Wenn die Zahl etwas Sinnliches wäre, könnte sie nicht Unsinnlichem beigelegt werden."
6. We shall consider them in Section 10.2.
7. GRL, p. 33.
8. GRL, § 26.
9. GRL, § 27.
10. GRL, p. X.
11. Cf. title of § 26 in the analysis of contents of GRL.
12. GRL, p. VI.
13. GRL, § 25.
14. "Während für Mill die Zahl etwas Physikalisches ist, besteht sie für Locke und Leibniz nur in der Idee."
15. GRL, § 93.
16. "In diesem Gedankengange [Leibniz's view, cf. note 14] kommt man leicht dazu, die Zahl für etwas Subjectives anzusehen."
17. Leibniz [1], V (*Nouv. Ess.*), p. 76; "estre dans l'entendement" is obviously *objective*.
18. Cf. Section 2.51.
19. GRG I, p. 2: "In wessen Geiste?" This question is addressed to Dedekind, who spoke of sets as being "in the mind".
20. Frege usually characterizes *subjective* as that which is *Verschieden für verschiedene Menschen* (BG, *Vorwort*, first page; SUB, pp. 29, 31; GRL, p. 37, etc.). This is precisely *psychological* subjectivity as opposed to *transcendental* subjectivity, cf. Eisler [1], "Subjektiv" (p. 516). Psychological subjectivity is also the *strict* sense of "subjective" (*ibid.*). I think it is appropriate to call this the "strong" sense as well. It seems that Frege has understood "subjective" only in this way, leaving aside the minor exceptions we refer to in the present section. "Subjective" means for Frege *psychology*, *personal sensations*, *personal feelings*, and so on (cf. for instance GRL, § 93). GED indicates that this was Frege's understanding of that term until the end of his life. Of course in this sense numbers are "outside the subject" because they are in fact accessible to many thinkers.

21. "Wir beschäftigen uns in der Arithmetik mit Gegenständen, die uns nicht als etwas Fremdes von außen durch Vermittelung der Sinne bekannt werden, sondern die unmittelbar der Vernunft gegeben sind, welche sie als ihr Eigenstes völlig durschschauen kann.
Und doch, oder vielmehr grade daher sind diese Gegenstände nicht subjective Hirngespinnste. Es giebt nichts Objectiveres als die arithmetischen Gesetze" (GRL, § 105).
Frege acknowledges and introduces what philosophy has called transcendental subjectivity, but he does not wish to employ the term "subjective" to designate it. We could ask: "in whose *Vernunft*?" (cf. note 19).
Cf. also: "So verstehe ich unter Objectivität eine Unabhängigkeit von unserm Empfinden, Anschauen und Vorstellen, von dem Entwerfen innerer Bilder aus den Erinnerungen früherer Empfindungen, aber nicht eine Unabhängigkeit von der Vernunft; denn die Frage beantworten, was die Dinge unabhängig von der Vernunft sind, hieße urtheilen, ohne zu urtheilen, den Pelz waschen, ohne ihn naß zu machen" (GRL, § 26).
"Und wir kommen zu dem Schlusse, daß die Zahl weder räumlich und physikalisch ist [. . .] noch auch subjectiv wie die Vorstellungen, sondern unsinnlich und objectiv. Der Grund der Objectivität kann ja nicht in dem Sinneseindrucke liegen, der als Affection unserer Seele ganz subjectiv ist, sondern soweit ich sehe, nur in der Vernunft" (GRL, § 27).
22. "Dieses Subjektive der Erkenntnis [i.e., "subjectiv" in the kritisch-transzendentalen Sinne] ist *zugleich* objektiv [again, in the critical-transcendental sense] (Eisler [1], "Subjektiv").
23. GRL, p. 38, § 45, § 93 (title). In GED, Frege will apply the same dichotomy to *Gedanken.*
24. Cf. Section 10.52.
25. Cf. Section 10.3.
26. Cf. Section 10.52.
27. Cf. Section 2.7. Frege associates both issues in GRL, § 106.
28. ". . . läßt sich die Zahl als eine Eigenschaft desjenigen Begriffes auffassen, unter welchem die gewählten Individuen vereinigt werden." (Hilbert-Ackermann [1], pp. 115–116).
29. Aristotle [3] (*Anal. Priora* A, Ch. 27).
30. Anscombe–Geach [1], p. 130.
31. GRL, p. 5.
32. *Ibid.* Up to now Frege has not provided any hint as to what number is, except a vague reference to numbers "lying beyond intuition" ($DISS_2$, p. 1) and the statement of his program of research in BG (*Vorwort*).
33. GRL, § 12, *in fine*, p. 57, § 89.
34. "Spricht man nicht in einem ganz andern Sinne von 1000 Blättern als von grünen Blättern des Baumes?" (GRL, p. 28; cf. also p. 29, in the middle).
35. "In dem Satze "dem Begriffe *F* kommt die Zahl 0 zu" ist 0 nur ein Theil des Prädicates, wenn wir als sachliches Subject den Begriff *F* betrachten. Deshalb habe ich es vermieden, eine Zahl wie 0, 1, 2 *Eigenschaft* eines Begriffes zu nennen" (GRL, § 57, italics Frege's).
Cf. § 46: "Aber dem Begriffe Venusmond wird dadurch eine Eigenschaft beigelegt, nämlich die, nichts unter sich zu befassen."
36. Cf. Section 6.6.

37. Cf. Section 6.43.
38. Cf. Chapter 6.
39. Cf. Chapter 6.
40. "Trotz dieser Unräumlichkeit und Unwirklichkeit ist 1/2 kein Begriff in dem Sinne, daß Gegenstände unter ihn fallen könnten. Man kann nicht sagen: "dies ist eine 1/2", wie man sagen kann: "dies ist ein rechter Winkel", ebensowenig sind Ausdrücke wie "alle 1/2", "einige 1/2" zulässig; sondern 1/2 wird als bestimmter einzelner Gegenstand behandelt . . ." (UFT, pp. 103–104). For an interesting criticism of Frege, cf. Kneale [1], p. 458f.
41. It is curious to observe that authors such as Wittgenstein [1] (p. 186) or Carnap [4] (p. 301) have erroneously assigned to Frege the thesis that number is a property of a concept, as if it were a second-level concept (cf. also Goodstein [1], p. 3). Numbers appear, so to speak, at the second level; but this means only that their names are proper names which occur in the name of a second-level property. Of course Frege's language in GRL is in many instances loose enough to suggest that numbers are properties of concepts. For example, "beilegen" numbers to concepts is a frequent turn in his text (GRL, §§ 46, 53). Numbers also "zukommen" to concepts (GRL, §§ 51, 54). Frege also speaks of the *Träger* or *Substrat* of number (GRG II, p. 150), and this may erroneously suggest that concepts or classes are "subjects" of a property like *two*.
42. Cf. Section 10.4.
43. Cf. Section 10.51.
44. Benacerraf [1] and a paper mentioned therein by Ch. Parsons (unpublished) indicate an increasing interest in Frege's intuitive philosophy of number.
45. I arrange the various possibilities indicated by Frege without considering his division given at the end of GRL § 28; this division will become a distinction of sub-cases in the interpretation of the Euclidean definition.
46. I use the following terminology (*The Concise Oxford Dictionary*): "unit" = "individual entity regarded for purposes of calculation as single and complete"; "unity" = "oneness, being formed of parts that constitute a whole" (*indivisum*). Frege uses "Einheit", which covers both, as the term "unitas".
47. Also in English "(the) unity" (*The Concise Oxford Dictionary*).
48. Cf. Section 8.1, especially note 5 of Chapter 8.
49. Cf. Section 10.11.
50. Aristotle [2], I, 6, 1057a, 2.
51. "unde etiam multitudo absolute dicta videtur comparari ad quantitatem discretam per modum generis, seu praedicati superioris essentialiter . . ." (Suarez [1], 41, sectio 1).
52. Cf. Section 3.62.
53. GRL, § 28 *in fine* or § 29.
54. Cf., for instance, GRL § 51.
55. Where numbers are defined as classes of concepts.
56. Cf.: "numerum definio unum et unum et unum, etc.", Leibniz quoted in Achsel [1], p. 11.
57. GRL, § 51. Cf.: "Ferner soll dasselbe Element nicht mehrfach vorkommen dürfen" (Kamke [1], § 1).
58. P. 8.
59. ". . . if $a = b$, we have $\{a, b\}=\{a, a\}=\{a\}$ (Sierpiński [1], p. 7, example 2). Frege has often attacked the notion of a set of units (or abstract units, i.e.,

"number ones") conceived as an abstract "equivalent" of a concrete set of entities. Precisely, Cantor [1] (p. 283) speaks of *lauter Einsen*: (1, 1, . . ., 1). Frege in CANT, p. 270 calls them "jene unglücklichen Einsen", and he asserts that Cantor asks *impossible abstractions.* Cf. Zermelo in Cantor [1], p. 351. For more recent implications, see Beth [2], p. 259.

60. GRL, p. 40. Cf. GRL, § 49 (*in fine*), now for the "transcendental" *ens.*
61. This is the core of Frege's argument from § 34 to § 45. The dilemma is stated in § 39.
62. GRL, p. 58.
63. GRL, p. 50.
64. "Wenn wir die Zahl durch Zusammenfassung von verschiedenen Gegenständen entstehen lassen wollen, so erhalten wir eine Anhäufung, in der die Gegenstände mit eben den Eigenschaften enthalten sind, durch die sie sich unterscheiden, *und das ist nicht die Zahl*" (GRL, p. 50 (italics mine); cf. also p. 51).
65. Especially GRL, p. 57 bottom. Cf. pp. 49, 53.
66. The argument is reiterated for instance in SCHU, pp. 8–12.
67. GRL, § 45.
68. GRL, § 54; Frege's speculation is familiar in classical ontology: "Sed Plato ex consideratione universalium deveniebat ad ponendum principia sensibilium rerum. Unde, cum diversitatis multorum singularium sub uno universali causa sit divisio materiae, posuit diversitatem ex parte materiae, et unitatem ex parte formae" (Aquinas [1], n. 168).
69. Cf. note 57.
70. GRL, § 51.
71. Cf. GRL, § 54.
72. Cf. Section 8.31.
73. Of course, this does not mean that numbers are second-level or *n*-level predicates. Frege requires, in my view, that they be *individuals* but individuals "appearing" at the second level. That numbers appear (whatever this may mean) at the second level is a traditional doctrine. Cf. Springer [1], p. 33, where, nevertheless, Maimonides' having in mind a second-level predicate is not duly appreciated. Maimonides, like Geach [1], p. 159, speaks in ambiguous terms of *being incidental to*, or *being supervenient upon.* This is justifiable in Maimonides' traditional approach to the higher predicates, but one wonders why Prof. Geach deliberately uses the Avicennian phraseology. Burkamp [1] is an important criticism of Frege's view on numbers as they concern concepts. But, unfortunately, I do not understand what Burkamp (p. 203) means by "synthetic" and "analytic", or "(un)wesentliche" predicates of predicates. He is aware of the distinction *Merkmal–Eigenschaft* (p. 304) and thus he should not use "unwesentlich" as traditional philosophers used "accidere" (cf. Section 9.2, note 18), but on p. 205 (lines 10–12 from the bottom) we are surprised to find that a "synthetic" higher predicate is that which is not . . . a mark! But of course, by this brief negative remark I do not intend to diminish the contribution of Burkamp [1], a book worthy of a special analysis, both for its interest and because it is dedicated to Frege. Krenz [1] gives a presentation of some of Burkamp's ideas.
74. GRL, 55f.
75. Cf. Section 2.7.
76. Cf. Section 10.13.

77. Which may be illustrated by Frege's first phrases in GRL § 62: "Wie soll uns denn eine Zahl gegeben sein, wenn wir keine Vorstellung oder Anschauung von ihr haben können?"
78. Marcel [1], p. 162. Cf. Geach [1], p. 158. Professor Geach probably has in mind GRL, § 107 (*in fine*), but perhaps Frege is referring there to his proposal of substituting "Begriff" for "Umfang des Begriffes" (GRL, p. 80 note). Still, I fully agree with Prof. Geach's interpretation that the famous definition is "only a secondary and doubtful point". I would add only the following qualification: as "essential" definition it is unimportant (i.e., it is not intended by Frege to express what numbers really are), but as "coffret" it is essential, as indicated by the last words of the *Nachwort* (GRG II).
79. GRL, § 62f.
80. Cf. Section 10.3, in particular note 63.
81. Cf. Section 10.2.
82. GRL, p. 80 note. GRL, p. 65 provides an example of what number one would be if identified with the concept *having as many individuals as the concept moon of the Earth*. Number one would be the second-level concept *Einzigkeit*, under which the concept *moon of the Earth* falls. But on p. 65 Frege does *not* say that *Einzigkeit* is number one. There he is trying to *see*; on such a phenomenological level he cannot say that *Einzigkeit* is 1. But on page 80 his method is different: he is trying the "logistic" definition.
In my interpretation of Frege (10.2) such a thing as "instances" of numbers were excluded, but now the "definition" – if taken as a statement about the real nature of numbers – calls for a new discussion. I do not think that the Frege who suggests that numbers are ultimate subjects of predication (10.2) would readily admit that a trio of men is an instance of number 3 (to use Russell [3]'s example). Of course it is not thereby implied that a trio of men is an instance of number, which would be the rough traditional view of "concrete numbers" (cf. 10.51). Still, to view a trio of men as an "instance" of 3 is obviously a partial relapse into that traditional view, a relapse of course with respect to the Frege we have tried to understand in 10.2.
83. GRG II, p. 265, Frege says "fassen".
84. For instance, Becker [3], p. 20, n. 3.
85. Quoted by Gilson [3], p. 284. Incidentally, the same famous authors are mentioned by Cantor [1] (p. 396), in a context of philosophy of number.
86. Cf. Chapter 3.
87. Cf. preceding section.
88. Sanchez Sedeño [1], Liber V, quaestio XXIII ("dissoluuntur argumenta").
89. Cornford [2], p. 8, note 2.
90. This is suggested by an examination of books on the history of mathematics (M. Cantor's, to begin with). It is most significant that the Euclidean definition is not apparent in Becker [2]. In mathematically oriented research such as Levi [1] (p. 87), the definition does not lead to any perplexities. Probably the only impact of that definition on mathematics has been the traditional exclusion of 0, and perhaps 1, from the class of numbers. Simplicius [2], (220 a 7) clearly explains that 0 and 1 cannot be numbers *if* number is a set of units. Cf. Ross in Aristotle [4] (p. 604). Chrysippus is said to have introduced 1 as a number (Becker [1], p. 45). All this, and recent history as well (cf. Gigli [1], p. 105), enables one to understand Frege's concern in saying that 0 and 1 are numbers

(for instance, title of GRL, § 44). I am grateful to Dr. F. Olivieri for valuable information on this matter.

91. Aristotle [2] Z, 13, 1039a, 11–14. Heath [1] (p. 113) is richly informative on this. The mass of commentaries on this passage would provide an interesting *liaison* between traditional metaphysics and GRL. Aristotle's solution is to distinguish units *in act* and *in potency*. But I believe that act and potency are used here as a psychologistic expedient. Are they not the same as "paying attention to" (i.e., the units are in act) or "not paying attention to" (i.e., the units are in potency)? The culmination of traditional philosophy of number, Husserl [4] (p. 84, 156), proposes a solution (now, of Frege's *aporia* in GRL) quite like that of Aristotle. Frege's reply, in HUSS (p. 325), is an accusation of psychologism. Whitehead–Russell [1] (I, p. 72, note) prefer to eliminate classes.
92. This definition will also be successful (Euler, Lagrange . . .) and its effect will be to weaken the Aristotelian separation between discrete and continuous quantity.
93. Cf. Schütz [1], "numerus".
94. Cf. Fernandez Garcia [1], "numerus".
95. "Difficultas in qua discordant diversi" (*ibid.*).
96. *Ens* if and only if *unum*; but cf. Frege's lack of interest in such transcendental properties, note 60.
97. Cf. Section 10.51.
98. As far as I know, the term "class" originally designated the Aristotelian ten categories. (Cf. for instance Eust. a Sto Paulo, quoted by Gilson [3], p. 35f.)
99. Keckermann [1], Lib. I, Sectio I, cap. 8.
100. ". . . unde quis non immerito concludat numerum non esse ens verum et per se . . ." (*ibid.*).
101. Fonseca [2], Tomus II, in Met. 5, cap. XIII, qu. IV, sectio IV: "Posteriorem sententiam [the subjectivist one] ex recentioribus quidem scholasticis plurimi amplectuntur . . .". Our author remarks that even within a single lifetime (that of Duns Scotus) there was a similar process. And Fonseca himself adheres to this subjectivist interpretation, according to which *in rerum natura* there are only "heaps" (of substances or other real entities), and it is our mind which transforms a mere *acervum lapidum aut frumenti* into a number (always, of course, within the Euclidean definition).
102. If number "outside the mind" is only a "heap" (cf. preceding note), then: "dices, ergo, numerus ut numerus, et ut aliquid unum, est ens rationis, et non rei, et consequenter non poterit dici quantitas realis". Answer: "Nam licet multitudo unitatum, ut multitudo, a parte rei sit, tamen, ut habens aliquam unitatem per se, secundum aliquem ordinem vel constitutionem, non est nisi per intellectum, et dependenter ab intellectu" (Suarez [1], 41).
103. Cf. Sections 10.12 and 10.13.
104. Cf. Section 1.43.
105. The number three is supposed to be a property (an accident) inhering in more than one subject: "numerus trinarius non habet esse in uno subiecto sed in tribus." In a reply to this argument, someone said: "Dico quod illa tria habent rationem illius subiecti respectu numeri, quae [ratio] est forma discreta; quia haec est ratio formae discretae quod habeat esse in subiecto diviso in actu in plures partes non copulatas in aliquo termino communi" (Nicolaus D'Orbellis [1] "quantitas discreta").

106. Fonseca [2] (*ibid.*, as in note 13, sectio II) mentions the *accidens discretum*, but he finds this meaningless: "... tamen quia hoc ipsum mens capere non omnino videtur, ut unius accidentis non sit unum subiectum ..." The notion of an "accidens partialiter existens in pluribus subiectis" is indeed hardly conceivable: "You will not, I believe, admit an accident which is in two subjects at once" (Russell [1], p. 206; the text is Russell's translation of Leibniz). Incidentally, this is a good occasion to observe the divergency between the two ontological dimensions (cf. Chapter 1); *per definitionem*, a property (predicate, universal) is something which may exist in several subjects.
107. UFT, GRG II, p. 156 ("Formal" = "rein logisch").
108. "In der That kann man so ziemlich Alles zählen, was Gegenstand des Denkens werden kann: Ideales so gut wie Reales, Begriffe wie Dinge, Zeitliches so gut wie Räumliches, Ereignisse wie Körper, Methoden so gut wie Lehrsätze; auch die Zahlen selbst kann man wieder zählen" (UFT, p. 94).
109. UFT, pp. 94–95: "Daraus ist doch wohl so viel zu entnehmen, daß die Grundsätze, auf denen sich die Arithmetik aufbaut, sich nicht auf ein engeres Gebiet beziehen dürfen [...] sondern jene Grundsätze müssen sich auf alles Denkbare erstrecken; und einen solchen allgemeinsten Satz zählt man doch wohl mit Recht der Logik zu." This has been clearly appreciated by Bocheński [1], 39.04. To be able to appreciate Frege's logicism, it is necessary to know that *it is not trivial*. And it is not trivial with respect to the philosophical past, which Frege (along with other philosophers) combatted in order to vindicate the metaphysical significance of numbers (cf. next section). Outside of this perspective, I believe that "logicism" (vs. intuitionism, etc.) loses its original significance.
110. Suarez [1], 41, sect. II. Cf. Martin [1], § 8, and Maritain [2].
111. *Ibid.*
112. There will be sets of supra or non-sensible entities ("multitudo, quatenus ex unitatibus transcendentalibus consurgit", *ibid.*); but the question remains whether such abstract sets may be called *numbers*. Our use of "proper" finds support, for instance, in Fonseca's distinction between "unum transcendens" and "unum *proprie* dictum". At least in the 16th century this was a rather artificial situation, because ordinary language, as Suarez points out, allows one to speak of the number of angels and to compare that number with the number of human beings (*ibid.*).
113. I mean those philosophers supporting the *sententia negans* (the universal applicability of number proper, Suarez [1], *ibid.*). There were also many who held the opposite position (cf. *ibid.*).
114. Cf. Section 3.62.
115. Cf. Suarez [1], *ibid.*
116. Leibniz's view is quoted by Frege in GRL, § 24.
117. Husserl [3], § 24, p. 68 note.

11. THE MAIN RESULTS OF THE PRESENT INVESTIGATION

The primary question motivating the present research was: What is Frege's significance with respect to the philosophical tradition? This question was restricted to some aspects of Frege's thought; in particular, the formal logical aspects of Frege were not considered since their importance has long been established.

In accord with the *analytical* method used, the results obtained are stated in each of the single particular investigations making up this work. Nevertheless, for more clarity and in order to present some results which are in some way more general than any of the particular investigations, it seems advisable to survey here the main conclusions. These results may be classified into groups. At the beginning of each group the chapters mainly concerned are indicated.

I. **Predication Theory** (Chapters 3, 4, 5, 9)

Ia. *Higher predicates and the problem of universals*

(1) From the point of view of Frege's predication theory it is possible to re-examine the traditional problem of universals. This re-examination is, I believe, a far-reaching clarification which could not be achieved as long as the accepted predication theory was the Aristotelian (traditional) one. The problem of universals is intimately associated with predication theory in that *to be a universal* is a predicate (property) which has to be assigned to *some* subject (*cui convenit ratio generis . . .*). Our conclusion is that the choice and the way of considering this subject has been negatively influenced, in the philosophical tradition, by a defective predication theory. By "defective" I mean that traditional predication theory did not have adequate instruments for dealing with predicates of predicates. In 1884 Gottlob Frege definitely introduced into logic a more adequate predication theory.

(2) In view of clarifying the traditional problem of universals, the most powerful Fregean distinction is that of *Merkmal* and *Eigenschaft*. This, and its immediate applications (the first antepredicamental rule, the *triplex status naturae*) are discussed in Chapter 5. Both the first antepredicamental rule and the important doctrine on the *triplex status naturae* are interpreted in a new way by means of Frege's doctrines. Also the traditional approach to *second intentions* may be viewed from a new perspective; this is to be found in Chapter 7.

(3) Another significant application of Frege's (higher) predication theory is our thesis that many ideas of traditional metaphysics concerning existence as a property of properties could *not* be adequately *formulated* because of the predominance of an Aristotelian, and not a Fregean, theory of predication. In particular, some aspects of Gilson's research in metaphysics and its history may be viewed from a new perspective (Chapter 9).

Ib. *First-level predication* (Chapter 4)

(1) Frege's complaint that traditional logic did not distinguish the relation between an individual and a concept from the relation between two subordinate concepts, is answered by pointing out the fact that traditional logic has been influenced by an extremely powerful idea, namely, the idea of *essence*. The idea of essence has the effect of blurring the sharp distinction of individuals and properties, because there will be some privileged properties – the essential or "constitutive" ones – which will be "identified" with their individuals. In other words, we shall not have "Petrus ε homo", but "Petrus = homo". This is the ontology underlying mediaeval logic as well as such a significant textbook as Port-Royal Logic. It is plausible to think that the lack of the above mentioned distinction in traditional logic is due to these metaphysical presuppositions.

(2) In connection with this conclusion, it is also pointed out that if one rejects the idea of essence, then there is no known reason why the properties (of an object *a*) should still be classified according to, say, "external" and "internal". This is a pertinent remark because in later periods of his life Frege was momentarily attracted by the distinction between "extrinsic" and "intrinsic" properties.

(3) Some consequences of the absence of the distinction, denounced

by Frege, are stated, for instance: (1) why traditional philosophy could not have a clear concept of class, and (2) what is the source of the problem of "Locke's triangle", etc.

Ic. *The hierarchy of the predicates of an object* (Chapter 3)

(1) It is shown that a central point in the Frege-Husserl polemic was a different approach to predication theory. This disagreement appears to be much more interesting than other issues, such as "psychologism". The point is closely related to the idea of essence mentioned above. In fact, traditional predication theory was dominated by the idea of a *hierarchy* of predicates (essential, accidental, *denominationes extrinsecae*). The misunderstanding between both thinkers was due to the fact that Frege did not assume such a hierarchy, while Husserl did.

II. **Ontology** (Chapter 1)

IIa. *The ontological square* (Chapter 1)

(1) It is shown that the Aristotelian ontology included two fundamental ontological relations: not only the individual–universal, but also the relations of inherence between substance and accident. This results in a classification of entities into four groups: *the ontological square.*

(2) From the point of view of the main motivation of the present research, the conclusion to be derived from the existence of the "ontological square" is that any comparison of contemporary logic or philosophy with the philosophical past should take into account the existence of those two relations. What Frege or contemporary philosophy would call "the" relation between an individual and a property splits into *two* different relations as soon as one looks back into the philosophical tradition.

(3) One of the applications of this in the present work, is that Frege's notion of unsaturatedness (*Ungesättighteit*), as a feature of properties, cannot be directly transplanted into the Aristotelian tradition; first, one must determine to what extent Frege's (or modern logic's) unique relation coincides with one or the other Aristotelian relation (Chapter 6.77).

(4) A far-reaching consequence of the "ontological square" is that the term "property" ("predicate", etc.) becomes equivocal. In one sense

"property" means accident, in another it means property in the usual present-day sense. According to the latter, properties are abstract (ideal) entities, universals which exist in Plato's heaven and are opposed to their "many" individuals. But in the sense of accident, a property may be an individual, just as concrete (real) as "its" substance.

(5) For instance, this aids in understanding an otherwise unintelligible use of the term "Eigenschaft" in Frege's *Grundlagen der Arithmetik* (Chapter 10.11).

(6) It is also shown that ambiguities involved in the term "property" may be found also in other contemporary philosophers (Carnap, Reichenbach, Ingarden, F. Kaufmann).

(7) Russell's interpretation of Leibniz is shown to be erroneous in one of its main points because it neglects the "bi-dimensionality" of classical ontology.

(8) All this tends to confirm the conclusion that the Aristotelian idea of categories (not, of course, the "rhapsodical" list of eight or ten, but the essential opposition of substance–accident) should be taken into account as much as the platonic distinction of universals and singulars. Contemporary philosophy of logic has stressed only the platonic relation.

(9) But, while pointing out the importance of the Aristotelian doctrine, it must be admitted that the extant works of Aristotle do tend to blur the clear distinction of the two ontological relations. The same applies to history of philosophy in general.

IIb. *Logic and ontology* (3.1, 5, 7.54, 7.58, 9.3)

The traditional opposition between logic and ontology (or metaphysics) was a consequence of a peculiar way of dealing with predicates of predicates, i.e. the Avicennian (5.4) as opposed to the Fregean approach. Clauberg's abyss (1, note 13) was the separation introduced by traditional logicians between *man-in-the-mind* and *man-in-itself* (7.54), which was required not to have predicates of predicates falling down to Socrates.

III. **Semantics** (Chapter 2)

IIIa. *Results concerning Frege*

(1) *Sinn–Bedeutung* is primarily an ontological distinction.

(2) The term "Bedeutung" is ambiguous; in some cases it should be translated by "importance" without any semantic import. This enables us to better understand some points of Frege's semantics: the semantics of sentences (truth–values as the "importance" of sentences) and the semantics of predicate-terms (classes as the "importance" of predicates).

(3) The theory of sense is not independent of the theory of unsaturatedness. In particular, senses cannot be identified with concepts because senses may have saturated names ("the sense of the expression *A*" is the name of a sense), while concepts cannot. But if senses are not concepts, what are they? In such a case Frege's ontology would not be able to provide a satisfactory answer, as it lacks a theory of concrete properties (aspects).

(4) The fame of the "semantic principle of *Grundlagen der Arithmetik*" (i.e., "names have meaning only in context") is shown to be due to an insufficient consideration of the Fregean text.

IIIb. *Results concerning Frege and the philosophical tradition*

(1) Frege's hasty association of the Leibnizian principle of interchangeability *salva veritate* with identity is objectionable; in other words, the antinomy of the name-relation (in the case of Frege) lacks plausibility.

(2) As a conclusion following from the preceding point, one may formulate this program (not undertaken in the present work): the convenience of re-introducing in the philosophical discussion the old schema of *reduplicatio*. This should begin with an examination of Leibniz's acquaintance with *reduplicatio* and his principle of substitutivity.

(3) "Frege's Platonism" is not a legitimate expression because "Platonism" cannot be assigned a unique meaning with respect to Frege.

IV. **Unsaturatedness of functions** (Chapter 6)

In this question the critical discussion of Frege's own view is much more extensive and difficult than the establishment of its connections with the philosophical tradition.

IVa. *Results concerning Frege*

(1) A careful analysis of the genesis of Frege's idea of unsaturatedness indicates that it was not necessary that Frege arrived at the paradoxes of *Begriff und Gegenstand*. Kerry's criticism appear to have had a catalytic effect upon Frege in this question.

(2) As a plausible explanation of Frege's difficulties with unsaturatedness the following hypothesis is proposed: Frege has not freed himself of his initial view of functions as *signs*.

IVb. *Results concerning Frege and the philosophical tradition*

(1) In each of the two ontological relations of classical ontology the idea of unsaturatedness has been considered. Both universals and accidents are unsaturated, at least in the Aristotelian tradition.

(2) But for *ancient* semantics the fact that an entity is unsaturated does not require that the names of that entity have an empty argument place, as Frege demands. In this, mediaeval semantics coincides with contemporary post-Fregean semantics. Nevertheless, in mediaeval semantics a reason is explicitly assigned for that fact: the *modus intelligendi*. This is a reason which does not seem to be explicitly considered in contemporary logic or semantics.

V. **Levels of functions** (Chapters 6 and 7)

Va. *Results concerning Frege*

(1) In Frege, the idea of levels of functions is essentially dependent on the unsaturatedness of functions.

(2) There are two ways in which levels of functions may be introduced, while preserving unsaturatedness (6.8).

Vb. *Results concerning the philosophical tradition*

(1) Frege's remark that "no logician has considered the distinction of first and second level" is a starting point for a far-reaching re-examination of the philosophical tradition, in an aspect which had been completely forgotten by modern philosophy. This concerns in particular *second intentions*.

(2) The traditional treatment of levels of predicates, at least in the most familiar version, is vitiated by the defective Aristotelian theory of

higher predication. Because of such a theory of predication, higher properties are put, so to speak, "beside" and not "above" the first-level properties, which reveals itself in the curious and scarcely known *eleventh* category.

(3) Self-predication is a particular point where neither the philosophical tradition nor Frege, in spite of their profound insights, may provide valuable information: the philosophical tradition because of the heavy predication theory, Frege because of unsaturatedness.

VI. **Class** (Chapter 8)

VIa. *Results concerning Frege*

(1) Frege has two different approaches to the notion of class (*Wertverlauf* of propositional or logical functions), a formal and an intuitive one. His philosophy of class is describable as a sort of tension between both approaches.

(2) Frege chooses to understand classes as abstract objects. But he could have considered a different interpretation, more akin to his former insights. Some reasons are given explaining why Frege was led to view classes as abstract objects.

VIb. *Results concerning Frege and the philosophical tradition*

(1) The idea of class in the philosophical tradition was not, or rather could not, be clearly formulated because of the Aristotelian theory of predication (cf. Ib, 3).

(2) Therefore, not many applications of the Fregean view can be expected with respect to the idea of class and the philosophical tradition. However, an important application may be made with respect to *contemporary* philosophy where the idea of classes as abstract objects is unanimously accepted. Such an idea is largely due to Frege, and the analysis of Frege's reasons for adopting it may be instructive in order to discuss this idea in post-Fregean philosophy.

(3) It is stressed that Frege, in agreement with his early intuitions, could have developed a philosophy of class which makes classes neither abstract nor concrete entities. This might be called the "Sinn-Bedeutung" interpretation of classes. It is only hinted at in the present work.

VII. **Number** (Chapter 10)

VIIa. *Results concerning Frege*

(1) As a result of an analysis of the nature of natural numbers Frege arrives at a sort of *impasse*: numbers appear to him in a way quite similar to the *substantiae immateriales* of the mediaeval philosophers. Like the Aristotelian Callias, they are ultimate subjects of predication, but unlike Callias they are not perceptible objects.

(2) The famous definition "classes of classes" (or equivalent versions) is only introduced as a technical device for "grasping" or being able to "deal with" those unattainable and invisible Callias which are Fregean numbers. The idea comes from Mill.

(3) Numbers are for Frege entities having a transcendental character in the mediaeval sense. This is the reason why arithmetic – qua science dealing with *transcendentalia* – is likely to be "derivable" from logic or ontology. And this is the only acceptable way of understanding the overworked term "logicism", i.e., by contrast with a past philosophical tradition where numbers were not generally regarded as transcendentals.

VIIb. *Results concerning Frege and the philosophical tradition*

(1) Frege's criticism of the Euclidean definition concerns not precisely the history of arithmetic but the history of metaphysics.

(2) His analysis of the past philosophies of number in *Grundlagen der Arithmetik* is defective. Thus it may be observed that the defect ultimately consists in Frege's inability to distinguish empirical and transcendental subjectivity, or, in terms of earlier philosophies, to realize that "to be in the mind" is not necessarily subjectivism in the psychological sense.

(3) The philosophical tradition has ambiguously spoken of "concrete" and "abstract" numbers. Frege clarifies this confused situation. Nevertheless, his actual "definitions" of number seem to be a partial relapse into that tradition. (But Frege would reply that his "definitions" were not intended to say what numbers really are. Cf. VIIa, 2.)

(4) In his philosophical logicism Frege follows Leibniz, and, in general, the idea of the universal applicability of number may be regarded as heterodox with respect to traditional standards.

The primary question at the basis of the present investigation may now be finally answered.

The significance of Frege with respect to the philosophical tradition is very great, *also in those aspects which are not formal logic proper*.

It is indeed a remarkable fact that Frege's significance for philosophy is not restricted to his formal logical creation, in other words, that he is not only to be inserted into the history of philosophy as continuing *Analytica Priora*, Stoic Logic or Paulus Venetus, but also as continuing other classical themes thereby obtaining new insights in several important areas.

The ancient discussion on *the one and the many* appears in *Grundlagen der Arithmetik*, § 54, which is, perhaps, the decisive text in Frege's philosophy. Numbers "concern" concepts, not the individuals falling under the concepts. This insight helps to clarify many traditional topics: universals, predication theory, existence, to mention only the more important fields where Frege's insight may be applied.

There are aspects of Frege's thought which may be unacceptable, which in fact have been unanimously rejected by philosophy before and after Frege: for instance, the Fregean idea of unsaturatedness. Nevertheless, this Fregean thesis is not a mere curiosity or a mistake; it is one of the most interesting "footnotes to Plato" ever proposed.

There are aspects of Frege's thought which may be negatively criticized from the point of view of a comparison with philosophy: for instance, his failure to clarify his use of the term "Eigenschaft", or his being pre-Kantian in the sense of not being able to distinguish empirical and transcendental subjectivity, or his naive adoption of the Leibnizian association of identity with interchangeability. Nevertheless, it remains that the analysis and clarification of these defects, *qua Fregean* mistakes or defects, is an appropriate task for philosophy today.

APPENDIX

The appendix of this work was prepared while the author was 'Forschungsstipendiat' of the Alexander von Humboldt-Stiftung (German Federal Republic), at the 'Philosophisches Seminar' of the University of Erlangen-Nürnberg.

The English text of this book has been completely revised and corrected three times, successively by P. Briday, J. McCarthy, H. Glover, and T. W. Bynum: to all of them I wish to express my gratitude.

University of Notre Dame IGNACIO ANGELELLI
October, 1966

Fregean bibliography includes three books: the excellent C. Thiel, *Sinn und Bedeutung in der Logik G. Freges* (Hain, Meisenheim 1965, 171 pp.); J. Walker, *A Study of Frege* (Blackwell, Oxford 1965, XIV+201 pp.); and R. Egidi, *Ontologia e conoscenza matematica. Un saggio su G. Frege* (Sansoni, Firenze 1963, 274 pp.)

I was not able to take into account Egidi's important research except for some minor points. Thiel's and Walker's books appeared when the present work was already finished.

In this appendix some aspects of these books and other publications will be discussed, and complementary remarks concerning different aspects of my work will be added. All this will be ordered according to the chapters of the present work.

Ad 1.2:

The ontological square is discussed by M. Novak, *Toward Understanding Aristotle's Categories* (Philosophy and Phenomenological Research, XXVI) (1965), pp. 117–123.

Ad 1.43:

The standard misunderstanding of Leibniz's problems in his philosophy of relations is to be found in the following text of such a distinguished scholar as the late professor Beth:

> Leibniz refused to recognize relations as original and irreducible predicates but attempted to reduce them to properties inherent in each separate substance. [...] The recognition of the original character of the relations would have permitted a much more satisfactory construction of Leibniz's system. (*Mathematical Thought*, Reidel Publ. Co., Dordrecht 1965, p. 65).

But *how* would professor Beth have dealt with *individual* relations?

G. Parkinson (*Logic and Reality in Leibniz's Metaphysics*, Oxford 1965), seems not to consider the problems of the ontological square in Leibniz (cf. my review in *Documentación Crítica Iberoamericana*, Sevilla, received 1965).

Russell's criticism of Leibniz has been criticised several times in various ways. Cassirer, in his *Leibniz' System in seinen wissenschaftlichen Grundlagen* (Marburg 1902, XIV+548+2 pp.), accuses Russell of viewing faults in Leibniz which for Cassirer are his very merits. "Es ist daher Russell, nicht Leibniz, der die volle Freiheit und Reinheit der Beziehungen verkennt und beschränkt, indem er von ihnen ein anderes Sein, als ihre rein 'ideale' Geltung verlangt" (p. 537). My interpretation is different; I claim Leibniz's "idealization" of relations was not a consequence of a preference for *Idealität*, but just a way of avoiding the ontological difficulties of relations *as individual accidents* by throwing them into the shadowy realm of *entia rationis*. Cassirer's interpretation fails as soon as we see that it is based on a confusion concerning the term "ideal". Cassirer wants to interpret Leibniz as an idealist by basing himself on the occurrence of the word "ideal" in Leibniz's work. On pp. 208–209 we see how Leibniz, as an old Schoolman, opposes *ens rationis* to *ens reale*, calling the former *ens ideale* too and dividing it into *sine fundamento in re* (chimaera) and *cum fundamento in re* (*entia mathematica*). A minimal knowledge of the scholastic tradition indicates that the *fundament* is to be viewed in the *real* being; in other words, the *entia rationis* are secondary entities. Curiously, Cassirer suggests that Leibniz is viewing ideal being as the fundamental one (cf. also pp. 203, 205, 207).

Ad 1.45:

H. Weyl, *Das Kontinuum*, 1918, reprint Chelsea Publ. Co. s.a., p. 1: "Eine besonders wichtige Kategorie von Sachverhalten . . . wird von den *Eigenschafts-Sachverhalten* gebildet: ein Eigenschafts-Urteil behauptet, dass ein gewisser Gegenstand eine gewisse Eigenschaft besitzt. 'Dies (mir in einem gegenwärtigen Akt der Wahrnemung gegebene) Blatt hat diese bestimmte (mir in eben dieser Wahrnemung gegebene) grüne Farbe, mag als Beispiel dienen."

Obviously "Eigenschaft" here means something *concrete*, non-abstract, having a *hic et nunc*, an individual accident as the Aristotelian tradition would say. (It should be observed that Weyl was philosophically dependent on Husserl; cf. for instance p. 2 note.) As it may be assumed that Weyl is not always using "Eigenschaft" in the sense of individual accident, one may affirm that his use of this term is ambiguous. It is not immediately apparent whether such ambiguity has had consequences on other views of Weyl; though it is interesting to consider that a main point of Weyl's thought, his "vicious circle", is formulated in terms of properties of properties, that is to say in terms where the ambiguity of "Eigenschaft" is likely to become actually dangerous (cf. Weyl, 'Über die neue Grundlagenkrise der Mathematik', *Math. Zeits.* **10**, 1921, 39–79; reprint Wiss. Buchges. 1965, p. 1–4; cf. especially I, 1: 'Der circulus vitiosus').

Another example of the ambiguities determined by the ontological square is to be found in E. Beth, *Mathematical Thought* (Reidel, Dordrecht 1965), p. 56. The author gives:

An apple is sour
Sour is a taste
―――――――――
An apple is a taste

as an instance of the form

$$\frac{\begin{array}{l} S \,\varepsilon\, M \\ M \,\varepsilon\, P \end{array}}{S \,\varepsilon\, P,}$$

but it is obvious that, if *sour* is an abstract property, then it cannot be a taste, unless one grants that tastes are abstract entities. *Sour* would be better viewed as an individual property or individual accident; then one may still say that tastes are "tastable" — this is not possible if tastes are predicates of predicates.

Ad 1.46:

Walker (*op. cit.*) identifies Frege's relation between objects and properties with the traditional distinction of substance and qualities (p. 97). But, as I hope to make clear in my work, this is not possible, unless qualifications are introduced. Moreover, if Frege's relation may be compared with anything at all, the dimension singularity–universality should be considered rather than the dimension substance–accident.

Ad 2:

(a) Section 2 of Thiel's book is devoted to Frege's semantics. My basic objection is that the author does not clarify enough the Fregean notion of *Sinn*; the latter remains as something mysterious: "Was auch immer hier unter 'Sinn' verstanden werden mag" (p. 89). This lack of information as to what the *Sinn* really is, becomes particularly apparent when Thiel affirms that "Frege den Sinn von Sätzen genauer erläutert hat als den Sinn der grammatischen Eigennamen" (p. 132) or when the author sums up his results at the end of the book (p. 164: "Was Frege . . . sollen"). Actually, it should be observed that Thiel, as many other students of Frege, is curiously reluctant to take advantage of a Fregean formula which he knows very well. I mean Frege's description of sense as *Art des Gegebenseins* (quoted by Thiel on pp. 85, 86).

Thiel asserts that if we knew what *Sinn* really is, then the question of the identity of sense of two given expressions would be easily decidable (p. 121, "denn wäre . . ."). This is also a mistake in my view, because although Frege *does* say what the sense is, it is clear that senses are entities which *per definitionem* cannot be dealt with by means of decidable or undecidable algorithms. All the problems which presuppose absolute precision in the notion of *Sinn* are pseudo-problems.

Thiel's unwillingness to see what senses really are leads him to two other false positions. The first is that he does not sufficiently contest the Fregean thesis that propositions are senses of sentences. The second is that he excludes *to be a sense* from the ontological properties, or, in the authors's language, from the "ontological table" (p. 161). This is a main argument supporting the author's tendency toward an *ontologiefreie Semantik* (p. 165). Against such a thesis, I claim that Frege's semantics – *Sinn* and *Bedeutung* – arose within a certain *ontology* according to which entities are complex structures, not mere geometrical points.

(b) Frege and Frege's critics sometimes talk of unsaturated or incomplete *senses* (Rivetti Barbó [1], § 24, following Dummett; Jackson, H., 'Frege on sense-functions', *Analysis*, **23**, 1962, 84–87; Resnik, M., 'Frege's theory of incomplete entities', *Philos. of Science*, **32**, 1965, note 6). Perhaps the first Fregean important text where one finds complete and incomplete senses is *Begriff und Gegenstand*, p. 205. But unfortunately this depends on Frege's semantics of sentences. I do not think that any student of Frege is able to *see* what a "part" of a *Gedanke* is at all, and ultimately what a *Gedanke* is once the *Bedeutungen* of the parts of the sentence are excluded from the *Gedanke*. One may follow Frege up to a certain point, for instance, one may be pleased by his explanations (including metaphors) of unsaturatedness; but it lies beyond any possible intuition to combine this with the already unintelligible doctrine of *Gedanke* as sense (*Art des Gegebenseins*) of the sentence. The combination consists in calling the *Gedanke* a "complete" sense (*Begriff und Gegenstand*, *ibid.*) and viewing it as composed of the senses of the parts of the sentence, one of which (senses and parts) must be incomplete in order that they *haften aneinander* (*ibid.*) This chaos is likely to have a merely accidental origin, i.e. that in the context of explaining to Kerry that unsaturatedness cannot be dispensed with, Frege chooses the way of showing that it cannot be dispensed with *at the level of the meaning of the sentence*. Such a vague meaning or *Inhalt* of a sentence like "die Zahl Zwei fällt unter den Begriff Primzahl" could be obviously described as composed of the elements: *die Zahl Zwei*, *Fallen unter einen Begriff*, *Primzahl*. But at the time of BGGE *Inhalt* or meaning of a sentence is already divided into sense and reference, truth-value, and *Gedanke*. Thus, the indispensability of unsaturatedness must be shown *either* at the level of the truth-value *or* at the level of the *Gedanke*. Now it is difficult to conceive how Frege can show that the truth-values are entities including at least one unsaturated part (although in SUB, p. 35, one finds a brief reference to "parts" of truth-values). The task of showing to Kerry that in the meaning of sentences there is unsaturatedness must be achieved at the level of the *Gedanke*. Now the *Gedanke* is an entity which *per definitionem* excludes from itself the *Bedeutungen* of (at least some of) the parts of the sentence (SUB, p. 33). If the *Gedanke* is made up of anything at all, it must include *senses*. In the above example, the *Gedanke* must include some of the senses of "die Zahl Zwei", "Primzahl" and "fällt unter den Begriff". Thus, in trying to show that the set of units of meaning making up {*die Zahl Zwei, Fallen unter einen Begriff, Primzahl*} requires at least one unsaturated element, Frege has two alternatives: (1) either to view this set as made up of *Bedeutungen*, but then it is *not* the *Gedanke* (and not either the truth-value); (2) or, if he wants to view it as the *Gedanke*, to take at least some of its elements as senses. Frege must choose the second possibility: this is how the distinction complete–incomplete senses appears in the Fregean world. This distinction even looks plausible because in introducing it Frege simultaneously calls the *Gedanke* "complete", "abgeschlossen", which looks intuitively adequate. In other contexts Frege chooses the first possibility, momentarily forgetting his semantics of sentences. Thus in UGG_1, p. 372, he puts the "aneinander haften" of the meanings of the parts of a sentence at the level of the *Bedeutungen* of, not the *Sinn* of, these parts: "Ein Gegenstand – z.B. die Zahl 2 – kann an einem andern Gegenstande – z.B. Julius Caesar – logisch nicht haften ohne ein Bindemittel . . .." Obviously here Frege talks about the *Bedeutung* of "die Zahl 2", namely *die Zahl 2*, and not about the sense of it, as he did in BGGE, p. 205.

Ad. 2.3:

In SUB, p. 35, Frege refers to the *Gedanken* as *Weise der Zerlegung* of the truth-values. This shows his efforts to preserve "sense" for sentences according to the original meaning of *Art des Gegebenseins*.

Ad. 2.43:

If in ". . . *A* . . ." "*A*" denotes its sense, it would seem that one might replace "A" by a name of the same sense, for instance "the sense of '*A*'" or by any other conceivable name of the sense of "*A*" (in a natural or artificial language). But obviously this substitution will result in absurd sentences. For example, consider the sentence "Peter thinks that *A* is the same as *B*"; here "*A*" denotes its sense, but it is absurd to claim that therefore "Peter thinks that the sense of '*A*' is the same as *B*". Now, Frege himself has clearly pointed out that in indirect contexts "it is not permissible to replace one expression in the subordinate clause by another having the same customary reference, *but only by one having the same indirect reference, i.e. the same customary sense*" (SUB, in *Translations of the Philosophical Writings of G. Frege*, Blackwell, Oxford 1960, p. 67, italics mine). Thus, in our example "*A*" cannot be replaced by "the sense of '*A*'". This important point is not taken into account by Bartlett [1], 1.3225 (p. 19), by Resnik, 'Frege's theory of incomplete entities', *Philos. of Science*, **32** (1965), note 6, and in general by those scholars who wish to eliminate the ambiguity of "*A*" denoting once its *Bedeutung* and another time its sense. This ambiguity cannot be eliminated by constructing any special names whose usual reference would be the sense of other names.

Ad 2.7:

Contrary to Schwaider ['Uses of language and uses of words, with application to a problem of Frege', *Theoria*, **26**, 1960, 31–43 (p. 36, n. 3)], GRG I, § 29 cannot be viewed as a restatement of the semantic principle of GRL; the first lines of § 30 show that Frege in § 29 is not defining "meaning" (*Bedeutung*) but merely securing the meaningfulness of new names once some initial names are assumed as being meaningful independently of their context.

Ad 5:

Professor G. Patzig has kindly authorised me to publish here his list of Aristotelian texts relevant for the distinction *Merkmal–Eigenschaft*:

> Der Unterschied zwischen Eigenschaft und Merkmal ist sachlich bei Aristoteles in der Topik Z, Kap. X, 148a 14f. im Blick. Es wird davon gesprochen, dass eine Definition in gegebenen Fällen nicht auf die Idee anwendbar sei; so seien zwar die Lebewesen sterblich, aber die Idee eines sterblichen Lebewesens sei nicht sterblich. Ganz ähnliche Unterschiede sind in Kap. XII, 149a 38f. Gegenstand der Betrachtung, wobei man davon sprechen kann, dass Aristoteles unterscheidet zwischen der Existenz von Begriffen und der objektiven Realität von Begriffen. Eine Reihe von weiteren Stellen die in einem gewissen Zusammenhang mit diesen Problemen stehen, finden sich in der Auseinandersetzung über das Verhältnis von Genos und Diaphora im Kap. *Δ*, 2.

Ad 5.42:

Walker (*op. cit.*, p. 17) affirms that according to Frege existence is "a predicate of predicates, *in the old terms*, and not a predicate of objects" (italics mine). To which of the two senses of "predicate of predicate" is he referring? (cf. Caietanus' text, and cf. Section 5.42).

Ad. 6.7:

In Hilbert–Bernays, *Grundlagen der Mathematik* I, Berlin 1934, one may find suggestive examples of unsaturatedness. The latter is apparent when the authors introduce the notion of *Nennform* (p. 89), as may be confirmed by a later statement concerning the symbol "$A(a)$". This symbol generally represents a *Formel*, but in a particular case (p. 383) it is intended to represent a predicate symbol: "Die Variable *a* dient hier, so wie eine Individuenvariable einer Nennform, nur zur Festlegung einer Argumentstelle." Concrete examples of unsaturated functional signs are: "$\varphi(.\,,.)$" (with two arguments) and "$\varphi(.)$" (with one argument), pp. 288–289. A more precise presentation of the notion of *Nennform* is to be found in Vol. II, Berlin 1939, p. 377.

Ad 6.8:

There seems to be a Fregean influence on Hilbert's use of the term "Stufe". In Hilbert–Bernays I, p. 155, systems of first *Stufe* are those where the variable predicates have been replaced by constants; in fact, axiom systems with *Formelvariablen* (variable predicates) are, in Fregean terms, names of functions of second *Stufe*. But this use of "Stufe" clashes with the usual one (already in Hilbert–Ackermann, 1928), according to which "first *Stufe*" refers to systems where predicate variables are not quantified; thus on p. 413 of volume I "zweite Stufe" means quantification over functional variables. The resulting ambiguity is cleared up at the very beginning of the second volume (Berlin 1939, p. 1 note): "Logik erster (zweiter) Stufe" shall mean that quantification applies only to individual variables (or to functional signs also), whereas "Axiomsystem erster Stufe" shall be reserved to the axiom systems without variable predicate terms.

Ad 6.83:

Sluga (H. D. Sluga, 'Frege und die Typentheorie', in *Logik und Logikkalkul*, Alber, Munich 1962, pp. 195–209) affirms that *Freges Theorie, konsequent durchgedacht, führt zur Annahme einer unendlichen Hierarchie von Typen* (p. 197). More recently, M. Resnik ('Frege's theory of incomplete entities', *Philos. of Science*, **32**, 1965, 329–341) refers to a "denumerable infinity of types", which is certainly "only implicit" or "only in principle infinite "(notes 4 and 5). Thiel (*op. cit.*, chapter 1.3) promises a "Vermutung" concerning the reasons why Frege did not consider more levels than three, but no such "Vermutung" is obvious in the following pages (p. 56f).

The question is: is there such a thing as a Fregean function of the 4th or 5th level? The authors who affirm that there are infinite Fregean levels should provide actual examples – but they do not. In *Principia Mathematica* one could find a suggestion that Fregean functions go upwards infinitely. In chapter II of the introduction (first ed.), as well as in chapter 12, we find a curious fact: all examples of functions of higher level (functions of functions) are *à la Frege*, namely they presuppose that a function-sign must always have the "Argumentstelle(n)" (*Ungesättigtheit*). A reader who is puzzled by this may think it is mere coincidence or arbitrariness, and apparently nothing prevents the reader of *Principia* (first ed., *loc. cit.*) from interpreting the symbol "$f(f(\hat{z}))$" – a function of a function – in a *non*-Fregean way. In the introduction to the second ed. one understands why that choice of examples was not a mere coincidence. Such examples *à la Frege* are in fact the only possible functions of functions available without "going outside logic". I think this is clear on page XXXII (supra). Now, in the introduction to the second ed. a new approach (due to Wittgenstein) is discussed, according to which a function can only occur through its values, and consequently a function must be always accompanied by its "Argumentsstellen" (p. XXXI, infra). This means that Frege's *Ungesättigtheit* is at work. Thus it may be said that in the second ed. *Principia's* world of functions of functions reduces to the Fregean world of functions of functions.

Now, in the introduction to the second ed. (p. XXXIV) it is asserted that the "hierarchy" of functions can be developed infinitely. This would imply that, as the above mentioned authors claim, Fregean functions of functions go upward in infinitum. Unfortunately, like those authors, the introduction to the second ed. of *Principia* does not provide actual examples. They only provide a general scheme, which does not even respect Frege's unsaturatedness.

Ad 7.54 (*or 11, conclusion IIb*)

According to my interpretation, the sharp distinction between the logical and the ontological levels has been the way in which traditional students of Aristotle have tried to enrich their master's predication theory by adding authentic predicates of predicates. A recent work, *La teoria aristotelica della scienza*, by Mario Mignucci (Sansoni, Milano 1965), has as its main thesis that the distinction "logical–ontological" is *not* Aristotelian but belongs to the so-called Aristotelian tradition. Let us quote the final words of Mignucci's book:

> Non è poi scopo di questa ricerca valutare da un punto di vista teoretico se la distinzione tra piano logico e piano reale introdotta dalla filosofia posteriore a quella aristotelica sia da considerarsi un'ulteriore conquista nel difficile cammino verso la verità, oppure sia da intendersi come un'involuzione, un mancato riconoscimento [. . .] Molto più modestamente ci si limita a dire che una tale distinzione in Aristotele non c'è, o meglio, che non è necessaria per una sensata lettura delle sue opere. (p. 329)

Ad 8:

Thiel's remarkable discussion of the interpretation of *Wertverlauf* contains an inconsistency. Thiel welcomes the Fregean identification of $\grave{\varepsilon}(\varepsilon = \neg\!\overset{\mathfrak{a}}{\smile}\!\!-\, \mathfrak{a} = \mathfrak{a}))$ with *das Falsche*, and of $\grave{\varepsilon}(-\varepsilon)$ with *das Wahre* as "in voller Übereinstimmung" with intuitive requirements. This is expressed three times on pages 64–65. But it is important to observe that that Fregean "Festsetzung" is "intuitive" only in so far as one identifies unit-classes with their members, an identification which Thiel definitely rejects on p. 68 (cf. the example of the *Kölner Dom*).

However, the chapter ends with a passage (p. 84) suggesting that *Wertverlauf*-signs do have, independently of the formal development of the *Begriffsschrift*, a quite familiar meaning as in the case of other logical signs (negation, assertion, etc.). The reader gets the impression that the author knows (although he does not say it) what that meaning is (cf. "Aus dieser Kenntnis und der Kenntnis der Bedeutung eines bestimmten Funktionsnames ergibt sich dann von selbst die inhaltliche Bedeutung des entsprechenden Wertverlaufsnamens", p. 84).

On p. 73 (note 12) there is a curious suggestion of a possible interpretation of *Wertverläufe*. The latter would be *sequences*, namely the set of the values of the function *ordered* by means of a basic order introduced in the set of arguments (cf. p. 60 line 14). But such an interpretation cannot be accepted because in the special case of *Wertverläufe* of propositional functions the result would depart too much from the interpretation which Frege *did* intend to preserve, at least until the *Nachwort*, namely *der Begriffsumfang im hergebrachten Sinne des Wortes* (GRG II, p. 260).

Thereby I am assuming that we are able to know what Frege meant by "traditional" interpretation of classes and extensions. I think that this "traditional" notion included at least the two following requirements: (1) in a class or set (when it has more than one element) the idea of *many* is preserved, (2) the class is viewed as made up of its elements too. This second condition implies that *Wertverläufe* of logical functions are the collection of arguments, or in other words, the *Wertverlauf* of a logical function is the set of arguments (not the "sequence", not the set of couples, etc.)

The two above mentioned conditions look very trivial, but this is not the case as soon as one takes into account that they are not consistent with any prevailing philosophy of class in contemporary philosophy. Moreover, although Frege did intend to preserve the "traditional" notion of class (which I believe may be said to fulfil at least those two conditions), he was unable to achieve such a program because he preferred to go into a philosophy of classes as abstract objects. When classes are conceived as abstract objects it is no longer possible to think of them (if they have more than one element) as involving or preserving somehow the idea of *many*. Such a thing would be to ask for "unmögliche Abstraktionen" (to use Frege's own language, which he used in his criticism of Cantor). Of course condition (2) also must be given up, because otherwise, *inter alia*, classes of concrete objects would be concrete.

Now, if one accepts Frege's actual view of classes as *logische Gegenstände*, not only the familiar notion of classes as pluralities, but also other intuitive interpretations such as sequences, sets of couples (arguments and truth-values), etc. disappear.

Ad 8.2:

Walker stresses the term "Wert" in "Wertverlauf", understanding it in the sense of *value* (*of a function*), and finds in it a key to interpreting the meaning of the whole compound term "Wertverlauf" in the sense of identifying it with the values of a function rather than with the arguments; cf. p. 12: "But whatever a *value*-range is, it is not simply a set of *arguments* . . .", and p. 180: "But in introducing the notion of a value-range he was certainly talking not about the arguments of functions but about their values." But this is a mistake due to not considering the actual use of "Wertverlauf" in German. Against Walker's reading of the German term "Wertverlauf" we may take into account Hilbert–Bernays, *Grundlagen der Mathematik*, I and II, Springer, Berlin 1934 and 1939). The term is introduced in vol. I, p. 9, in a way which stresses precisely the reading of "Wert" in "Wertverlauf" as referring to the values which the *argument* may take: "Des weiteren hat man zu beachten, dass es bei der Bestimmung eines Prädikates nur auf seinen 'Wertverlauf' ankommt, dass heisst darauf, für welche *Werte der* (*an den Subjektstellen auftretenden*) Variablen das Prädikat zutrifft bzw. nicht zutrifft ('wahr' bzw. 'falsch' ist)" (italics mine). The term "Wertverlauf" continues to be used by Hilbert–Bernays on many occasions. The resulting general impression is that they mean a set of couples, whose first elements are values of the argument of the function, and whose second elements are properly the values of the function. But it is clear that "Wert" in "Wertverlauf" does not imply a reference to the values of the function *only*, but also to the values which the arguments may take. This is perhaps the complete list of occurrences: p. 9 below; p. 10 (here the expression "die Anzahl der in Betracht kommenden Systeme von Wertverläufen" is abbreviated into "die Anzahl der verschiedenen möglichen Prädikatensysteme"), p. 11 (= sets of couples whose second elements are *true* or *false*); p. 12, below (stressing again "Wert" in the sense of the values which may be taken by the arguments!); p. 14; p. 17; p. 35 below (*Wertverlauf* of a function which is not a logical or propositional function; here the authors suggest that "Wertverlauf" means a set of couples, where both the first and second elements are "values": ". . . die Werte der Funktion nur *für vorgelegte Argumentswerte* . . ."); p. 45 ("der Verlauf dieser Funktion", referring to the truth-table of conjunction); p. 88 (the "Wertverlauf eines Prädikates" is a function which maps some domain into the truth-values); etc.

Ad 11:

(A. Frege's Works) In the 1964 reprint of Frege's *Begriffsschrift* ("reprographischer Nachdruck") unfortunately some logical symbols have disappeared. I m grateful to Terrell Ward Bynum for having detected these and other misprints, which will be listed here.

(1) In the reprint the following signs have disappeared. On p. 1 reads "—", should read "$\vdash$" (*Urteilsstrich*). On p. 62 reads "$\equiv\genfrac{}{}{0pt}{}{\gamma}{\beta}$", should read "$\equiv\genfrac{}{}{0pt}{}{\gamma}{\tilde{\beta}}$". On p. 81 first line, reads "$\genfrac{}{}{0pt}{}{\gamma}{\tilde{\beta}}$", should read "$\frac{\gamma}{\tilde{\beta}}$", and the seventh line of formula 125 should be negated. On p. 84 the second line should be negated (cf. formula 129). On p. 91, the formula following "Durch" should be negated.

(2) Moreover, the first edition (1879) still contains errata which have not been "verbessert" in the 1964 reprint. On p. 58 each of the two formulae separated by "oder" includes one mistake: in the first, the two Greek letters in the extremes of the vertical line should be interchanged; in the second, the "lateinische" *d* should be replaced by a German letter. On p. 63, the list of substitutions at the left of formula 79 includes, in the line corresponding to "c", a "F(y)" which should be replaced by "F(α)". On p. 67, reads "F-Reihe", should read "f-Reihe". On p. 81, the fifth line of formula 125 lacks an "ε".

Other minor misprints are not of a logical nature, such as on p. 9 "mau" instead of "man", etc. A doubtful case is whether parentheses should be added to the identity statements on pp. 72, 73. According to Frege's explanations about the *Inhaltsstrich* (p. 2) that would not be necessary, but Frege's definition on p. 15 seems to imply that parentheses should be added.

BIBLIOGRAPHY

A. Frege's works

A complete list of Frege's *publications* is to be found in G. Frege, *Kleine Schriften* (ed. by I. Angelelli), Wissenschaftliche Buchgesellschaft, Darmstadt, 1967. Here are mentioned only the items actually quoted in the present work, and the abbreviations are explained.

$DISS_1$ *Über eine geometrische Darstellung der imaginären Gebilde in der Ebene.* Diss. Göttingen 1873.

$DISS_2$ *Rechnungsmethoden, die sich auf eine Erweiterung des Größenbegriffs gründen.* Diss. *Venia Docendi* Jena 1874.

BG *Begriffsschrift, eine der arithmetischen nachgebildete Formelsprache des reinen Denkens.* Halle 1879, VIII+88 pp. Reprinted in *Begriffsschrift und andere Aufsätze* (ed. by I. Angelelli), Olms 1964. [Cf. 'Appendix'.]

UWB 'Über die wissenschaftliche Berechtigung einer Begriffsschrift', *Zeits. f. Philos. u. phil. Kritik* **81** (1882) 48–56.

UZBG 'Über den Zweck der Begriffsschrift', *in Sitz. d. Jenaischen Ges. f. Med. u. Naturwiss. für das Jahr 1882*, Jena 1883, pp. 1–10.

GRL *Die Grundlagen der Arithmetik*, Breslau 1884, XI+119 pp.

COH Review of H. Cohen, *Das Prinzip der Infinitesimal-Methode und seine Geschichte*, in *Zeits. f. Philos. u. phil. Kritik* **87** (1885) 324–329.

UFT 'Über formalen Theorien der Arithmetik', in *Sitz. d. Jenaischen Ges. f. Med. u. Naturwiss. für das Jahr 1885*, Jena 1885, pp. 94–104.

UTG 'Über das Trägheitsgesetz', *Zeits. f. Philos. u. philos. Kritik* **98** (1891) 145–161.

FUB *Function und Begriff*, Jena 1891, 31 pp.

SUB 'Über Sinn und Bedeutung', *Zeits. f. Philos. u. philos. Kritik* **100** (1892) 25–50.

CANT Review of G. Cantor, *Zur Lehre vom Transfinitem*, in *Zeits. f. Philos. u. philos. Kritik* **100** (1892) 269–272.

BGGE 'Über Begriff und Gegenstand', *Viertelj. f. Wiss. Philos.* **16** (1892) 192–205.

GRG I *Grundgesetze der Arithmetik*. I. Band, Jena 1893, XXXII+253 pp.

HUSS Review of E. Husserl, *Die Philosophie der Arithmetik*, in *Zeits. f. Philos. u. philos. Kritik* **103** (1894) 313–332.

KSCH 'Kritische Beleuchtung einiger Punkte in E. Schroeders Vorlesungen über die Algebra der Logik', *Archiv. f. system. Philos.* **1** (1895) 433–456.

LNE 'Le nombre entier', *Revue de Mét. et Mor.* **3** (1895) 73–78.

SCHUB *Über die Zahlen des Herrn Schubert*, Jena 1899, VI+32 pp.
GRG II *Grundgesetze der Arithmetik*, II. Band, Jena 1903, XV+265 pp.
UGG_1 'Über die Grundlagen der Geometrie', *Jahresbericht der Deutschen Mathematiker-Vereinigung* **12** (1903) 319–324, 368–375.
WIF 'Was ist eine Funktion?', in *Festschrift L. Boltzmann*' Leipzig 1904, pp. 656–666.
UGG_2 'Über die Grundlagen der Geometrie, I, II, III', *Jahresbericht der Deutschen Mathematiker-Vereinigung* **15** (1906) 293–309, 377–403, 423–430.
JOURD 'Notes to Ph. Jourdain, *The development of the theories of mathematical logic and the principles of mathematics*', *The Quarterly Jour. of Pure and Applied Math.* **43** (1912) 237–269.
GED 'Der Gedanke', *Beitr. z. Philos. d. deut. Ideal.*, **1** (1918) 58–77.
VERN 'Die Verneinung', *Ibid.*, 143–157.
UBR 'Unbekannte Briefe Frege's über die Grundlagen der Geometrie und Antwortbrief Hilbert's an Frege (aus dem Nachlass her. von M. Steck)', *Sitz. der Heidelberger Akad. der Wiss., Math.-naturw. Klasse*, 1941.

B. Other Works

AARON, R. [1]: *The Theory of Universals*, Clarendon Press, Oxford 1952, VIII+247 pp.

ACHSEL, R. [1]: *Über den Zahlbegriff bei Leibniz*, Inaug.-Diss. Rostock, Burg. b. M. 1905, 21 pp.

ALBERTUS MAGNUS [1]: *Opera Omnia* (ed. A. Borgnet) Vives, Paris 1890. Volumen sextum: *Metaphysicorum libri XIII*, 798 pp.

ALCORTA, J. I. [1]: *La teoria de los modos en Suarez*, C.S.I.C., Madrid 1949, 335 pp.

ALEXANDER [1]: *Alexandrini Aphrodisiensis in Aristotelis metaphysica commentaria* (Commentaria in Aristotelem Graeca I) 1891, XIII+919 pp.

ALFARABI [1]: *Alfarabis Philosophische Abhandlungen.* Aus dem Arabischen übersetzt von F. Dieterici, Leiden 1892, XLVII+223 pp.

ALGAZEL [1]: *Algazel's Metaphysics. A Medieval Translation* (ed. by J. T. Muckle), Toronto 1933.

AMMONIUS [1]: *Ammonius in Aristotelis categorias commentarium* (Commentaria in Aristotelem Graeca, vol. IV, pars IV, 1895, XXII+143 pp.

AMMONIUS [2]: *Ammonius in Aristotelis de interpretatione commentarius* (Commentaria in Aristotelem Graeca, vol. IV, pars V) 1897, LIV+316 pp.

ANGELELLI, I. [1]: 'Leibniz's misunderstanding of Nizolius' notion of *multitudo*', *Notre Dame Journal of Formal Logic* **6** received 1964.

ANGELELLI, I. [2]: 'On identity and interchangeablity in Leibniz and Frege', *ibid.*, received 1965.

ANONYMOUS [1]: *Anonymi in Aristotelis Categorias Paraphrasis* (Commentaria in Aristotelem Graeca, vol. XXIII, pars II) 1883, IV+87 pp.

ANSCOMBE, G. E. M., GEACH, P. T. [1]: *Three philosophers* (*Aristotle, Aquinas, Frege*), Blackwell, Oxford 1961, XX+162 pp.

AQUINAS [1]: *In duodecim libros Metaphysicorum Aristotelis Expositio*, Ed. Marietti, Romae-Taurini 1950, XXIII+648 pp.

AQUINAS [2]: *Opuscula philosophica*, Ed. Marietti, Romae-Taurini 1954, XXXI+379 pp.

AQUINAS [3]: *Le 'De Ente et Essentia' de St. Thomas d'Aquin.* Texte établie d'après les manuscrits parisiens. Introd., notes et études historiques par M. D. Roland Gosselin, Vrin, Paris 1948, XIII+215 pp.

AQUINAS [4]: *In Aristotelis libros Perihermeneias et Posteriorum Analyticorum Expositio*, Ed. Marietti, Romae-Taurini 1955, XVIII+439 pp.

AQUINAS [5]: *De natura verbi intellectus*, in Aquinas [2].

ARISTOTLE [1]: *Categoriae et Liber de Interpretatione* (ed. Minio-Paluello), Oxford 1949, XXIII+96 pp.

ARISTOTLE [1.1]: *Aristotle's Categories and De Interpretatione*. Translated with notes and Glossary by J. C. Ackrill, Oxford 1963, VI+162 pp.

ARISTOTLE [2]: *Aristotle's Metaphysics*. A revised text with introduction and commentary by W. D. Ross, 2 vols., Oxford, first ed. 1924, reprinted 1948.

ARISTOTLE [2.1]: *La Métaphysique*. Nouvelle édition [...] avec commentaire, par J. Tricot, Vrin, Paris 1953, 2 vols.

ARISTOTLE [3]: *Aristotle's Prior and Posterior Analytics*. A revised text with introduction and commentary by W. D. Ross, Oxford 1949, X+690 pp.

ARISTOTLE [3.1]: *The Works of Aristotle. Vol. I* (*Organon*). Oxford Univ. Press, Oxford 1955, Becker's pagination.

ARISTOTLE [3.2]: *Logique d'Aristote*. Traduite [...] par J. Barthélemy de St. Hilaire, 4 vols., Paris, first volume published 1864.

ARISTOTLE [4]: *Aristotle's Physics*. A revised text with introduction and commentary by W. D. Ross, Oxford 1936, XII+750 pp.

ARISTOTLE [4.1]: *The Works of Aristotle. Vol. II* (*Physica*, etc.), Oxford Univ. Press, Oxford 1947, Becker's pagination.

ARISTOTLE [5]: *Aristotelis Topica et Sophistici Elenchi* (ed. W. D. Ross), Oxford 1958, X+260 pp.

ARISTOTLE [6]: *The Works of Aristotle. Vol. XII (Select Fragments)* Oxford 1952, XII+162 pp.

ASCLEPIUS [1]: *Asclepii in Aristotelis metaphysicorum libros A–Z commentaria* (Commentaria in Aristotelem Graeca, Vol. VI, pars II) VII+505 pp.

AVERROES [1]: *Aristotelis Opera cum Averrois Commentariis*. Venetiis, apud Juntas, 1562–1574. Minerva Buchhandlung, unveränderter Nachdruck, 1962. 9 vols. +3 vols. *Supplementum*.

AVICENNA [1]: *Opera philosophica*, Venise 1508. Reprinted (with a *clé des abréviations*) by Edition de la Bibliothèque S.J., Louvain 1961.

BARTLETT, J. M. [1]: *Funktion und Gegenstand. Eine Untersuchung in die Logik von G. Frege*. Dissertation München 1961.

BAUDRY, L. [1]: *Lexique Philosophique de Guillaume d'Ockham* (*Etude des notions fondamentales*), Lethielleux, Paris 1958, 298 pp.+table.

BAUMGARTEN, A. [1]: *Metaphysica*, editio VII, 1779. Nachdruck G. Olms, Hildesheim 1963.

BECKER, O. [1]: *Das mathematische Denken der Antike*, Vandenhoeck & Ruprecht, Göttingen 1957, 128 pp.

BECKER, O. [2]: *Grundlagen der Mathematik* (*in geschichtlicher Entwicklung*), Karl Alber Verlag, Freiburg–München 1954, V+422 pp.

BECKER, O. [3]: *Zwei Untersuchungen zur antiken Logik*, Wiesbaden 1957, 55 p.

BENACERRAF, P. [1]: 'What Numbers Could Not Be', *The Philosophical Review* **74** (1965) 47–74.

BERGMANN, Gustav [1]: 'Russell's Examination of Leibniz Examined', *Philosophy of Science* **23** (1956) 175–203.

BERGMANN, Gustav [2]: 'Frege's Hidden Nominalism', *The Philosopical Review* **67** (1958) 437–459.

BERGMANN, Julius [1]: *Die Grundprobleme der Logik*, zweite, völlig neue Bearbeitung, Berlin 1895, 232 p.

BERNAYS, P., FRAENKEL, A. [1]: *Axiomatic Set Theory*, North Holland Publ. Comp., Amsterdam 1958, VIII+226 pp.

BERNAYS, P. [2]: 'Sur le platonisme dans les mathématiques', *L'enseignement mathématique* **34** (1935–6) 59–62.

BETH, E. W. [1]: *The Foundations of Mathematics*, North-Holland Publ. Comp., Amsterdam 1959, XXVI+741 pp.

BETH, E. W. [2]: 'A propos d'un "Traité de Logique", *Methodos* **2** (1950) 258–264.

BIRJUKOV, B. V. [1]: *Two Soviet Studies on Frege*. Translated and edited by I. Angelelli, D. Reidel Publ. Comp., Dordrecht 1964, XXII+100 pp.

BOCHEŃSKI, I. M. [1]: *Formale Logik*, Verlag K. Alber, München 1956, XV+639 pp.

BOCHEŃSKI, I. M. [2]: *La logique de Théophraste*, Librairie de l'Université, Fribourg en Suisse 1947, 138 pp.

BOCHEŃSKI, I. M. [3]: *Ancient Formal Logic*, North-Holland Publ. Comp., Amsterdam 1951 (second printing 1957), VI+122 pp.

BOCHEŃSKI, I. M. [4]: 'Non-analytical laws and rules in Aristotle', *Methodos* **3** (1951) 70–80.

BODEMANN [1]: *Die Leibniz-Handschriften der Königlichen Oeffentlichen Bibliothek zu Hannover*, Hannover 1895.

BOETHIUS [1]: *In Categorias Aristotelis* (Patrologia Latina, Tomus 64).

BOETHIUS [2]: *Anicii Manlii Severini Boethii In Isagogen Porphyrii Commentaria.* (Corpus Scriptorum Ecclesiasticorum Latinorum, Vol. 48) Vindobonae, Lipsiae 1906, LXXXVI+423 pp.

BOLZANO, B. [1]: *Wissenschaftlehre*, 4 vols., Sulzbach 1837.

BONITZ, H. [1]: *Index Aristotelicum*, Wissenschaftliche Buchgesellschaft, Darmstadt 1960, 878 pp. (a reprint of the 1870 edition).

BONITZ, H. [2]: *Aristotelis Metaphysica*, 2 vols., Bonn 1848–1849.

BORTOLOTTI, E. [1]: 'Definizioni di numero (cardinale)', *Periodico di matematiche per l'insegnamento secondario* **4** (1922) 413–429.

BORTOLOTTI, E. [2]: 'Definizioni di numero (ordinale)', *Esercitazioni Matematiche* (*Circolo matematico di Catania*) **2** (1922) 253.

BOURBAKI, N. [1]: *Elements de Mathématique* (XVII), Première partie, livre I, ch. IV, Hermann, Paris 1957, 124 pp.

BRENTANO, F. [1]: *Die Lehre vom richtigen Urteil*, Francke Verlag, Bern 1956, XXIV+344 pp.

BRENTANO, F. [2]: *Von der mannigfachen Bedeutung des Seienden nach Aristoteles*, Freiburg i.B. 1862, VIII+220 pp.

BRENTANO, F. [3]: *Vom Dasein Gottes* (Philos. Bibliothek), Meiner, Leipzig 1929, LIX+546 pp.

BRENTANO, F. [4]: *Psychologie* (Philos. Bibliothek) 2 vols. Meiner, Leipzig 1924–1925, XCVII+278 pp., XXIII+337 pp.

BURGERSDICIUS [1]: *Fr. Burgersdicii Institutionum logicarum libri duo*, Cantabrigiae 1668, 219 pp.

BURIDAN [1]: *Tractatus de suppositionibus*, La Nuova Italia Editrice Firenze, 1957, 68 pp.

BURKAMP, Wilhelm [1]: *Begriff und Beziehung. Studien zur Grundlegung der Logik*, Meiner 1927, XVI+306 pp.

CAIETANUS [1]: *Thomae de Vio, Caietani, In De Ente et Essentia D. Thomae Aquinatis Commentaria*. Cura et studio P. M. H. Laurent, Marietti, Taurini 1934, XVI+260 pp.

CAIETANUS [2]: *Commentaria in Porphyrii Isagogen et Praedicamenta Aristotelis*, apud Instit. "Angelicum", Romae 1934, LXXXIV+140 pp.+Index.

CANTOR, Georg [1]: *Gesammelte Abhandlungen* (herausg. von E. Zermelo), Reprint G. Olms, Hildesheim 1962, VII+486 pp.

CARNAP, R. [1]: *Meaning and Necessity*, Enlarged edition, The Univ. of Chicago Press, Chicago 1956, VIII+258 pp.

CARNAP, R. [2]: *The Logical Syntax of Language*, Fifth impression, Routledge & Kegan Paul Ltd., London 1959, XVI+352 pp.

CARNAP, R. [3]: *Introduction to Semantics and Formalization of Logic* (2 vols. in one). Harvard U.P., Cambridge, Mass. 1959, XIV+259 pp,; XV+159 pp.

CARNAP, R. [4]: 'Die Mathematik als Zweig der Logik', *Blätter für dt. Philos.* **4** (1930) 298–310.

CARNAP, R. [5]: *Der logische Aufbau der Welt*. Reprint (first edition 1928) together with *Scheinprobleme in der Philosophie*, Felix Meiner, Hamburg 1961, XX+336 pp.

CARNAP R. [6]: 'Überwindung der Metaphysik', *Erkenntnis* **2** (1932) 219–241.

CARNAP, R. [7]: 'Alte und neue Logik', *Erkenntnis* **1** (1930) 12–26.

CASSIRER, E. [1]: *Substanzbegriff und Funktionsbegriff*, Verlag B. Cassirer, Berlin 1923, XV+459 pp.

CATON, Charles [1]: 'An Apparent Difficulty in Frege's Ontology', *The Philosophical Review* **71** (1962) 462–475.

CHUNG-HWAN CHEN [1]: 'On Aristotle's two expressions *καθ' ὑποκειμένου λέγεσθαι* and *ἐν ὑποκειμένῳ εἶναι*', *Phronesis* **2** (1957) 147–159.

CHURCH, A. [1]: *Introduction to Mathematical Logic*. Vol. 1, Princeton University Press, Princeton 1956, X+378 pp.

CHURCH, A. [2]: 'A Formulation of the Logic of Sense and Denotation', in *Structure, Method and Meaning, Essays in honour of H. Sheffer*, New York 1951.

CHURCH, A. [3]: 'Intention' in Runes [1].

CORNFORD, F. M. [1]: *Plato's Theory of Knowledge*, Routledge, London 1960 (first published 1935), XIV+336 pp.

CORNFORD, F. M. [2]: 'Mysticism and Science in the Pythagorean Tradition', *The Classical Quarterly* **17** (1923) 1–13.

COUTURAT, L. [1]: *Opuscules et fragments inédits de Leibniz*, G. Olms, Hildesheim 1961 (reprint), XIV+682 pp.

CRAHAY, F. [1]: *Le formalisme logico-mathématique et le problème du non-sens*, Ed. "Les Belles Lettres", Paris 1957, 152 pp.

CRAMER, Wolfgang [1]: *Das Problem der reinen Anschauung* (Heidelberger Abhandlungen zur Philos. und ihrer Geschichte, 27), Tübingen 1937, V+89 pp.

DESCARTES [1]: 'Les Principes de la Philosophie (Première Partie)', in *Oeuvres de Descartes*. Publiées par C. Adam et P. Tannery, vol. IX, Paris 1904.

DEXIPPUS [1]: *Dexippi in Aristotelis Categorias commentarium* (Commentaria in Aristotelem Graeca, vol. IV, pars II) 1887, LVI+181 pp.

DUMMETT, M. [1]: Review of *Translations from the Philosophical Writings of Frege*, in *Mind* **63** (1954) 102–105.

DUMMETT, M. [2]: 'Frege on Functions, a Reply', *The Philosophical Review* **64** (1955) 96–107.
DUMMETT, M. [3]: 'Note: Frege on Functions', *The Philosophical Review* **65** (1956) 229–230.
DUNS SCOTUS [1]: *Obras del Doctor Sutil Juan Duns Escoto*, B.A.C., Madrid 1960, 129*+712 p. [Reproduces the critical edition, two first volumes.]
DUNS SCOTUS [2]: *Questiones Scoti Super Universalia Porphyrii necnon Aristotelis Predicamenta ac Peryhermeneias*, Venetiis 1508, 100 ff. [The volume includes other works.]

ECHAURI, R. [1]: *El ser en la filosofia de Heidegger*, Rosario (Argentina) 1964, 173 pp.
EGIDI, R. [1]: *Ontologia e conoscenza matematica. Un saggio su G. Frege*, Sansoni editore, Firenze 1963, 274 p.
EISLER, R. [1]: *Kant-Lexikon*, Olms, Hildesheim 1961 (reprint), VIII+642 pp.
EISLER, R. [2]: *Wörterbuch der Philosophischen Begriffe*, 3 vols., Berlin 1927.
ELIAS [1]: *Eliae in Porphyrii Isagogen et Aristotelis Categorias Commentaria* (Commentaria in Aristotelem Graeca, vol. XVIII, pars I) 1900, XXXI+288 pp.
EUCKEN, R. [1]: *Geschichte der philosophischen Terminologie*, Olms, Hildesheim 1960 (reprint), IV+226 pp.

FERNANDEZ GARCIA, M. [1]: *Lexicon scholasticum philosophico-theologicum in quo termini, distinctiones, [. . .] philosophiam ac theologiam spectantes a b. Ioanni Duns Scoto declarantur*. Ad Claras Aquas (Quaracchi) 1910, LIV+1055 pp.
FERRATER MORA, J. [1]: 'On the Early History of "Ontology"', *Philosophy and Phenomenological Research* **24** (1963) 36–48.
FITCH, F. B. [1]: *Symbolic Logic. An introduction*, The Ronald Press Company, New York 1952, X+238 pp.
FØLLESDAL, D. [1]: *Husserl and Frege*, Oslo 1958, 60 pp.
FONSECA, P. [1]: *Institutionum dialecticarum libri octo*, apud Cl. Morillon, Lugduni 1611, 358 pp.+Indexes. [Bibl. Cantonale, Fribourg, Switzerland].
FONSECA, P. [2]: *Petri Fonsecae Commentariorum in libros Methaphysicorum Aristotelis*, Tomus I–IV, Olms, Hildesheim 1963 (reprint).
FRAENKEL, A. A., BAR-HILLEL, Y. [1]: *Foundations of Set-Theory*, North-Holland Publ. Comp., Amsterdam 1958, X−415 pp.
FRIES, J. F. [1]: *System der Logik*, Heidelberg 1819, XII+124+650 pp.

GARDEIL, H. D. [1]: *Initiation à la Philosophie de St. Thomas d'Aquin. Introduction, Logique*, Ed. du Cerf, Paris 1956, 253 pp.
GASCONIUS, Ioannes [1]: *In Logicam sive Dialecticam Aristotelis commentaria*, Oscae, 1576, 3 f.+errata+22 f. (a general introduction)+334 ff. By "I" we refer to the set of 22 fol., by "II" to the set of 334 f. There is a copy of this book in Univ. of Pennsylvania Library (cf. *Aristotle Texts and Commentaries up to 1700*, Univ. of Pennsylvania Press, Philadelphia 1961, 324A).
GEACH, P. Th. [1]: see Anscombe–Geach [1].
GEACH, P. Th. [2]: *Reference and Generality. An Examination of Some Medieval and Modern Theories*, Cornell Univ. Press, Ithaca 1962, XX+202 pp.
GEACH, P. Th. [3]: 'On Frege's way out', *Mind* **65** (1956) 408–409.
GIACON, C. [1]: *La seconda scolastica*, Bocca, Milano 1944–1950.
GIGLI, Duilio [1]: 'Aritmetica Generale', in *Enciclopedia delle Matematiche Elementari*,

Hoepli, Milano 1930, Volume I, parte I, 81–212 pp.

GILSON, E. [1]: *L'Etre et l'essence*, Vrin, Paris 1962, 328 p.

GILSON, E. [2]: *Jean Duns Scot*, Vrin, Paris 1952, 700 pp.

GILSON, E. [3]: *Index Scholastico-Cartesien*, Alcan Paris 1912, IX+324 pp.

GOMEZ CAFFARENA, J. [1]: *Ser participado y ser subsistente en la metafísica de Enrique de Gante*, Univ. Gregoriana, Rome 1958, XII+283 pp.

GOODSTEIN, R. L. [1]: *Recursive Number Theory*, North-Holland Publ. Comp., Amsterdam 1957, XII+190 pp.

GOUDIN, [1]: *Philosophia. Tomus Primus, Logica*, Parisiis 1886, 272 pp.

GREDT, J. [1]: *Elementa Philosophiae Aristotelico–Thomisticae*, 2 vols., Ed. nona, Herder, Augsburg 1951.

GRENIEWSKI, H. [1]: *Elementy logiki formalnej*, P.W.N., Warszawa 1955, 492 pp.

GRIMM, J. and W. [1]: *Deutsches Wörterbuch.*

GROSSMANN, R. [1]: 'Frege's Ontology', in *Essays in Ontology* (Iowa Publications in Philosophy, I) 1963 106–121.

GRUCHIUS, [1]: *Operum Aristotelis Stagiritae* [. . .] nova editio, Graece et Latine, Tomus I. G. Laemarius, 1597, 1517 pp. [Gruchius is the translator of the *Organon.*]

HAUSDORFF, F. [1]: *Grundzüge der Mengenlehre*, Leipzig 1914, VIII+476 pp.

HAYEN, A. [1]: *L'Intentionnel dans la Philosophie de St. Thomas*, Museum Lessianum, Louvain 1942, 317 pp.

HEATH, Th. [1]: *Mathematics in Aristotle*, Oxford 1949, XIV+291 pp.

HEGEL, [1]: *Phänomenologie des Geistes* (Philos. Bibl.), Meiner, Leipzig 1952, XLII+598 pp.

HEIDEGGER, M. [1]: *Die Frage nach dem Ding*, M. Niemeyer Verlag Tübingen, 1962, VII+189 pp.

HEIDEGGER, M. [2]: *Kants These über das Sein*, V. Klostermann, Frankfurt 1963, 36 pp.

HEIDEGGER, M. [3]: *Sein und Zeit*, Siebente unver. Auflage, M. Niemeyer Verlag, Tübingen 1953, XI+437 pp.

HEIDEGGER, M. [4]: 'Neuere Forschungen über Logik', *Literarische Rundschau für das Katholische Deutschland* **38** (1912) 465–472, 517–524, 565–570.

HEIMSOETH, H. [1]: *Los seis grandes temas de la metafísica occidental* [Die sechs großen Themen der abendländischen Metaphysik], *Rev. de Occidente* (Madrid), 1959, 341 pp.

HERING, Jean [1]: 'Bemerkungen über das Wesen, die Wesenheit und die Idee', *Jahrbuch für Philosophie und phänomenologische Forschung* **4** (2. Ausgabe) (1930), 495–543.

HILBERT, D., ACKERMANN, W. [1]: *Grundzüge der theoretischen Logik*, Dritte Aufl., Springer, Berlin 1949, VIII+155 pp.

HILLEBRAND, F. [1]: *Die neuen Theorien der kategorischen Schlüsse*, 1891.

HÖFLER, A. [1]: *Logik*, Second ed., Wien–Leipzig 1922, XII+936 pp.

HUSSERL, E. [1]: *Logische Untersuchungen*, 2 vols., Niemeyer Verlag, Tübingen 1928.

HUSSERL, E. [2]: 'Bericht über die deutsche Schriften der Logik 1895–1899', *Archiv für systemat. Philosophie* **9** (1903) 393–408; **10** (1904) 101–125.

HUSSERL, E. [3]: *Formale und transzendentale Logik*, M. Niemeyer Verlag, Tübingen 1929, XI+298 pp.

HUSSERL, E. [4]: *Philosophie der Arithmetik*, Halle–Saale 1891, XVI+324 pp.

HUSSERL, E. [5]: *Erfahrung und Urteil*, Hamburg 1954.

INGARDEN, R. [1]: 'Vom formalen Aufbau des individuellen Gegenstandes', *Studia Philosophica*, Leopoli, 1935, 30–106.

IOANNES A STO. Thoma [1]: *Cursus philosophicus thomisticus. Tomus primus* (ed. Reiser), Marietti, Torino 1930, XXVI+839 pp.

JACKSON, H. [1]: 'Frege's Ontology', *The Philosophical Review* **69** (1960) 394–395.

JACOBY, G. [1]: *Allgemeine Ontologie der Wirklichkeit*, Erster Band, M. Niemeyer Verlag, Tübingen 1925, 576 pp.

JACOBY, G. [2]: 'Denkmal Hans Pichler zum 5. Todestag', *Zeits. f. philos. Forschung* **17** (1963) 462–476.

JAVELLUS [1]: *Chrysostomi Javelli Canapitis Tractatus de Transcendentibus, praevius Metaphysices*. Fol. 149–174 of a volume without title containing several works of the same author, Venetiis 1569, 395 ff.

JAVELLUS [2]: Idem, *Epitome in Metaphysicem Aristotelis*, Fol. 175–395.

JOFFRE, Petrus [1]: *Ars Syllogistica Demonstrata*, Tarbiae 1712, Index+errata+ 208 pp.

JOHN OF SALISBURY [1]: *The Metalogicon*. Translated by D. Mc.Garry, University of California Press, Berkeley 1962, 304 pp.

JOSEPH, H. W. B. [1]: *An Introduction to Logic*, Second ed. revised, Clarendon Press, Oxford 1916, XII+608 pp.

JUNGIUS, Joachimus [1]: *Logica Hamburgensis* (ed. R. Meyer) Hamburg 1957, 673 pp.

KAMKE, E. [1]: *Mengenlehre* (Sammlung Göschen), Berlin 1962.

KANT, I. [1]: *Der einzig mögliche Beweisgrund zu einer Demonstration des Dasein Gottes*, in Kant's *Gesammelte Schriften*. Her. von der Kön. Preus. Akad. der Wiss., Band II, Berlin 1905.

KANT, I. [2]: *Logik*, *Ibid*., Band IX, Berlin 1923.

KANT, I. [3]: *Kritik der reinen Vernunft*. Zweite Auflage, *Ibid*., Band III, Berlin 1904.

KANT, I. [4]: *Über eine Entdeckung, nach der alle neue Kritik der reinen Vernunft durch eine ältere entbehrlich gemacht werden soll*, *Ibid*., Band VIII, Berlin 1912.

KASTIL, Alfred [1]: *Die Philosophie Franz Brentanos*, Salzburg 1951, 337 pp.

KAUFMANN, David [1]: *Geschichte der Attributenlehre in der jüdischen Religionsphilosophie des Mittelalters von Saadja bis Maimûni*, F. A. Perthes, Gotha 1877, XIV+537 pp.

KAUFMANN, Felix [1]: *Das Unendliche in der Mathematik und seine Ausschaltung. Eine Untersuchung über die Grundlagen der Mathematik*, Leipzig and Vienna 1930, X+203 pp.

KAUFMANN, Felix [2]: 'Bemerkungen zum Grundlagenstreit in Logik und Mathematik', *Erkenntnis* **2** (1931–32) 262–290.

KAUPPI, Raili [1]: *Über die Leibnizsche Logik, mit besonderer Berücksichtigung des Problems der Intension und der Extension*, Societas Philosophica Fennica, Helsinki 1960, 279 pp.

KECKERMANN, B. [1]: *Systema Logicae* [...], ed. secunda [...], Hanoviae 1602, Indices+598 pp.+Indices.

KENT SPRAGUE, R. [1]: *Plato's Use of Fallacy*, Routledge and Kegan Paul, London 1962, XI+106 pp.

KERRY, B. [1]: 'Über Anschauung und ihre psychische Verarbeitung. Vierter Artikel', *Vierteljahrschrift für wissensch. Philosophie* **11** (1887) 249–307.

KLEMKE, E. D. [1]: 'Prof. Bergmann and Frege's "Hidden Nominalism"', *The Philosophical Review* **68** (1959) 507–514.

KNEALE, W. and M. [1]: *The Development of Logic*, Clarendon Press, Oxford 1962, VIII+761 pp.
KÖRNER, S. [1]: *The Philosophy of Mathematics*, Harper & Brothers, New York 1962, 198 pp.
KRENZ, E. [1]: *Der Zahlbegriff bei Frege*, Diss. Vienna 1942, 116 pp.
KÜNG, G. [1]: *Ontologie und logistische Analyse der Sprache. Eine Untersuchung zur zeitgenössischen Universaliendiskussion*, Springer Verlag, Wien 1963.
KÜNG, G. [2]: 'Concrete and Abstract Properties', *Notre Dame Journal of Formal Logic* **5** (1964) 31–37.

LASK, E. [1]: *Gesammelte Schriften*, II. Band, Tübingen 1923, IV+463 pp.
LEIBNIZ, G. [1]: *Die Philosophischen Schriften von G. W. Leibniz*. Herausgegeben von C. J. Gerhardt, 7 vols., Berlin 1875–90, reprint G. Olms, Hildesheim 1960.
LEVI, Beppo [1]: *Leyendo a Euclides*, Ed. Rosario S.A., Rosario (Argentina) 1947, 224 pp.
LINKE, P. [1]: 'Gottlob Frege als Philosoph', *Zeits. für philos. Forschung* **1** (1946) 75–99.
LINSKY, L. (editor) [1]: *Semantics and the Philosophy of Language*, Urbana, Ill., 1952, 289 pp.
LOCKE, J. [1]: *An Essay Concerning Human Understanding* (ed. Fraser), Dover Public., New York 1959, 2 vols.
LORENZEN, P. [1]: *Formale Logik* (Sammlung Göschen) Berlin 1962, 165 pp.
LOTZE, R. [1]: *Grundzüge der Logik und Enzyklopädie der Philosophie*, Fünfte Auflage, Berlin 1912, 130 pp.
LUSCHEI, E. [1]: *The Logical Systems of Leśniewski*, North-Holland Publ. Comp., Amsterdam 1962, VII+361 pp.

MAIMON, Salomon [1]: *Versuch einer neuen Logik*. Herausg. von Kant-Gesellschaft, Berlin 1912, XXXVIII+445 pp.
MARCEL, G. [1]: *Journal Métaphysique*, Gallimard, Paris 1927, 342 pp.
MARITAIN, Jacques [1]: *Eléments de Philosophie. II. L'ordre des concepts. I. Petite logique (logique formelle)*, Quinzième édition, Paris 1946, 355 pp.
MARITAIN, Jacques [2]: 'Préface' to R. Le Masson, *Philosophie des nombres*, Desclée, Paris 1932, XII+82 pp.
MARSCHALL, W. [1]: 'Frege's Theory of Functions and Objects', *The Philosophical Review* **62** (1953) 374–390.
MARSCHALL, W. [2]: 'Sence and Reference, a Reply', *The Philosophical Review* **65** (1956) 342–361.
MARTIN, G. [1]: *Klassische Ontologie der Zahl* (Kantstudien, Ergänzungshefte) Köln 1956, 159 pp.
MARTIN, R. M. [1]: 'On the Frege–Church Theory of Meaning', *Philosophy and Phenomenological Research* **23** (1963) 605–609.
MARTINUS DE DACIA [1]: *Martini de Dacia Opera*. Nunc primum edidit H. Roos (Corpus philosophorum danicorum Medii Aevi, II). Hauniae 1961, XL+365 pp.
MARTY, A. [1]: *Gesammelte Schriften*. II. Band, 1. Abteilung, Halle 1918, XXI+364 pp.
MARTY, A. [2]: *Satz und Wort*, Francke Verlag, Bern 1950, 92 pp.
MATES, B. [1]: *Stoic Logic*, Univ. of California Press, Berkeley 1961, VI+148 pp.
MAUTHNER, F. [1]: *Zur Sprache und zur Psychologie*, Dritte . . . vermehrte Aufl., 3 vols., Meiner, Leipzig 1923.

MEINONG, A. [1]: 'Selbstdarstellung', in *Die Philosophie der Gegenwart in Selbstdarstellungen*, her. von R. Schmidt, Leipzig 1923.
MERCIER, D. [1]: *Cours de Philosophie*. Volume 1 *Logique*, Louvain 1897, VII+285 pp.
MILL, J. S. [1]: *A System of Logic Ratiocinative and Inductive*, Longmans, Grene and Co., London 1916, XVI+622 pp.
MORAVCSIK, J. M. E. [1]: 'The "Third Man" Argument and Plato's Theory of Forms', *Phronesis* **8** (1963) 50–63.
MORTAN, G. [1]: *Gottlob Freges philosophische Bedeutung*, Diss. Jena 1954.
MUÑOZ DELGADO, V. [1]: *La logica nominalista en la universidad de Salamanca* (*1510–1530*), Ed. Revista Estudios, Madrid 1964, 448 pp.+20 photocopies.
MURALT, André de [1]: 'Adéquation et intentions secondes', *Studia Philosophica* (Switzerland) **20** (1960) 88–114.

NESFIELD, J. C. [1]: *English Grammar Past and Present*, MacMillan, London 1949, VIII+470 pp.
NICOLAUS DE ORBELLIS (or DORBELLUS) [1]: *Summulae Philosophiae rationalis seu logica excellentissimi artium et theologiae professoris Magistri Nicolai Dorbelli secundum doctrinam doctoris subtilis Scoti*, Basilee 1494 (no pagination). [Stadtbibliothek, Bern.]
NIZOLIUS, Marius [1]: *Marii Nizolii Antibarbarus Philosophicus, sive Philosophia Scholasticorum impugnata, libris IV. De veris principiis et vera ratione philosophandi contra Pseudo-Philosophos* [. . .]. Francofurti 1674, 360 pp. [with Leibniz's introduction and notes].

OLYMPIODORUS [1]: *Olympiodori Prolegomena et in Categorias Commentarium* (Commentaria in Aristotelem Graeca, vol. XII, pars 1) 1902, XII+163 pp.
OWEN, G. E. L. [1]: 'Inherence', *Phronesis* **10** (1965) 97–105.
OWENS, Joseph [1]: *The Doctrine of Being in the Aristotelian Metaphysics*, Toronto 1951, 450 pp.

PACIUS, Julius [1]: *Aristotelis Organon*. Translation and notes by Pacius, Francofurti 1598. 951 pp.
PACIUS, Julius [2]: *Institutiones Logicae in usum scholarum Bernensium*, Bern 1600, 10+183 pp. [Stadtbibliothek, Bern.]
PACIUS, Julius [3]: *Commentarius Analyticus in Universum Organum*, Francofurti 1597, 532 pp. [Stadtbibliothek, Bern, in one vol. with another ed. of Pacius [1]].
PAPST, W. [1]: *G. Frege als Philosoph*, Diss. Berlin 1932.
PATZIG, G. [1]: *Die Aristotelische Syllogistik*, 2. Auflage, Vandenhoeck & Ruprecht, Göttingen 1963, 208 pp.
PAULUS VENETUS [1]: *Logica parva*, Venetiis 1552, 111 ff.
PAULUS VENETUS [2]: *Logica Magna*, Venetiis 1499, 200 ff. [Universitätsbibliothek, Basel.]
PEANO, Giuseppe [1]: *Formulario Mathematico*, Ed. Cremonese, Roma 1960, XLVIII+459 pp.
PEREIRA GOMEZ, J. [1]: *Os professores de filosofia da Universidade de Evora* (*1559–1759*), Evora 1960, 622 pp.
PETRUS HISPANUS [1]: *Summulae Logicales, quas e codice manu scripto . . .* edidit I. M. Bocheński, Marietti, Roma 1947, XXIII+143 pp.

PHILOPONUS [1]: *Ioannis Philoponi in Aristotelis Analytica Posteriora Commentaria* (Commentaria in Aristotelem Graeca, vol. XIII, pars III), 1903, XXX+620 pp.
PHILOPONUS [2]: *Philoponi in Aristotelis categorias commentarium* (Commentaria in Aristotelem Graeca, Vol. XIII, pars 1), 1898, XVI+232 pp.
PICHLER, Hans [1]: *Über C. Wolffs Ontologie*, Leipzig 1910, 91 pp.
PORPHYRY [1]: *Porphyrii Isagoge et in Aristotelis categorias commentarium* (Commentaria in Aristotelem Graeca, vol. IV, pars I), 1887, LVI+181 pp.
PORT-ROYAL [1]: *La Logique ou l'Art de Penser* [. . .]. Cinquième édition, chez G. Desprez, Paris 1683, 471 pp.
PORT-ROYAL [2]: *Logica sive Ars Cogitandi* [. . .], Post duodecimam Gallicam [. . .] editio tertia Veneta, Venetiis 1765, XXII+318 pp.
PRANTL, K. [1]: *Geschichte der Logik im Abendlande*, 4 vols., *Nachdruck*, Berlin 1957.
PRIOR, A. [1]: *Formal Logic*, Clarendon Press, Oxford 1955, IX+329 pp.
PRIOR, A. [2]: 'Some Problems of Self-reference in J. Buridan', *Proc. of the British Acad.* **48**, 1962, 281–296.

QUINE, W. V. O. [1]: *Methods of Logic*. Revised with a new appendix, Routledge and Kegan Paul, London 1958, XIX+272 pp.
QUINE, W. V. O. [2]: *Mathematical Logic*. Revised ed., Harvard Univ. Press, Cambridge, 1955, XII+346 pp.
QUINE, W. V. O. [3]: *From a Logical Point of View*, Harvard Univ. Press, Cambridge, 1961, VIII+184 pp.
QUINE, W. V. O. [4]: *Set Theory and Its Logic*, Harvard Univ. Press, Mass., 1963, XV+359 pp.
QUINE, W. V. O. [5]: 'On Frege's way out', *Mind* **64** (1955) 145–159.

RABUS, L. [1]: *Logik und Metaphysik*, Erlangen 1868, XVI+528 pp.
REICHENBACH, H. [1]: *Elements of Symbolic Logic*, Macmillan Co., New York 1956, XIII+444 pp.
REICHENBACH, H. [2]: *Introduction à la logistique*, Hermann, Paris 1939, 65 pp.
REID [1]: *Essays on the Intellectual Powers of Man, to Which Is Annexed an Analysis of Aristotle's Logic*, London 1843, XXXII+600 pp.
RESNIK, M. [1]: 'Some Observations Related to Frege's Way Out', *Logique et Analyse* **27** (1964) 138–144.
RIEFFERT, J. B. [1] 'Logik', in *Die Philosophie in ihrer Einzelgebieten* (her. von M. Dessoir), Berlin 1925, pp. 1–294.
RIJK, L. M. de [1]: *The Place of the Categories of Being in Aristotle's Philosophy*, Diss. Utrecht 1952.
RIJK, L. M. de [2]: 'The Authenticity of Aristotle's Categories', *Mnemosyne*, IV Series, **4**, fasc. II (1951), 129–159.
RISSE, W. [1]: *Die Logik der Neuzeit. Band* 1: *Die Geschichte der Logik von 1500–1640*, Frommann, Stuttgart 1965, 574 pp.
RIVETTI BARBÓ, F. [1]: 'Il "Senso e Significato" di Frege', in *Studi di Filosofia e di storia della filosofia in onore di F. Olgiati*, Soc. ed. Vita e Pensiero, Milano 1962 [Rivetti Barbó's paper has 64 pages.]
RUNES, D. [1]: *Dictionary of Philosophy*, Littlefield, Adams and Co., Paterson, N.J., 1961, 343 pp.
RUSSELL, B. [1]: *A Critical Exposition of the Philosophy of Leibniz*. Third impression (second edition), Allen and Unwin, London 1949, 311 pp.

RUSSELL, B. [3]: *Introduction to Mathematical Philosophy*. Ninth impression, Allen and Unwin, London 1956, XIII+208 pp.

RUSSELL, B. [4]: *The Principles of Mathematics*. Second edition, seventh impression, Allen and Unwin, London 1956, XXXIX+534 pp.

RUSSELL, B. [5]: 'The Philosophy of Logical Atomism', in *Logic and Knowledge* (ed. by R. Marsh). Allen and Unwin, London 1956, VII+382 pp.

SANCHEZ SEDEÑO [1]: *Aristotelis Logica Magna*, Salmanticae 1600. [A copy in Biblioteca Nacional, Madrid.]

SCHOLZ, H., HASENJAEGER, G. [1]: *Grundzüge der Mathematischen Logik*, Springer, Berlin 1961, 504 pp.

SCHOLZ, H. [2]: *Die Auffassungen der Mathematik von Leibniz und Kant bis zu Hilbert und Brouwer*. Sommervorlesung 1931, [...] als Manuskript gedruckt. Die freie mathematische Fachschaft zu Münster, 238 pp.+Anhang (7 pp.).

SCHOLZ, H. [3]: *Vorlesungen über Grundzüge der mathematischen Logik I*. Zweite, neu verfaßte Auflage, 1950, XIV+276 pp.

SCHOLZ, H. [4]: *Abriß der Geschichte der Logik*. Zweite, unver. Auflage, K. Alber, München 1959, VII+78 pp.

SCHOLZ, H. and SCHWEITZER, H. [5]: *Die sogenannten Definitionen durch Abstraktion*, Münster 1935, 109 pp.

SCHOLZ, H. [6]: *Mathesis Universalis*, Wiss. Buchgesell., Darmstadt 1961, 483 pp.

SCHOLZ, H. [7]: *Logik, Grammatik, Metaphysik*. In Scholz [6].

SCHÜLING, H. [1]: *Bibliographie der im 17. Jahrhundert im Deutschland erschienenen logischen Schriften*, Universitätsbibliothek, Giessen 1963, 143 pp. [Cf. W. Risse's review in: *Philos. Rundschau* **12** (1965) p. 298.]

SCHÜTZ, L. [1]: *Thomas-Lexikon*. Zweite, sehr vergrösserte Auflage. Reprint Fromman Verlag, Stuttgart 1958, X+889 pp.

SCHWEGLER, A. [1]: *Die Metaphysik des Aristoteles*. Grundtext, Übersetzung und Commentar [...], 3 vols., Tübingen 1847–1848.

SIERPIŃSKI, W. [1]: *Cardinal and Ordinal Numbers*, Warszawa 1958, 487 pp.

SIGNORIELLO, N. [1]: *Lexicon peripateticum philosophico-theologicum*. Editio novissima, Neapoli 1893, VI+423 pp.

SIGWART, Ch. [1]: *Logik*. 2 vols., Tübingen 1924.

SIMPLICIUS [1]: *Simplicii in Aristotelis Categorias Commentarium* (Commentaria in Aristotelem Graeca, vol VIII), 1907, XXI+575 pp.

SIMPLICIUS [2]: *Simplicii in Aristotelis Physicorum libros* [...] *commentaria* (Commentaria in Aristotelem Graeca, vols. IX and X), 1882–1895.

SIMPSON, T. M. [1]: *Formas logicas, realidad y significado*, Eudeba, Buenos Aires 1964, 301 pp.

SLUGA, H. D. [1]: 'Frege und die Typentheorie', in *Logik und Logikkalkül*, K. Alber, München 1962, 249 pp.

SŁUPECKI, J., BORKOWSKI, L. [1]: *Elementy Logiki Matematycznej i Teorii Mnogości*, Warszawa 1963, 285 pp.

SOBOCIŃSKI, B. [1]: 'L'analyse de l'antinomie russellienne par Leśniewski', *Methodos* **1** (1950) 94–107, 308–316; **2** (1950) 237–257.

SPINOZA [1]: *Ethica*, in *Opera quotquot reperta sunt*. Recognoverunt J. van Vloten et J. P. N. Land, ed. tertia, Nijhoff, The Hague 1914.

SPRINGER, M. [1]: *Die Attributenlehre des Moses Maimonides beleuchtet vom Standpunkt der modernen Logik*, Diss. Zurich (under Prof. K. Dürr), Solco Press, New

York 1942.
STEGMÜLLER, W. [1]: *Das Wahrheitsproblem und die Idee der Semantik*, Springer, Wien 1957, X+328 pp.
STEGMÜLLER, W. [2]: *Hauptströmungen der Gegenwartsphilosophie*, Zweite Auflage, Kröner Verlag, Stuttgart 1960, XLVIII+532 pp.
STEINER, H. G. [1]: 'Frege und die Grundlagen der Geometrie I, II', *Mathem.-Phys. Semesterbericht* **10** (1963–4) 175–186; **11** (1964) 35–47.
STENIUS, E. [1]: *Wittgenstein's Tractatus.* (*A critical exposition of the main lines of thought*). Blackwell, Oxford 1960, IX+241 pp.
STEPHANUS ALEXANDRINUS [1]: *Stephani Alexandrini in librum Aristotelis de Interpretatione commentarium* (Commentaria in Aristotelem Graeca, vol. XVIII, pars III), 1885, VIII+92 pp.
SUAREZ [1]: *Disputationes Metaphysicae.* 6 vols., Gredos, Madrid 1960.
ŚWIEŻAWSKI, Stephan [1]: 'Les intentions premières et les intentions secondes chez J. D. Scot', *Archives d'hist. doctr. et litt. du moyen âge*, 1934, 205–260.

TOMÁS DE ERFURT [1]: *Gramatica Especulativa*, Losada, Buenos Aires 1947, 173 pp.
TONQUEDEC, J. [1]: *La Critique de la Connaissance*, Troisième édition, G. Beauchesne, Paris 1929, XXX+565 pp.
TRENDELENBURG, A. [1]: *Historische Beiträge zur Philosophie. Erster Band. Geschichte der Kategorienlehre*, Berlin 1846, XVI+384 pp.
TRENDELENBURG, A. [2]: *Elementa Logices Aristoteleae*, Ed. tertia, Berolini 1845, XVI+150 pp.

VAIHINGER, H. [1]: *Commentar zur Kritik der Reinen Vernunft.* 2 vols., 1881.
VAN AUBEN, Madeleine [1]: 'Accident, catégories et prédicables dans l'oeuvre d'Aristote', *Revue Philosophique de Louvain* **61** (1963) 361–401.

WELLS, R. [1]: 'Frege's Ontology', *The Review of Metaphysics* **4** (1951) 537–573.
WHITE, Morton G. [1]: 'The Analytic and the Synthetic: An Untenable Dualism'. Reprinted in Linsky [1], 272–286.
WHITEHEAD, A. N., RUSSELL, B. [1]: *Principia Mathematica.* Second ed., 3 vols., Cambridge 1925.
WILPERT, P. [1]: 'Die Neugestaltung des "Überweg"', *Archiv f. Geschichte der Philosophie* **43** (1961) 85–99.
WIENPAHL [1]: 'Frege's Sinn und Bedeutung', *Mind* **59** (1950) 483–494.
WITTGENSTEIN, L. [1]: *Remarks on the Foundations of Mathematics*, Blackwell, Oxford 1956, XIX+204 pp.
WITTGENSTEIN, L. [2]: *Philosophical Investigations*, Blackwell, Oxford 1958, X+232 pp.
WOLFF, Christian [1]: *Philosophia prima sive Ontologia* (ed. by Jean Ecole) Olms 1962, 774 pp.
DE WULF, M. [1]: *Storia della Filosofia Medievale*, 3 vols., Libreria Editrice Fiorentina, s.a.
DE WULF, M. [2]: *Histoire de la philosophie scolastique dans les Pays Bas et la principauté de Liège jusqu'à la Révolution Française*, Louvain 1895, XX+404 pp.
WUNDT, Max [1]: *Die deutsche Schulmetaphysik des 17. Jahrhunderts*, Mohr, Tübingen 1939, XXVI+288 pp.

INDEX OF NAMES

INDEX OF SUBJECTS